perspectives

Personality

Academic Editor
Sabrina Zirkel
Saybrook Graduate School
and Research Center

coursewise
publishing
inc.

Bellevue • Boulder • Dubuque • Madison • St. Paul

Our mission at **coursewise** is to help students make connections—linking theory to practice and the classroom to the outside world. Learners are motivated to synthesize ideas when course materials are placed in a context they recognize. By providing gateways to contemporary and enduring issues, **coursewise** publications will expand students' awareness of and context for the course subject.

For more information on **coursewise,** visit us at our web site: http://www.coursewise.com

To order an examination copy, contact:
Houghton Mifflin Sixth Floor Media: 800-565-6247 (voice); 800-565-6236 (fax).

coursewise publishing editorial staff

Thomas Doran, ceo/publisher: Environmental Science/Geography/Journalism/Marketing/Speech
Edgar Laube, publisher: Geography/Political Science/Psychology/Sociology
Linda Meehan Avenarius, publisher: **courselinks**™
Sue Pulvermacher-Alt, publisher: Education/Health/Gender Studies
Victoria Putman, publisher: Anthropology/Philosophy/Religion
Tom Romaniak, publisher: Business/Criminal Justice/Economics
Kathleen Schmitt, publishing assistant

coursewise publishing production staff

Lori A. Blosch, permissions coordinator
Mary Monner, production coordinator
Victoria Putman, production manager

Note: Readings in this book appear exactly as they were published.
Thus, inconsistencies in style and usage among the different
readings are likely.

Library of Congress Catalog Card Number: 99-90063

ISBN 0-395-97207-8

Printed in the United States of America by **coursewise publishing,** Inc.
1559 Randolph Avenue, St. Paul, MN 55105

10 9 8 7 6 5 4 3 2 1

from the
Publisher

Edgar Laube
coursewise publishing

My wife and I have twin girls, now almost sixteen months old. They are completely different from one another. Anne is outgoing, curious, assertive, and a bit chunky. She wants to do things herself. I'm sure that she can pinch as well as any other one-year-old in the lower forty-eight states. Julia is much more the observer. She's quiet and operates independently, and she's much better coordinated. She's happy to build a tower out of blocks or boxes and watch her sister knock it over. The two of them play together and seem to communicate quite well without benefit of words. (We'll see how long this lasts. . . .)

Many of these behaviors could not have been "learned," but rather are part of each baby's DNA. Anne and Julia showed up on the planet with these rudiments of personality intact. (The articles in Section 3 of this reader elaborate on this theme.) But there's so much more to the subject of personality: what it is, how internal and external influences shape it, how it changes over time, and how people end up thinking about themselves as a result.

This reader offers selections on the major approaches to the study of personality, resulting in a integrated look at the "whole" person. The result is a body of information that you will find useful daily, even hourly. It will help you make sense of your environment, see through the barrage of messages that modern society puts in your way, and understand your own behavior and that of others. There's plenty of science here, but a lot of practical stuff, too. I'm grateful to be the publisher of such a blend.
I'd like to extend a special "thank you" to Sabrina Zirkel for her admirable work on this volume. The selection and presentation of articles here reflect Sabrina's professionalism and awareness of students' attitudes and concerns. In addition, Sabrina assembled a first-rate Editorial Board and really brought board members into the selection process.

And so, students, *bon appetit.* Please feel free to let Sabrina and me know what you think of the reader and the rich collection of resources available at www.courselinks.com. And if any of you out there is a twin, I'm especially interested in your feedback. I have a lot of homework to do on this issue. . . .

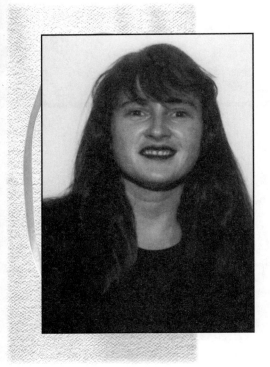

from the
Academic Editor

Sabrina Zirkel

*Saybrook Graduate School
and Research Center*

Welcome to a new kind of supplemental text for personality! When Ed Laube approached me about joining the **coursewise** team and putting together a reader about personality, I was very excited. I had served on the **coursewise** Editorial Board for *Perspectives: Social Psychology,* and so I knew that this reader would be different and exciting for students. First, the emphasis would be on finding articles that illustrate what personality psychology has to say about the parts of our lives we care about—including such topics as love and relationships, work, health, identity, and raising children. I knew that this reader would allow undergraduates to see why this is such an exciting field in which to teach and learn. Second, this reader was to have a strong Internet connection—helping students to wend their way through the mass of Internet sites to find those that provide reliable, interesting information, and helping faculty to take their courses "to the twenty-first century" without spending all their time surfing the web for quality, relevant sites.

Personality psychology grabbed my attention as a student because it is probably the only area of psychology that examines the "whole" person. Personality psychologists integrate information about a person's genetic makeup, biological processes, cognitive processes and thoughts, affect or emotional life, early childhood experiences, social relationships, culture, and place in the life cycle to understand who the person is as an individual. Other areas of psychology take one of these areas and focus on it in detail— but rarely does psychology try to "put it all together." Personality psychology is nature *and* nurture, childhood *and* adulthood, development *and* culture, change *and* consistency. As I put together the readings in this volume, I focused on making sure that each one has something interesting and important to say about ourselves or those we love. Included here are readings that might help you understand how our personalities are shaped by our parents, our genes, and the historical time in which we live. The readings explore how and with whom we fall in love, and why it's so hard for some people to develop friendships. I'm hoping you'll find this readings and ideas as exciting as I do!

I'm also very pleased to have this opportunity to blend the Internet directly into your readings and the topics you cover in class. No one polices the quality of the information on the web. Some web sites are commercial ventures with the goal of selling you something—for example, sites about depression run by drug companies that produce antidepressants. Others are put together by individuals who may not be concerned about providing unbiased, empirically validated information. Learning to navigate through and around these web sites can be difficult without some guidance.

Moreover, anyone who has spent any time on the web knows how many hours it can take to get the most basic piece of information. The sites I've chosen for this book and for the **courselinks**™ web site will all provide you with reliable information and link you to other reliable sites. This way, you can use the web as a tool for learning, rather than as a way to spend countless, fruitless hours.

I'm very excited about what the Editorial Board and I have put together here, and hope that you enjoy it!

Editorial Board

WiseGuide Introduction

Question Authority

Critical Thinking and Bumper Stickers

The bumper sticker said: Question Authority. This is a simple directive that goes straight to the heart of critical thinking. The issue is not whether the authority is right or wrong; it's the questioning process that's important. Questioning helps you develop awareness and a clearer sense of what you think. That's critical thinking.

Critical thinking is a new label for an old approach to learning—that of challenging all ideas, hypotheses, and assumptions. In the physical and life sciences, systematic questioning and testing methods (known as the scientific method) help verify information, and objectivity is the benchmark on which all knowledge is pursued. In the social sciences, however, where the goal is to study people and their behavior, things get fuzzy. It's one thing for the chemistry experiment to work out as predicted, or for the petri dish to yield a certain result. It's quite another matter, however, in the social sciences, where the subject is ourselves. Objectivity is harder to achieve.

Although you'll hear critical thinking defined in many different ways, it really boils down to analyzing the ideas and messages that you receive. What are you being asked to think or believe? Does it make sense, objectively? Using the same facts and considerations, could you reasonably come up with a different conclusion? And, why does this matter in the first place? As the bumper sticker urged, question authority. Authority can be a textbook, a politician, a boss, a big sister, or an ad on television. Whatever the message, learning to question it appropriately is a habit that will serve you well for a lifetime. And in the meantime, thinking critically will certainly help you be course wise.

Getting Connected

This reader is a tool for connected learning. This means that the readings and other learning aids explained here will help you to link classroom theory to real-world issues. They will help you to think critically and to make long-lasting learning connections. Feedback from both instructors and students has helped us to develop some suggestions on how you can wisely use this connected learning tool.

WiseGuide Pedagogy

A wise reader is better able to be a critical reader. Therefore, we want to help you get wise about the articles in this reader. Each section of *Perspectives* has three tools to help you: the WiseGuide Intro, the WiseGuide Wrap-Up, and the Putting It in *Perspectives* review form.

WiseGuide Intro

In the WiseGuide Intro, the Academic Editor introduces the section, gives you an overview of the topics covered, and explains why particular articles were selected and what's important about them.

Also in the WiseGuide Intro, you'll find several key points or learning objectives that highlight the most important things to remember from this section. These will help you to focus your study of section topics.

At the end of the WiseGuide Intro, you'll find questions designed to stimulate critical thinking. Wise students will keep these questions in mind as they read an article (we repeat the questions at the start of the articles as a reminder). When you finish each article, check your understanding. Can you answer the questions? If not, go back and reread the article. The Academic Editor has written sample responses for many of the questions, and you'll find these online at the **courselinks**™ site for this course. More about **courselinks** in a minute. . . .

WiseGuide Wrap-Up

Be course wise and develop a thorough understanding of the topics covered in this course. The WiseGuide Wrap-Up at the end of each section will help you do just that with concluding comments or summary points that repeat what's most important to understand from the section you just read.

In addition, we try to get you wired up by providing a list of select Internet resources—what we call R.E.A.L. web sites because they're **R**elevant, **E**xciting, **A**pproved, and **L**inked. The information at these web sites will enhance your understanding of a topic. (Remember to use your Passport and start at http://www.courselinks.com so that if any of these sites have changed, you'll have the latest link.)

Putting It in *Perspectives* Review Form

At the end of the book is the Putting It in *Perspectives* review form. Your instructor may ask you to complete this form as an assignment or for extra credit. If nothing else, consider doing it on your own to help you critically think about the reading.

Prompts at the end of each article encourage you to complete this review form. Feel free to copy the form and use it as needed.

The courselinks™ Site

The **courselinks** Passport is your ticket to a wonderful world of integrated web resources designed to help you with your course work. These resources are found at the **courselinks** site for your course area. This is where the readings in this book and the key topics of your course are linked to an exciting array of online learning tools. Here you will find carefully selected readings, web links, quizzes, worksheets, and more, tailored to your course and approved as connected learning tools. The ever-changing, always interesting **courselinks** site features a number of carefully integrated resources designed to help you be course wise. These include:

- **R.E.A.L. Sites** At the core of a **courselinks** site is the list of R.E.A.L. sites. This is a select group of web sites for studying, not surfing. Like the readings in this book, these sites have been selected, reviewed, and approved by the Academic Editor and the Editorial Board. The R.E.A.L. sites are arranged by topic and are annotated with short descriptions and key words to make them easier for you to use for reference or research. With R.E.A.L. sites, you're studying approved resources within seconds—and not wasting precious time surfing unproven sites.

- **Editor's Choice** Here you'll find updates on news related to your course, with links to the actual online sources. This is also where we'll tell you about changes to the site and about online events.

- **Course Overview** This is a general description of the typical course in this area of study. While your instructor will provide specific course objectives, this overview helps you place the course in a generic context and offers you an additional reference point.

- **www.orksheet** Focus your trip to a R.E.A.L. site with the www.orksheet. Each of the 10 to 15 questions will prompt you to take in the best that site has to offer. Use this tool for self-study, or if required, email it to your instructor.

- **Course Quiz** The questions on this self-scoring quiz are related to articles in the reader, information at R.E.A.L. sites, and other course topics, and will help you pinpoint areas you need to study. Only you will know your score—it's an easy, risk-free way to keep pace!

- **Topic Key** The Topic Key is a listing of the main topics in your course, and it correlates with the Topic Key that appears in this reader. This handy reference tool also links directly to those R.E.A.L. sites that are especially appropriate to each topic, bringing you integrated online resources within seconds!

- **Web Savvy Student Site** If you're new to the Internet or want to brush up, stop by the Web Savvy Student site. This unique supplement is a complete **courselinks**™ site unto itself. Here, you'll find basic information on using the Internet, creating a web page, communicating on the web, and more. Quizzes and Web Savvy Worksheets test your web knowledge, and the R.E.A.L. sites listed here will further enhance your understanding of the web.

- **Student Lounge** Drop by the Student Lounge to chat with other students taking the same course or to learn more about careers in your major. You'll find links to resources for scholarships, financial aid, internships, professional associations, and jobs. Take a look around the Student Lounge and give us your feedback. We're open to remodeling the Lounge per your suggestions.

Building Better Perspectives!

Please tell us what you think of this *Perspectives* volume so we can improve the next one. Here's how you can help:

1. Visit our **coursewise** site at: http://www.coursewise.com

2. Click on *Perspectives*. Then select the Building Better *Perspectives* Form for your book.

3. Forms and instructions for submission are available online.

Tell us what you think—did the readings and online materials help you make some learning connections? Were some materials more helpful than others? Thanks in advance for helping us build better *Perspectives*.

Student Internships

If you enjoy evaluating these articles or would like to help us evaluate the **courselinks** site for this course, check out the **coursewise** Student Internship Program. For more information, visit:

http://www.coursewise.com/intern.html

Contents

At **coursewise**, we're publishing *connected learning tools*. That means that the book you are holding is only a part of this publication. You'll also want to harness the integrated resources that **coursewise** has developed at the fun and highly useful **courselinks**™ web site for *Perspectives: Personality*. If you purchased this book new, use the Passport that was shrink-wrapped to this volume to obtain site access. If you purchased a used copy of this book, then you need to buy a stand-alone Passport. If your bookstore doesn't stock Passports to **courselinks** sites, visit http://www.courselinks.com for ordering information.

section

1

Self and Identity

section 2

Personality, Depression and Mental Health

section 3

Genetic and Evolutionary Models of Personality

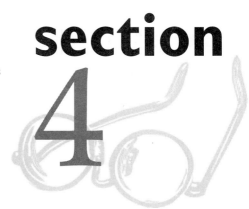

section 4

Personality Development and Change

section 5

Personality and Motivation

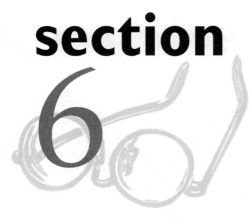

section 6

Personality and Social Relationships

section 7

Resilience and Psychological Defense

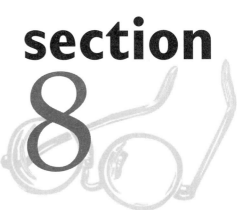

section

8

Sociocultural Aspects of Personality

Topic Key

This Topic Key is an important tool for learning. It will help you integrate this reader into your course studies. Listed below, in alphabetical order, are important topics covered in this volume. Below each topic, you'll find the reading numbers and titles, and also the R.E.A.L. web site addresses, relating to that topic. Note that the Topic Key might not include every topic your instructor chooses to emphasize. If you don't find the topic you're looking for in the Topic Key, check the index or the online topic key at the **courselinks**™ site.

Adolescence
13 Linking Individual Development and Social Changes

Successful Pathways through Middle Childhood
http://midchild.soe.umich.edu/index.html

Adult Development
12 Eight Ages of Man
13 Linking Individual Development and Social Changes
15 The Stability of Personality: Observations and Evaluations

Adult Attachment Lab at UC Davis
http://psychology.ucdavis.edu/Shaver/lab.html

Laboratory of Personality and Cognition
http://lpcwww.grc.nia.nih.gov/

Attachment
21 The Loving Ties That Bind
22 Stages of Friendship Growth in Preadolescence as Related to Attachment History

Adult Attachment Lab at UC Davis
http://psychology.ucdavis.edu/Shaver/lab.html

Behavioral Genetics
9   Were You Born That Way?
10 Moving Beyond the Heritability Question: New Directions in Behavioral Genetic Studies of Personality

Society for Neuroscience
http://www.sfn.org

Biological Approaches to Personality
9   Were You Born That Way?
10 Moving Beyond the Heritability Question: New Directions in Behavioral Genetic Studies of Personality

Society for Neuroscience
http://www.sfn.org

Child Development
12 Eight Ages of Man
13 Linking Individual Development and Social Changes
14 Introduction and How to Test Your Own Propensity to Rebel
18 Babies, Bonds, and Brains: The Relationship between Love and Development
21 The Loving Ties That Bind
22 Stages of Friendship Growth in Preadolescence as Related to Attachment History
23 Basic Behavioral Science Research for Mental Health: Vulnerability and Resilience
27 Commentary: Tending the Garden of Personality
28 Growing Up in Black and White
31 A Collective Fear of the Collective: Implications for Selves and Theories of Selves

Successful Pathways through Middle Childhood
http://midchild.soe.umich.edu/index.html

Clinical Psychology
7   Women and Depression

Comparative Psychology and Personality
Human Behavior and Evolution Society
http://psych.lmu.edu/hbes.htm

Culture and Personality
13 Linking Individual Development and Social Changes
28 Growing Up in Black and White
29 The Death of the Profane: A Commentary on the Genre of Legal Writing
31 A Collective Fear of the Collective: Implications for Selves and Theories of Selves

International Association for Cross-Cultural Psychology
http://www.fit.edu/CampusLife/clubs-org/iaccp/

Depression
6   Personal History: Anatomy of Melancholy
7   Women and Depression

Wing of Madness: A Depression Guide
http://www.wingofmadness.com/

Discrimination
28 Growing Up in Black and White
29 The Death of the Profane: A Commentary on the Genre of Legal Writing

Stereotypes and Prejudice: A Resource Page for Teachers
http://ucsub.colorado.edu/~schneidn/

Dreams
26 Dream Analysis by Mail: An American Woman Seeks Freud's Advice

Association for the Study of Dreams
http://www.asdreams.org/

Eastern vs. Western Psychology
31 A Collective Fear of the Collective: Implications for Selves and Theories of Selves

Evolutionary Psychology
11 Psychological Sex Differences: Origins through Sexual Selection

Human Behavior and Evolution Society
http://psych.lmu.edu/hbes.htm

Family Dynamics
14 Introduction and How to Test Your Own Propensity to Rebel

Freud
24 Resistance and Repression
26 Dream Analysis by Mail: An American Woman Seeks Freud's Advice

Association for the Study of Dreams
http://www.asdreams.org/

section

1

Learning Objectives

- Learn about the concept of multiple identities and how this view departs from traditional psychological theories positing that the goal of development is one, true, coherent self.

- Describe how discrimination can influence the development of young people's identities.

- Discuss why people might prefer to have a *consistent* rather than a *positive* self-view.

- Name and describe some of the key components of narcissism.

Self and Identity

 *Personality* can be defined in terms of one's characteristic actions, interests, goals, emotions, and "ways of being." You'll see it defined in all these ways and more in the articles ahead and as you study the ideas presented in your textbook and in class. We begin this first section of the reader by focusing on identity: one's own perception of oneself and "who one is." The ways we define ourselves and think about ourselves play a large role in how others see us and vice versa. It will be helpful to begin our review of topics within personality by examining what and how people think about themselves.

The articles in this first section represent a broad range of ideas about identity and the self, showcasing how personality psychology connects with fields as diverse as philosophy, education, and social, clinical, and counseling psychology. The authors of these articles focus on understanding identity from a number of points of view. They ask such questions as: What is identity? What is the role of others in shaping our identity? What is the role of our identity in shaping our social relationships with others? Finally, the last two articles describe the effects of relatively mild or more severe levels of obsession with the self.

In "To Thine Own Selves Be True," Stephens notes that a number of psychologists have been questioning psychology's focus on "finding oneself" and "being true to oneself." They argue that it is false to assume that we have "one true self" to which we can be true. Rather, each of us has multiple selves that we access at different times in different situations. If you have moved away for college, you may have noticed this the first time you went home for a holiday. We may be a "different" person with our friends than with our parents, or we may seem like quite different people if one were to meet us giving an aggressive sales presentation vs. taking our kids to the park on the weekend. These theorists note that we all have different "sides" to, or aspects, of our personalities that come out in some situations but not others. For example, we may feel shy at school but not when at home with our families. Which is our "true" self? Neither, says these authors. Each of these different "selves" is equally "true," and it is misguided to expect people to be the same in all situations. O'Hara discusses the way this can apply to the treatment of psychotherapy patients—rather than helping people "find themselves" in what may seem a confusing number of roles, therapists might help them understand how their different selves all represent important parts of their personalities.

Woo discusses the role that discrimination can play in the development of students' identities and goals in "Can Racial Stereotypes Psych Out Students?" She reports on research conducted by Claude Steele of Stanford University on the experiences of racial minority students and women. He notes the burden that discriminatory stereotypes place on those they are meant to be describing: the fear of confirming a negative stereotype about oneself places an enormous burden on people, making them anxious and sapping precious mental

Reading 1. How do theories of multiple selves differ from traditional psychological theories? How might this idea be applied to therapeutic settings?

Reading 2. What is "stereotype threat"? What are some of the ways that stereotype threat can be eliminated or at least lessened?

Reading 3. Which marriages showed the greatest level of commitment in this study? Why does Swann argue that people want to confirm negative self-images?

Reading 4. What happens when narcissists are given the opportunity to look at themselves? How do narcissists perceive their contribution to a group project?

Reading 5. What was narcissistic in Ted Kaczynski's behavior? What is the relationship between Narcissistic Personality Disorder, as defined in this article, and the narcissism found among many college students in the previous article?

and emotional energy from the business at hand. He has conducted several studies examining the effects of this burden, demonstrating again and again that merely reminding students of the negative stereotype can impair performance. However, the story also has a positive side—it also describes the conditions necessary to help alleviate the burden of negative stereotypes for students.

Swann has taken a fairly radical position in personality and social psychology: He argues that people would rather be around others who confirm their own view of themselves, even if that view is negative, than to be around people who will bolster their self-esteem. In "Embracing the Bitter 'Truth,' " Swann and colleagues demonstrate a rather sinister version of this. People are more committed to marriage if their partner's view of them is consistent with their own self-view, even if their own self-view is quite negative. That is, people who view themselves in relatively negative terms are more committed to their marriage when their partner also thinks very little of them than when their partner thinks highly of them. Read about this and see if it helps you to make sense of any of your family or friends' relationships!

Robins and John conducted an interesting study of college students. First, nearly half of their college student sample scored fairly high on a narcissism scale. Narcissists are individuals who are pathologically focused on themselves—you'll recall the myth of Narcissus, who was infatuated with his own reflection. In their work, Robins and John showed that these narcissists enjoyed looking at themselves (as you might expect) and showed especially inflated views of their own abilities and contributions to a group project when they were able to watch themselves on tape. See if reading this article helps you to understand the way the last group project you worked on may have run into trouble!

Finally, compare the "garden-variety" narcissists represented in this article with that of the Unabomber in Scarf's article: "The Mind of the Unabomber." How do you think the two kinds of narcissism differ—is one simply a more extreme version of the other, or are they fundamentally different types?

How do theories of multiple selves differ from traditional psychological theories? How might this idea be applied to therapeutic settings?

To Thine Own Selves Be True

A new breed of psychologists says there's no one answer to the question "Who am I?"

Mitchell Stephens

Pick a late-20th-century city, better an American city, even better a California city, and study one of the inhabitants. Note the range of people this individual is exposed to: the different ethnic backgrounds, the different lifestyles, the different beliefs. Then observe the variety of behaviors the subject exhibits: from vegetarianism to weightlifting, or from bungee jumping to helping the homeless. And note how often and how easily these behaviors change.

Now move in closer, close enough to hear the specimen's thoughts. A jumble of voices will become audible: some bold, some whiny; some mature, some immature; some naive, some cynical. You'll pick up echoes of parents, friends and talk-show hosts; rapper-like boasts and Woody Allen-like anxieties.

Keep listening and eventually you will hear a question. Perhaps it will arrive during a session with a therapist or a heart-to-heart with a friend, perhaps in some lonely moment late at night. (The older and the more self-satisfied the subject, the longer you may have to wait.) But at some point that person will wonder: "Who am I?" And if you have been paying attention, you will understand why no good answer comes.

"Who am I?" Snuggled up behind this question is a comfortable, mostly unnoticed assumption: that we each have a kernel of identity, a self. It is a supposition that has long lain at the center of Western culture: "Know thyself," advised the Delphic oracle, classical Greece's version of self-help therapy. "To thine own self be true," Shakespeare counseled.

However, mutating lifestyles and changing intellectual currents have led a group of increasingly influential psychologists—postmodern psychologists seems to be the name that is sticking—to the conclusion that we have no single, separate, unified self. They maintain that we contain many selves and that the proper response to the suggestion "Get in touch with yourself" or "Be yourself" is "Which one?"

Hazel Rose Markus, professor of psychology at the University of Michigan, calls this "the most exciting time in psychology in decades and decades." We have begun to realize, she says, that "there isn't just one answer to the 'Who am I?' question."

Consider, as an example, the individual named Mick Jagger. The Rolling Stones' lead singer was and, if the tabloids are to be believed, remains a classic libertine, but he is also a father and, until recently at least, a family man. Jagger is a rock 'n' roller, a bohemian, whose songs and lifestyle challenge traditional standards of behavior; yet he travels in upper-class British circles, hobnobbing with dukes and princesses. Jagger can be coarse and crude, yet he knows his nonfiction and his vintages.

Which is the real Mick? His answer: all of the above. "People find it very hard to accept that you can be all these things at almost the same time," Jagger has complained.

Relax, Mick. The times seem to be catching up with you once again. This new group of psychologists starts from the assumption that there is no single Mick, just a rotating bunch of possible Micks, changing as the people you are with and the situations you are in change. And, these psychologists believe, similarly disparate groups of selves, if less wealthy and less famous, inhabit us all. Like Walt Whitman, we "contain multitudes."

Healthy multitudes. We are not talking here of those who suffer from "multiple personality disorder." That nightmarish condition (chronicled in popular books and movies) is characterized by dissociative states in which a personality "splits" into different selves with different memories, some of which appear to know nothing about the other selves. No, we are talking about healthy people, like Jagger, who don't blank out, who are quite aware of everything they are doing, but who have, quite naturally, created different selves to relate to different aspects of their multifaceted lives.

"There are people who can live very comfortably and successfully with a multiple vision of who they are," says Cal State Northridge psychology professor Edward Sampson. "And they don't go to traditional therapists unless they want to get that knocked out of them." This is not, its proponents contend, just another provocative theory. It is a response to some feelings that, in this fractured, complicated, media-saturated, post-"Ozzie and Harriet" world, are very much in the air. There is the sense that we are often, if not always, playing—at work, at our relationships, even at parenthood; the sense that each of us can switch roles as easily as we switch costumes—from business person to jock, from backpacker to sophisticate, from nurturer to sex object.

The implications of the theory are large: It's not just that we each have different sides to our personality; it's that we have no central personality in relation to which all our varied behaviors might be seen as just "sides." We are, in other words, not absolutely anything.

"The true self is dead," proclaims Walter Truett Anderson, author of *Reality Isn't What It Used to Be*, a primer on postmodernism.

If you find this somewhat difficult to swallow, you're not alone. Some psychologists consider the whole issue a waste of time. "It doesn't matter if it's one self or two or three or 5,000," scoffs Robert Zajonc, director of the Institute for Social Research at the University of Michigan and Markus' husband. Zajonc, who has spent much of his life in Europe, finds this preoccupation with the self—or selves—typically American. "I don't think of my self, as such," he says. "I may think of my schedule, my obligations, my meetings, but I don't really spend too much time asking, 'Who am I?' "

Others who do spend time asking are disturbed by the suggestion that there isn't one answer. After all, the idea that we each have a single identity, one true self—just as we each have one true nose and one true medical history—does have a certain seductiveness. Our friends and acquaintances don't seem to have much trouble dealing with each of us as if we were a constant, consistent entity. Why should we?

"People certainly are capable of experiencing themselves as having a relative unity," says Louis Sass, a Rutgers clinical psychology professor who has been critical of some of these new ideas. "They have in the past, and I doubt that has changed much."

Kenneth Gergen, a Swarthmore psychology professor whose book, *The Saturated Self: Dilemmas of Identity in Contemporary Life*, provides the best introduction to postmodern psychology, notes a similar resistance to his postmodern perspective among some of his students. " 'It's just empirically wrong,' they say, or, 'That's just your point of view.' I've had students who've complained to the deans that this idea was really so antithetical to their values that they felt it was injurious to the student body."

Gergen, who is wont to question traditional notions of truth and reality as well as identity, understands his students' disquiet. Belief in a single self is so basic to our culture, to the ways each of us has of thinking and talking about what we call "ourself," that it cannot be easily surrendered.

Gergen "himself," however, began having trouble with the "Who am I?" question, and therefore came into conflict with this language, when he was only 9. "I grew up in a family that was very educated, very cultured," Gergen says. His father was a professor and one of his brothers is David Gergen, the former Reagan media wizard, now a MacNeil/Lehrer NewsHour commentator. "I had a whole way of being in that family which was virtually required, but then I got deposited in a county school in rural North Carolina. And there was no way I could be the person I was at home in that school system, so I kind of fought to stay alive by changing my whole accent, my way of talking, my way of being.

That made two selves: the self Gergen used at home and the self he used in school.

"Then there was another transition," Gergen recalls. "This time to a city school, which had a whole different set of concerns, which again weren't the ones in my family. And then I went from that city school to Yale, which required that I leave the Southern thing behind." So Gergen had to "make" yet another identity for himself.

While in graduate school at Duke, he read the psychological literature that argued the importance to our mental well-being of maintaining a unified, centralized, coherent self. "But it just made no sense, given my experience," he explains. "Now I could either say, 'I'm very sick,' or I could say, 'This literature has got to be wrong.' " Gergen has been challenging the traditional psychological understanding of the self off and on ever since. And lately he has had lots of help.

A group of counselors and therapists, for example, has begun noting that we all must "create" other selves as we leave our families in search of friendship, success and love—and then move on to new friendships, new successes and new loves. Social psychologists have begun studying not only our "child selves," our "professional selves," our "friendship selves" and our "parent selves," but also what Hazel Markus labels our "possible selves," our "feared possible selves," our "ideal selves," our "fleeting selves," our "tentative selves" and our "chronically accessible selves."

Philosophers have pointed out that the self divides the moment we start looking for it: There is the self that we're trying to find plus the self that is doing the looking, plus the self within which this game of hide and seek is being played. Even the practice of placing an alarm clock out of reach in the bedroom implies that we have at least two selves—a responsible nighttime self and a lazy morning self.

But perhaps the most interesting support for Gergen's position has come from those philosophers of mind, cognitive psychologists and biologists who investigate the workings of consciousness. When they examine the gray matter or interrogate their computer models in search of something that might pass for a self, they come up empty. It's not there.

"Our common-sense notion is of the self as a sort of inner boss, a sort of puppeteer inside the body, who is in charge," says Daniel Dennett, author of *Consciousness Explained*. "So that, for instance, when I talk my vocal apparatus is being controlled as if there was some homunculus, sitting at a mighty theater organ, making the words come out, as if my body speaks on behalf of this sort of central meaner on the inside. But as soon as you look closely at this notion of self, it seems to break down."

Dennett's research into the workings of consciousness has convinced him that there is no "homunculus" or little person, no "central meaner," no "ghostly supervisor," no "benevolent dictator," sitting there at the center of the brain, making decisions for the rest of the mind and watching consciousness like an audience might watch a movie. There is, in other words, no point of pure Dennettness, no "brain pebble," somewhere in Dennett's head that contains his identity or self. Consciousness, instead is a rather sloppy, multilayered thing in which various takes on reality, supplied by our various perceptual and cognitive organs, supersede each other.

But if there is no kernel of selfness inside our brains, why do we all seem to start with this common-sense notion of a single, separate, unified self? The answer may be that not all people do. Here Gergen's view has gotten some support from anthropology and our increasing awareness of other cultures.

"I took a trip to Japan," says Markus, "and that, as a social psychologist, is a journey that alters your world altogether. That's where I really saw great differences in the answer that gets given to the 'Who am I?' question." The Japanese, Markus learned and confirmed in subsequent research projects, do not look upon the self as being nearly as separate and self-contained as Americans do.

"Here, there's a real press to individuate yourself, to be special and unique, to separate from others, to be your own person," Markus says. "It's encoded in all our sacred texts and documents: We want independence and liberty and to be free. As Americans we're absolutely fearful of showing that we're a social or a group product in some way. We need to see ourselves as bounded wholes. But in Japan, the common view is that the individual is just a fraction. You can only be whole there when you fit in with groups."

From an anthropological or historical perspective, it is the American conception of an isolated, unified self—the conception most of us take for granted—that may be the exception. "Our view of the self has a history," says Philip Cushman, of the California School of Professional Psychology in Berkeley. "It comes from a tradition of self-contained individualism." That I-gotta-be-me! tradition, a compulsion to do things "my way," may never have been stronger than it has been in 20th-century America.

An escape from this exaggerated individualism is, for Gergen, one of the major benefits of the theory of multiple selves. Gergen defines those various selves as "the capacities we carry within us for multiple relationships." We have, for example, selves for relating with our bosses, selves for our subordinates, selves reserved for our friends and selves that come to life only in the presence of certain someones.

These selves, despite what we like to think here in America, are not our property alone. They are not just "discovered" within us. They are "created" in our relationships with other people. It probably will take a child, or at least the thought of a child, to help you create yourself as a parent. You may never have an opportunity to create a certain romantic, moonstruck, poetry-writing self unless you pick up the scent of Mr. or Ms. Right. "You can't be a self by yourself," Markus concludes.

Our selves are the product of what Gergen calls—with a nod to the Japanese—"relatedness." And Gergen (exhibiting a hopeful self) believes that acknowledging our various selves and accepting our "relatedness" is a route to the psychologist's ever-present goal: improved mental health.

This San Diego woman was frazzled, anxious and depressed— "at times really anxious and deeply depressed," reports psychologist Maureen O'Hara. "She exhibited, in other words, typical late-20th-century symptoms."

The woman worked in the Navy, as a medic. She went home to a husband and three children. And on holidays she returned to the village in Mexico where she had been reared. Tough sailor one moment, gentle, nurturing mom the next, deferential daughter every few months—perhaps not the typical late-20th-century life, but characteristically wide-ranging and scattered.

The woman's problem, it soon became apparent, was the tension, the conflict, between her disparate roles. Which of these selves was really her? "She couldn't reconcile them," O'Hara says. She had no good answer to the "Who am I?" question. O'Hara, president of the Assn. for Humanistic Psychology, is one of those who have begun to use the ideas of postmodern psychology to treat patients. She says acceptance of multiple selves turned out to be the key to relieving that San Diego woman's anxiety and depression. "We worked for a while, and she realized she didn't have to reconcile the three worlds she lived in," O'Hara says. "She didn't have to worry about being consistent. She could honor all these different selves. The woman described it as 'allowing each personality to get out of the way of the others.' "

Sass, of Rutgers and author of the forthcoming book *Madness and Modernism*, acknowledges that there might be some "rigid" people for whom learning that they can allow themselves to express different sides of their personality might have therapeutic value. "But," he asks in a recent critique of "the postmodern turn in contemporary psychoanalysis": "What of those who suffer from problems of a different sort—for example, from feelings of emptiness, meaninglessness and unrelatedness; from the inability to form stable relationships, or from a lack of sustaining interests or continuing goals, values and ideals?" These problems, too, as Sass notes, are "characteristic of our age." By surrendering our belief in a true self, don't we risk aggravating them?

Maybe not. Maybe it is the separate, unified self—the one that traditional psychotherapists are still trying to help us "find" or "realize" —that is causing these feelings of "emptiness, meaninglessness and un-relatedness." Maybe our feelings of inadequacy have grown with the inevitable frustrations of the effort to locate and bolster this mythical "true self." Maybe we have spent too many hours on too many couches trying to determine who we really are. Maybe by accepting, as that San Diego woman did, the idea that our identities come from our relationships, we could find a way out of the psychological desert in which some of us now wander.

The word *postmodern* has been stretched over a lot of different ideas, but the central one seems to be that our way of looking at the world is not a given, that we create what we see as "reality" through language. This view has at least as many detractors among academics as supporters. Berkeley philosopher John Searle, for example, has debated angrily with Gergen at academic conferences whether "reality" is in fact just a creation of language. "Science is based on the supposition of an independently existing reality," Searle maintains. "If you don't believe in that then you're out of business."

Gergen, however, argues that we "construct" reality through the stories—the narratives—we tell about it. Other societies, for example, have told other stories about such seemingly basic matters as mental illness, emotions, and thought—and therefore these concepts had a different "reality" for them. Our identities, too, Gergen maintains, are constructed—products of different stories we tell ourselves about ourselves.

Postmodernism is based on some difficult theories (poststructuralism, deconstruction, etc.) hatched, for the most part, in France, but somehow this new view of psychology seems most at home in America, particularly California. In an insular, homogeneous Old World town it might have been possible for people to define themselves in terms of a single belief, a single way of life, but not here. Not where we are tugged at by so many possible belief systems and lifestyles—each of which presents us with new "possible selves."

"California has always been where the idea of the possible came from," says Markus, who grew up in San Diego. "There is a bit of Hollywood in everyone in California—the sense that you can be other than who you are now, that you can kind of create yourself."

And why settle for creating just one self? Indeed, how could you settle for creating just one self in a world where even adults are encouraged to play, a world where we can trade in our one "true" nose for a shorter version, a world where we can move from one identity to another—with a change of clothes, a change of channel, an unexpected phone call—as easily as we might move from Main street to Adventureland at Disneyland? Gergen and friends say they did not invent this new postmodern world. They are just trying to help us adjust to it. Don't agonize over consistency or authenticity, they advise. Enjoy yourselves!

But if this is indeed where we're headed, some questions must be answered. Questions about ethics and morality, to begin with. Sass, for one, is not at all sanguine about this acceptance of inconsistency and inauthenticity. "There are clearly dangers in giving up that notion of a single self," he notes. "You absolve the person of responsibility for making judgments." Imagine the excuses people might make: "Hey, it wasn't my fault. One of my other selves did it."

Absolving people of responsibility for their behavior, however, is not at all what O'Hara has in mind for postmodern psychology. Instead, she hopes these new views of identity will cause us to reopen "the ethical conversation" and produce some original ideas on how people—multiselved people—can be held "accountable to each other." The issue might not be who we really are but whether our various selves can ethically share the same body.

Gergen attempts to construct an ethics of postmodernism upon a slightly different foundation: He places his faith in the concept of "relatedness." If we become aware of the extent to which our selves are created with others, Gergen contends, perhaps

we'll be more, not less, responsible in our dealings with those others—more aware of the debt we owe them, less likely to think we can "find ourself" by leaving them behind.

Perhaps. Still, the issue of how our various selves are going to deal with others' various selves in this new postmodern world remains problematic. If everybody is plural, how do we decide whom we like and whom we dislike? How, if our identities are constantly subject to change, do we know whom it is we're talking to, whom we're taking a shine to? These questions might be combined into one question: How can two people who know all this be, gulp, in love?

"My wife and I went through this painfully at first," confesses Gergen, whose wife, Mary, is also a psychology professor. "This is a second marriage for both of us, kind of a romantic thing: We ran away from the world. So, early on in our marriage, she'd frequently ask me whether I still loved her." And Gergen, who was trying to think out some of these psychological issues, didn't know how to respond: "What exactly as a psychological event could love mean? And how could I do an introspective examination of all my interior to know whether it was still there or not?

"Finally, she said, 'Look, when I ask you whether you love me, don't go through these tortuous questions of what's really real about love and how you'd know. Just say the words meaningfully, and I'll be a lot better off." And that may be the key to life in the postmodern world. We will have to do our best to say words like "I love you" meaningfully even though we sense there are dozens of "I's," not all of whom can be in agreement on anything, even though we know we'll never pin down whom "you" really might be. We will have to learn to make do, in other words, with rituals and approximations.

"I don't think we need someone to love all 93 of our selves," Markus says. "If someone just takes three or four of them real seriously, that's enough to keep most of us going on most days."

 Article Review Form at end of book.

What is "stereotype threat"? What are some of the ways that stereotype threat can be eliminated or at least lessened?

Can Racial Stereotypes Psych Out Students?

Elaine Woo

Two students, one black and the other white, sit next to each other in a college classroom. Both are bright and from middle-class families. They went to decent high schools and did well on college placement exams. But the black student is flunking, and the white one is not.

Why do they perform so differently?

Stanford University social psychologist Claude Steele believes he has an answer. And it isn't genetics, social class, lack of academic skills, family dysfunction or segregation—the usual suspects in the lineup of explanations for the stubborn problem of black underachievement.

Steele says that blacks—or any member of a group freighted with negative stereotypes—constantly labor under the suspicion that the stereotypes about them are true. Thus, women contend with the image of being mathematical klutzes, the elderly with insinuations of forgetfulness, blacks with the specter of intellectual inferiority. This burden alone, he believes, can make an otherwise competent student flounder.

His work is likely to stir up the scientific community, where many researchers believe that a number of factors underlie group differences in academic performance. But Steele's theory, tested in the lab and on campus, turns some common psychological assumptions on their head. In the process, it offers ammunition to both sides of the affirmative action debate.

Steele argues that the possibility of being judged by a stereotype—or inadvertently fulfilling it—can cause an anxiety so disruptive that it impairs intellectual performance. The victim may reject the stereotype, yet can't avoid its glare.

Steele calls this condition "stereotype threat." For black college students, it can deaden the commitment to academics, becoming a barrier as effective, he says, as a lock on the schoolhouse door.

In a paper published last month in the *Journal of Personality and Social Psychology*, Steele and Joshua Aronson of the University of Texas offer proof that pervasive negative stereotypes about blacks' intellectual ability create a "situational pressure" that distracts them and depresses their academic performance.

The trigger can be astonishingly trivial—asking a student to identify his race before taking a test, or suggesting that the test will measure intellectual performance. But defuse the stereotype threat by removing those triggers, their research says, and black students score as well as whites.

Suggesting the phenomenon's universality, Steele and professor Steven J. Spencer of Hope College in Holland, Mich., found the same results in experiments examining women and the image that they are mathematically inept. Steele and Aronson have found even white men may be stereotype-vulnerable: Their scores plummeted in testing situations that implied their math ability would be measured against that of Asians.

"If they can feel stereotype vulnerability," Aronson says, "anybody can."

Yet it is Steele's and Aronson's work involving blacks that has received the most enthusiastic attention, in part because of the promise it holds for solving what has seemed an intractable problem.

Dropout Rate a Problem

Nationally, the college dropout rate for African Americans is 70%, almost twice that of whites, despite three decades of efforts aimed at boosting their academic success.

"It is an extremely encouraging program of research," said Jennifer Crocker, a University of Michigan social psychologist. "It suggests this is a problem we can do something about . . . these group differences in achievement."

The harshest criticism so far has come from a painfully close source: Shelby Steele, the conservative essayist who is Claude's identical twin brother.

In an extraordinary outburst, the San Jose State English professor, an ardent foe of affirmative action, has accused Claude of stealing his ideas and applying them to a more politically correct agenda.

"This has stood between us for some time," Shelby wrote in a scathing letter to the *New York Times* in October, after the newspaper ran an article contrasting their views. What his brother now calls "stereotype threat," Shelby claimed, is really his idea of "racial vulnerability," which Shelby explored in a series of essays published five years ago.

Then Stanford's Steele replied with his own letter, denying the charges and spelling out the differences between his theory and his brother's ideas.

Trying to patch up their relationship, Claude initially declined to be interviewed for this article without assurances that Shelby would not be mentioned. He relented after reaching an agreement with Shelby that neither would comment on the other's work.

Claude began investigating the problem of black underachievement in the late 1980s, while on the faculty at the University of Michigan. Asked to join a committee studying student retention and recruitment, he came upon some astounding statistics: grades and Scholastic Achievement Test scores of blacks and whites who were flunking out.

The conventional wisdom said that when black college students failed it was because they were ill-equipped, felled by sub-standard schooling since kindergarten.

But Steele found that those with the best preparation—reflected in high SAT scores—were failing more frequently than those with lower scores, and at a rate more than three times that of whites with similar scores.

Among black students, 18% to 33% were bombing out, compared to 2% to 11% of whites. And the dropout rate was the highest among students ranked in the top third by SAT scores.

"That pattern surprised me," Steele said recently. "Something else was going on in that situation beyond just skill preparation."

At Stanford, which hired him in 1991, Steele embarked on a series of experiments with Aronson, then a postdoctoral student, to test the hypothesis that social stigma was hampering blacks' intellectual performance.

In the first two experiments, three groups of undergraduates were recruited to take a test made up of the toughest items from the verbal portion of the Graduate Record Exam, used by graduate programs to assess aptitude.

The first group was told that the test would provide a genuine measure of verbal reasoning ability—a cue that researchers thought could trigger in blacks fear of being judged according to a stereotype about their intelligence.

The second group was given no suggestion that intellectual prowess was being measured. It was told that the test would merely evaluate the factors involved in solving verbal problems.

The third group's students got the same instructions as the second with one addition: The test would challenge them.

The researchers theorized that stereotype vulnerability works, in part, by preying on self-doubt any test-taker may feel when struggling to answer a difficult question.

Giving students an alternative context for evaluating their performance—that their frustration might be caused by the test's difficulty rather than any mental deficiencies—could be another way of shielding them from stereotype anxieties.

Researchers said the results of the study confirmed their hunches. Black students who thought the test would measure verbal ability scored significantly lower than whites in their group, and lower than blacks given other introductions.

"This was the first clear demonstration that we had something," Steele said.

In their next experiment, Steele and Aronson wanted to establish what psychological process was unleashed by the murmur of stereotypes. Did cuing blacks that their intelligence was being measured set off thoughts about the relevant, damning stereotype?

They invited 35 undergraduates to take a difficult test. But just before they began, the students were asked to complete 80 word fragments, some associated with negative black stereotypes (such as race, lazy), and others suggesting self-doubts (such as dumb, shame).

The students also filled out questionnaires asking for personal information, such as musical preferences.

These exercises were meant as a sort of racial Rorschach test, "to find out what is psychologically active in a person's mind" during the exam, Steele said.

He and Aronson found that blacks who were told the test would assess mental abilities completed the most word fragments related to negative stereotypes and self doubt. And they recorded fewer stereotype-related preferences (such as rap music) than other blacks or whites.

Those results, the researchers said, suggested that the mere threat of having their intelligence measured aroused in blacks thoughts of stereotypes about intellectual inferiority. And these students tried to distance themselves from those thoughts by disavowing stereotypical interests.

Fears Can Be Eased

Coming just as their mental powers are being stretched by the exam, self-doubt causes blacks to labor twice as hard, but to ill effect, Steele theorizes: They reread questions and recheck answers, in the end working less efficiently and making more mistakes.

"When a black kid sits down to take an ability test," Steele concludes, "bang! Racial stereotypes are activated . . . and are probably driving their emotions and behavior in that situation. . . . You're self-conscious, you don't have as much to allocate" to the task at hand.

In the final experiment in this series, all subjects were told they would take a test that would not reflect their ability. The only variable was that half of the subjects were asked to identify their race on the test sheet.

When blacks were asked to state their race, they scored dramatically lower than whites. But when the race question was absent, their scores matched those of whites.

In other words, the barest hint of stigma seemed to dampen blacks' achievement, but lifting it was the key that opened the lock.

"I think that is the major contribution of our work, really," said Steele, "showing that stereotype threat is a situation that can be turned on and off."

Even some proponents of a competing theory—that genetics account for group differences in intelligence—such as UC Berkeley professor emeritus Arthur Jensen, concede that Steele's research may have some merit and is worth further study.

But Jensen—an educational psychologist who caused an uproar in 1969 when he wrote an article suggesting that black children had low IQs that were largely inherited—also said that "stereotype vulnerability" is, at best, a "minor contributor" to racial differences in standardized tests. He cited a recent study showing that the gap appears as early as age 3, "before any conscious awareness of societal (attitudes) toward blacks have been imbibed."

How well Steele's theory holds up won't be known for years. To answer some of his critics, he is in the midst of replicating his experiments using classic intelligence tests, which Jensen and others consider truer gauges of the ability to think and reason.

What is certain is that the theory already is challenging common views of prejudice and how it affects achievement.

Richard Nisbett, a University of Michigan social psychologist and noted authority on the psychology of stereotypes, observed that Steele's "is really quite a different notion about prejudice than the way people thought in the past."

Black underachievement previously has been tied to prejudice in two ways: Racism shortchanges black children, who wind up with the worst teachers and the most dilapidated campuses. And black students internalize negative stereotypes, which gives rise to crippling self-loathing.

The latter idea informs much of the movement to eliminate affirmative action. Shelby Steele has written powerfully of the danger of such "racial vulnerability" in his 1990 book, *The Content of Our Character: A New Vision of Race in America.*

Affirmative action, he wrote, has perpetuated blacks' "inner realm of racial doubt." That doubt itself, he said, "becomes an unrecognized preoccupation that undermines their ability to perform. . . ."

This debilitating power of stereotypes was part of "an entire framework of ideas lifted without attribution" by his brother, Shelby alleged in his letter to the *New York Times.* Asked in a recent interview whether he still believed his brother's theories borrow from his, he would only say, "We do not comment on each other's work."

In Nisbett's view, Claude's take on the problem is distinctly different from Shelby's, and suggests a different solution than a wholesale scrapping of affirmative action.

Stereotype threat rejects self-victimization as an explanation for black failures: The problem arises from imperfect situations rather than imperfect psyches.

"The brilliance of it (is) to locate the problem out there," Nisbett said. "There are circumstances that can trigger susceptibility to those stereotypes, and there are things institutions can do to make it more or less likely that people will feel vulnerable to them."

Steele and colleagues at Michigan are five years into a comprehensive effort to demonstrate how that vulnerability can be lessened.

Michigan's 21st Century Program is based in large part on Steele's research. Blacks and whites, randomly recruited, live and study together. They discuss personal and social issues in weekly rap sessions or seminars. Their regular course work is supplemented by evening "mastery workshops" in English, calculus, chemistry and physics, taught by upper-class students and emphasizing collaborative study.

Dramatic Results

By avoiding the self-segregation that is standard at most colleges, the program works against what Steele calls "pluralistic ignorance"—the racial isolation that can lead blacks, for instance, to assume their poor grades are the result of a racist professor. When blacks and whites room and study together, they have the opportunity to see their struggles in a different, nonracial light.

The benefits for blacks have been striking. Last year, the average GPA for 21st Century students was 2.89, almost a point higher than that of other blacks. For the top two-thirds of blacks, it eliminated the grade gap with whites. And in the program's first two years, 90% of blacks went on to graduate.

Whites in the program also earned higher grade averages than other white students, but Steele said the increase was not statistically significant. Some observers say the workshops are responsible for blacks' improved performance. Others credit the unique group culture—the value placed on studying, the collaborative ethic, the socializing that cuts across race.

Steele, who is analyzing the program, believes that black students' strong gains are caused by a combination of these factors.

The effort—which will be doubled to 50 students next fall—embraces what Steele calls "wise schooling": education must have at its heart the belief that every student is "up to the challenge of school."

Stereotypes, he reasons, threaten that principle. So do the remedial program into which so many minorities are funneled.

Instead, Steele says, schools should strive to reinvent themselves in ways that eliminate the stereotype threat. That means ending remedial programs that set minimal goals and rethinking those affirmative-action efforts that, in subtler ways, send minorities the message that they are not up to the competition.

And it means encouraging in students the idea that their ability to learn is not fixed, but expandable—an optimistic counterpoint to *The Bell Curve,* the 1994 book that renewed debate over the genetic basis of intelligence.

The success of these principles, Steele notes, has already been demonstrated by a number of prominent educators, such as former Garfield High teacher Jaime Escalante, who motivated underachieving East Los Angeles math students.

"If there is any single principle involved," Steele said, "it is 'Challenge them, don't remediate them.' Challenge conveys faith in their potential."

 Article Review Form at end of book.

Which marriages showed the greatest level of commitment in this study? Why does Swann argue that people want to confirm negative self-images?

Embracing the Bitter "Truth"

Negative self-concepts and marital commitment

**William B. Swann, Jr.,
J. Gregory Hixon,
and Chris De La Ronde**

University of Texas at Austin

Abstract

We propose that because self-concepts allow people to predict (and thus control) the responses of others, people want to find support for their self-concepts. They accordingly gravitate toward relationship partners who see them as they see themselves. For people with negative self-views, this means embracing relationship partners who derogate them. Our findings confirmed this reasoning. Just as persons with positive self-concepts were more committed to spouses who thought well of them than to spouses who thought poorly of them, persons with negative self-concepts were more committed to spouses who thought poorly of them than to spouses who thought well of them.

I flee who chases me, and chase who flees me. (Ovid. ca. 8/1925, line 36)

Ovid's remarks raise eyebrows because they seem to defy a basic truth of social conduct. That is, over the years, everyone from poets and philosophers to grandmothers has noted that people love to be loved. In the last few decades, social scientists have documented this proposition so many times that it is now a bedrock assumption of most theories of social behavior (e.g., Berscheid, 1985). This is what makes Ovid's commentary so puzzling; surely, all other things being equal, rational people do not flee from loving partners in favor of indifferent ones.

Or do they? Recent theorizing has suggested that people want more than adoration from their relationship partners; they also want verification and confirmation of their self-concepts. This research suggests that there may be a grain of truth to Ovid's commentary. That is, if people with negative self-concepts truly look to their relationships for self-verification, they may shun partners who appraise them favorably and embrace those who appraise them unfavorably.

Self-Verification Processes and the Search for Feedback That Fits

Self-verification theory (Swann, 1990) begins with the assumption that the key to successful social relations is the capacity for people to recognize how others perceive them (e.g., Cooley, 1902; Mead, 1934; Stryker, 1981). To this end, people note the reactions of others and use these reactions as a basis for inferring their own self-concepts. From this vantage point, self-concepts are cognitive distillations of past relationships.

Because self-concepts are abstracted from the reactions of others, they should allow people to predict how others will respond to them in the future. Recognizing this, people come to rely on stable self-concepts and view substantial self-concept change as a threat to intrapsychic and interpersonal functioning (for related accounts, see Aronson, 1968; Festinger, 1957; Lecky, 1945). Consider, for example, how a woman who perceives herself as socially inept might feel upon overhearing her husband characterize her as socially skilled. If she takes his comment seriously, she will probably find it thoroughly unsettling, as it challenges a long-standing belief about who she is and implies that she may not know herself after all. And if she does not know *herself*, what does she know?

Even if she lacked such existential concerns, she might still want her husband to recognize her social ineptitude for purely pragmatic or interpersonal reasons (e.g., Goffman, 1959). That is, as long as he recognizes her limitations, he will form modest expectations of her and their interactions will proceed smoothly. In contrast, should he form an inappropriately favorable impression, he might develop unrealistic expectations that she could not meet.

Both intrapsychic and interpersonal considerations may therefore motivate people to prefer self-verifying appraisals over self-discrepant ones. This reasoning leads to an unusual prediction: Although people with negative self-views may find that unfavorable evaluations frustrate their desire for praise, they may nevertheless seek such evaluations because they find them to be reassuring—particularly when they contemplate the intrapsychic and interpersonal anarchy that inappropriately favorable appraisals may bring. People with negative self-views may accordingly prefer relatively negative evaluations and relationship partners who provide such evaluations.

Although laboratory studies have shown that people with firmly held negative self-views prefer interaction partners who evaluate them unfavorably (e.g., Swann, Hixon, Stein-Seroussi, & Gilbert, 1990; Swann, Stein-Seroussi, & Giesler, in press; Swann, Wenzlaff, Krull, & Pelham, in press), no one knows whether or how this tendency influences people's choice of relationship partners outside the laboratory.[1] This issue is not trivial, as some theorists have argued that these findings are a product of idiosyncratic features of laboratory settings and would not generalize to naturally occurring situations (e.g., Raynor & McFarlin, 1986). To address this issue, we moved outside the laboratory to examine people's reactions to appraisals from persons with whom they were involved in ongoing relationships. In particular, we focused on the extent to which married persons with negative, moderate, or positive self-concepts seemed committed

to spouses who appraised them relatively favorably or unfavorably.

Self-Verification at the Horse Ranch and Mall

We recruited 95 married couples from a sample of patrons of a horse ranch (41 couples) and shopping mall (54 couples) in the central Texas area by offering them $5 apiece. Participants ranged in age from 19 to 78, with a mean of 32.1 years. Most participants were Caucasians (87.8%) and had at least some college education (91%). Spouses had known one another for an average of 9 years and had been married for an average of 6 years. Members of 3 couples misunderstood the instructions, and members of 6 other couples gave conflicting responses (e.g., reported having a different number of children); we accordingly deleted their data.[2]

The experimenter seated the members of each couple at opposite ends of a long table so they could not discern one another's responses. After obtaining informed consent and assuring participants that their partners would never see their responses, the experimenter presented each participant with an identical questionnaire as part of an investigation of "the relation between personality and close relationships." In addition to the items described below, the questionnaire included items pertaining to the structure of self-knowledge, interpersonal accuracy, and related issues.

The measure of self-concepts was the short form of the Self-Attributes Questionnaire (SAQ; Pelham & Swann, 1989). The SAQ is a measure of a confederacy of five specific self-views central to self-worth: intellectual capability, physical attractiveness, athletic ability, social skills, and aptitude for arts and music. For each attribute, participants rated themselves relative to

other people their own age and gender on graduated-interval scales ranging from 0 (bottom 5%) to 9 (top 5%). Previous work has shown that the SAQ is stable over a period of 4 months (test-retest $r(50) = .77$). The scale is also internally consistent (co-efficient $\alpha = .64$), which permitted us to sum the five items and use the sum scores to distinguish participants with negative self-concepts (lower third, ≤ 27), moderate self-concepts (middle third, 28–32), and positive self-concepts (upper third, ≥ 33).

After completing the self-ratings, participants filled out the principle index of partner appraisal: the sum of their ratings of their partners on the five SAQ attributes. As expected, spouses rated participants with negative self-views less favorably ($M = 29$) than participants with moderate ($M = 32$) or positive ($M = 34$) self-views, $F(2, 159) = 10.39, p < .001$.

The measure of commitment focused on the participants' intentions, feelings, and actions regarding their relationships. On 9-point scales, participants responded to seven items tapping desire to remain in the relationship, plans to remain in the relationship, relationship satisfaction, time spent together, amount of talking, discussion of problems and worries, and disclosure of personal matters. Responses to these items were closely associated ($\alpha = .88$) and were summed.

The means plotted in Table 1 suggest that people were committed to spouses who verified their self-concepts. A simultaneous multiple regression with commitment as the criterion revealed the anticipated interaction between self-concept and spouse appraisal, $F(1, 157) = 15.15$, $p < .001$. Just as participants with positive self-concepts were more committed to their relationships insofar as their spouses thought well of them, $F(1, 51) = 9.40, p < .004$, $r = .39$, participants with negative self-concepts were more committed to the extent that their spouses thought poorly of them, $F(1, 52) = 9.31, p < .004, r = -.39$. Those with moderate self-concepts were not influenced by the nature of their spouses' appraisals, $F < 1$. The difference scores in row 4 of Table 1 highlight this interaction.

---

1. Although two investigations seem superficially relevant (Backman & Secord, 1962; Doherty & Secord, 1971), they are not because the investigators did not analyze the responses of people with positive and negative self-views separately.

2. Before combining these samples, we ensured that the participants in the ranch and mall samples responded similarly (i.e., our findings replicated across samples). Also, concurrent with this study, we collected data from dating couples as part of an independent investigation of the effect of relationship type on self-verification (Swann, Hixon, & De La Ronde, 1991).

Table I	Average Level of Marital Commitment by Self-Concept and Spouse's Appraisal		
	Self-Concept		
Spouse's Appraisal	**Negative**	**Moderate**	**Positive**
Unfavorable	52.4	52.8	52.0
Moderate	52.7	53.2	53.1
Favorable	43.8	53.8	58.7
Difference (favorable − unfavorable)	−8.6	+1.0	+6.7

Note. Higher values indicate more commitment.

Why People with Negative Self-Views Embraced Spouses Who Derogated Them

Our most provocative finding was that people with negative self-views were most committed to spouses who appraised them unfavorably. To better understand this finding, we examined our participants' responses to several questions that they completed after the major measures.[3] We found the following:

1. The more participants believed that their spouses' appraisals "made them feel that they really knew themselves" rather than "confused them" (summed over the five SAQ attributes), the more committed they were to the relationship, $r(106) = .35, p < .001$, for all participants; $r(35) = .37$, $p < .01$, for those with negative self-views only.

2. There was no evidence that people were committed to partners who appraised them unfavorably because they thought such partners would help them improve themselves. In fact, participants with negative self-views were less confident that feedback from their spouses would help them improve themselves ($M = 6.56$) than were participants with moderate ($M = 7.28$) and positive ($M = 7.49$) self-views, $F(2, 161) = 3.69, p < .04$.

3. In the interests of brevity, some of these items were included in the ranch or mall sample only.

3. People with negative self-views were not especially committed to spouses who rated them negatively because they hoped to win their spouses over. Indeed, participants with negative self-views showed a marginally reliable tendency to be more committed to spouses to the extent that they expected their spouses' appraisals on the five SAQ attributes would worsen, $r(35) = -.25, p < .06$.

4. People with negative self-views did not commit themselves to spouses who rated them unfavorably because they took expressions of negativity as signs of perceptiveness; that is, commitment was unrelated to ratings of spouse perceptiveness, $r(36) = .08$, *ns*.

5. Self-verification was not the exclusive province of women or men. Specifically, gender had no main or interactive effects (all $Fs < 1.15$) when added to the regression equation that related commitment to participants' self-concepts and their spouses' ratings of them.[4] Moreover, when we performed separate regressions on the commitment of women and men, reliable interactions between self-concept and spouse's

4. The modest correlation ($r = .24$) between the residual scores of women and men indicated that the error terms for testing the interactions between gender and the other predictors in our design were minimally biased (D. A. Kenny, personal communication, April 1991). This reassured us that our gender interactions were truly nonsignificant.

appraisal emerged for both genders. $Fs > 5.30, ps< .03$. By showing that our effects obtained even when only one member of each dyad was examined, these findings also suggest that the p values associated with our primary findings were not spuriously inflated by interdependency between the responses of members of dyads (Kenny & Judd, 1986).

General Discussion

In our investigation, married people with negative self-views responded in a remarkable fashion. Whereas participants with positive self-concepts displayed more commitment to spouses who evaluated them favorably than to spouses who evaluated them unfavorably, participants with negative self-views displayed more commitment to spouses who evaluated them *un*favorably, than to spouses who evaluated them favorably. Our findings therefore suggest that people embrace spouses who appraise them in a self-verifying manner, even if this means committing themselves to persons who think poorly of them. This tendency may have undesirable consequences, especially for people who want to improve their self-esteem. Such people may discover, for example, that they are unable to benefit from therapy because their spouses reinforce their negative self-concepts (for a related experiment, see Swann & Predmore, 1985).

Skeptics could, of course, note that our design was correlational and that it is thus hazardous to assume that the spouses' appraisals caused the level of commitment. Although we agree that caution is in order, we are reassured by the evidence we report that casts doubt on several alternative explanations of our effects and by the fact that recent laboratory research has yielded findings that parallel our own (see Swann, 1990, for a review). To us, a more troubling issue is the discrepancy between our findings and the voluminous literature indicating that people prefer favorable evaluations. One reason for this discrepancy may be that past researchers have typically examined participants' reactions to evaluations from complete strangers in laboratory settings. Clearly, it is one thing to express attraction for a stranger who offers an inappropriately favorable evaluation. It is quite another to pursue a relationship with such a person (e.g., Huston & Levinger, 1978), because doing so may invite the undesired intrapsychic and interpersonal consequences associated with discrepant feedback. Thus, for example, the same flattering remarks that seem harmless and pleasant when delivered by a stranger may seem disturbing and unsettling when delivered by someone who should know the person well.

Of course, some laboratory studies, including those we have conducted, *have* shown evidence of self-verification strivings. Why? Perhaps because we have focused on our participants' choice of feedback and interaction partners rather than on immediate, affective reactions to evaluations, as most past researchers have done. Recent research and theorizing (e.g., Swann, 1990; Swann et al., 1990) have suggested that when people with negative self-views first receive favorable evaluations, they are quite enamored with them; only after they have had time to compare such evaluations with their self-concepts has a preference for self-verifying evaluations emerged. Similarly, immediately after receiving unfavorable feedback, people with negative self-views report being distressed by it, yet shortly thereafter they go on to seek additional unfavorable feedback (e.g., Swann, Wenzlaff, Krull, & Pelham, in press)!

This research, then, suggests that people with negative self-views are enveloped in a psychological cross fire between a desire for positive feedback and a desire for self-verifying feedback. For such persons, it seems that the warmth produced by favorable feedback is chilled by incredulity, and that the reassurance produced by negative feedback is tempered by sadness that the "truth" could not be more kind. Given this dilemma, it seems likely that people with negative self-concepts may seek unfavorable (self-verifying) evaluations in some contexts and positive appraisals in others (e.g., Swann, Hixon, & De La Ronde, 1991). When they do court unfavorable evaluations, however, it is not out of masochism, as it seems that they engage in such activities in spite of rather than because of the unhappiness that such appraisals foster.

References

Aronson, E. (1968). A theory of cognitive dissonance: A current perspective. In L. Berkowitz (Ed.), *Advances in experimental social psychology* (Vol. 4, pp. 1–34). New York: Academic Press.

Backman, C. W., & Secord, P. F. (1962). Liking, selective interaction, and misperception in congruent interpersonal relations. *Sociometry, 25,* 321–335.

Berscheid, E. (1985). Interpersonal attraction. In G. Lindzey & E. Aronson (Eds.), *Handbook of social psychology* (Vol. 2, pp. 413–484). New York: Random House.

Cooley, C. H. (1902). *Human nature and the social order.* New York: Scribner's.

Doherty, E. G., & Secord, P. F. (1971). Change of roommate and interpersonal congruency. *Representative Research in Social Psychology, 2,* 70–75.

Festinger, L. (1957). *A theory of cognitive dissonance.* Evanston, IL: Row, Peterson.

Goffman, E. (1959). *The presentation of self in everyday life.* New York: Anchor Books.

Huston, T. L., & Levinger, G. (1978). Interpersonal attraction and relationships. *Annual Review of Psychology, 29,* 115–156.

Kenny, D. A., & Judd, C. M. (1986). Consequences of violating the independence assumption in the analysis of variance. *Psychological Bulletin, 99,* 422–431.

Lecky, P. (1945). *Self-consistency: A theory of personality.* New York: Island Press.

Mead, G. H. (1934). *Mind, self and society.* Chicago: University of Chicago Press.

Ovid. (1925). *The Loves* (Book II) (J. Lewis May, Trans.). Burgay, England: John Lane The Bodley Head. (Original work published ca. 8)

Pelham, B. W., & Swann, W. B., Jr. (1989). From self-conceptions to self-worth: On the sources and structure of global self-esteem. *Journal of Personality and Social Psychology, 57,* 672–680.

Raynor, J. O., & McFarlin, D. B. (1986). Motivation and the self-system. In R. M. Sorrentino & E. T. Higgins (Eds.), *Motivation and cognition: Foundations of social behavior* (pp. 315–349). New York: Guilford Press.

Stryker, S. (1981). *Symbolic interactionism.* Menlo Park, CA: Benjamin/Cummings.

Swann, W. B., Jr. (1990). To be adored or to be known: The interplay of self-enhancement and self-verification. In R. M. Sorrentino & E. T. Higgins (Eds.), *Motivation and cognition* (Vol. 2, pp. 408–448). New York: Guilford Press.

Swann, W. B., Jr., Hixon, J. G., & De La Ronde, C. (1991). *Dating games and marital reality.* Manuscript submitted for publication.

Swann, W. B., Jr., Hixon, J. G., Stein-Serouossi, A., & Gilbert, D. T. (1990). The fleeting gleam of praise: Behavioral reactions to self-relevant feedback. *Journal of Personality and Social Psychology, 59,* 17–26.

Swann, W. B., Jr., & Predmore, S. C. (1985). Intimates as agents of social support: Sources of consolation or despair? *Journal of Personality and Social Psychology, 49,* 1609–1617.

Swann, W. B., Jr., Stein-Seroussi, A., & Giesler, R. B. (In press). Why people self-verify. *Journal of Personality and Social Psychology.*

Swann, W. B., Jr., Wenzlaff, R. M., Krull, D. S., & Pelham, B. W. (in press). The allure of negative feedback: Self-verification strivings among depressed persons. *Journal of Abnormal Psychology.*

Article Review Form at end of book.

What happens when narcissists are given the opportunity to look at themselves? How do narcissists perceive their contribution to a group project?

Effects of Visual Perspective and Narcissism on Self-Perception

Is seeing believing?

Richard W. Robins[1] and Oliver P. John[2]

[1]University of California, Davis,
and [2]University of California, Berkeley

Abstract

Would people still see themselves through rose-colored glasses if they had the same perspective as others do? We contrast predictions from narcissism theory with cognitive-informational accounts of self-perception bias. Study 1 showed that Narcissists enjoy situations in which they can view themselves from an external perspective, and report that such situations boost their self-confidence. In Study 2, subjects evaluated their performance in a group task from the normal visual perspective of the self and from a "reversed" perspective (manipulated via videotape). Narcissists overestimated their performance, and reversing visual perspective did not reduce this self-enhancement bias. Instead, we found a person-situation interaction: Narcissists became even more positively biased in the reversed-perspective condition, whereas nonnarcissists showed even less bias. Thus, allowing narcissistic individuals to observe themselves on videotape further increased their

self-admiration, just as the mythical Narcissus admired his reflection in the pond.

The eye cannot see its own lashes.
—Chinese adage

Other men's sins are before our eyes; our own are behind our back.
—Seneca

A classic distinction in psychology is that between the self as perceiver (the "I") and the self as object of perception (the "Me"). According to Mead (1934), "the essential problem of selfhood or of self-consciousness" is for the individual to "get outside himself (experientially) in such a way as to become an object to himself" (p. 138). Yet, under normal circumstances, people cannot literally become objects of their own perception; that is, we cannot physically perceive ourselves from the same perspective as others do. But what if we could "see ourselves as others see us" (Robert Burns)? Would our self-perceptions become more accurate? Would seeing

Address correspondence to Richard W. Robins, Department of Psychology, University of California, Davis, CA 95616-8686; e-mail: rwrobins@ucdavis.edu.

ourselves from the perspective of others clear up the rose-colored glasses through which many of us perceive ourselves?

Popular admonishments such as "take a look at yourself in the mirror" and "try to see yourself from their perspective" suggest that taking an external view of oneself will reveal more clearly one's faults, flaws, and limitations.[1] Consistent with this folk belief, researchers studying self-focused attention have argued that "it is clear that perceiving yourself as others perceive you is usually a blow to self-esteem" (Buss, 1995, p. 261). In contrast, the myth of Narcissus suggests a rather different possibility. According to Greek mythology, when Narcissus saw his reflection in a pond, he fell in love with his own image; he enjoyed looking at himself so much that he stopped eating and eventually died. Thus, the myth suggests that seeing oneself from the

---

1. For example, when undergraduates were asked, "If people could see themselves from the same perspective as others see them, would this give them a more or less accurate view of themselves?" we found that 67% responded "more accurate," 14% "less accurate," and 19% "about the same."

Robins, R. W., and John, O. P. (1997). "Effects of Visual Perspective and Narcissism on Self-Perception." *Psychological Science*, 8, 37–42. Reprinted by permission of Blackwell Publishers.

perspective of others increases self-admiration and self-love.

We tested these contrasting views in two studies. Study 1 examined whether narcissists seek out situations in which they can see themselves from an external perspective, and whether they do so because such situations boost their self-confidence. Study 2 experimentally manipulated visual perspective and examined the consequences for accuracy and bias in self-evaluation.

Perceptual-Informational Influences on Self-Evaluation

The idea that self-perception becomes more accurate when people see themselves from an external perspective follows from cognitive-informational accounts of the self-perception process. The basic premise of Bem's (1972) self-perception theory is that individuals acquire self-knowledge by observing their own behavior in much the same way as would an objective observer. However, compared with the normal self-perspective, the external perspective provides the individual with additional information that is usually available only to an observer (e.g., nonverbal cues such as facial expressions). Storms (1973) found that "reversing" the visual orientation of subjects via videotape produced a corresponding reversal in the typical actor-observer difference in causal attributions: Individuals who observed themselves on videotape (i.e., from the same perspective as an observer) were more likely to attribute their behavior to dispositional causes than individuals who had the normal self-perspective. Storms interpreted this effect as evidence that visual perspective influences the availability and salience of informational cues (cf. Nisbett & Ross, 1980). This observation raises an intriguing possibility: Do distorted self-perceptions result from the unique visual perspective of the self?

Surprisingly, visual perspective has received little empirical attention in the literature on self-perception biases. However, Kolar, Funder, and Colvin (1996) have argued that the unique visual perspective of the self

may be responsible for the limited accuracy of self-reports: "Individuals may be in a poor position to see their own consistent personality attributes . . . because of the literal angle from which . . . they view themselves" (p. 314). Similarly, Kenny (1991) predicted that self-other agreement will be lower when the self and observer judges have different information available (Robins & John, 1996). When the individual has the same visual perspective as an observer, the informational difference between self and other judges is reduced. Thus, if informational factors underlie the divergences between self and other judgments found in previous research (Funder & Colvin, in press; John & Robins, 1993), then self-judgments formed from an observer perspective should be more accurate and less biased.

Self-awareness theory (Duval & Wicklund, 1972; see also Buss, 1980; Carver & Scheier, 1981) makes similar predictions, but for somewhat different reasons. According to self-awareness theory, seeing oneself on videotape induces a state of self-focused attention, which heightens awareness of discrepancies between what one believes one is like and what one wishes one were like. The self-focused state leads to a drop in self-evaluation because attention is focused on one's failure to meet internal standards. Thus, the general positivity bias should be reduced or eliminated when subjects evaluate their behavior on videotape. Self-awareness theory also predicts that self-focused attention will improve the correspondence between self-reports and behavior, implying more accurate self-perception (see Buss, 1980; Gibbons, 1983).

Self-Enhancement and Individual Differences in Narcissism

The myth of Narcissus provides a portrait of the self-focused individual that contrasts sharply with that provided by self-awareness theory. The myth suggests that rather than feeling acutely self-conscious and uncomfortable when confronted with their own image, some individuals enjoy focusing attention on them-

selves. Narcissism theories of the self provide a general account of the psychological dynamics of self-enhancement motivation and offer an individual differences framework for research on self-perception biases. Narcissistic individuals are assumed to hold unrealistically positive beliefs about their abilities and achievements (e.g., Freud, 1914/1953; Kohut, 1971; Millon, 1990). According to the fourth edition of the *Diagnostic and Statistical Manual of Mental Disorders* (American Psychiatric Association, 1994), they have "a grandiose sense of self-importance" (p. 658) and tend to "exaggerate their achievements and talents, and expect to be recognized as superior without commensurate achievements" (p. 661); they are "preoccupied with fantasies of unlimited success, power, brilliance, and beauty" (p. 658).

Narcissists are particularly prone to positive distortions because their inflated sense of self-importance and superior competence is easily threatened (e.g., Western, 1990). In other words, narcissism reflects individual differences in sensitivity and responsiveness to threats to self-worth. In ego-involving contexts, narcissistic individuals will be particularly motivated to bolster their self-image by positively distorting their self-perceptions. Recent research has provided empirical support for these accounts. Relatively narcissistic individuals respond to threats to their self-worth by perceiving themselves more positively than is justified (Gabriel, Critelli, & Ee, 1994; John & Robins, 1994) and by denigrating others (Morf & Rhodewalt, 1993). These studies have assessed the normal range of narcissistic tendencies and thus focused on narcissistic modes of self-evaluation in the general population, rather than on the clinical syndrome of narcissistic personality disorder.

Narcissism theories suggest several predictions about the effects of visual perspective that contrast with those generated by the perceptual-informational account. First, reversing visual perspective should not eliminate self-enhancement bias; presumably, individuals are motivated to enhance their self-worth regardless of the visual perspective from which they evaluate themselves. Second, individuals should vary in the degree to which they show self-enhancement bias, with narcissistic individuals showing the highest levels of bias. Third, the effect of visual perspective should depend on the individual's level of narcissism. Self-admiration and exhibitionism are central characteristics of the narcissistic personality. Thus, just as the mythical Narcissus enjoyed looking at his reflection in the water, narcissistic individuals should enjoy seeing themselves on videotape, which should activate their aggrandized self-views and further inflate their self-perceptions.

Study 1

Do narcissists indeed enjoy the self-focused state, and are they more inclined than other people to seek out situations that involve seeing themselves from an external perspective? We predicted that narcissists would prefer to look at themselves (rather than another person) on videotape and that they would look at themselves in the mirror more frequently than less narcissistic individuals. We also examined whether they do so in order to admire themselves and boost their confidence.

Method

One hundred thirty undergraduates (64% women) participated in an experimental session including several ostensibly unrelated parts. In the first part, subjects were told about another researcher seeking subjects who would be videotaped performing a group task and later watch the performance of one group member on videotape. Subjects were asked to choose one of two videotape conditions in this study: viewing their own performance or viewing the performance of another group member. In addition, subjects rated (on 7-point scales) the importance of five reasons for their choice; two of the reasons were designed to test whether subjects experience watching themselves as pleasurable or as aversive. To make the situation realistic, subjects were asked to provide telephone numbers and were told that a researcher would call to sign them up for the fictitious videotaping study.

In the second part, subjects rated how often they look at themselves in a mirror on a typical day. Subjects also rated (on 7-point scales) the importance of seven reasons for looking in a mirror; three of these reasons reflected self-admiration.

In the third part, subjects completed a 38-item version of the Narcissistic personality Inventory (NPI; α = .86; Raskin & Terry, 1988)[2] and the 10-item Rosenberg Self-Esteem Scale (RSE; α = .88; Rosenberg, 1979). The NPI is the best validated self-report measure of narcissism for nonclinical populations and predicts psychologists' ratings of narcissism (e.g., John & Robins, 1994). An example item is "If I ruled the world it would be a much better place," which was endorsed by 45% of the subjects. Level of narcissism (high vs. low) was defined by a median split.[3] The RSE Scale was used as a control variable to test whether the effects of narcissism were independent of self-esteem. The NPI correlated .37 with the RSE Scale.

In both Studies 1 and 2, there were no main or interactive effects of sex, and all results are reported for men and women combined.

Results

As predicted, individuals in the high-narcissism group were more than twice as likely to choose to participate in the "watch self" condition than in the "watch other" condition (69% vs. 31%); individuals in the low-narcissism group showed the opposite pattern (40% vs. 60%), $\chi^2(1, N = 130) = 11.2$, $p < .01$. When asked about the reasons for their choice, high-narcissism individuals were more likely than low-narcissism individuals to report that "it would be fun to watch myself" (Ms = 3.8 vs. 2.8), $t(128) = 2.9$, $p < .01$, and less likely to report that "I might feel uncomfortable seeing myself on videotape" (Ms = 3.2 vs. 4.2), $t(128) = 3.1$, $p < .01$.

2. This version of the NPI did not include two items that involve looking at oneself.

3. The average NPI item was endorsed by 41% of the sample, suggesting that almost half of the subjects showed narcissistic tendencies. Thus, a median split was used in Studies 1 and 2 to simplify presentation of the findings. All main effects and interactions from both studies were replicated when the NPI was used as a continuous variable.

Also as predicted, high-narcissism individuals reported looking at themselves in the mirror more frequently than did low-narcissism individuals (Ms = 5.7 vs. 4.8), $t(128)$ = 1.9, $p < .05$. Moreover, high-narcissism individuals rated the three reasons reflecting self-admiration as more important than did low-narcissism individuals, all $ts(128) > 2.0$, all $ps < .01$: "I like looking at myself" (Ms = 4.0 vs. 3.3), "I am proud of the way I look" (4.1 vs. 3.0), and "To build my confidence" (3.6 vs. 2.6). Finally, a series of analyses of covariance showed that the effects of narcissism were independent of self-esteem for all dependent variables.

Discussion

When given the choice between watching themselves or another person on videotape, narcissistic individuals preferred to watch themselves. Moreover, the reasons they gave for their choice indicate that narcissists do not perceive the self-focused state as aversive, but rather think it is "fun." Parallel findings emerged when subjects reported about looking at themselves in mirrors; the reasons narcissistic subjects gave for looking in the mirror suggest that they use self-focused attention to make themselves feel better and bolster their self-esteem. What do these findings suggest for the self-evaluation process? Seeing one's reflection may fuel narcissistic self-admiration. Study 2 tested this hypothesis.

Study 2

We examined two potential influences on accuracy and bias in self-perception: individual differences in narcissism (measured via questionnaire) and visual perspective (manipulated via videotape). Specifically, we asked: Are the self-evaluations of individuals high and low in narcissism differentially influenced by the visual perspective from which they perceive themselves?

Cognitive-informational accounts of self-perception predict that reversing visual perspective will increase accuracy and produce more negative self-evaluations, which will, in turn, decrease self-enhancement bias. In contrast, narcissism theory predicts a main effect of narcissism on self-enhancement bias that is independent of visual perspective, and an interaction between narcissism and visual perspective. Specifically, relatively narcissistic individuals should show even higher levels of self-enhancement bias in the reversed-perspective condition, whereas less narcissistic individuals (who are less defensive in response to negative information about themselves) should show the drop in self-evaluation predicted by self-awareness theory.

Method

Subjects

The experiment was conducted using two samples (total $N = 124$; 56% women): Sample 1 included 49 M.B.A. students (median age = 29), who on average had more than 3 years of postcollege work experience, and Sample 2 included 75 undergraduates (median age = 19). Sample (1 vs. 2) did not interact with visual perspective or narcissism in its effect on self-evaluation, indicating that the pattern of findings held in both samples. Thus, we report results for the two samples combined.

Group Discussion Task

Subjects participated in a simulation of a committee meeting in a large organization; six-person groups were used in Sample 1, and four-person groups were used in Sample 2. Subjects were told that the purpose of the meeting was to allocate a fixed amount of money to candidates for a merit bonus. Each subject was assigned the role of supervisor of one candidate and was instructed to present a case for that candidate at the meeting. Subjects received a realistic written summary of the employment backgrounds of all six (or four) candidates, including salary, biographical information, and appraisals of prior job performance, and were given 10 (or 5) min to review this information. At the beginning of the meeting, subjects gave 3- to 5-min presentations on the relative merits of their candidates. The groups then had 40 (or 30) min to reach a consensus on how to allocate the bonus money. Instructions emphasized that subjects should try to achieve two goals: obtain a large bonus for the candidate they represented and help the group achieve a fair overall allocation of the money. Thus, effective performance required behaviors that promoted the achievement of both goals.

Manipulation of Visual Perspective

Visual perspective was manipulated in a repeated measures design. In the *normal-perspective* condition, subjects evaluated their performance immediately after the group discussion; this condition provided a direct replication of our previous research (John & Robins, 1994). In the *reversed-perspective* condition, subjects returned to the lab at least 2 weeks later and evaluated themselves after privately viewing videotapes of themselves taken from the perspective of an external observer (i.e., each subject viewed a videotape taken with a camera focused on the subject's face and upper body). This design allowed us to measure change in self-evaluation from the normal- to the reversed-perspective condition.

Narcissism and Self-esteem

Several weeks prior to the experiment, subjects completed the 33-item version of the NPI (α = .71) and a 5-item version of the RSE Scale (α = .80), which was used as a control variable. The NPI correlated .33 with the RSE Scale. Level of narcissism (high vs. low) was defined by a median split.

Dependent Variable; Self-Evaluation of Performance

In both visual-perspective conditions, subjects privately ranked their own performance in the task and the performance of the other group members. The ranking procedure required subjects to compare their own performance directly with that of the other group members, rather than with some unspecified reference group or norm. Prior or privileged knowledge about the self (e.g., intentions, motives, past behavior) was irrelevant to the evaluations (see John & Robins, 1994, pp. 209–210). To calibrate the self-evaluation scales used in the two samples, the 4-point ranking scale used in Sample 2 was rescaled to a 6-point scale.[4]

Performance Criteria

Because any one criterion can provide only an imperfect measure of a subject's true level of performance (see Robins & John, in press, for a review), we used three criteria to assess accuracy and bias. The first was the average ranking of each subject's performance by the other group members (peers). The alpha reliability of this peer criterion was .79 in Sample 1 (based on rankings by the five peers in each group of six) and .74 in Sample 2 (rankings by the three peers in each group of four). The second criterion (Sample 1 only) was the average ranking of each subject's performance by a staff of 11 psychologists trained to evaluate performance in the task (α = .93). Because the peer and staff criteria correlated very highly (.77 in Sample 1 and .81 in John & Robins, 1994), the staff criterion was omitted for Sample 2.

The third criterion was based on an objective task outcome: the amount of bonus money each subject obtained for his or her candidate. This criterion allowed us to rule out an alternative explanation of our earlier narcissism effects. Specifically, when narcissists evaluated their performance, they may have emphasized the egocentric task goal (trying to get the most money for their candidate) and ignored the other task goal (working toward a fair overall allocation). If narcissists succeeded in getting more bonus only and weighed this factor heavily in their self-evaluations, they would have appeared to overestimate their performance relative to the peer and staff judgments, which reflected the attainment of both task goals. Thus, the bonus criterion provided a stringent test of whether narcissists over-estimate their performance.

Results and Discussion

Self-Evaluation Accuracy

Accuracy was defined by the correlation between the self-rankings and

---

4. For each subject in Sample 2, we subtracted 1 from the original self-ranking, multiplied this value by 5.3, and then added 1.

the performance criteria. The results supported the overall accuracy of the self-evaluations: We found strong correlations with the peer and staff criteria in both conditions, and weak but significant correlations with the bonus criterion. More important, did the self-evaluations become more accurate in the reversed-perspective condition? Although the accuracy correlations were indeed higher in the reversed-perspective condition, the differences between the correlations were small, and none reached significance (.57 vs. .51 for the peer criterion, .61 vs. .52 for the staff criterion, and .22 vs. .20 for the bonus criterion). These results do not support either the argument that visual perspective is central to self-perception accuracy (Kolar et al., 1996) or the prediction that self-judgments should agree more with judgments by others when self and others have similar information available (Kenny, 1991).

General Self-Enhancement Bias

Bias was defined by directional deviations (i.e., over- vs. underestimation) from the criteria. Subjects generally overestimated their performance. Subjects in the normal-perspective condition evaluated their performance about one-half rank more positively than they were evaluated by their peers, $t(123) = 3.7$, $p < .01$; by the staff, $t(49) = 2.1$, $p < .05$; or relative to the bonus criterion, $t(123) = 2.5$, $p = .01$. The magnitude of this self-enhancement bias is similar to that found in our previous research (John & Robins, 1994).

Effects of Visual Perspective and Narcissism on Self-Evaluation

Figure 1 shows self-evaluation as a function of visual perspective and narcissism. Hypotheses were tested using a repeated measures analysis of variance, with visual perspective (normal vs. reversed) as a within-subjects factor and narcissism (low vs. high) as a between-subjects factor. There was no main effect of the visual-perspective manipulation. $F < 1$. Contrary to self-awareness theory, subjects did not evaluate themselves less positively when they viewed

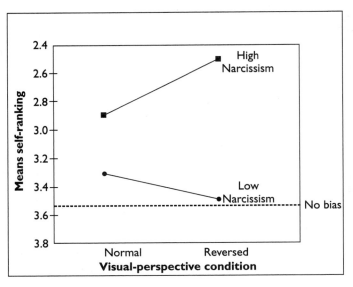

Fig. 1. Self-evaluation of performance as a function of visual perspective and narcissism. Low ranks imply better self-perceived performance. The "no bias" line is based on the mean of the three performance criteria and indicates what the mean self-ranking would have been if subjects' self-evaluations were unbiased. N = 124.

themselves from the perspective of an external observer. Instead, the general self-enhancement bias was equally strong from the two perspectives.

Next we consider the findings separately for the high- and low-narcissism groups. As predicted, high-narcissism individuals evaluated themselves more positively than low-narcissism individuals in both conditions. $F(1, 122) = 8.2$, $p < .01$. Did narcissists evaluate themselves more positively simply because they performed better? No. Narcissistic individuals did not perform better than less narcissistic individuals on any of the three performance criteria, all $ts < 1.3$. The finding that narcissists did not receive more bonus money for their candidates is particularly important because it replicates our previous research using a criterion based on an objective task outcome. Thus, differences in the self-evaluations of individuals high and low in narcissism cannot be attributed to differences in actual performance but must reflect biased self-perception.[5] Figure 1 shows that the self-evaluations of high-narcissism individuals were positively biased relative to the mean criterion ranking, whereas low-narcissism individuals were relatively unbiased.

5. Including the performance criteria as covariates did not affect any of the findings significantly.

Most important, the effect of the visual-perspective manipulation depended on the subject's level of narcissism, as indicated by a significant interaction. $F(1, 122) = 6.0$, $p = .01$. Specifically, reversing visual perspective accentuated the effect of individual differences in narcissism, producing an even wider gap between the self-evaluations of high and low narcissists. The self-evaluations of high-narcissism individuals became even more positively biased in the reversed-perspective condition, whereas the self-evaluations of low-narcissism individuals became less positively biased and moved closer to the no-bias line.[6] In correlational terms, individual differences in narcissism predicted change in self-evaluation across the two visual-perspective conditions: Higher narcissism scores (using the NPI as a continuous variable) predicted increases in self-evaluation, $r = .28$, $p < .01$. All effects in Study 2 were independent of self-esteem.

6. To ensure that the interaction between narcissism and visual perspective was not due to differential memory effects, we ran a control condition in which 36 M.B.A. subjects participated in the group discussion task and 2 weeks later were asked to remember their earlier self-evaluations. Neither narcissists nor nonnarcissists showed memory-based distortions; for both groups, the remembered self-evaluations were slightly worse (0.2 of a rank, n.s.) than the actual self-evaluations.

General Discussion

The present research examined two influences on accuracy and bias in self-perception: the visual perspective from which individuals perceive themselves (a situational variable manipulated via videotape) and individual differences in narcissism (a person variable measured via questionnaire). Thus, this research integrates a situational variable from social-psychological theory with an individual difference construct from personality and clinical psychology. In both studies, we found evidence of a person-situation interaction (Caspi & Bem, 1990; Snyder & Ickes, 1985). Study 1 shows a *proactive* interaction (or selection) effect: Individuals often select situations that fit their personality. We found that narcissistic individuals seek out and enjoy situations (e.g., looking in the mirror) in which they can focus their attention on themselves. As a result, compared with less narcissistic individuals, they more often find themselves in situations that reinforce their grandiose self-perceptions. This form of situation selection may be one mechanism through which individuals form and maintain positively distorted self-perceptions.

Study 2 demonstrated a *reactive* person-situation interaction: Individuals often experience and react to the same situation differently. When we required subjects to focus attention on themselves (thus overriding the selection effect), they reacted differently than in the normal-perspective condition: Narcissists evaluated themselves in an even more positive manner, whereas nonnarcissists tended to see themselves more negatively. This reactive interaction effect is illustrated in the free-response comments subjects wrote after watching themselves on videotape. One of the low narcissism subjects wrote: "I don't think I performed as well as I thought I did. The only impressions I got from watching myself on videotape were the bad ones. It was quite a sobering experience." In contrast, a high-narcissism subject wrote: "I came across more or less the way I would want to: stern but compassionate, matter of fact, busi-

ness-like and effective. I liked watching myself very much. Not too many surprises." It is clear from the tone of these comments that the two individuals experienced the situation quite differently.

Why did these two individuals react so differently to the experimental situation? More generally, why do people self-enhance? Self-enhancement bias is often seen as an attempt to regulate self-esteem, and our findings are consistent with the growing body of evidence supporting this claim. The present findings extend this research by showing that individuals continue to enhance their self-worth even when they are provided with all the information that is usually available only to an external observer: Seeing oneself from an external perspective is not sufficient to eliminate self-enhancement bias. Thus, self-enhancement bias cannot result solely from limitations in the information available to the self. Overall, then, our findings do not support a purely cognitive-informational view of self-perception bias, and they are not fully consistent with theories that conceptualize the self-perceiver as a scientist seeking out information in a dispassionate search for truth about the self (e.g., Bem, 1972; see Robins & John, in press, for a review of the scientist metaphor).

Instead, the findings seem more consistent with theories that conceptualize the self-perceiver as an egoist distorting information to enhance self-worth (e.g., Greenwald, 1980; Robins & John, in press). However, the apparent contrast between the scientist and egoist conceptions can be reconciled through an individual difference account: The scientist metaphor may better capture the self-perception process of relatively nonnarcissistic individuals, whereas the egoist metaphor may be more appropriate for narcissistic individuals. Specifically, the motive to enhance self-esteem is stronger and more easily activated in narcissistic individuals because of their heightened sensitivity to threats to their aggrandized self-views. Study 2 showed that the most powerful drive toward

self-enhancement occurred when narcissistic individuals evaluated themselves from an external perspective. This finding implies that the reversed-perspective condition served to activate the self-enhancement motive in narcissists, leading to even more inflated self-evaluations.

This interpretation is consistent with self-concept theories in which attentional processes play a central role in the self-regulation of behavior. These theories argue that the self-focused state triggers self-evaluative processes, and heightens awareness of the discrepancy between reality and internal standards. According to Carver and Scheier (1981), self-focus activates mechanisms that reduce discrepancies between one's perceived self and one's ideal self; discrepancies can be reduced by changing internal standards, modifying behavior, or distorting self-perceptions. The inflated internal standards of narcissists are unlikely to change, and the behavior in Study 2 could not be changed to fit the standard because the group discussion had already occurred when the self-evaluations were made. Thus, the only remaining option for regulating self-esteem was to distort self-perceptions to bring reality in line with narcissistic ideals.

In conclusion, although our manipulation of visual perspective altered the physical perspective of the self, it did not eliminate the motives that drive self-perception. Thus, even when subjects viewed themselves from the visual perspective of others, they still saw themselves from the emotionally charged perspective of the self. It is said that "seeing is believing," but, as Santayana pointed out, people often see what they believe, rather than believe what they see. The present research suggests that narcissistic individuals are unable to truly see themselves as others see them because they are blinded by their need for self-worth. Thus, rather than reducing self-enhancement bias, allowing narcissistic individuals to observe themselves on videotape further increased their self-admiration, just as the mythical Narcissus admired his reflection in the pond.

References

American Psychiatric Association. (1994). *Diagnostic and statistical manual of mental disorders* (4th ed.). Washington, DC: Author.

Bem, D. J. (1972). Self-perception theory. In L. Berkowitz (Ed.), *Advances in experimental social psychology* (Vol. 6, pp. 1–62). New York: Academic Press.

Buss, A. H. (1980). *Self-consciousness and social anxiety.* San Francisco: W. H. Freeman.

Buss, A. H. (1995). *Personality: Temperament, social behavior, and the self.* Boston: Allyn & Bacon.

Carver, C. S., & Scheier, M. F. (1981). *Attention and self-regulation: A control-theory approach to human behavior.* New York: Springer-Verlag.

Caspi, A., & Bem, D. J. (1990). Personality continuity and change across the life course. In L. A. Pervin (Ed.), *Handbook of personality: Theory and research* (pp. 549–575). New York: Guilford Press.

Duval, S., & Wicklund, R. A. (1972). *A theory of objective self-awareness.* New York: Academic Press.

Freud, S. (1953). On narcissism: An introduction. In J. Strachey (Ed. and Trans.), *The standard edition of the complete psychological works of Sigmund Freud* (Vol. 14, pp. 69–102). London: Hogarth Press. (Original work published 1914).

Funder, D. C., & Colvin, R. C. (in press). Convergence of self and others' judgments of personality. In R. Hogan, J. A. Johnson, & S. R. Briggs (Eds.), *Handbook of personality psychology.* New York: Academic Press.

Gabriel, M. T., Critelli, J. W., & Ee, J. S. (1994). Narcissistic illusions in self-evaluations of intelligence and attractiveness. *Journal of Personality, 62,* 143–155.

Gibbons, F. X. (1993). Self-attention and self-report: The "veridicality" hypothesis. *Journal of Personality, 51,* 517–542.

Greenwald, A. G. (1980). The totalitarian ego: Fabrication and revision of personal history. *American Psychologist, 35,* 603–618.

John, O. P., & Robins, R. W. (1993). Determinants of interjudge agreement on personality traits: The Big Five domains, observability, evaluativeness, and the unique perspective of the self. *Journal of Personality, 61,* 521–551.

John, O. P., & Robins, R. W. (1994). Accuracy and bias in self-perception: Individual differences in self-enhancement and the role of narcissism. *Journal of Personality and Social Psychology, 66,* 206–219.

Kenny, D. A. (1991). A general model of consensus and accuracy in interpersonal perception. *Psychological Review, 98,* 155–163.

Kohut, H. (1971). *The analysis of self.* New York: International Universities Press.

Kolar, D. W., Funder, D. C., & Colvin, C. R. (1996). Comparing the accuracy of personality judgments by the self and knowledgeable others. *Journal of Personality, 64,* 311–337.

Mead, G. H. (1934). *Mind, self, and society.* Chicago: University of Chicago Press.

Millon, T. (1990). The disorders of personality. In L. A. Pervin (Ed.), *Handbook of personality: Theory and research* (pp. 339–370). New York: Guilford Press.

Morf, C. C., & Rhodewalt, F. (1993). Narcissism and self-evaluation maintenance: Explorations in object relations. *Personality and Social Psychology Bulletin, 19,* 668–676.

Nisbett, R. E., & Ross, L. (1980). *Human inference: Strategies and shortcomings of social judgment.* Englewood Cliffs, NJ: Prentice-Hall.

Raskin, R., & Terry, H. (1988). A principal-components analysis of the Narcissistic Personality Inventory and some further evidence of its construct validity. *Journal of Personality and Social Psychology, 54,* 890–902.

Robins, R. W., & John, O. P. (1996). Toward a broader agenda for research on self and other perception. *Psychological Inquiry, 7,* 279–287.

Robins, R. W., & John, O. P. (in press). The quest for self-insight: Theory and research on accuracy and bias in self-perception. In R. Hogan, J. A. Johnson, & S. R. Briggs (Eds.), *Handbook of personality psychology.* New York: Academic Press.

Rosenberg, M. (1979). *Conceiving the self.* New York: Basic Books.

Snyder, M., & Ickes, W. (1985). Personality and social behavior. In E. Aronson & G. Lindzey (Eds.), *Handbook of social psychology* (3rd ed., Vol. 2, pp. 883–947). New York: Random House.

Storms, M. D. (1973). Videotape and the attribution process: Reversing actors' and observers' points of view. *Journal of Personality and Social Psychology, 27,* 165–175.

Westen, D. (1990). The relations among narcissism, egocentrism, self-concept, and self-esteem: Experimental, clinical, and theoretical considerations. *Psychoanalysis and Contemporary Thought, 13,* 183–239.

 Article Review Form at end of book.

What was narcissistic in Ted Kaczynski's behavior? What is the relationship between Narcissistic Personality Disorder, as defined in this article, and the narcissism found among many college students in the previous article?

The Mind of the Unabomber

Narcissism and its discontents

Maggie Scarf

Was it, as many people believe, the Unabomber's overwhelming vanity—his pressing need to remind us all that he was the wiliest, most sophisticated and terrifying bomber in the nation—that ultimately exposed him? Certainly, it was in the wake of Oklahoma City that the serial murderer suddenly found a voice—a mocking, embittered voice, bubbling with self-righteous rage, but a distinctive voice nonetheless.

Until then, he had been striking out at a despised society for seventeen years without ever making the nature of his grievances clear. In the agonized aftermath of the Oklahoma explosion, though, he seemed to need to command our attention, to say, "I exist, and you forget me at your peril." In quick succession, another bomb, several taunting letters (one to David Gelernter), some threatening notes (among them, a threat to blow up an airliner) and his grandiose, rambling manifesto followed. The Unabomber had once again transfixed the attention of the nation; but, in doing so, he had emerged just far enough from the shelter of his silence to allow himself to be identified. Given the type and amount of evidence gathered in the

alleged Unabomber's Montana shack, the FBI does appear to have its man. What we still don't know, in any psychological detail, is why he did what he did. And why, after seventeen years of secret attacks, did the Unabomber break cover and begin to explain himself? Did Kaczynski, as some journalists have suggested, have the "urge to purge" himself—that is, did he want to be caught? Or did he yearn to prove himself ever more brilliant and elusive by dancing closer and closer to the edge of discovery?

One explanation, which many find satisfactory, is that the unabomber is just plain crazy—a "full-service maniac," as Joe Klein of Newsweek phrased it. Time advanced the idea that suspected Unabomber Theodore J. Kaczynski's strange life story was "the Odyssey of a Mad Genius."

But the question remains (and it is a question that experts in psychiatry and the law have wrangled about endlessly over the years): Is bizarre behavior of this kind to be understood as lying within the realm of "madness" or of "badness"? Is this serial terrorist who is responsible for twenty-three injuries and three deaths to be viewed as someone fundamentally deranged or, as one of his victims, Yale professor David

Gelernter, has called him, "an evil coward"?

If, in an effort to distinguish between "what is mad" and "what is bad," one turns to the psychiatric literature on homicide, the pickings are surprisingly sparse, especially when compared to the vast literature on suicide. An excellent exception, however, is a new book called Homicide: A Psychiatric Perspective, by Carl P. Malmquist, M.D., M.S., Dr. Malmquist is a forensic psychiatrist who states in his preface that he has "personally evaluated" over 500 individuals who have committed homicide. He argues that murderers are frequently not "mad" in the formal sense of the word—that is, they are generally not suffering from schizophrenia or some other psychotic illness that leads them to experience hallucinations, delusions or both. When it comes to psychiatric disorders, a much larger number of murderers meet the diagnostic criteria for one or more of the severe personality disorders (e.g., Borderline Personality Disorder, Antisocial Personality Disorder, Narcissistic Personality Disorder and so forth).

In my own view, the diagnosis of Narcissistic Personality Disorder seems to be the most illuminating explanation of the Unabomber's seemingly incomprehensible behavior.

Scarf, Maggie (1996, June 10). "The Mind of the Unabomber: Narcissism and Its Discontents." *New Republic,* 214, p. 20. Reprinted by permission of *The New Republic,* © 1996, The New Republic, Inc.

Narcissistic Personality Disorder, as delineated in DSM-IV (the most recent version of the American Psychiatric Association's Diagnostic and Statistical Manual of Mental Disorders), is "A pervasive pattern of grandiosity (in fantasy or behavior), need for admiration, and lack of empathy beginning by early adulthood and present in a variety of contexts. . . ." The characteristic features of narcissistic disturbances are, in brief, an overinflated sense of uniqueness, self-importance and personal entitlement.

The narcissistic person is, nevertheless, deeply injured at the core and suffering from sorely depleted supplies of self-esteem. His overweening grandiosity is, for this reason, intermingled with a sense of inner emptiness and painful feelings of unworthiness, despair and desolation. His internal world contains only two views of the self: he is either great, powerful, brilliant, the very best, or he is a nothing—someone who is not at all special, a nobody. And since being nobody exceptional or special is experienced as profoundly threatening—it may indeed be equated with an annihilation of the self—the narcissistic person experiences an ever-present tension and inner pressure, which will fluctuate in intensity over the course of time, sometimes proving manageable and at other times completely intolerable.

Narcissists are hungry, voraciously in need of adulation—but theirs is a kind of hunger that can never, under any circumstances, be fully seated. For, even in instances where the narcissist does earn applause for what may be very real accomplishments and talents, the intensity of his needs for admiration and praise—which are never going to be met at the required level—eventually leave him feeling estranged, barren, depressed and resentful. And frequently, as his suffering intensifies, a brooding anger (he is not receiving his due!) begins to grow and develop. He looks for the person, or situation, to blame for his terrible pain.

"Narcissistic components are present more frequently in homicides than is usually believed," writes Malmquist. "The key seems to be an

experience of some type of threat to one's vulnerable self that becomes magnified far beyond the nature of the threat."

One can imagine young Teddy John Kaczynski, the precociously bright little "genius" of the household, as he grew up and slowly retreated into adolescent fantasies of the wonderful mathematician he would one day become. And one can picture the emotionally immature Harvard undergraduate, so morbidly isolated that he seems to have become invisible; hardly anyone who knew him there can remember a thing about him (aside from the stench of garbage emanating from his room). It is in fact not hard to envisage why and how a pathologically shy, relatively poor young man from the Midwest, who was suddenly encountering other people just as smart and gifted—perhaps more so, and socially competent, too—might have withdrawn completely to nurture his soothingly self-inflating fantasies in private.

As Malmquist writes,

[N]arcissistic individuals may develop an indifferent or cool exterior as an initial response to threats to their self-esteem. However, when their composure gives way, it is striking to see the intensity of their anger and their need for revenge. . . . [T]he trigger can be when the narcissistic individual perceives people or organizations as not living up to his or her expectations, following which the narcissistic individual perceives them as behaving badly. . . . Such individuals then develop a sense of self-righteous morality or take up causes to reform others, both of which reactions only thinly conceal their power-seeking needs.

The narcissist's special vulnerability is linked to his conviction that he is someone special and to his vast sense of entitlement. He feels he is supposed to be recognized not only for his remarkable talents and gifts but for his superior qualities; he is someone quite distinctive, far better and brighter than any and all of his peers. But if such recognition isn't forthcoming—if he isn't being endlessly admired or, worse yet, is receiving outright criticism—the stage is gradually set for depressive feelings to leak into consciousness and then perhaps for impulsive acting out

to occur. It is at this juncture that the narcissistically compromised person's anger may begin to kindle and eventually erupt in acts that are either curiously destructive to the self (such as Kaczynski's sudden resignation from his academic career) or senselessly destructive to others.

Did Kaczynski impulsively bolt from the Berkeley faculty in 1969 because his need for recognition of his total and complete superiority was not being gratified? Did Kaczynski realize that, while he was a competent and hardworking mathematician, he was never going to be counted among the great mathematicians of our time—to be appreciated as someone who towered, by everyone's reckoning, above all others in the field?

Or did he decide to leave academia because he was so harshly criticized by his students? Assistant Professor Kaczynski's students had complained, in their course evaluations, that his lectures were "useless and right from the book" and that he completely refused to answer questions and ignored the questioners. To the individual suffering from NPD, any criticism, however mild, is experienced as utterly intolerable.

And as forensic expert Malmquist notes, the narcissist's perception that he is being criticized or threatened usually leads him to "singl[e] out someone or something in the external world which becomes viewed as the source of the hostile aggression." That aggressor "might actually be a person or situation that develops because of the narcissistic person's sensitivity." The narcissist's sensitivities are enormous. Any hint of a negative reaction arouses such intense feelings of shame and humiliation that it may undermine his sense of self profoundly (hence, one supposes, the Unabomber's final withdrawal from a social world in which we all have to endure our occasional bumps and put-downs). "When narcissistically vulnerable individuals are put in extreme positions where their self-esteem is severely threatened," writes Malmquist, "they seem to respond in two ways: via a shame mechanism that leads to withdrawal and hiding, or via an outburst of rage that leads to some aggressive action."

Perhaps, when the hermit-mathematician struck out in the bizarre fashion that he did, it was his only means of asserting that he was truly alive—of saying, "I am intact, I am special, and I am important." The string of unexplained bombs, the taunting letters and finally the anti-technology diatribe that capped the sequence may well have been part of a desperate attempt to deliver this bulletin: "You'd better recognize me as someone uniquely clever and powerful, because you fail to do so at your own peril."

Was the Unabomber, in the wake of the Oklahoma explosion, feeling isolated and ignored—was he clamoring, at that moment, for some fresh acknowledgment of his own special place in the fantasy life of this nation? His pressing need was to point out the stupidity of others—to let us know that he was not only an immensely gifted person, able to elude an 18-year-old manhunt and force *The New York Times* and *The Washington Post* to publish his manifesto—but a gifted person bringing us a special message.

This need, a godlike need—for the theme of grandiosity permeates his behavior—was to educate us and explain how we were going astray. At first, he rained down catastrophes like an angry deity, without telling us what we had done to deserve them. But now—since we didn't seem to be getting the point—he decided to help us out by dispatching more lethal "communications" (bombs, mocking and threatening letters, the manifesto), all of which said, essentially, "Look stupid, it's technology that's at the heart of this society's problems—what do I have to do to get the message across?" In paragraph forty-four of his manifesto, the Unabomber writes, "[F]or most people it is through the power process—having a goal, making an autonomous effort and attaining the goal—that self-esteem, self-confidence and a sense of power are acquired. When one does not have adequate opportunity to go through the power process the consequences are . . . boredom, demoralization, low self-esteem, inferiority feelings, defeatism, depression, anxiety, guilt, frustration, hostility. . . ." This, and other passages in the manifesto, have a self-revealing, deeply tormented quality.

Kaczynski certainly sought, and found, autonomy—a self-imposed solitary confinement (even in prisons, solitary confinement is viewed as punishment) during which his major social engagements consisted, if he is indeed the Unabomber, of murdering people anonymously and from a distance. But his stated moral purpose—to return our technological/industrial society to a state of "wild nature"—was ludicrously inconsistent. For in his tiny 10-by-12-foot cabin the alleged Unabomber had, as we now know, a virtual bomb factory, including books on bomb-making and hand-drawn diagrams, lengths of pipe, soldering wire and chemicals used in explosives, such as potassium chlorate, sulfur, ammonium nitrate and saltpeter. He was not exactly rubbing two sticks together to create fire. No less tellingly, the FBI found a bottle of trazodone (Desyrel), an antidepressant prescribed for people suffering from agitation, depression and sleep disorders. Wouldn't someone whose goal was to destroy our modern society, and restore a state of pre-industrial simplicity, prefer some kind of plant or herbal remedy for whatever it was that was ailing him?

In fact, if one surveys the Unabomber's trajectory over the years, it seems clear that his actual motivation was not so much to demolish technological society as it was to maim or kill certain individuals who seemed to be flourishing in that society—one in which he had no hope of ever really belonging. Paradoxically, though, it is by virtue of his exposure and capture that the Unabomber is "in the world" again, and once more at the center of our collective attention.

 Article Review Form at end of book.

WiseGuide Wrap-Up

- The idea that people have "one true self" has been called into question by many psychologists. People have many "selves" that they enact in different settings and with different groups of people.

- Our identities are formed in a social context. Discrimination can lead to dis-identifying with the relevant domain, because identifying with it can feel too threatening.

- Our desire to "know" ourselves can be greater than our desire to feel good about ourselves. We sometimes choose to be around people who hold a familiar—even if negative—view of us rather than an unfamiliar but positive view.

- Narcissism is a particular kind of self-absorption. It can be seen in relatively mild levels among a certain percentage of college students—and more seriously dysfunctional levels among people like the Unabomber.

R.E.A.L. Sites

This list provides a print preview of typical **coursewise** R.E.A.L. sites. There are over 100 such sites at the **courselinks**™ site. The danger in printing URLs is that web sites can change overnight. As we went to press, these sites were functional using the URLs provided. If you come across one that isn't, please let us know via email to: webmaster@coursewise.com. Use your Passport to access the most current list of R.E.A.L. sites at the **courselinks**™ site.

Site name: Association for Humanistic Psychology
URL: http://ahpweb.bestware.net/

Why is it R.E.A.L.? Dr. O'Hara, quoted in the first article in this section, is a past president of the Association for Humanistic Psychology. The organization is dedicated to a particular vision of psychology emphasizing individual growth and development and with attention to "mind, body, and soul." The association's web site includes information on the society and links to related web sites focused on health and healing, related student organizations, graduate programs in the field, humanistic psychology journals, recent scholarships, and more.

Key topics: personality theories, humanistic psychology, clinical psychology

Site name: Stereotypes and Prejudice: A Resource Page for Teachers
URL: http://ucsub.colorado.edu/~schneidn/

Why is it R.E.A.L.? In "Can Racial Stereotypes Psych Out Students?" the author reports on research demonstrating the powerful effects stereotypes can have on students' developing identities. This web site is dedicated to eradicating that threat from classrooms. The site provides information on racial stereotypes and how they affect school classrooms and resources, as well as links to relevant videos, books, activities for classrooms, and teaching methods to combat the role of racism in the classroom. It is a comprehensive site—especially relevant to aspiring and current teachers but is also relevant to college students, as many of the issues apply to their classrooms.

Key topics: race and ethnicity, discrimination, personality and education

section

2

Learning Objectives

- Describe some of the major symptoms of depression.

- Learn some of the theories concerning why men and women have different rates of depression.

- Discuss some of the ways that personality can affect one's health and well-being.

Personality, Depression, and Mental Health

 **WiseGuide Intro**

Since its inception, the field of personality psychology has had strong links to clinical psychology. The distinction between normal personality and serious mental health problems is not a clean one. We saw in the previous section that a mild version of narcissism may be a relatively common characteristic of college students but that a more severe version of it can have a far more devastating impact. The three articles in this section are focused on personality as it relates to depression and health. These are areas in which personality psychology has contributed a great deal. Personality psychology offers an opportunity to understand the ways people characteristically behave and perceive the world and how that shapes important health and mental health outcomes. These three articles provide three different ways of looking at this relationship. We will return to a similar set of issues in Section 7, when the articles center on psychological resilience and defense.

In "Personal History: Anatomy of Melancholy," Solomon provides a first-person account of the experience of a major depression. We all have periods of time in life when we are "down" or even "depressed." During such times, we may feel lethargic and sad and not show any interest in those around us. For most of us, these periods follow a clear, noticeable event, such as the loss of a loved one or a personal failure in an area that is important to us. However, most of us do not remain in this state very long, and even "in the thick of it" we have some awareness of the kinds of things that will "shake us out of it"—exercise, spending time with friends, eating and sleeping properly. Those who experience a major depression are experiencing something quite different, however, and one purpose of this article is to help you grasp the difference. Solomon's descriptions of his depression are vivid and can help you grasp the difference between "being blue" and experiencing a major depression. Clinical depression is a serious, potentially fatal problem. Approximately 10 percent of people suffering from depression eventually kill themselves. See the web site at the end of this section for information on how to get help if you or someone you know is suffering from depression.

Strickland provides a very brief overview on some current research into the reasons women are more likely to experience depression than are men in "Women and Depression." Women are more than twice as likely as men to experience depression. Strickland reviews work that examines biological differences between men and women, that examines differences in their styles of coping with adversity, and that has focused on differences in the social status of men and women. Think about which explanations make the most sense to you. Perhaps you'll have some time in class to discuss these different lines of research and their strengths and weaknesses.

Questions

Reading 6. How does Solomon's experience of depression differ from what you expected? What strikes you as particularly moving in this personal account of a major depression?

Reading 7. How much more likely are women to be depressed than are men? Identify two of the reasons women are more likely than men to be depressed.

Readiing 8. What are the three components of explanatory style? What are two ways explanatory style might influence well-being and death?

Finally, Peterson and his colleagues report on a study of the relationship between a personality style known as "catastrophizing" and early death. They demonstrate that a personality style in which one attributes bad events to global causes—"Nothing ever goes right for me," "Life is never fair"—is associated with relatively early death among a healthy sample followed over the course of their lives. This article suggests that a personality style colloquially referred to as "being a Cassandra"—because of Cassandra's role in Greek tragedy—may indeed have deleterious, even fatal, effects. Don't worry if you don't understand all the statistical techniques the authors used to analyze their data—instead, for purposes of this class, pay more attention to the findings and the interpretations they make of the data. Perhaps reading about this relationship between personality and death will be sobering enough to get you to rethink the wisdom of such an approach to life!

How does Solomon's experience of depression differ from what you expected? What strikes you as particularly moving in this personal account of a major depression?

Personal History

Anatomy of melancholy

Depression afflicts millions of Americans each year, and many don't know where to turn when it strikes. The author recalls the greatest struggle of his life.

Andrew Solomon

I did not experience depression until I had pretty much solved my problems. I had come to terms with my mother's death three years earlier, was publishing my first novel, was getting along with my family, had emerged intact from a powerful two-year relationship, had bought a beautiful new house, was writing well. It was when life was finally in order that depression came slinking in and spoiled everything. I'd felt acutely that there was no excuse for it under the circumstances, despite perennial existential crises, the forgotten sorrows of a distant childhood, slight wrongs done to people now dead, the truth that I am not Tolstoy, the absence in this world of perfect love, and those impulses of greed and uncharitableness which lie too close to the heart—that sort of thing. But now, as I ran through this inventory, I believed that my depression was not only a rational state but also an incurable one. I kept redating the beginning of the depression: since my breakup with my girlfriend, the past October; since my mother's death; since the beginning of her two-year illness; since puberty; since birth. Soon I couldn't remember what pleasurable moods had been like.

I was not surprised later when I came across research showing that the particular kind of depression I had undergone has a higher morbidity rate than heart disease or any cancer. According to a recent study by researchers at Harvard and the World Health Organization, only respiratory infections, diarrhea, and newborn infections cost more years of useful life than major depression. It is projected that by the year 2020 depression could claim more years than war and AIDS put together. And its incidence is rising fast. Between six and ten per cent of all Americans now living are battling some form of this illness; one study indicates that nearly fifty per cent have experienced at least one psychiatric disorder in their lifetime. Treatments are proliferating, but only twenty-eight per cent of all people who have a major depression seek help from a specialist; fifteen per cent of hospitalized patients succeed in killing themselves. Attempting to understand this strange malady, I plunged into intensive research shortly after my recovery. I started by attempting a coherent narrative of my own experience.

In June, 1994, I began to be constantly bored. My first novel had recently been published in England, and yet its favorable reception did little for me. I read the reviews indifferently and felt tired all the time. In July, back home in downtown New York, I found myself burdened by phone calls, social events, conversation. The subway proved intolerable. In August, I started to feel numb. I didn't care about work, family, or friends. My writing slowed, then stopped. My usually headstrong libido evaporated.

All this made me feel that I was losing my self. Scared, I tried to schedule pleasures. I went to parties and failed to have fun, saw friends and failed to connect; I bought things I had previously wanted and gained no satisfaction from them. I was overwhelmed by messages on my answering machine and ceased to return calls. When I drove at night, I constantly thought I was going to swerve into another car. Suddenly feeling I'd forgotten how to use the steering wheel, I would pull over in a sweat.

In September, I had agonizing kidney stones. After a brief hospitalization, I spent a vagabond week migrating from friend to friend. I would stay in the house all day, avoiding the street, and was careful never to go far from the phone. When they came home, I would cry. Sleeping pills got me through the night, but morning began to seem increasingly difficult. From then on, the slippage was steady. I worked even less well, cancelled more plans. I began eating irregularly, seldom feeling hungry. A psychoanalyst I was seeing told me, as I sank lower, that avoiding medication was very courageous.

At about this time, night terrors began. My book was coming out in the United States, and a friend threw a party on October 11th. I was feeling too lack-lustre to invite many people, was too tired to stand up much during the party, and sweated horribly all night. The event lives in my mind in ghostly outlines and washed-out colors. When I got home, terror seized me. I lay in bed, not sleeping and hugging my pillow for comfort. Two weeks later—the day before my thirty-first birthday—I left the house once, to buy groceries; petrified for no reason, I suddenly lost bowel control and soiled myself. I ran home, shaking, and went to bed, but I did not sleep, and could not get up the following day. I wanted to call people to cancel birthday plans, but I couldn't. I lay very still and thought about speaking, trying to figure out how. I moved my tongue, but there were no sounds. I had forgotten how to talk. Then I began to cry without tears. I was on my back. I wanted to turn over, but couldn't remember how to do that, either. I guessed that perhaps I'd had a stroke. At about three that afternoon, I managed to get up and go to the bathroom. I returned to bed shivering. Fortunately, my father, who lived uptown, called about then. "Cancel tonight," I said, struggling with the strange words. "What's wrong?" he kept asking, but I didn't know.

If you trip or slip, there is a moment, before your hand shoots out to break your fall, when you feel the earth rushing up at you and you cannot help yourself—a passing, fraction-of-a-second horror. I felt that way hour after hour. Freud once described pleasure as the release of tension; I felt as though I had a physical need, of impossible urgency and discomfort, from which there was no release—as though I were constantly vomiting but had no mouth. My vision began to close. It was like trying to watch TV through terrible static, where you can't distinguish faces, where nothing has edges. The air, too, seemed thick and resistant, as though it were full of mushed-up bread.

My father came to my apartment with my brother, his fiancéee, and a friend; fortunately, they had keys. I had had nothing to eat in almost two days, and they tried to give me smoked salmon. I ate a bite, then threw up all over myself. The next day, my father took me to my analyst's office. "I need medication," I said, diving deep for the words. "I'm

sorry," she said, and she called a psychopharmacologist.

Dr. Alfred Wiener agreed to see me in an hour. He seems to have come out of some "Spellbound"-era shrink movie: he is in his late sixties, smokes cigars, has a European accent, and wears carpet slippers. He has elegant manners and a kindly smile. He asked me a string of specific questions. "Very classic indeed," he said calmly as I trotted out my atrocities. "Don't worry, we'll soon have you well." He wrote a prescription for Xanax, then handed me some Zoloft. "You'll come back tomorrow," he said. "The Zoloft will take some time. The Xanax will alleviate anxiety almost immediately. Don't worry, you have a very normal group of symptoms."

Once upon a time, depression was generally seen as a purely psychological disturbance; these days, people are likely to think of it as a tidy biological syndrome. In fact, it's hard to make sense of the distinction. Most depressive disorders are now thought to involve a mixture of reactive (so-called neurotic) factors and internal ("endogenous") factors; depression is seldom a simple genetic disease or a simple response to external troubles. Resolving the biological and the psychological understanding of depression is as difficult as reconciling predestination and free will. If you remember the beginning of this paragraph well enough to make sense of the end of it, that is a chemical process; love, faith, and despair all have chemical manifestations, and chemistry can make you feel things. Treatments have to accommodate this binary structure—the interplay between vulnerability and external events.

Vulnerability need not be genetic. Ellen Frank, of the University of Pittsburgh, says, "Experiences in childhood can scar the brain and leave one vulnerable to depression." As with asthma, predisposition and environment conspire. Syndrome and symptom cause each other: loneliness is depressing, but depression also causes loneliness. "When patients recover from depression by means of psychotherapy," Frank says, "we see the same changes in, for example, sleep EEG as when they receive medication. A socially generated depression does not necessarily

need psychosocial treatment, nor a biologically generated one a biological treatment."

The day after my birthday, I moved to my father's. I was hardly able to get up for the next week. The days were like this: I would wake up panicked. Xanax would relieve the panic if I took enough, but then I would collapse into thick, confusing, dream-heavy sleep. I wanted only to take enough to sleep forever. Whenever I woke up, I took more pills. Killing myself, like taking a shower, was too elaborate an agenda to entertain. All I wanted was for it to stop, but I could not say what "it" was. Words, with which I have always been intimate, seemed suddenly like complex metaphors, the use of which entailed much more energy than I had.

Little has been written about the fact that depression is ridiculous. I can remember lying frozen in bed, crying because I was too frightened to take a shower and at the same time knowing that showers are not scary. I ran through the individual steps in my mind: You sit up, turn and put your feet on the floor, stand, walk to the bathroom, open the bathroom door, go to the edge of the tub . . . I divided it into fourteen steps as onerous as the Stations of the Cross. I knew that for years I had taken a shower every day. Hoping that someone else could open the bathroom door, I would, with all the force in my body, sit up; turn and put my feet on the floor; and then feel so incapacitated and frightened that I would roll over and lie face down. I would cry again, weeping because the fact that I could not do it seemed so idiotic to me. At other times, I have enjoyed skydiving: it is easier to climb along a strut toward the tip of a plane's wing against an eighty-mile-an-hour wind at five thousand feet than it was to get out of bed those days.

Evenings, I was able to rise. Most depression has a diurnal rhythm, improving over the course of the day and descending overnight. I could sit up for dinner with my father. I could speak by then. I tried to explain; my father implacably assured me that it would pass, and told me to eat. When I was defeated by the difficulty of getting a piece of lamb chop onto my fork, he would do it for me. He would say he remembered feeding me when I was a child, and would make me promise, jesting, to cut up his lamb chops when he was old and toothless. "I used to work twelve hours, go to four parties in an evening," I would say. He would assure me that I would be able to do it all again soon. He could just as well have told me that I would soon be able to build a helicopter of cookie dough and fly to Neptune, so clear was it to me that my real life was definitely over. After dinner, I would return some calls. It is embarrassing to admit depression; to all but my closest friends I said that I'd developed an "obscure tropical virus."

When you are depressed, the past and the future are absorbed entirely by the present, as in the world of a three-year-old. You can neither remember feeling better nor imagine that you will feel better. Being upset, even profoundly upset, is a temporal experience, whereas depression is atemporal. Depression means that you have no point of view.

Since that first visit to Dr. Wiener, I have been playing the medicine game. I have been on, in various combinations and doses, Zoloft, Xanax, Paxil, Navane, Valium, BuSpar, and Wellbutrin. This is a relatively short list. I do well with SSRIs ("selective serotonin-reuptake inhibitors," the growing family of drugs that includes Prozac, Zoloft, Paxil, and Luvox) and have good experiences with benzodiazepines (such as Xanax and Valium). I have never been on a tricyclic (which chiefly affects the neurotransmitters serotonin and norepinephrine) or on an MAO inhibitor (which influences serotonin, norepinephrine, and dopamine). I have never taken a mood stabilizer/anticonvulsant (such as lithium or Depakote), or had shock treatments or psychosurgery. "Depression these days is curable," people told me. "You take antidepressants the way you take aspirin for a headache." Depression these days is treatable; you take antidepressants the way you take chemotherapy for cancer. They sometimes do miraculous things, but the treatment can be painful and difficult, and inconsistent in its results. Trying out different medications makes you feel like

a dartboard. "If many remedies are prescribed for an illness," Chekhov wrote, "you may be certain that the illness has no cure."

Side effects arrive with the first pill and sometimes fade away with time. The real effects, at best, fade in with time. We cannot predict which medications will work for whom. Zoloft made me feel as though I'd had fifty-five cups of coffee. Paxil gave me diarrhea, but fortunately Xanax, though it made me exhausted, was also constipating. Paxil seemed better than Zoloft, and I soon adjusted to its making me feel as though I'd had *eleven* cups of coffee—which was definitely better than feeling as though I couldn't brush my own teeth. Only after a year did I discover Effexor, which made me appreciate that Paxil had been only partly effective for me. The side effects for which antidepressants are known (tension, irascibility, sexlessness, headaches, indigestion) are easily confused with the complaints for which they are taken (anxiety, irritability, and sexlessness, accompanied sometimes by headaches and indigestion), and so it was easy for me to conclude, two weeks after I began on Effexor, that I was probably having an adverse reaction to the drug. Dr. Weiner suggested that I might be having no reaction at all to the drug. He said, "Let's try doubling your dose. If you don't feel terrible, we'll keep going up. If you do, we'll come straight down." I'm now on triple the original dose.

The most constant side effect of the SSRIs is sexual dysfunction, and it is a serious side effect. It is damaging to your existing relationships and hell if you want to get into a new one. It doesn't matter much when you're first recovering, when you have other things on your mind, but to get over unbearable pain at the cost of erotic pleasure is not a happy arrangement. Robert Boorstin, a senior adviser to the Secretary of the Treasury, is manic-depressive and is an outspoken advocate for the mentally ill, and he told me that during four years on Prozac he did not have an orgasm in intercourse—"which I considered a fairly major drawback."

Popular articles seem to suggest that the neurotransmitter serotonin is the key to happiness—that giving serotonin boosters to depres-

sives is like giving iron to anemics, or insulin to diabetics. This is wrong. It appears that depressed people do not have low serotonin levels, which explains what would otherwise be a puzzling phenomenon. For three weeks, you're on Prozac, a drug that has an instant effect on your serotonin levels, and you feel as lousy as you did before. Then things improve. Why this delay? When the serotonin levels go up, the brain appears to reduce the number of receptors, or decreases the sensitivity of existing receptors, which suggests that the brain is seeking a balance between output and receptivity. Over-all serotonin function is probably not very different from what it was before—and yet there are important subtle changes. Indeed, the most plausible explanation for the SSRIs is that they work indirectly. The human brain is stupefyingly plastic: cells respecialize and change; they "learn" new patterns of responding. When you raise serotonin levels, and cause some receptors to close up shop, other things happen elsewhere in the brain, and those other things are presumed to correct the imbalance that makes you feel bad.

Less is known about an herb called St. John's wort (hypericum), which has become popular lately among fans of alternative medicine. "These treatments can sound batty," Tom Wehr, at the National Institute of Mental Health, acknowledges. "But, frankly, if you said to someone, 'I'd like to put wires on your head and run electricity through your brain to induce a seizure because I think that might help your depression,' and if that were not a well-established treatment, you might have a hard time getting it going."

But the precise mechanism of effect remains elusive even for the intensively studied mainstream pharmaceuticals. "It is in these subtle adaptations to nerve cells, these compensations meant to handle increased serotonin, that the actual healing process lies," Steve Hyman, the director of the N.I.M.H., says of the SSRIs, "just as a pearl results from the adaptation of an oyster to the irritation caused by a grain of sand." Bill Potter, who until recently headed a research group in clinical psychopharmacology at the N.I.M.H., says "Drugs that work by very different mechanisms produce antidepressant effects. It is possible for drugs with acutely different spectrums of biochemical activity to produce very similar long-term effects. It's like a weather system. Something changes wind speeds or humidity, and you get a completely different kind of weather a hundred miles away, but even the best meteorologists can't calculate all the variables." There is an ongoing quest for drugs that affect the brain with greater specificity. "The existing medications are just too indirect for us to fully understand how they are working," Potter says.

"It was amazing," Sarah Gold, a young editor, said of her first months on Wellbutrin, a drug that affects the neurotransmitters dopamine and norepinephrine but not serotonin. "I could pick up the phone and make calls—my life was no longer governed by fear. It was like my first experience of sunlight." But she was one of those people for whom medication is effective for only a limited time. She got a lift again from Effexor, but that, too, wore off after a year or so. "One of my roommates told me I had a black aura and she couldn't stand to be in the house when I was up in my room," she recalled. Gold went through other combinations of medications, only to end up taking Wellbutrin again, along with Zoloft and small doses of Risperdal. Sometimes, especially when she is dancing—and she is a wonderful dancer—she reaches the unsustainable height of normal feelings. Having lived them, she says, "I have them to aspire to."

One woman who works in the mental-health field and takes a panoply of SSRIs and mood stabilizers told me, "I have two children who also suffer from this disease, and I don't want them to think it's a reason for not having a good life. I get up every single day and make breakfast for my kids. Some days I can keep going, and some days I have to go back to bed afterward. I come into this office at some point every day. Sometimes I miss a few hours, but I've never missed a whole day from depression." We were in a cubicle at the hospital where she works. Her eyes were wide as she held forth. Her hands, folded in her lap, trembled from all the medicines she was on at the time. She soon had

tears rolling down her face but went right on speaking. "One day last week, I woke up and it was really bad. I managed to get out of bed, to walk to the kitchen, counting every step, to open the refrigerator. And then all the breakfast things were near the back of the refrigerator, and I just couldn't reach that far. When my kids came in, I was just standing there, staring into the refrigerator."

Two separate but inseparable matters come into play here: depression and personality. Some people are disabled by levels of depression that others can handle, and some contrive to function despite serious symptoms. Antidepressants help those who help themselves. To take medications as part of the battle is to battle fiercely, and to refuse them is as ludicrous as entering a modern war on horseback. "It may be a sign of character, not of weakness, to know when you have to ask for help," says Martha Manning, whose book, "Undercurrents," chronicles her depression.

Two years before my first severe episode, a friend with an apparently terrific life, a regular old Richard Cory, committed suicide. It was no cry for help: he slit his wrists crosswise, and then went up to the roof of his building and jumped off. Suicide is a seductress, and those who have sailed near it stay alive only when they stop up their ears and flee from its Siren song. Even with chemical assistance, it's a fight against the wind and the tide to stay off the rocks. I don't believe that this friend's life had become more intolerable than Manning's, or mine. His life was not, however, strong enough in him to defy annihilation, and our lives, so far, are.

It is possible to keep yourself alive without modern technologies, but the price can be high. At a cocktail party in London, I saw an acquaintance and mentioned to her that I was writing this article. "I had terrible depression," she said. I asked her what she had done about it. "I didn't like the idea of medication," she said. "My problem was stress-related. So I decided to eliminate all the stresses in my life." She counted off on her fingers. "I quit my job," she said. "I broke up with my boyfriend and never really looked for another one. I gave up my roommate and moved to

a smaller place. I stopped going to parties that run late. I dropped most of my friends. I gave up, pretty much, on makeup and clothes." I was looking at her in bewilderment. "It sounds bad, but I'm much less afraid than before," she went on, and she looked proud. "I'm in perfect health, really, and I did it without pills."

Someone who was standing in our group grabbed her by the arm. "That's completely crazy. That's the craziest thing I've ever heard. You must be crazy to be doing that to your life," he said. Is it crazy to avoid the behaviors that make you crazy?

Inconveniently, I had a reading tour to do after that birthday, and antidepressants usually take about a month to kick in. Still, I was determined to get through it, because I believed that, meds or no meds, if I started giving up on things I would give up on everything and die. Before the first reading, in New York, I spent four hours taking a bath, and then a friend helped me take a cold shower, and then I went and read. I felt as though I had baby powder in my mouth, and I couldn't hear very well, and I kept thinking I might faint, but I did it. Then I went to bed for three days. Though I could keep the tension under control if I took enough Xanax, I still found mundane activities nearly impossible. I woke up every day in a panic, early, and needed a few hours to conquer my fear before getting out of bed. But I could force myself out in public for an hour or two in the evening.

I had thought I could not possibly go to California for a reading the next week. My father took me there: he got me on and off the plane and to the hotel. So drugged up that I was almost asleep, I could manage these changes, which would have been inconceivable a week earlier. I knew that the more I managed to do, the less I would want to die. During my first dinner in San Francisco, I suddenly felt my depression lift. I chose my own food. I had been spending days on end with my father, but I had no idea what had been happening in his life, except me; depression is a disease of self-obsession. We talked that night as though we were catching up after months apart. When I finally went to bed, I was almost ecstatic. I had some chocolates from my mini-bar, wrote a letter. I felt ready for the world.

The next morning, I felt just as bad as I had ever felt. My father helped me get out of bed and turned on the shower. He tried to get me to eat, but I was too frightened to chew. I managed to drink some milk. These days, a quarter of a milligram of Xanax will put me to sleep for eight hours. That day, I took seven milligrams of Xanax and was still so tense I couldn't sit still. Dr. Wiener had by then started me on Navane, an antipsychotic drug that we hoped would allow me to take the Xanax less often. (I was then taking it every forty-five minutes or so, and in higher doses at bedtime.) The perpetual sensation of tension was completely exhausting, and the cumulative sedative effects of the Xanax and the Navane began to overwhelm me.

The third week of my tour, I lost the ability to remain upright for very long. I would walk for a few minutes and then I would have to lie down. I could no more control that need than I could the need to breathe. At my readings, I would cling to the podium. I would start skipping paragraphs to get through. When I was done, I would sit in a chair and hold on to the seat. As soon as I could leave the room, on any excuse, I would lie down again, often on a bathroom floor. I remember going for a walk with a friend outside Berkeley, hoping that nature might do me good. I had not left my bed for the previous fifty-eight hours; because I'd reduced my Xanax substantially, I was beginning to experience high anxiety again. We got out of my friend's car and walked for almost fifteen minutes, and then I couldn't go any farther. I lay down, fully dressed in nice clothes, in the mud. "Please let me stay here," I said, and I didn't care about standing up ever again. For an hour I lay in that mud, feeling the water seep through, and then my friend pretty much carried me back to the car. Those same nerves that had been scraped raw now seemed to be wrapped in lead.

During my reading tour, I took a lot of cold showers, which got me through the necessary hours. As soon as I could drag myself out of bed, I'd do exercises, or, if I could manage it, I'd go to a gym. I felt as though the exercise filtered the depression out of my blood, helped me to get cleaner. "Most people feel that," Norman Rosenthal, at the N.I.M.H., says. "It's very strong anecdotally."

In the end, I cancelled only one reading. Between November 1st and December 15th, I visited eleven cities. Doing those readings was the most difficult endeavor of my life. My publisher's publicist, who had organized my reading tour, came with me for more than half of it, cheering me through; my father came with me the rest of the time, and when we were apart he called me every few hours. I was never alone for long. The knowledge that I was loved was not in itself a cure, but without it I would not have been able to complete the tour. I would have found a place to lie down in the woods and I would have stayed there until I froze and died. Recovery depends enormously on support. The depressives I've met who have done the best were cushioned with love. Nothing taught me more about the love of my father and my friends than my own depression.

After Thanksgiving, I felt better earlier in the day, and for longer, and more often. My great-aunt Beatrice is remarkable because she's ninety-seven and lives alone; gets up and gets dressed every day; will walk as much as sixteen blocks. Emerging from a depression, you get up and get dressed every day, but this triumph no more implies that you're leading your regular life than Aunt Bea's ability to dress up for lunch implies that she is the all-night dancer she was at seventeen.

The terror lifted in mid-December. Whether that was because the Paxil had really kicked in or because the reading tour was over, I do not know. The poet Jane Kenyon, who suffered from devastating depressions, wrote, "With the wonder and bitterness of someone pardoned for a crime she did not commit I come back to marriage and friends . . . to my desk, books, and chair." So in mid-December I walked into a Christmas party on the Upper West Side and I had an O.K. time. I took hope not from the O.K. time I was having but from the fact that I was having it. I had lost eighteen pounds, and now I was putting on weight. My father and my friends congratulated me on my progress. I thanked them. Privately, however, I was convinced that only the worst symptoms were gone. I was back to about where I had been in September, except that now I understood how bad it could get. I was determined never again to go through such a thing.

Accuracy of perception is not an evolutionary priority. Too optimistic a world view results in foolish risk-taking, but moderate optimism gives you a strong selective advantage. "Normal human thought and perception," Shelley Taylor writes in her 1989 book, "Positive Illusions," "is marked not by accuracy but by positive self-enhancing illusions about the self, the world, and the future. Moreover . . . these illusions are not merely characteristic of human thought; they appear actually to be adaptive." As she notes, "The mildly depressed appear to have more accurate views of themselves, the world, and the future than do normal people. [They] clearly lack the illusions that in normal people promote mental health and buffer them against setbacks."

The phase of depressive realism that I entered after Christmas is the dangerous time. During the worst of my depression, when I could hardly eat, I could not have done myself real harm. In this emerging period, I was feeling well enough for suicide. I could push myself to do pretty much all of what I had always been able to do, but I was unable to experience pleasure. Now I had the energy to wonder *why* I was pushing myself, and I could find no good reasons. One February evening, an acquaintance persuaded me to attend a party. I went to prove my own gaiety, and for several hours kept up every appearance of sharing in the fun that others were having. When I came home, I felt a return of panic, and a sadness that felt almost menacing. In the bathroom, I threw up repeatedly, as though my acute understanding of my own loneliness were a toxin; and when I tried to catch my breath I inhaled my own bile. I lay on the bathroom floor for about twenty minutes, and then I crawled out and lay down on my bed. It was clear to me that I was going crazy again, and the awareness tired me further; but I knew that it was bad to let the craziness run wild. I needed to hear another voice, which could penetrate my fearful isolation. I didn't want to call my father, because I knew he would worry. I picked up the phone and, shaking, dialed one of my oldest friends. It was about three-thirty in the morning. "Hello?" she said.

"Hi," I said, and paused.

"Has something happened?" she asked.

It was immediately clear that I could not explain. "I've got to go," I said, and hung up.

Later, I climbed laboriously up to my roof and wrapped myself around a pipe. As the sun came up, I realized that if you lived in New York there was no point in attempting suicide from the top of a six-story building. Drenched with sweat and developing what would soon become a raging fever, I returned to my bedroom. I knew that the voice of reason was the voice of reason; that depression was ludicrous; and that it would be sad for my father to have worked so hard at saving me and not to have succeeded. I had promised to cut up lamb chops for him someday; he had never broken a promise to me, and that, finally, led me downstairs. When I called my old friend, the next day, to apologize, she demanded an explanation. I could not explain. She told me I had gone too far, and did not speak to me for two years.

It is hard to talk to friends about depression during depression, so there's solace to be found in strangers. In recent years, support groups have proliferated. Mood Disorders Support Group, Inc. (MDSG), is the largest such organization in the United States, with more than a hundred support-group meetings annually. I never went to one when I was ill, but in researching this piece I went to the MDSG/New York meetings at Beth Israel Medical Center for eight weeks at seven-thirty on Friday night, which is when depressed people are not having dates. Members pay four dollars, get a sticky label bearing their first names only (to further protect privacy, I've changed those names), and go into a room with about a dozen others and a facilitator.

This crowd looked as run-down as it felt, especially in the hospital light. At one meeting, Jaime talked first. Forced to resign from his job with "a government agency" after missing too many days, Jaime had been on disability leave for three years. People wouldn't understand. He pretended to have his old job—didn't answer the phone during the day. "If I couldn't keep up appearances," he said, "I'd kill myself." Maggie, who was too depressed to talk, pulled her knees up under her chin.

John, who came often and spoke seldom, had been stroking his coat all evening. At forty, he had never had a full-time job. Two weeks ago, he'd announced that he was about to take one, be like a normal person. We'd told him to go for it, but tonight he said that it was just too frightening. Maggie asked whether his moods improved on vacation. "I've never had a vacation," he said. He shuffled his feet. "I'm sorry. I mean, I guess I've never really had anything to take a vacation from."

Anne said, "I hear people talking about cycling, and I feel really jealous. For me, it's never been like that. I was a morbid, unhappy, anxious child. What's the point?" She was on Nardil, and had found that Catapres-TTS in microdoses saved her from heavy sweating, a side effect. She had originally been on lithium but had gained about fifteen pounds a month, and stopped. Someone thought she should try Depakote, which can be helpful with Nardil, even though the Physicians' Desk Reference discourages the combination. No one could tell her "the point."

A longtime MDSG member, Polly, asked the group, "Do you have friends outside? Only one other person and I said that we did. Polly said, "I try to make new friends, but I don't know how it works. I took Prozac, and it worked for a year, and then it stopped. I think I did more that year, but I lost it." She was sad and sweet-natured and intelligent—clearly a lovely person, as someone told her encouragingly. "How do you meet people, besides here?" she wanted to know. Before I could answer, she added, "And, once you've met them, what do you talk about?"

And then it was Howie's turn. He looked around, but you could tell that he wasn't seeing any of us. His wife had brought him here, hoping it would help, and she was waiting outside. "I feel," he said, in a flat voice sounding like a slowed-down old record-player, "as though I died a few weeks ago but my body hasn't found out yet."

The basic feeling at the support group—I have my mind today, do you have yours?—was as familiar as a native language, and, almost in spite of myself, I began to relax into it. There is so much that cannot be said during depression, that can be intuited only by others who know about it. "If I were on crutches, they wouldn't ask me to dance," one woman said about her family's relentless efforts to get her out. We all held each other up with what we said.

Talk is not cheap, medication is not cheap, and often even the two together are not enough. Only one person at MDSG had tried electroconvulsive therapy, or ECT, and the others were mostly too upset by the thought of it even to discuss it. Most people I met elsewhere who had done ECT, however, were enthusiasts. "I didn't want to die because I hated myself—I wanted to die because I loved myself enough to want this pain to end," Martha Manning says of the day she found the address of a gun shop. "I listened to my daughter singing in the shower and knew that if I killed myself I would stop that song. The next day, I checked myself in for ECT." Antidepressants are effective about seventy per cent of the time. Among people who are severely depressed, ECT seems to work about seventy-five per cent of the time or more. It is used as a recourse for people who have not had success with medications. Patients normally get six to twelve treatments over about a month. ECT often works much more rapidly than medication; its effects can be sustained with meds.

After some routine exams and blood work, a cardiogram, often a chest X-ray for older patients, and some neuroanesthesia-related tests in a hospital, a patient judged suitable for ECT signs elaborate consent forms. The patient is taken to the

ECT suite, usually in the morning. After he has been hooked up to monitors, nurses put an electrolyte jelly on his temples, and then electrodes are attached. A short-acting general anesthetic, which puts the patient out completely for about ten minutes, is administered, along with a muscle relaxant to prevent physical spasms. (The only movement during treatment is a slight wiggling of the fingers and toes.) The patient is connected to EEG and EKG monitors. The electrical stimulus usually lasts no more than several seconds. It causes a seizure in the brain, which usually lasts about fifty seconds—long enough to change brain chemistry, not long enough to create trouble. Why ECT works is unclear, but it seems to have a strong enhancing effect on the major neurotransmitters. Within ten minutes, the patient wakes up in the recovery room. Once he's awake, he's given breakfast and taken to his room—"feeling hung over, knowing it's going to be a Tylenol day," Manning says. The session lasts about thirty minutes, from start to finish; afterward, there is real disorientation for about twenty minutes, and some minor memory loss, which is usually recovered during the day. In fact, the only lasting memory loss is usually of the ECT period itself; patients are often blurry about the whole treatment period.

ECT is considered easier and safer—especially in elderly patients—than antidepressants, and it is now sometimes done on an outpatient basis. But ECT is still the most stigma-loaded of the popular treatments. "You do feel like Frankenstein on the table there," Manning says. "And people don't want to hear about it. Nobody brings you casseroles when you're in for ECT. It's very isolating." But it can be miraculously effective. "Before, I was aware of every swallow of water, that it was just too much work," she goes on. "Afterward, I thought, Do regular people feel this way all the time? It's like you've been not in on a great joke for the whole of your life." The effects start quickly. "Vegetative symptoms got better fast, although mood took longer, then my body felt lighter; then I really wanted a Big Mac," Manning says. "I felt like I'd been hit by a truck, but that was,

comparatively speaking, not so bad." And researchers have begun imagining a possible new-generation device that would accomplish the effects of ECT without the trauma. Robert Post, chief of biological psychiatry at the N.I.M.H., has been working on repeated transcranial magnetic stimulation, or R.T.M.S., which uses fluxes in magnetic fields to stimulate the brain without producing seizures. While electric current has to be turned up quite high to get through the scalp and the skull, magnetic fluxes travel through easily. Since R.T.M.S. avoids the brain seizure, it appears that there are no memory-loss side effects, and that alone makes it an attractive alternative.

Like all illnesses, depression is a great equalizer, but I met no one who seemed a less likely candidate for it than Ted Winstead—thirty, a Northwestern graduate, soft-spoken, polite, good-natured, and good-looking. "So you want inside my head?" he wrote in a notebook once. "Welcome . . . Not exactly what you expected? It's not what I expected either." Six months after he graduated from college, his first depression hit him. In the seven years since, he has been hospitalized more than thirty times. He puts his hands up and presses hard on his forehead and the back of his head, then just above his ears. "It's like my head's in a vise, squeezing together. All I can do is obsess on the negative, and the pain is petrifying and physical. It's like I'm in a locked room and I can't get out and the walls are closing in and in and I'm being compressed and destroyed under the pressure."

His first episode came on abruptly: "I'd been to a movie, and on the way home I realized I might drive into a tree. I felt a weight pushing my foot down, someone pulling my hands around. I knew I couldn't drive home because there were too many trees, so I headed for the hospital." In the following years, Winstead went through every medication in the book and got nowhere. In the hospital, he tried to strangle himself. He finally had ECT, which made him briefly manic. "I attacked another patient and had to go into the quiet room for a while," he recalls. For the last five years, Winstead has been getting booster ECT whenever the depression hits—usually about every

six weeks. When we met, he was also taking lithium, Wellbutrin, Adapin, Cytomel, and Synthroid. "ECT is totally safe and I would recommend it, but they're putting electricity into your head, and that's scary," he says. "I hate the memory problems. It gives me a headache. I keep journals so I can remember what happened. Otherwise, I'd never know."

Winstead was unable to work from late 1994 to the middle of 1996, but before this he researched and wrote part of a history book. "The people I've worked with and for have been really supportive, and have made allowances," he says. "Everyone was great: parents, friends, doctors. The attention has gotten me through."

First, you might try talking, then you might try pills, then ECT; at some point, you try the experimental odds and ends; then you try surgery. In the late nineteen-forties and early fifties, patients diagnosed with severe neuropsychiatric disorders were prime candidates for having their prefrontal lobes severed. In the heyday of lobotomies, about five thousand were performed annually in the United States, causing between two hundred and fifty and five hundred deaths a year. Psychosurgery lies under this shadow. When I first met Winstead, he was just back from having a cingulotomy. In that procedure, the scalp is frozen locally and the surgeon drills a small hole in the front of the skull. He then puts an electrode directly into the brain to destroy areas of tissue, usually measuring about eight by eighteen millimeters. The leading place for this surgery is Massachusetts General Hospital, and that is where Winstead was operated on by the neurosurgeon Rees Cosgrove. "About sixty to seventy per cent of patients have at least some response," Cosgrove told me. "Thirty per cent show marked improvement. This procedure is for people whose illness has failed to respond to everything thrown at it, so those are encouraging statistics." It is difficult to get into the cingulotomy protocol; Mass. General, the most active center, does only fifteen or twenty of the procedures a year. The surgery usually has a delayed effect, often showing benefits only several weeks, or even months, later. Like ECT, such surgery probably causes disruption of brain function, but how, exactly, this trauma causes a change for the better is not clear. "We don't understand the pathophysiology," Cosgrove says. "But the effect on other parts of the brain is indirect, whatever it is."

"I have real hopes for the cingulotomy," Winstead told me when we met. He was having a pretty good day, laughing from time to time in gentle self-deprecation. He pushed back his red hair to show me the scar near the front of his scalp, centered over his eyes. "I heard the drill going into my skull, like when you're at the dentist's office. I thought, This is creepy, and I asked to be put further under. So they did before they started burning my brain. I hope it works. If it doesn't, I have a plan for how to end it all, because I just can't keep going like this."

In the spring of 1995, I stopped taking drugs cold turkey. I knew that this was dumb, but I wanted desperately to find out again who I "really" was. At first, all I was conscious of was the awful withdrawal symptoms from the Xanax. I couldn't sleep for four days, and my eyes and stomach hurt, and my sense of balance was off. Unrelenting nightmares seemed to penetrate my wakefulness, and I kept sitting up abruptly with my heart pounding. Dr. Wiener had told me that when I was ready to go off the drugs I should do it gradually, but I was afraid that if I went slowly I'd never really make it.

It was a bad mistake. If you stimulate seizures in an animal every day, the seizures become automatic: the animal will go on having them even if you withdraw the stimulation. Similarly, a brain that has gone into depression several times may return to depression. Brain-imaging scans have indicated that depression changes both the structure and the biochemistry of the brain. Medication-responsive patients may cease to respond over the long term if they cycle on and off the medications; with each episode, there is a ten-percent increase in the risk that the depression will become chronic. "It's analogous to a primary cancer that's very drug-responsive but once it transforms itself and metastasizes is less responsive," Bob Post explains. "People worry about side effects from staying on medication for a life-time, but these effects seem insubstantial compared with the lethality of undertreated depression. It would be like asking someone to go off his digitalis, seeing if he has another heart attack, and restarting medication when his heart is too flabby to recuperate."

At this point, I entered what is commonly called "agitated depression." I developed in rapid succession all the typical symptoms—hatred, anguish, guilt, self-loathing. I stopped speaking to at least six people. I took to slamming down the phone when someone said something I didn't like. I criticized everyone. It was hard to sleep, because my mind was racing with tiny injustices from my past: irritability kept me awake every night, and the lack of sleep made me more irritable still.

It is not unusual for really depressed people to have no deep sleep at all. Does one sleep oddly just because of depression or does one sink into depression in part because of sleeping oddly? Many people occasionally wake up too early with a sensation of ominous dread; that momentary fearful, despairing state may be the closest that healthy people come to depression. "By not letting someone go to sleep, you extend the diurnal improvement," Tom Wehr, who heads sleep research at the N.I.M.H., says. "Though depressed people seek the oblivion of sleep, it is in sleep that the depression is maintained and intensified." There has been limited research in this area (because it is non-patentable and hence unprofitable), but studies suggest that manipulating the timing of sleep can be a way to treat depression.

In my agitated state, with my sleep disrupted and my time in the daylight altogether irregular, I found that I couldn't really concentrate on anything. I started doing my laundry every night, to keep busy. When I got a mosquito bite, I scratched it until it bled, then picked off the scab; I bit my nails so far down that my fingers were always bleeding. I had open wounds and scratches everywhere, though I never actually cut myself with a knife. Yet, being free of the vegetative symptoms of my breakdown, I did not imagine that I might still be depressed.

In retrospect, this seems odd, since I had developed the ultimate hallmark of depression, which is an obsession with suicide. I had had more than enough of life, and wanted to figure out how to end it with the least damage to those who loved me. I decided that a fatal disease would be a valid excuse for suicide. I knew that it would be devastating for my family and sad for my friends, but felt that they would understand, whereas I knew that if I did something while I was "healthy" they would not. I couldn't figure out how to give myself cancer or M.S., but I knew just how to get AIDS. The particular behavior I chose was related to my own neuroses, but the decision to behave in so systematic a way, with such a sustained hunger to die, was typical of agitated depression. After my first episode of unsafe sex, I had a burst of fear and called a good friend and told him what I had done. He talked me through it, and I went to bed. When I woke up in the morning, I felt much as I had felt on the first day of college or summer camp or a new job. This was to be the next phase of my life. There was something I genuinely wanted, and the end was at hand. Over the next three months, I took ever more direct risks. I was sorry to have no pleasure from encounters some of which I knew I would have once enjoyed. Casual with life, I also walked through Central Park at night, crossed highways against the traffic, and drank myself into unconsciousness.

In early October of 1995, after a bout of unpleasant unsafe sex, I realized that I might be infecting others. Dismayed at how numb I had become to their vulnerability, I again withdrew into physical isolation. I'd had four months to get infected; I'd had a total of about eighteen encounters; and knowing I would die had, ironically, diminished the urgency of my wish to die. I put that period of my life behind me, became gentler again. On my thirty-second birthday, I looked at the many friends who had come to celebrate it, and was able to smile, knowing I would never have a birthday again. The celebrations were tiring; the gifts I left in their wrappings.

When major depression with high-level anxiety—in the argot of the clinicians—started coming around the second time, I recognized it. I didn't want to go back on meds, and tried to ride it out. I knew about three days ahead of the total crash that I was going all the way down. I started taking Paxil. I called Dr. Wiener. I warned my father. I addressed the practicalities: losing your mind, like losing your keys, is a hassle. Out of the terror I heard my voice holding on tight when friends called, "I'll have to cancel Wednesday," I said. "I'm afraid of lamb chops again." The symptoms came fast. In about a month, I lost a fifth of my body weight—some thirty pounds. I had just moved into the new house I'd been restoring for five years. I stayed there three nights, then had to move in with my father again. There was a lot of talk about hospitalization, which terrified me further: I believed that once I went into Payne Whitney I'd never return, and I didn't want to die slowly in a padded room.

Dr. Wiener started me on Effexor, and also added BuSpar, an antianxiety medication. Anxiety is not paranoia; people with anxiety disorders assess their own position in the world much as people without them do. What changes in anxiety is how one feels about that assessment. It's possible to distinguish between anxiety and depression, but, according to Jim Ballenger, a leading expert on anxiety, "they're fraternal twins." George Brown, of the University of London, has said succinctly, "Depression is usually a response to a current loss. Anxiety is a response to a threat of future loss." About half the patients with anxiety or panic disorders develop major depression within five years. The diseases appear to have overlapping genotypes.

Depression exacerbated by anxiety has a much higher suicide rate than depression alone, and is much harder to recover from. "If you're having panic every day," Ballenger says, "it's gonna bring Hannibal to his knees." One in ten Americans has a panic attack of some kind every year. Because the locus coeruleus in the brain, which controls much of norepinephrine production, has a strong influence on lower-bowel function, almost half of panic-disorder patients have irritable-bowel symptoms as well. "Two out of three times, life events are implicated in the onset of panic disorder, and it's always a loss of personal security," Ballenger says.

Xanax is, in my view, a lifesaver. There is popular prejudice against the benzodiazepines, partly because they have often been given without proper patient evaluation. They can be addictive, so withdrawing from them abruptly can be an enormous problem; some can affect short-term memory. Despite these drawbacks, the rapid relief they provide is extraordinary, and for people who are not inclined toward abuse they save lives. "Nonsense, nonsense," Dr. Wiener said when I dithered about Xanax. "Take it as I tell you to and we'll deal with these problems when your symptoms have lifted."

When I was heading for my second breakdown, everyone, including Dr. Wiener, told me firmly that I should find a new shrink for talking therapy. Finding a new shrink when you are feeling up and communicative is burdensome, but doing it when you are in the throes of a major depression is beyond the pale. Nonetheless, I was lucky that I could afford to follow that advice. Most managed-care companies are keen on medication, which is, comparatively speaking, cheap, and are not very keen on talking therapies or hospitalizations.

"I spend more and more time on the phone with managed-care companies trying to justify patients' need to stay in the hospital," Sylvia Simpson, a physician at Johns Hopkins, says. "Frequently, when a patient is still very, very ill and unable to function—if he's not acutely suicidal that day, authorization for coverage of further in-patient stay is denied." Depressed people are usually in no condition to argue their own cases with insurers—and depression is one expensive illness. My first breakdown cost me five months of work, five thousand dollars' worth of visits to the psychopharmacologist, twelve thousand dollars of talking therapy, thirty-five hundred dollars for medications. My guess is that I've used up about seventy thousand dollars on this disease so far.

The result of treatment dictated by cost-economizing managed-care companies is that more and more people are taking medication with little context. "Medicines treat depression," said the therapist I now see. "I treat depressives." More

people are treated for depression now because it is more acceptable and medicines are available, and, over all, public health may be going up in consequence, but the idea that the option of psychotherapy can go on a back burner is "lunacy," according to Kay Jamison, the author of "An Unquiet Mind" and an authority on manic depression; she believes that she would be dead without psychotherapy. Therapy helps someone to make sense of the new self attained on meds and to accept the loss of self that occurs during a breakdown. Antidepressants are not amnesiac drugs. If real experience has triggered your descent into depression, you have a human yen to understand it even when you have overcome acute symptoms. Dr. Robert Klitzman, of Columbia University, says, "Pills should not obviate insight; they should enable insight."

The week of my H.I.V. test, I was taking between twelve and eighteen milligrams of Xanax every day, so that I could sleep most of the time. On Thursday of that week, I woke up at four in the afternoon and checked my messages. The nurse from my doctor's office: "Your cholesterol is down, cardiogram is normal, and your H.I.V. test turned out fine." I had to call her the next morning to make sure that that hadn't been another Xanax dream.

I knew then that I wanted to live, and I was grateful for the news. But I went right on feeling terrible for two more months. Gritting my teeth against what is quaintly termed "suicidal ideation," I decided I was sufficiently well to go to Turkey to do research, but I went feeling infinitely burdened by the work I had there. Then, in the perfect Turkish sunshine, the depression finally evaporated. That was the last I heard from it.

In a poem entitled "Back" Jane Kenyon writes, "Suddenly I fall into my life again, like a vole picked up by a storm then dropped three valleys and two mountains away from home. I can find my way back. I know I will recognize the store where I used to buy milk and gas. I remember the house and barn, the rake, the blue cups and plates, the Russian novels I loved so much, and the black silk nightgown that he once thrust into the toe of my Christmas stocking." And so it was for me: everything seemed strange, then became abruptly familiar, and I realized that the deep melancholy that had started when my mother got ill, had worsened when she died, had built beyond grief into despair, and had disabled me was not disabling me anymore. I was still sad about the sad things, but I was myself again.

"Pharmaceutical wonders are at work," Kenyon writes in another poem, "but I believe only in this moment of well-being. Unholy ghost, you are certain to come again . . . and turn me into someone who can't take the trouble to speak; someone who can't sleep, or who does nothing but sleep; can't read, or call for an appointment for help. There is nothing I can do against your coming." You are never the same once you have acquired breakdown knowledge. We are told to learn self-reliance, but it's tricky if you have no self on which to rely. Friends, doctors, and my father have helped me, and some chemistry has wrought a readjustment, and I feel O.K. for the moment, but the recurring nightmares are no longer about the things that will happen *to* me, from outside, but about the things that happen *in* me. What if tomorrow I wake up as a manure beetle? Every morning starts with a check for cancers, a momentary anxiety about which nightmares might be true. It's as if my self, like the friend I called that late night in 1995, had said, "Don't push it, don't count on me for much, I have problems of my own to take care of."

I hope not to have to go off my medications. I'm not addicted, because addicts are prone to symptoms caused by the removal of the drug, but I am dependent, because without the drug I would probably develop symptoms. I have some side effects, which may eventually become intolerable. I get terrible hives, which seem to be getting worse, and have to apply cortisone creams and ointments every six hours; I also have to take antihistamines several times a day, and am therefore perpetually groggy. The way that SSRIs undermine your capacity for sustained sexual fantasy means that you can climax only when you're in the presence of someone to whom you're strongly attracted. I gain weight more easily than I used to. I sweat

more. My memory, which was never good, is impaired: I frequently forget in the middle of a sentence what I am saying. I get headaches often, and occasional muscular cramps. It's not ideal, but it seems to have put a real wall between me and depression.

Slowly, I catch up. When two friends died recently, both in freak accidents, I felt sad, but to feel just grief was almost (this sounds terrible, but it is true) a kind of joy. "Will you become depressed doing your depression piece?" everyone has asked me. I have not. I have felt blue sometimes, and on some days I have chosen not to work on this difficult subject, but I feel far away from the reality described here, and, were it not for notes I wrote when I was ill, I would have been unable to describe it fully.

Once you stop being depressed, you can notice in isolation those sensations which were previously blurred. What is it like to feel tired? To be frightened by something frightening? To be hungry, annoyed, hung over, bored? You learn them all over again. And what is it like to hope? Hope is the belief in a future without loss; it defends against its oblique cousin dread—the dread of a recurrence. "I am overcome by ordinary contentment," Jane Kenyon has written. "What hurt me so terribly all my life until this moment? How I love the small, swiftly beating heart of the bird singing in the great maples; its bright, unequivocal eye."

I wonder constantly whether these experiences have served any purpose. Is depression a mood state that nature or God willed us to have for some reason? Is it useful? "Organisms have a selective advantage if they have different states that give them the upper hand in particular circumstances," Randolph Nesse, of the University of Michigan, says. Is depression one of those states? Is it merely a derangement, like cancer, or can it be defensive, like nausea? Some people argue that it's best seen as a mixture of maladaptive or pathological withdrawal and so-called conservation withdrawal, which may be useful in some circumstances: hibernating, avoiding danger, saving energy.

This is an idea that has been elaborated in Emmy Gut's book

"Productive and Unproductive Depression," which proposes that the long pause brought about by a depression causes people to change their lives in useful ways, especially after a loss. It can draw people away from unproductive pursuits and relationships. For her, the question is which depressions should be normalized and which should be left untouched. There are probably people who don't have enough anxiety and sadness to keep them out of trouble, and it seems likely that they don't do well. Leprosy is a disease in which you do not feel enough physical pain: lepers become deformed and then die because crucial warnings do not get through to them. I suspect that the most important function of grief is in the formation of attachment. If you do not fear loss, you cannot love intensely. Homesickness showed how much I loved my parents; losing my mother not only depressed me but also intensified my love for her and for people still alive.

We now identify as pathology many things that were previously accepted as personality. The supermodel has damaged our images of ourselves by setting unrealistic expectations, and the psychological supermodel is even more dangerous than the physical one. People are constantly examining their own minds and rejecting their own moods. The use of antidepressants is going up as people seek to normalize what used to be deemed normal. Thirty million people worldwide have been on Prozac, and millions more on the other SSRIs—not to mention a substantial number on non-SSRI antidepressants. SSRIs are now prescribed for homesickness, eating disorders, PMS, household pets who scratch too much, chronic joint pain, and ordinary grief. They are prescribed not only by psychiatrists but also by G.P.s and gynecologists; someone I met had been put on Prozac by his podiatrist. When T.W.A. Flight 800 went down, families waiting for news of their loved ones were offered drugs with the same palliative expression with which they might have been offered extra pillows or blankets.

Is the grand-scale social experiment of eliminating a state from the human mood spectrum dangerous? George Brown says, "Social systems can play a powerful role in generating both psychiatric and physical disorder. For example, in the U.K., the rate of major depression among single mothers is double that of women raising children with a partner. I have nothing against Prozac, but there needs to be a recognition that what may well be a rising tide of depression is related to the fact that basic social and psychological needs are not being met." More generally, modernity has wrought changes to which we are not yet adequately adapted; depression appears to increase far more rapidly in technological cultures than in others. "The investment to achieve modern life goals, the number of opportunities we have, is probably beyond the range our mind was designed to handle," Randolph Nesse says.

The question of what functions depression serves is not the same as the question of what functions antidepressants are coming to serve. Are they restoring the normal self or are they changing the self? It's said that everyone has the virtues of his faults. If one eliminates the faults, do the virtues go as well? "We are only at the dawn of pharmacological exuberance," Nesse says. "New medications that are being developed may likely make it quick, easy, cheap, and safe to block many unwanted emotions. We should be there within the next generation. And I predict we'll go for it, because if people can make themselves feel better they usually do. I could imagine the world in a few decades being a pharmacological utopia, controlling viciousness, fear, and pain. I can equally imagine people so mellowed out that they neglected all their social and personal responsibilities." Robert Klitzman says, "Not since Copernicus have we faced so dramatic a transformation. In centuries to come, there may be new societies that look back at us as creatures that were slaves to and crippled by uncontrolled emotions."

The survivors stay on pills, waiting. "I'm reconciled to a lifetime of medicine," Martha Manning says, suddenly fervent. "And I'm thankful. Sometimes I look at those pills and wonder, Is this all that stands between Hell and me? You don't defeat depression, you learn to manage it. When you come so close to taking your life, if you get it back you'd better claim it."

Striving to claim it, we hold on to the idea of productive depression, something not only normal but vital. "I lost a great innocence when I understood that I and my mind were not going to be on good terms for the rest of my life," Kay Jamison says, with a shrug. "I can't tell you how tired I am of character-building experiences. But I treasure this part of me. Whoever loves me loves me with this in it."

"My wife has never seen me severely depressed," Robert Boorstin says. "I've walked her through it, and other people have talked to her about what it's like. I've done my best to prepare her, because doubtless I'll have another depression. Sometime in the next forty years, I'm going to be crawling across the room again. And it scares me a lot, because the thought of being without your mind is a lot scarier than being without anything else. I mean, if somebody said to me, 'I'll take away your mental illness if you'll cut me off your leg,' I don't know whether I'd make the exchange. And yet, before I was ill, I was intolerant beyond comparison, arrogant beyond belief, with no understanding of frailties. I'm a better person as a result of having been through all this, but I would not recommend the experience."

"If I had it to do over, I wouldn't do it this way," Ted Winstead said the last time I saw him. I had spent the afternoon with him and his parents and his psychiatrist, and we were discussing the grim reality: that his first cingulotomy still hadn't worked, that he'd been hospitalized three times in the months after it, and that he might have to have a second surgery. In his gently courageous way, he was making plans to be up and running in six months. "I have this experience with my doctor that's been very good," he said gamely. "There really are up sides to depression. It's just hard to see them when you're in it."

On the happy day when we lose depression, we will lose a great deal with it. As the sun seems brighter and clearer when it comes on a rare day of English summer after ten months of gray skies than it can ever seem in the tropics, so recent happiness feels enormous and embracing and beyond anything I have ever imagined. In the course of my depression, I reached a strange point at which I could not see the line between my own tendency to theatricality and the reality of my illness. The line is still not clear, but there is someone or something here writing these words, a unionist me that held on until the rebel chemicals had been brought back into line. Some ropy fibre holds fast even when most of the self has been stripped from it; we know what chemistry is and how deep it runs, and yet anyone who lives through this knows that the shifting self reaches beyond serotonin and dopamine. I'm more confident, in some odd way, than I've ever imagined being. I do not think that I will ever again try to kill myself, nor do I think that I would give my life up readily if my plane crashed in a desert. I would struggle tooth and nail to survive. The opposite of depression is not happiness but vitality, and my life, as I write this, is vital, even when it's sad. I may wake up sometime next year without my mind again. But I know what is left of me when my mind is gone and my body is going. I was not brought up religious, and think that when you die you're dead, yet I have also discovered what I guess I would have to call a soul—something I had never imagined until one day, two and a half years ago, when Hell came to pay me a surprise visit. It's a precious discovery. This week, on a chilly night when I was overtired, I felt a momentary flash of hopelessness, and wondered, as I so often do, whether I was slipping; for a petrifying instant, a lightning-quick flash, I wanted a car to run me over, and I had to clench my teeth to stay on the sidewalk until the light turned green. Nevertheless, I cannot find it in me to regret entirely the course my life took.

 Article Review Form at end of book.

How much more likely are women to be depressed than are men? Identify two of the reasons women are more likely than men to be depressed.

Women and Depression

Bonnie R. Strickland

During this year, some 10 million Americans will be clinically depressed and could be diagnosed with an affective disorder. The experience of depression is the most common complaint of people seeking mental health care and the third leading reason individuals see physicians. The emotional toll of the affective disorders in terms of human suffering is incalculable. In addition to the despair and loss of pleasure suffered by depressed individuals (and their families), two thirds of the 30,000 reported suicides in this country each year may be linked to clinical depression. The economic expense to American society in lost productivity and health care is staggering. Annual costs for "mental illness" exceeded $129 billion in 1988. Depression and the affective disorders are recurrent and constitute a major public and mental health problem. Still, they are often unrecognized, undiagnosed, and untreated.

The predominant affective disorders are major depressive disorder, affecting some 3% of our adult population; dysthymia, affecting another 3%; and bipolar disorder (manic-depression), which affects about 1% of our citizens. Depression also often accompanies physical illness and may be a response to high-stress and disruptive life events. No sex differences are found for bipolar disorder, but females make up about two thirds of those individuals who suffer major depression and dysthymia. Around the world, whether rich or poor, black or white, of high or low socioeconomic status, women are, on the average, twice as likely to be depressed as men.[1] One of four women and one of eight men will be clinically depressed at some time in their lives. The reasons for this discrepancy are complex and poorly understood, but likely arise from an interaction of biological, cultural, and psychological factors that may be different for males and females.[2]

Biological Perspectives

Research suggests that the affective state of depression, such as feelings of sadness, results from both biogenic and psychosocial factors. Arousal and reactions to stress are a function of physiological responses and one's cognitive appraisal of the events that lead to such arousal. Neurotransmitter substances, such as norepinephrine, dopamine, and serotonin, cross excitatory and inhibitory neuronal synapses and are taken up by specific receptors. A dysfunction in transmission across the synapses, whether a function of the transmitter substances, the mechanisms of synaptic activity, or the uptake or reuptake of the neurotransmitters, may lead to mood dysregulation.

Gender differences in neurophysiological functioning could account for some of the reasons that women are more likely to be depressed than men. Yet little research is available on neurochemical differences. We do know that reproductive-related events, such as menstruation, pregnancy, childbirth, and menopause, are linked to the reproductive hormones and may influence mood. Seasonal affective disorder, perhaps associated with light change and biological cycling, is also particularly pronounced for women. Those precise interactions of reproductive cycling and depression are difficult to assess, however, in view of our limited knowledge of the basic mechanisms of the reproductive hormones. Moreover, social and cultural influences may bias women's cognitive and affective descriptions of their reproductive experiences and sexual functioning.

Most women, especially in their late 20s and early 30s, report mild to minimal mood changes premenstrually, with about 5% reporting serious and severe symptoms. Typical premenstrual and menstrual symptoms are similar to those of clinical depression but are generally more mild. They include depressed mood, irritability, hostility, anxiety, and changes in sleep, eating habits, and energy.[3]

The use of oral contraceptives may also lead to depressive symptoms for some women. Pregnancy, in contrast, is associated with a low incidence of psychiatric disorders. Following childbirth, some 50% to

80% of women report mild depressive symptoms; as many as 10% experience severe postpartum depression. Depressive symptoms are also reported by women who wish to conceive and fail or cannot carry a fetus to term. The incidence of infertility appears to be increasing among young women and is a major life crisis similar to other high-stress events.[4] Many women who find themselves infertile report this to be the most upsetting experience of their lives.

A prevalent myth in regard to reproductive cycling and depression is that menopausal women are ill-tempered and depressed. Women experiencing early, surgically induced menopause may report depression, but depression does not seem to occur as a function of natural changes from pre- to postmenopause. About 15% of menopausal women report themselves to be depressed, a rate almost identical to that of women at the same ages who are not menopausal.[5]

Depression and a sense of guilt and loss have also been assumed to be related to abortion. These feelings may occur for some women, but are typically mild and transitory. By far, the feeling most reported by women who choose to terminate their pregnancies is relief. Those factors implicated in increased risk of depression after abortion, such as lack of support for the decision and self-blame, seem similar to factors reported in research on other stressful life events.[6]

The arena of hormones and behavior is further complicated by the ways in which the reproductive hormones may be related to fat placement and weight gain. The role of adipose (fat) tissue in the storage of cholesterol and the uptake of the stress catecholamines needs continued research as a physiological mechanism involved in the regulation of mood and eating disorders.

Research on the occurrence of depression in relation to reproductive hormones and cycling is intriguing but limited. Generally, the empirical evidence that hormonal changes directly contribute to depression is weak.

Psychological and Cultural Perspectives

Psychological research on gender differences and depression is relatively recent. Findings suggest that socialization patterns for males and females reinforce certain stereotypes of appropriate sex role behavior. Males are encouraged toward independence and mastery behavior; females are expected to present themselves as attractive, sensitive to other people, and passive in relationships. Because depression is identified as lack of activity and energy, it is not surprising to find that women may be more depressed than men. (Note that men are overrepresented in those psychiatric disorders that involve active, and sometimes impulsive, behavior, namely, conduct disorders and substance abuse.)

The cognitive revolution in psychology has framed much of the current research on depression. Findings from clinical practice mesh with theoretical notions of the role of cognition and motivation in emotion. Certain cognitive styles (e.g., constructive thinking, emotional self-focus, learned helplessness or learned optimism, mindfulness, perceived control) and various self-evaluative or self-esteem variables appear to be related to health and depression.[7] Yet few of these constructs have been related systematically to gender, although one might expect differences in view of the assumed differential social cognitions of men and women. For example, *irrational thinking* is assumed to be related to depression; therapeutic interventions involve changing or reframing distorted thoughts. Yet many women live in aversive situations that they may be perceiving accurately. As with other oppressed groups, these women's perceptions may be realistic in view of the social conditions in which they live. Thus, therapeutic change for these women may demand behavioral action to escape or improve stressful life conditions as well as changing cognitions.

Within a diathesis-stress model, Abramson, Metalsky, and Alloy[8] have developed a theory of *hopeless-ness depression* in which a proximal sufficient cause of depressive symptoms is an expectation that one cannot change highly aversive life situations and desired and valued outcomes will not be available. Hammen and her colleagues[9] also have suggested that specific depressive self-schemas lead to vulnerability to depression and that self-schemas may be generally different for men and women depending on their life situations. If a woman finds value in social relationships, for example, an interpersonal loss may be particularly distressful. Lowered self-esteem may also be a function of specific, self-focused disappointments rather than generalized unhappiness. Nolen-Hoeksema[1] also found women engage in more ruminative, brooding responses to negative events than do men, perhaps leading to more severe depression for a longer duration of time than for men.

Thus, social influences such as cultural expectations about women's roles appear to be major factors in the excess of depression for women as opposed to men. In our contemporary American society, stress is ubiquitous in our lives, but women may be disproportionately affected because of the generally lower power, respect, and esteem that accrue to women. Women and girls experience more discrimination, poverty, sexual harassment, and abuse than men and boys. Women also experience more stress in marriages and interpersonal relationships and are more likely than men to be the caretakers of children and the frail elderly. They often feel responsible when intimates are emotionally needy or psychologically distressed, thus living with prolonged, unremitting stress that can lead to both physical and emotional difficulties expressed as depression.

Individuals and family members with economic difficulties are often depressed, and three quarters of the people living in poverty in this country are women and children. A single mother, with unpredictable or limited economic support, is at particularly high risk for depression. Even controlling for income, research suggests that job loss and "money problems" are strongly associated with high levels of depressive symptoms. Women still have a difficult time entering the workplace, escaping sexual harassment, and advancing to positions of status and appropriate economic reward.

Sexual and physical violence against women are epidemic in this country, and women with a history of abuse are significantly more likely to be depressed than women with no such victimization. More than 90% of adult rape victims are women, and 80% of child sexual abuse involves girls. Almost two thirds of adult women recall at least one experience of sexual abuse or assault before age 18, and one third of adult women will be raped, sexually assaulted, or both. One of three married women is battered or abused during her marriage, as is one of four females in dating relationships. Moreover, regardless of whether women have personally experienced violence or abuse, they are likely to learn from friends, family, and the media that women's safety cannot be guaranteed in many situations. The burden of vigilance to ensure one's security is quite different for women than men and may be a continued source of stress resulting in depression for women.[10]

Treatment

The effective treatment of the affective disorders is one of the welcomed success stories of modern advances in mental health. Some 80% of individuals who are depressed and find appropriate mental health care recover in a period of a few weeks to a few months. However, depression is still often unrecognized and misdiagnosed, so that only about one in four depressed individuals will be properly treated.

The various psychotropic medications in use since the early 1950s have been one of the leading reasons for improved treatments for the affective disorders. Lithium and some of the antiseizure medications seem to be particularly useful for bipolar disorders. Psychopharmacological medications have also been effective in the treatment of major depressive disorder and dysthymia. Drugs of choice have included tricyclic antidepressants and the monamine oxidase inhibitors. Fluoxetine (Prozac) is now the drug most likely to be prescribed for depression because its effects are comparable to those of the older tricyclic antidepressants, but there are fewer unpleasant side effects. Estimates suggest that 60% of depressed individuals will respond to appropriate medication. Yet, although two thirds of antidepressant prescriptions are written for women, almost no research is available to ascertain differential responses for females versus males; little, if anything, is known about the interactions of antidepressant medications and the reproductive hormones.

Various brief cognitive-behavioral psychotherapies, especially those that focus on action and mastery behaviors, have also proven effective in treating depression. One example is feminist therapy, which addresses social and cultural aspects of depression as well as individual experiences and responses.

Psychopharmacology and psychotherapy, alone or in combination, are usually superior to placebo in the treatment of clinical depression. Cognitive therapy seems better than both other psychotherapies and pharmacology for mild and moderate depression, but appropriate antidepressant medications may be needed for the severe biological depressions and disruptive somatic symptoms. In the largest study completed to date comparing imipramine, cognitive-behavioral therapy, and brief interpersonal therapy, 57% to 69% of patients who completed 16 weeks of treatment were symptom free. Results were remarkably similar across the therapies except that drug treatment seemed to relieve symptoms earliest. No sex differences were noted.[11]

Little systematic information is available as to whether men and women respond differently to various psychosocial treatments. A meta-analysis of a decade of short-term psychodynamic psychotherapy studies did find behavioral treatments for depression to be twice as effective as short-term psychodynamic psychotherapy when treatment ends and at 1-year follow-up, although this finding was reduced for samples of female patients.[12]

Preventive efforts would also be expected to influence the occurrence of depression among women. Young people are significantly more likely to be depressed than older cohorts. Girls, in particular, have diminished self-esteem and become more depressed as they move into adolescence. Changing the social conditions that limit opportunities for girls and women or devalue women's contributions should lead to enhanced well-being and less depression. Increased support for women who are disadvantaged in this society, especially special populations such as single mothers in poverty, would improve not only their well-being but also that of their children.

Conclusions

Despite the continued difficulties of definition and delineation of the affective disorders, empirical evidence from biological, psychological, and sociological perspectives suggests that the complex etiology and treatment of the depressions are steadily beginning to be understood. Despite the fact that women are twice as likely to be depressed as men, however, little research has focused on gender differences in depression. Reproductive cycling appears to be related to depression for some women. Social roles and life experiences also influence depression and the duration of dysphoric affect. Women and men may use different cognitive strategies and coping responses to negative events and thus may be differentially dysphoric or depressed. Although both psychosocial and pharmacological treatments for depression lead to the remediation of symptoms, few data are available on the issue of whether men and women respond differently to psychotherapy or antidepressant medication. Systematic basic and applied research on gender and depression must continue and be expanded if we are to understand the affective disorders and answer the age-old question as to why women are more often depressed than men.

Notes

1. S. Nolen-Hoeksema, *Sex Differences in Depression* (Stanford University Press, Stanford, CA, 1990).
2. E. McGrath, G. P. Keita, B. R. Strickland, and N. F. Russo, *Women and Depression: Risk Factors and Treatment Issues*, report of the American Psychological Association Task Force (American Psychological Association, Washington, DC, 1990).
3. J. A. Hamilton, B. L. Parry, and S. L. Blumenthal, The menstrual cycle in context: I. Affective syndromes associated with reproductive hormonal changes, *Journal of Clinical Psychiatry, 49,* 474–480 (1988).
4. A. L. Stanton and C. A. Dunkel-Schetter, Psychological adjustment to infertility: An overview of conceptual approaches, in *Infertility: Perspectives From Stress and Coping Research,* A. L. Stanton and C. A. Dunkel-Schetter, Eds. (Plenum Press, New York, 1991).
5. J. B. McKinlay, S. M. McKinlay, and D. J. Brambilia, The relative contributions of endocrine changes and social circumstances to depression in mid-aged women, *Journal of Health and Social Behavior, 28,* 345–363 (1987).
6. N. E. Adler, H. P. David, B. N. Major, S. Roth, N. F. Russo, and G. E. Wyatt, Psychological responses after abortion, *Science, 248,* 41–44 (1990).
7. B. R. Strickland, Internal-external control expectancies: From contingency to creativity, *American Psychologist, 44,* 4–7 (1989).
8. L. Y. Abramson, G. I. Metalsky, and A. B. Alloy, Hopelessness depression: A theory-based subtype of depression, *Psychological Review, 96,* 358–372 (1989).
9. C. Hammen, T. Marks, A. Mayol, and R. deMayo, Depressive self-schemas, life stress, and vulnerability to depression, *Journal of Abnormal Psychology, 94,* 308–319 (1985).
10. M. L. Leidig, The continuum of violence against women: Psychological and physical implications, *American Journal of College Health, 40,* 149–155 (1992).
11. I. Elkin, T. Shea, J. T. Watkins, S. D. Imber, S. M. Stosky, J. F. Collins, D. R. Glass, P. Pikonis, W. R. Leber J. P. Docherty, S. J. Fiester, and M. B. Perloff, National Institute of Mental Health Treatment of Depression Collaborative Research Program: General effectiveness of treatments, *Archives of General Psychiatry, 46,* 971–982 (1989).
12. M. Svartberg and T. C. Stiles, Comparative effects of short-term psychodynamic psychotherapy: A meta-analysis, *Journal of Consulting and Clinical Psychology, 59,* 704–714 (1991).

Article Review Form at end of book.

What are the three components of explanatory style? What are two
ways explanatory style might influence well-being and death?

Catastrophizing and Untimely Death

Christopher Peterson,[1] Martin E. P. Seligman,[2] Karen H. Yurko,[3] Leslie R. Martin,[4] and Howard S. Friedman[5]

[1]University of Michigan, [2]University of
Pennsylvania, [3]Children's Hospital of
Michigan, [4]La Sierra University,
and [5]University of California, Riverside

Abstract

*Participants in the Terman Life-Cycle
Study completed open-ended questionnaires in 1936 and 1940, and these responses were blindly scored for
explanatory style by content analysis.
Catastrophizing (attributing bad events
to global causes) predicted mortality as of
1991, especially among males, and predicted accidental or violent deaths especially well. These results are the first to
show that a dimension of explanatory
style is a risk factor for mortality in a
large sample of initially healthy individuals, and they imply that one of the
mechanisms linking explanatory style
and death involves lifestyle.*

Explanatory style is a cognitive personality variable that reflects how
people habitually explain the causes
of bad events (Peterson & Seligman,
1984). Among the dimensions of explanatory style are

- internality ("it's me") versus
externality

- stability ("it's going to last
forever") versus instability

- globality ("it's going to undermine
everything") versus specificity

These dimensions capture tendencies
toward self-blame, fatalism, and catastrophizing, respectively. Explanatory style was introduced in the
attributional reformulation of helplessness theory to explain individual
differences in response to bad events
(Abramson, Seligman, & Teasdale,
1978). Individuals who entertain internal, stable, and global explanations for bad events show emotional,
motivational, and cognitive disturbances in their wake.

Explanatory style has been examined mainly with regard to depression, and all three dimensions
are consistent correlates of depressive
symptoms (Sweeney, Anderson, &
Bailey, 1986). More recent studies
have looked at other outcomes (no-
tably, physical well-being), and researchers have also begun to examine
the dimensions separately. Stability
and globality—but not internality—
predict poor health (Peterson &
Bossio, 1991). This is an intriguing
finding, but questions remain.

First, do these correlations mean
that explanatory styles are risk factors
for early death? Previous studies are
equivocal either because of small samples or because research participants
were already seriously ill.

Second, is the link between explanatory style and health the same or
different for males versus females?
Again, previous studies are equivocal
because they often included only male
or only female research participants.

Third, what mediates the link
between ways of explaining bad
events and poor health? The path is
probably overdetermined, but one
can ask if fatalism and catastrophizing predict differentially to particular
illness. These explanatory styles, as
cognates of hopelessness, may place
one at special risk for cancer, implying an immunological pathway
(Eysenck, 1988). Alternatively, these
explanatory tendencies, because of
their link with stress, may place one
at special risk for heart disease, suggesting a cardiovascular pathway
(Dykema, Bergbower, & Peterson,
1995). Or perhaps fatalism and catastrophizing predispose one to accidents and injuries and thus point to
an incautious lifestyle as a mediator.
Once again, previous studies are
equivocal either because illness was
deliberately operationalized in non-
specific terms or because only one
type of illness was studied.

We attempted to answer these
questions by investigating explanatory style and mortality among participants in the Terman Life-Cycle
Study (Terman & Oden, 1947). The
original sample of more than 1,500
preadolescents has been followed
from the 1920s to the present, with at-
trition (except by death) of less than
10% (Friedman et al., 1995). For most
of those who have died (about 50% of
males and 35% of females as of 1991),
year of death and cause of death are
known. In 1936 and 1940, the participants completed open-ended questionnaires about difficult life events,
which we content-analyzed for

explanatory style. We determined the associations between dimensions of explanatory style on the one hand and time of death and cause of death on the other.

Method

Sample

The Terman Life-Cycle Study began in 1921–1922, when most of the 1,528 participants were in public school. Terman's original objective was to obtain a reasonably representative sample of bright California children (IQs of 135 or greater) and to examine their lives. Almost every public school in the San Francisco and Los Angeles areas was searched for intelligent children. The average birth date for children in the sample was 1910 (SD = 4 years). Most of the children were preadolescents when first studied; those still living are now in their 80s. Data were collected prospectively, without any knowledge of eventual health or longevity.

In young adulthood, the participants were generally healthy and successful. In middle age, they were productive citizens, but none was identifiable as a genius. The sample is homogeneous on dimensions of intelligence (above average), race (mostly white), and social class (little poverty).

Content Analysis of Causal Explanations

We scored explanatory style of the responses to the 1936 and 1940 questionnaires using the CAVE (content analysis of verbatim explanations) technique (Peterson, Schulman, Castellon, & Seligman, 1992). A single researcher read through all responses in which bad events were described. Examples of questions that elicited such responses include

(from 1936): Have any disappointments, failures, bereavements, uncongenial relationships with others, etc., exerted a prolonged influence upon you?

(from 1940): What do you regard as your most serious fault of personality or character?

When a bad event was accompanied by a causal explanation, the event and the attribution were written down. These events, each with its accompanying attribution, were then presented in a nonsystematic order to eight judges who blindly and independently rated each explanation on a 7-point scale according to its stability, its globality, and its internality. The researchers (supervised by Peterson) who identified and rated attributions were independent of the researchers (supervised by Friedman) who collected and coded mortality information (see the next section).

A total of 3,394 attributions was obtained from 1,182 different individuals, an average of 2.87 attributions per person, with a range of 1 to 13. Each of these attributions was rated by each of the eight judges along the three attributional dimensions. We estimated coding reliability by treating the judges as "items" and calculating Cronbach's (1951) alpha for each dimension: alphas were satisfactory: .82, .73, and .94, for stability, globality, and internality, respectively. Ratings were averaged across raters and across different attributions for the same participant. These scores were intercorrelated (mean r = .52), as previous research has typically found (Peterson et al., 1982). The means (and standard deviations) were 4.52 (0.86) for stability, 4.46 (0.64) for globality, and 4.49 (1.29) for internality.

Cause of Death

Death certificates for deceased participants were obtained from the relevant state bureaus and coded for underlying cause of death by a physician-supervised certified nosologist using the criteria of the ninth edition of the International Classification of Diseases (U.S. Department of Health and Human Services, 1980) to distinguish among deaths by cancer, cardiovascular disease, accidents or violence, and other causes. For approximately 20% of the deceased, death certificates were unavailable; whenever possible, cause of death was assigned from information provided by next of kin. Among the 1,182 participants for whom explanatory style scores were available, mortality information was known for 1,179. The numbers of deaths as of 1991 were 148 from cancer (85 men, 63 women), 159 from cardiovascular disease (109 men, 50 women), 57 from accidents or violence (40 men, 17 women), 87 from other (known) causes (50 men, 37 women), and 38 from unknown causes (24 men, 14 women).

Results

Explanatory Styles and Mortality

To investigate the association between explanatory styles and mortality (through 1991), we used Cox Proportional Hazards regressions and checked them with logistic regressions. The Cox approach is nonparametric and assumes that the ratio of hazard functions for individuals with differing values of the covariates (stability, globality, and internality) is invariant over time. We used Tuma's (1980) RATE program for the Cox models, and LOGIST of SAS for the logistic regressions. When all three attributional dimensions were examined simultaneously for the entire sample, only globality was associated with mortality, with a risk hazard (rh) of 1.26 ($p < .01$). Results from the logistic regression analyses (predicting to a dichotomous variable of survival to at least age 65 vs. not) were consistent with this finding; only the odds ratio associated with globality was significant ($rh = 1.25$, $p < .05$).

Figure 1 depicts the probability of a 20-year-old in this sample dying by a given age as a function of sex and globality (top vs. bottom quartiles of scores). The point at which each curve crosses the .50 probability line represents the "average" age of death of individuals in the group. As can be seen, males with a global explanatory style were at the highest risk for early death.

To test whether the effects of globality were due to individuals being seriously ill or suicidal at the time of assessment, we conducted additional survival analyses that excluded individuals who died before 1945. The effects of globality remained for males.

Globality of Explanatory Style and Cause of Death

Next we investigated whether globality was differently related to causes

Table 1	Goodness of Fit for Gompertz Models Predicting (Age-Adjusted) Cause of Death from Sex and Globality of Explanatory Style (n = 1,179)		
Model		$\Delta\chi^2$	df
Model 1: predicting mortality from sex		705.44**	10
Model 2: predicting mortality		715.83**	11
from sex and globality, constraining the effect of globality to be equal across all causes of death			
Model 3: predicting mortality		726.62**	15
from sex and globality, not constraining the effects of globality to be equal across all causes of death			
Model 2 vs. Model 1		10.39**	1
Model 3 vs. Model 1		21.18**	5
Model 3 vs. Model 2		10.79*	4

*$p < .05$. **$p < .001$.

of death (cancer, cardiovascular disease, accidents or violence, other, and unknown) by comparing Gompertz models (see Table 1). When comparing a model with both sex and globality as predictors but constraining the effects of globality to predict equally across all causes of death (Model 2) with an unconstrained model in which globality was allowed to predict differentially to separate causes of death (Model 3), we found that the unconstrained model fit the data better than did the constrained model. This finding was also obtained when participants who did not survive until at least 1945 were excluded, $\Delta\chi^2(4, N = 1,157) = 13.29, p < .01$.

Globality best predicted deaths by accident or violence ($rh = 1.98, p < .01$) and deaths from unknown causes ($rh = 2.08, p < .01$). The risk ratios associated with other causes were 1.03 for cardiovascular disease (n.s.), 1.18 for cancer (n.s.), and 1.22 for other (known) causes (n.s.).

Finally, we computed a Cox model for prediction from globality specifically to suicide (which had been included in the accident-violence group). The result was marginally significant ($rh = 1.84, p < .06$), but only 25 individuals in the sample with globality scores available were known to have committed suicide. When these 25 individuals were excluded, along with individuals who died of accidents (some of which may have been suicides), and the

analyses already described were repeated, the same results were obtained: Globality predicted mortality for the entire sample ($rh = 1.20, p < .05$), especially for males ($rh = 1.31, p < .05$).

Additional Analyses

How might we explain the finding that globality of explanatory style predicted untimely death? In terms of simple correlations, men who had years earlier made global attributions experienced more mental health problems in 1950 ($r = .14, p < .001$), had lower levels of adjustment at this time ($r = -.11, p < .02$), and reported that they drank slightly more ($r = .07, p < .08$) than men who had made more specific attributions (see Martin et al., 1995). We examined other variables such as education, risky hobbies, and physical activity from 1940 through 1977, but none of the simple associations with globality was significant. The subsample of individuals for whom we had smoking data available was substantially smaller than the original sample because these data were collected in 1990–1991; however, within this group, no associations with globality were found.

Additional survival analyses were conducted, controlling for mental health and psychological adjustment. In these analyses, the association between globality and mortality risk remained stable and

significant. When mental health was controlled, the relative hazard associated with globality was 1.27 ($p < .05$). When level of adjustment was controlled, the relative hazard was 1.29 ($p < .01$). A final model controlling for both mental health and adjustment resulted in a relative hazard of 1.24 ($p < .05$). Globality, although related to these aspects of psychological well-being, was distinct, and its association with mortality was not substantially mediated by these other factors.

Finally, globality of explanatory style was inversely related to a measure of neuroticism constructed from 1940 data ($r = -.15, p < .001$) (Martin, 1996). This finding seems to rule out confounding of our measures by response sets involving complaints or exaggeration.

Discussion

The present results extend past investigations of explanatory style and physical well-being. They represent the first evidence from a large sample of initially healthy individuals that a dimension of explanatory style—globality—is a risk factor for early death, especially among males. Because globality scores were the least reliably coded of the three attributional dimensions and had the most restricted range, the present results may underestimate the actual association between globality and mortality. In any event, our findings were not due to confounding by neuroticism, suicide, or psychological maladjustment. Stability per se did not predict mortality, perhaps because it involves a belief that is circumscribed, that is, relevant in certain situations but not others.

In contrast, globality taps a pervasive style of catastrophizing about bad events, expecting them to occur across diverse situations. Such a style can be hazardous because of its link with poor problem solving, social estrangement, and risky decision making across diverse settings (Peterson, Maier, & Seligman, 1993). Supporting this interpretation is the link between globality and deaths due to accident or violence. Deaths like these are often not random. "Being in the wrong place at the wrong time" may be the result of a pessimistic lifestyle,

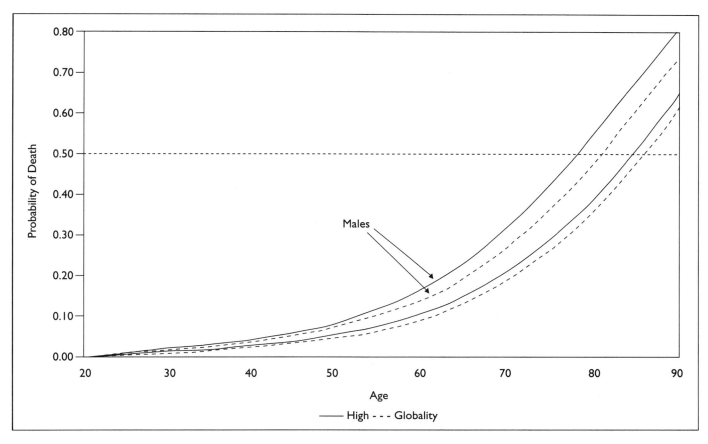

Figure 1. Probability of a 20-year-old dying by a given age as a function of sex and globality (upper vs. lower quartiles).

one more likely among males than females. Perhaps deaths due to causes classified as unknown may similarly reflect an incautious lifestyle.

Explanatory style, at least as measured in this study, showed no specific link to death by cancer or cardiovascular disease. Speculation concerning explanatory style and poor health has often centered on physiological mechanisms but behavioral and lifestyle mechanisms are probably more typical and more robust. We were unable to identify a single behavioral mediator, however, which implies that there is no simple set of health mediators set into operation by globality.

Previous reports on the health of the Terman Life-Cycle Study participants found that childhood personality variables predicted mortality (Friedman et al., 1993). Specifically, a variable identified as "cheerfulness" was inversely related to longevity. Its components involved parental judgments of a participant's "optimism" and "sense of humor." Because a

hopeless explanatory style is sometimes described as pessimistic and its converse as optimistic, these previous reports appear to contradict the present results. However, in this sample, cheerfulness in childhood was unrelated to explanatory style in adulthood. If cheerfulness and explanatory style tap the same sense of optimism, then this characteristic is discontinuous from childhood to adulthood. It is also possible, perhaps likely, that these two variables measure different things: An optimistic explanatory style is infused with agency: the belief that the future will be pleasant because one can control important outcomes.

In summary, a cognitive style in which people catastrophize about bad events, projecting them across many realms of their lives, foreshadows untimely death decades later. We suggest that a lifestyle in which an individual is less likely to avoid or escape potentially hazardous situations is one route leading from pessimism to an untimely death.

References

Abramson, L. Y., Seligman, M. E. P., & Teasdale, J. D. (1978). Learned helplessness in humans: Critique and reformulation. *Journal of Abnormal Psychology, 87,* 49–74.

Cronbach, L. J. (1951). Coefficient alpha and the internal structure of tests. *Psychometrika, 16,* 297–334.

Dykema, J., Bergbower, K., & Peterson, C. (1995). Pessimistic explanatory style, stress, and illness. *Journal of Social and Clinical Psychology, 14,* 357–371.

Eysenck, H. J. (1988). Personality and stress as causal factors in cancer and heart disease. In M. P. Janisse (Ed.), *Individual differences, stress, and health psychology* (pp. 129–145). New York: Springer-Verlag.

Friedman, H. S., Tucker, J. S., Schwartz, J. E., Tomlinson-Keasey, C., Martin, L. R., Wingard, D. L., & Criqui, M. H. (1995). Psychosocial and behavioral predictors of longevity: The aging and death of the "Termites," *American Psychologist, 50,* 69–78.

Friedman, H. S., Tucker, J. S., Tomlinson-Keasey, C., Schwartz, J. E., Wingard, D. L., & Criqui, M. H. (1993). Does childhood personality predict longevity? *Journal of Personality and Social Psychology, 65,* 176–185.

Martin, L. R. (1996). *Consonance of archival and contemporary data: A comparison of personality scales constructed from the Terman data set with modern personality scales.* Unpublished doctoral dissertation. University of California, Riverside.

Martin, L. R., Friedman, H. S., Tucker, J. S., Schwartz, J. E., Criqui, M. H., Wingard, D. L., & Tomlinson-Keasey, C. (1995). An archival prospective study of mental health and longevity. *Health Psychology, 14,* 381–387.

Peterson, C., & Bossio, L. M. (1991). *Health and optimism.* New York: Free Press.

Peterson, C., Maier, S. F., & Seligman, M. E. P. (1993). *Learned helplessness: A theory for the age of personal control.* New York: Oxford University Press.

Peterson, C., Schulman, P., Castellion, C., & Seligman, M. E. P. (1992). CAVE: Content analysis of verbatim explanations. In C. P. Smith (Ed.), *Motivation and personality: Handbook of thematic content analysis* (pp. 383–392). New York: Cambridge University Press.

Peterson, C., & Seligman, M. E. P. (1984). Causal explanations as a risk factor for depression: Theory and evidence. *Psychological Review, 91,* 347–374.

Peterson, C., Semmel, A., von Baeyer, C., Abramson, L. Y., Metalsky, G. I., & Seligman, M. E. P. (1982). The Attributional Style Questionnaire. *Cognitive Therapy and Research, 6,* 287–299.

Sweeney, P. D., Anderson, K., & Bailey, S. (1986). Attributional style in depression: A meta-analytic review. *Journal of Personality and Social Psychology, 50,* 974–991.

Terman, L. M., & Oden, M. H. (1947). *Genetic studies of genius: IV, The gifted child grows up: Twenty-five years follow-up of a superior group.* Stanford, CA: Stanford University Press.

Tuma, N. (1980). *Invoking RATE.* Unpublished manuscript, Stanford University, Stanford, CA.

U.S. Department of Health and Human Services. (1980). *International classification of disease* (9th revision, clinical modification, 2nd ed., DHHS Publication No. PHS 80-1260). Washington, DC: U.S. Government Printing Office.

 Article Review Form at end of book.

WiseGuide Wrap-Up

- Depression can arise in situations that make no logical sense. In fact, when people have clear reasons for feeling depressed, we don't usually call it depression. People can be struck by depression during some of the high points of their lives.

- Women are more than twice as likely as men to experience depression. One reason for this may be differences in the experiences men and women encounter.

- Personality has been demonstrated to affect health in dramatic ways—being linked to chronic illness, stress-related heart disease, and even death.

R.E.A.L. Sites

This list provides a print preview of typical **coursewise** R.E.A.L. sites. There are over 100 such sites at the **courselinks**™ site. The danger in printing URLs is that web sites can change overnight. As we went to press, these sites were functional using the URLs provided. If you come across one that isn't, please let us know via email to: webmaster@coursewise.com. Use your Passport to access the most current list of R.E.A.L. sites at the **courselinks**™ site.

Site name: National Institute of Mental Health

URL: http://www.nimh.nih.gov/

Why is it R.E.A.L.? This is the web site for the National Institute of Mental Health, the primary center for mental health research funding in the United States. The site provides a wealth of information on specific mental health problems, current research in the area, and grants and funding provided by the agency, and it provides links to other relevant government agencies. A comprehensive site, it highlights the role the federal government plays in funding research to understand and treat psychological disorders and problems.

Key topics: mental health, personality disorders, personality theories

Site name: Wing of Madness: A Depression Guide

URL: http://www.wingofmadness.com/

Why is it R.E.A.L.? This is a comprehensive site dedicated to providing people with information about the most common mental health problem in the United States. Many depression web sites are maintained by drug companies whose goal is to sell more antidepressant medication. While antidepressants can form an important part of a treatment program for some sufferers of depression, this site provides more than information on drugs. The site offers information about what clinical depression is, what it feels like, how to assess yourself or a loved one, resources for help, and more. It has links to many sites, including resource centers, ways of connecting with other sufferers, and the Wing of Madness bookstore. This is an extremely useful site for those who are experiencing depression or who have a loved one experiencing it. The site strongly advocates getting help and not trying to "fix it" yourself. Remember, depression is a serious problem that is potentially fatal.

Key topics: mental health, depression, psychological disorders, relationships, self-help

section

3

Learning Objectives

- Know which aspects of personality are most likely influenced by our genetic makeup.

- Understand that even aspects of our personality with some genetic influence are also influenced by the environment.

- Describe why it's important for behavioral geneticists to understand situational differences in behavior.

- Discuss how the environment in which humans evolved can influence personality today.

Genetic and Evolutionary Models of Personality

 **WiseGuide Intro**

Much of the focus in this reader up until this point has concerned environmental influences on our personalities. How do our experiences shape our personality characteristics, our motivation, and our development over time? The articles in this section focus on the potential genetic components of our personalities and those aspects of our personalities that may have been shaped by our evolutionary history. These ideas are relatively controversial, because they suggest that much of our behavior is caused by forces outside of our control. This runs counter to our cultural sense of our ability to "make ourselves" what we want. At the same time, it is consistent with our sense of competitiveness and individualism in which people are best understood without reference to the social context in which they live. As a result, Americans tend to have a "love-hate" relationship with such ideas.

The works in this section report on research suggesting that a portion of our personalities are shaped by genetic and/or evolutionary influences. There is an old adage that the parents of one child believe in nurture—thinking that every aspect of their child's personality is related to their parenting—but, with the birth of a second child, all parents believe in the influence of nature on personality. That is, with the birth of a second child, it becomes more obvious that children start out very differently and that parents' actions can be as much a result of the personality of their child as the force creating that personality. Right from the start, children differ in how fussy they are, how easily they can be soothed, and how interested they are in their surroundings. Nevertheless, personality is not fixed at birth. None of these authors in this section would suggest that behavior is completely controlled by our genes or our evolutionary history. None of these authors is arguing that environment plays no role in the development of personality. Rather, arguments center on the amount of influence that environment has on personality. Genetic and evolutionary approaches offer a way of understanding individuals' limits. For example, some people will never be completely anxiety-free in all social situations. However, that does not mean that shyness or timidity cannot be influenced by a supportive environment and by confidence building. Similarly, genetic models of addiction do not assume that some people have no choice but to live their lives as addicts. Rather, they suggest that those with a genetic propensity for addictive behavior slip more easily from social use of alcohol or drugs to addiction. This is especially true when other environmental factors, such as a history of trauma, are present. This point of view suggests that some people may need to take particular care in this area.

In "Were You Born That Way?" the authors provide an overview of current research on the genetic basis of personality. It outlines several areas in which researchers have looked for genetic influences on personality, including sociability, drug addiction, and obesity. The article also reviews comments from a number of researchers who speak about the ways that environment and genes work together to produce a particular characteristic of one's personality. In "Moving Beyond the Heritability Question," Saudino speaks about the future of the field of behavioral genetics more generally. He notes that researchers in behavioral genetics need to think in more sophisticated ways about personality in order to better understand the connection among genes, environment, and personality. His article will give you some ideas about the directions in which this exciting field is moving.

Buss conceptualizes personality as something that evolved along with our brains and the rest of our bodies. Thus, in his model, we can best understand personality by looking to the environment in which we evolved. Just as we can understand the shape of our hand and the presence of an opposable thumb in terms of certain problems we were trying to solve in the environment, we can ask what problems we were trying to solve psychologically. Specifically, what goals or tasks did people face in the environment of our evolutionary history and how might these tasks have selected for aspects of the personality characteristics we see today? He focuses on the fact that men and women faced different evolutionary challenges and that these differences might have helped shape men's and women's personalities today. Not surprisingly, his work is fairly controversial. As you read this work, note your reactions to the material—what appeals to you in his analysis? What feels uncomfortable and why? You may get some time in class to discuss your reactions to this material in more depth.

Questions

Reading 9. Identify at least three areas of personality in which genetics has been shown to demonstrate a role. What are some criticisms of the genetic approach noted in this article?

Reading 10. What are some of the more objective measures of personality Saudino suggests? Why does Saudino suggest exploring situational differences in personality?

Reading 11. Name two "adaptive problems" Buss identifies as differing for men and women. How might evolutionary history shape our personalities today?

Identify at least three areas of personality in which genetics has been shown to demonstrate a role. What are some criticisms of the genetic approach noted in this article?

Were You Born That Way?

It's not just brown eyes. Your inheritance could also include insomnia, obesity and optimism. Yet scientists are saying that genes are not—quite—destiny.

Karen Kuehn, George Howe Colt, Anne Hollister

In the debate over the relative power of nature and nurture, there may be no more devout believers in nurture than new parents. As my wife and I, suffused with a potent mix of awe, exhaustion and ego, gazed down at our newborn daughter in the hospital, it was hard not to feel like miniature gods with a squirming lump of figurative putty in our hands. We had long believed that people could make the world a better place, and now we firmly believed that we could make this a better baby. At home our bedside tables were sway-backed by towers of well-thumbed parenting manuals. A black-and-white Stim-Mobile, designed to sharpen visual acuity, hung over the crib. The shelves were lined with books, educational puzzles and IQ-boosting rattles. Down the line we envisioned museum visits, art lessons, ballet. And if someone had tapped us on the shoulder and told us that none of this would matter— that in fact we could switch babies in the nursery and send our precious darling home with any other new parents in the hospital, and as long as those parents weren't penniless, violent or drug addicted, our daughter would turn out pretty much the same

. . . well, we would have thwacked that someone with a Stim-Mobile.

Does the key to who we are lie in our genes or in our family, friends and experiences? In one of the most bitter scientific controversies of the 20th century—the battle over nature and nurture—a wealth of new research has tipped the scales overwhelmingly toward nature. Studies of twins and advances in molecular biology have uncovered a more significant genetic component to personality than was previously known. Far from a piece of putty, say biologists, my daughter is more like a computer's motherboard, her basic personality hardwired into infinitesimal squiggles of DNA. As parents, we would have no more influence on some aspects of her behavior than we had on the color of her hair. And yet new findings are also shedding light on how heredity and environment interact. Psychiatrists are using these findings to help patients overcome their genetic predispositions. Meanwhile, advances in genetic research and reproductive technology are leading us to the brink of some extraordinary—and terrifying— possibilities.

The moment the scales began to tip can be traced to a 1979 meeting between a steelworker named Jim Lewis and a clerical worker named Jim Springer. Identical twins separated five weeks after birth, they

were raised by families 80 miles apart in Ohio. Reunited 39 years later, they would have strained the credulity of the editors of Ripley's Believe It or Not. Not only did both have dark hair, stand six feet tall and weigh 180 pounds, but they spoke with the same inflections, moved with the same gait and made the same gestures. Both loved stock car racing and hated baseball. Both married women named Linda, divorced them and married women named Betty. Both drove Chevrolets, drank Miller Lite, chain-smoked Salems and vacationed on the same half-mile stretch of Florida beach. Both had elevated blood pressure, severe migraines and had undergone vasectomies. Both bit their nails. Their heart rates, brain waves and IQs were nearly identical. Their scores on personality tests were as close as if one person had taken the same test twice.

Identical twins raised in different families are a built-in research lab for measuring the relative contributions of nature and nurture. The Jims became one of 7,000 sets of twins studied by the Minnesota Center for Twin and Adoption Research, one of half a dozen such centers in this country. Using psychological and physiological tests to compare the relative similarity of identical and fraternal twins, these centers calculate the "heritability" of behavioral traits—the degree to which a trait in a given population is attributable to genes rather than to the environment. They have found, for instance, that "assertiveness" is 60 percent heritable, while "the ability to be enthralled by an aesthetic experience" is 55 percent heritable.

Studies of twins have produced an impressive list of attributes or behaviors that appear to owe at least as much to heredity as to environment. It includes alienation, extroversion, traditionalism, leadership, career choice, risk aversion, attention deficit disorder, religious conviction and vulnerability to stress. One study even concluded that happiness is 80 percent heritable—it depends little on wealth, achievement or marital status. Another study found that while both optimism and pessimism are heavily influenced by genes, environment affects optimism but not pessimism. A third study claimed a genetic influence for the consumption of coffee but not, it seems, of tea. Critics accuse researchers of confusing correlation with causation, yet they admit the data suggest a strong genetic influence on behavior. Far less clear is how it all works. Is there a gene for becoming an astronaut? For enjoying symphonies?

Molecular biologists around the world are trying to answer such questions, searching for specific bits of DNA that may contribute to particular behaviors. In a small, windowless laboratory cluttered with bottles of chemicals, back issues of scientific journals and bags of sterile rubber gloves, there sits an aged Sears Kenmore Coldspot refrigerator. Inside are 21 plastic trays labeled with Magic Marker: College Students. Gay Men. Smokers. Shy Kids. Each tray contains 96 almondize plastic vials. Each vial contains a smidgen of DNA. These are Dean Hamer's study subjects, his "people," as he refers to them. The refrigerator holds the blueprints for nearly 2,000 people, a database that Hamer, chief of Gene Structure and Regulation at the National Cancer Institute in Bethesda, Md., hopes will help him find the keys to why we smoke, why we get anxious, why we take risks. In what he describes as "a giant fishing expedition," Hamer is working his way through the human genome, tracking down any variation that may affect personality.

Even for someone like Hamer, who admits to genetic propensities for both optimism and risk-taking behavior, it is a daunting prospect. The human body has 100 trillion cells, each equipped with a complete set of DNA distributed among 23 pairs of chromosomes. (DNA is microscopic yet sizable: If set out in a continuous strand, the DNA from a single cell would be six feet long.) Each cell's DNA is made up of some three billion nucleic components. Most of these seem to be nonfunctioning—"junk" DNA, biologists call them—but about 3 percent are working genes. The total number of working genes is believed to be 80,000, give or take 20,000. The task: to pinpoint the one-in-three-billion bit that might contribute to a particular behavior.

Using DNA from groups of people with a high incidence of a certain trait, Hamer's lab has scanned hundreds of thousands of amplified strands of DNA, hoping to come across a variation common to those with the trait but absent in those without it. In 1993 his lab isolated a stretch of genes on the X chromosome that may be linked to male homosexuality. Three years later a gene on chromosome 11 was found to be consistently longer in people with a taste for novelty-seeking. Last year his lab linked anxiety to a gene involved in regulating levels of serotonin, a brain chemical affected by the antidepressant Prozac.

The hoopla with which these discoveries have been greeted—"GAY GENE!" the headlines blared—has obscured the fact that other institutions have had mixed results when trying to replicate the findings. It has also made it seem as if single genes dictate specific behaviors. The reality is more complicated. Genes don't make men gay or children timid. They make proteins, which kindle complex neurological events. Biologists now believe that any given trait is shaped by a constellation of different genes. "From twin studies, we know that anxiety is 40 to 50 percent genetic," explains Hamer. "And from our data we know that the gene we isolated accounts for about 5 percent of the effect. We think there may be ten genes altogether that influence anxiety. But there may be a hundred or a thousand." In any case, he says,

different people can have different combinations of those genes. People with just a few of those anxiety genes might feel nervous when they have to give a speech. Those with a few more might cringe when the phone rings. And those with a full complement might be so timid they rarely leave the house.

If, as twin studies suggest, the heritability of most personality traits is about 50 percent, that still leaves 50 percent to the environment—an environment, say behavioral geneticists, whose influence works far differently from what we once thought. Until recently the family was assumed to be the crucible in which personality was formed. In fact, children may shape parents' behavior as much as parents shape theirs. "If you are genetically a responsive, happy infant, you are going to get different mothering than if you are an irritable or rejecting child," says University of Minnesota psychologist David Lykken. The older a child gets, the more power he has to mold his own environment. "People seek out experiences and environments," Lykken says, "that are compatible with their genetic nature."

Studying adolescents adopted in infancy, University of Virginia psychologist Sandra Scarr was surprised to find that children adopted by well-educated, professional parents performed no better in school or on intelligence tests than children who had been adopted into working-class homes. "Providing children with super environments—private schooling, museum visits, lessons and so on—made no difference in their intelligence, adjustment or personality development," says Scarr. She concludes that if a child has "good enough parenting"—parents who aren't abusive or neglectful and provide a basic level of support—one set of parents is as good as another. The child will develop along paths set out by his genes. "It doesn't matter whether you take the kids fishing or to a Mozart concert," says Scarr. "As long as you do it with love, almost anything you do is going to be fine and functionally equivalent."

But don't throw out those Spock and Brazelton manuals. Even the most zealous behavioral geneticists admit that genes are not—

quite—destiny. "Depending on the other genes you inherit, and on your biology and on your in utero experience, the genes will have full force or less force," explains Harvard psychologist Jerome Kagan. Upbringing and circumstance may steer someone born with a predisposition for shyness to grow up into an agoraphobe —or a great poet. Someone with a propensity for aggression might become an Adolf Hitler, but he might become a General Patton.

In any case, if genes are not commands but nudges, we can nudge back. We are the only animals on earth that can over-rule our genes. And we do so constantly—whenever an alcoholic chooses not to drink or an obese person diets.

How important is it to understand our genetic makeup? Does it matter that our anxiety can be traced to a snippet of nucleic matter and not to the time Mommy spanked us for spilling our juice? Psychologist Thomas Bouchard, director of the Minnesota twin study, believes it does: "A lot of books say you can do anything you want, but we have real doubts about that. It's not that you can't, but we suspect it's done at a cost." He suggests that we not push kids in directions they're not inclined toward. "The job of a parent," says Bouchard, "is to look for a kid's natural talents and then provide the best possible environment for them."

Bethesda psychiatrist Stanley Greenspan is one of a growing number of therapists who have incorporated the findings of behavioral genetics into their practice. "When a trait appears to be influenced by genes, people assume it's not changeable," he says. "Well, we can't change the genes, but we can change the way genes express themselves. We can change behavior." Greenspan works with children and their parents to rechannel a child's genetic propensities. For a sensitive girl, so fearful of new sights and sounds that at age three she still clung to her mother for dear life, Greenspan prescribed rhythmic rocking, as well as extra doses of imaginative play. The rocking soothed the child; the play helped her to gradually become more assertive. For an aggressive girl who pushed, punched and bit her classmates—"she so craved sensory input

that she literally attacked her world," says Greenspan—he designed games of dancing, shouting and beating on drums, but part of the exercise was to gradually go from fast and loud to slow and soft. "We gave her socially appropriate ways to satisfy her needs, but we taught her how to learn control."

Greenspan's work illustrates an idea at the heart of behavioral genetics today—that heredity and environment are entwined, always reacting to and building on each other. "It's not a horse race between nurture and nature," he says. "It's a dance."

By the year 2005, scientists are expected to have mapped the entire sequence of the human genome. It will be many years before they know the functions of those 80,000 genes, but ways to take advantage of this information are already being developed. Within a few decades, people who feel ill will go to physician-geneticists who will run DNA scans to check the relevant genes, make pinpoint diagnoses and prescribe drugs targeted to precise genetic needs. This will be true for depression, phobias and life-threatening obesity, as well as for less crippling traits. Just as Mary Poppins had a magic bottle from which she dispensed spoonfuls of strawberry-flavored liquid to cure Michael's fussiness, parents may supply a pill to embolden their shy child before the school dance.

Before my wife and I had our daughter, genetic counselors were able to tell us whether she had the genes for Down syndrome or Tay-Sachs disease. By the time she is ready to be a mother, genetic counselors will be able to tell her whether her fetus is genetically inclined toward depression or addiction. Such knowledge will surely lead to an ethical morass. "Where does it stop?" asks a character in The Twilight of the Golds, a recent play in which a couple decide to abort a fetus whose genes suggest it will be gay. "What if you found out the kid was going to be ugly, or smell bad, or have an annoying laugh, or need really thick glasses?" (Not such a far-fetched question, given that three quarters of young couples in a recent survey said they would choose abortion if told their fetus had a 50 percent chance of growing up to be obese.) The morass will become still stickier when we

have the technology to tinker with the genes themselves. Clinical trials are already under way using gene therapy—the introduction of healthy new genes to counteract a mutated or missing gene—to repair disorders such as cystic fibrosis, cancer and AIDS. Most of us would welcome treatment that might eliminate these afflictions. But what about depression? Aggression? Timidity?

By the time my daughter's grandchild is ready to give birth, prospective parents may design their children at the computer, scrolling through genetic menus to pick and choose, from their own DNA pools, specific gene clusters for height, weight and eye color, as well as for assertiveness, extroversion, happiness and so on. "The question is not whether the science will happen—it will," says Princeton molecular geneticist Lee Silver. "The question is, will people use it?"

Have we ever been able to restrain ourselves? The first person to study twins, 19th century anthropologist Francis Galton, finding that "nature prevails enormously over nurture," recommended breeding quotas to weed out the "unfit." The eugenics movement gathered force— from 1907 to 1965, some 60,000 people were sterilized in the U.S. for such conditions as pauperism and "feeblemindedness"—and led to the extermination programs of the Third Reich, a horror that shadows the nature-nurture debate today. Critics of behavioral genetics say the risk of misuse should preclude further research. But that, journalist William Wright argues, "makes as much sense as rejecting electricity because of daytime television."

Weighed against the potential benefits—might we end war by getting rid of aggressive genes?—is a Pandora's box of misuse. After the discovery of the so-called gay gene, for example, religious fundamentalists called for techniques to "correct that genetic defect." Caution is needed. "Do we know enough to know what we are changing?" asks Ronald Green, director of the Ethics Institute at Dartmouth. "Are we going to be wise enough to do it well, in such a way that we don't impoverish the future? In trying to avoid a Ted Kaczynski, might we destroy an Einstein?"

Genes and Violence

No genetic link to criminality—other than being born male—has been proved. But that hasn't stopped people from making a connection. "The place to fight crime is in the cradle," says psychologist David Lykken, who has a controversial proposal: that biological parents be licensed. Lykken believes that a lot of crime is due to genetic predispositions for aggression and impulsiveness combined with incompetent parenting and the breakdown of the nuclear family. "We wouldn't let a crack addict, a teenager or a criminal adopt a child," he says. "Why not make the same minimal requirements for people having children biologically?"

One Minnesota state representative is trying to write a version of Lykken's views into law, while detractors have called Lykken a fascist. Indeed, when it comes to the subject of violence, behavioral genetics is particularly prickly. In 1992 a lawyer tried to stage a conference on genetics and crime, but civil rights groups forced its postponement. When it was finally held three years later, the symposium was disrupted by protesters, and a handful of attendees signed a statement labeling the proceedings "racist pseudoscience."

Critics say that linking genes and violence is blaming the victims and shifting the focus away from the real culprits: poverty, racism and unemployment. Brain research has shown that violent males tend to have low levels of the chemical serotonin, levels associated with depression, aggression and impulsivity—all traits with high heritability. But adoption studies show that children whose biological parents had trouble with the law have a far greater likelihood of having similar problems if their adoptive family had those problems too. Biology may contribute to antisocial behavior, the studies suggest, but environment helps tip the balance. In the same way, crime may be more pervasive in inner cities, not because of the genes of the people who live there but because inner cities tend to be fragmented, impoverished and racially polarized environments.

Neurobiologist Evan Balaban sees Lykken's proposal as a throwback to the early 1900s, when 15 states had laws permitting the sterilization of criminals. "The predominantly academic people making these suggestions seem to be ignorant of what attempts have been made to solve these problems by people on the firing line. It might behoove them to put some effort into learning what the real issues are."

A few nights ago, watching my daughter arrange her 37 Beanie Babies by color and species, I felt a shock of recognition—and glanced over at my wife, who wears the same expression when she arranges Shakespeare's plays in chronological order. My lump of putty is eight now, and I don't need a DNA scan to tell me she has inherited her mother's intelligence, her father's stubbornness, her grandfather's wit. The genes may be familiar, but the mix—thank heavens—is unique. Warts and all, she is exactly the child I want.

When I look at her, I see a part of me. When I look at myself, it seems there's less of me than there once was. At a recent party, schmoozing with one last guest on my way out the door, I suddenly thought, I'm acting exactly like my father! Having spent my youth fighting to forge my own identity, I find, increasingly, that I resemble the very parent against whom I worked so hard to rebel: his social ease, his sense of humor—and, now that I am in my forties, his thinning hair and slight potbelly. Indeed, as I get older, I feel that instead of adding layers, I am shedding skins. In becoming more like my parents, I am becoming more myself. I am surprised but delighted that it all feels so comfortable—not an imprisoning but a homecoming.

For Further Reading

Born That Way by William Wright. Knopf, 1998.

Galen's Prophecy by Jerome Kagan. Basic Books, 1994.

The Growth of the Mind by Stanley Greenspan. Addison-Wesley, 1997.

Living With Our Genes by Dean Hamer and Peter Copeland. Doubleday, 1998.

Remaking Eden by Lee Silver. Avon, 1997.

Twins by Lawrence Wright. John Wiley & Sons, 1997.

Article Review Form at end of book.

What are some of the more objective measures of personality
Saudino suggests? Why does Saudino suggest exploring situational
differences in personality?

Moving Beyond the Heritability Question

New directions in behavioral genetic studies of personality

Kimberly J. Saudino

*Department of Psychology, Boston
University, Boston, Massachusetts*

Most personality traits show some
genetic influence (i.e., are to some extent inherited). Studies of personality
and temperament in infancy, childhood, adolescence, adulthood, and
old age consistently yield heritabili-
ties in the range of .20 to .50, suggesting that genetic differences among
individuals account for between 20%
to 50% of the variability of personality within a population. The finding
of genetic influences on personality
has been replicated across American,
Australian, British, Finnish, Swedish,
and Russian cultures. However, the
conclusion that individual differences in personality are, in part, due
to genetic factors is just the beginning of the story. Behavioral genetics
has much more to offer to the study
of personality than heritability estimates, and in this article, I describe
three exciting new directions that
behavioral genetic studies of personality are taking. Although basic be-

havioral genetic terms are defined,
details of the theory and methods
cannot be described in this brief article; however, they are described in
textbooks on behavioral genetics
(e.g., Plomin, DeFries, McClearn, &
Rutter, 1997).

Using Objective Measures to Assess Personality

Behavioral genetic studies of personality have relied mainly on self-report questionnaires for adolescents
and adults and parent reports for
children. Although such measures
have provided ample evidence of genetic influences on personality, they
have been criticized as being subjective, reflecting raters' expectations in
addition to actual behavior. A key
question is whether more objective
measures of personality will also
show genetic influences. Thus far,
this question has been examined primarily in studies of infant and child
personality, or temperament, as it is
referred to in the developmental literature.

The use of objective measures of
temperament in behavioral genetic
studies arose as a result of some puzzling outcomes that occur when parents report on their children's
temperament. Identical twins typically show high correlations on ratings of temperament, whereas
fraternal twins show correlations that
are very low, often near zero or even
slightly negative (e.g., Neale &
Stevenson, 1989). Because identical
twins are more similar genetically
than fraternal twins, these results
imply genetic influence. However, the
low resemblance of fraternal twin
pairs is puzzling: The simple genetic
model predicts that their similarity
should be half that of identical twins
because fraternal twins are 50% similar genetically whereas identical twins
are genetically identical. Also puzzling is the finding that adoption
studies suggest little or no genetic influence on children's temperament as rated by their parents. For example, in the Colorado Adoption
Project, nonadoptive siblings, who
have the same biological parents and
are thus 50% related genetically, were

no more similar for parent-rated temperament than genetically unrelated adoptive siblings (Plomin, Coon, Carey, DeFries, & Fulker, 1991).

The problem of too-low resemblance of fraternal twin pairs and the higher heritability estimates in twin studies than adoption studies of parent-rated temperament can be explained by rating biases. Parents may either inflate the similarity of their identical twins (*assimilation effects*) or exaggerate the differences between their fraternal twins or nonadoptive siblings (*contrast effects*). Both assimilation effects and contrast effects artificially increase differences between the correlations for identical and fraternal twins and, therefore, result in overestimates of genetic influence in twin studies. Because contrast effects reduce the similarity of nonadoptive and adoptive siblings, adoption studies will underestimate heritability. Several recent articles have discussed assimilation and contrast effects (e.g., Saudino, McGuire, Reiss, Hetherington, & Plomin, 1995).

The puzzling outcomes can also be explained by the presence of *nonadditive* genetic effects, in which there is an interaction in the effects of genes. When genetic effects are nonadditive, the number of genes in common between family members does not directly translate into similarity among family members. An example of a nonadditive genetic effect is gene dominance, which occurs when one member of a gene pair is expressed and the other is not (e.g., a person with a brown-eyed gene and a blue-eyed gene will have brown eyes). Although full siblings other than identical twins have 50% of their genes in common, when nonadditive genetic influences are important to a trait, siblings will be dissimilar to the extent that one sibling has the dominant form of the gene and the other does not. Similarity of identical twins is not affected by nonadditive genetic effects because such twins are genetically identical. Nonadditive genetic effects reduce the similarity of fraternal twins and other first-degree siblings. Therefore, when nonadditive genetic effects are present, similarity of fraternal twins will be less than one half that of identical twins. Similarly, adoption designs, which are based on the difference in behavioral similarity

between nonadoptive and adoptive siblings, will not uncover as much genetic influence as will twin studies.

Objective measures of temperament can help us evaluate the possible explanations of the unusual outcomes from parent-rating studies of temperament. If the outcomes are due to parental rating biases, then objective measures should show a more reasonable pattern of results. However, if the low similarity of fraternal twins and nonadoptive siblings is due to nonadditive genetic effects, then objective measures of temperament would be expected to show a similar pattern of results.

The MacArthur Longitudinal Twin Study (MALTS; Emde, in press), a collaborative longitudinal study of twins that focuses on individual differences in temperament, emotion, and cognition from infancy to early childhood, provides an opportunity to evaluate the issue of possible parental rating biases because it includes many observed behavioral measures of temperament in addition to parent ratings. In MALTS, parent ratings of emotionality, activity level, shyness, and persistence produced a pattern of moderate correlations for identical twins and near zero or negative correlations for fraternal twins (Saudino & Cherny, in press-a). This pattern for fraternal twins is significant because it implies that they are perceived as no more similar—and, in some instances, less alike—than two randomly paired children. In fact, for some dimensions, fraternal co-twins are perceived as having opposing behavioral tendencies. Observational measures of the same temperament dimensions in the MALTS sample tell a different story, however. When temperament was assessed by observer ratings, correlations for fraternal twins were positive, and the difference between correlations for identical and fraternal twins was consistent with genetic expectations (Saudino & Cherny, in press-b).

Thus, the evidence from MALTS points toward parental contrast effects, a conclusion further supported by adoption research. Correlations for nonadoptive siblings are higher when measures such as observer or teacher ratings are employed than when parent ratings are used (e.g., Schmitz, Saudino, Plomin, Fulker, & DeFries, 1996). Moreover, adoption and twin studies

of objectively assessed temperament yield similar estimates of heritability (e.g., Braungart, Plomin, DeFries, & Fulker, 1992).

The finding that parent ratings and objective measures of temperament yield different results has implications more generally for personality research. The results strongly suggest that contrast biases affect parent ratings, at least for siblings. Researchers need to consider the possibility that parent ratings reflect parental expectations in addition to children's actual behavior. The lessons learned from studies of child temperament can also be applied to studies of adult personality, which have relied on self-report measures. Self-report questionnaires may be subjectively biased, and, therefore, research using more objective methods is needed to support the wealth of information that has been learned from self-report data.

Exploring Situational Differences in Personality

In addition to signaling the need for more objective measures of personality, the findings just reviewed remind us that a single mode of assessment may not paint a complete picture of personality. That is, there may be important contextual or situational factors that are overlooked when a single measure of personality is used. By applying genetic analyses to multiple measures of the same personality dimension, researchers can capture aspects of personality that operate across multiple measures (*measure-general effects*) as well as aspects of personality that are unique to specific measures (*measure-specific effects*). When different measures assess the same dimension of personality in different situations, analysis can address cross-situational and context-specific genetic effects.

Multivariate genetic analyses differ from traditional genetic analyses in that they assess the extent to which genetic effects on one variable overlap with genetic effects on another. Such analyses allow for the examination of genetic and environmental contributions to the covariance between two measures rather than the variance of each measure considered separately. For example, in MALTS, multivariate genetic analyses have explored the extent to which genetic effects on a measure of shyness in the laboratory overlap with genetic effects on shyness in the home environment (Cherny, Fulker, Corley, Plomin, & DeFries, 1994). The same genetic influences were found to be involved in the two situations. This finding of cross-situational genetic effects for shyness in the lab and the home means that genetic factors contribute to the stability of shyness across the two situations. Indeed, the observed correlation between the two measures of shyness was almost entirely due to overlapping genetic effects. In contrast, environmental factors contributed to differences between shyness in the lab and in the home.

Although genetic factors often contribute to cross-situational stability in personality, sometimes genetic factors contribute to change as well as continuity across situations. In a recent study, Schmitz et al. (1996) examined genetic effects on teacher ratings of temperament in the classroom and tester ratings of temperament in a laboratory test situation. Schmitz et al. found that the genetic influences on teacher ratings of activity level overlapped substantially with the genetic influences on tester ratings of activity level. In fact, genetic factors were entirely responsible for the covariance between teacher and tester ratings, indicating that what teachers and testers see in common in children's activity level is due to genetics. Despite this evidence of cross-situational genetic effects, there was also genetic influence unique to tester ratings, indicating context-specific genetic effects for activity level. Context-specific genetic effects are genetic effects that are unique to a situation and, therefore, contribute to changes or differences in personality across situations. Thus, with respect to teacher and tester ratings of activity level, genetics is involved in situational change as well as stability. Similar results have emerged from a recent application of a multitrait-multimethod approach to twin data for three temperament dimensions (emotional tone, activity level, socia-

bility), each assessed three different ways (examiner rating, playroom observation, parent rating). This study found substantial measure-specific genetic variance in addition to measure-general genetic variance (Philips & Matheny, 1997). However, the temperament measures in this study involved different methods (i.e., rating vs. observation plus rating) as well as different situations (lab vs. home vs. school), which makes it difficult to say whether the measure-specific genetic variance reflects situational change or method differences.

The fact that genes contribute to cross-situational stability for some dimensions of personality comes as no surprise because genetic factors are typically viewed as sources of stability. However, the finding of context-specific genetic effects on personality challenges the usual assumption that behavioral differences across situations are due to environmental influences. That is, situational variation in personality does not necessarily stem from environmental influences. Does this mean that there are personality genes unique to different situations or measures? Probably not. It is more likely that context-specific genetic influences arise because different measures provide different views of personality and thus detect different genetic effects specific to different contexts (Plomin & Nesselroade, 1990).

These findings offer an interesting perspective on what has been called the person-situation debate. At one time, psychologists were polarized with respect to the relative influence of the individual and situations on the individual's behavior; however, most would now agree that personality is a function of both the person (i.e., stable, enduring traits) and the specific characteristics of the situation. Multivariate genetic analyses allow us to examine the mechanisms that underlie cross-situational stability and change. Although more research is needed, initial applications of multivariate genetic analyses to personality suggest that we may have to change our conceptualization of situations to incorporate genetic influences.

Personality and the Interface between Nature and Nurture

One of the most provocative findings to emerge from recent behavioral genetic research is that genetic factors contribute substantially to many measures that assess the environments of individuals (see Reiss, this issue).* For example, genetic analyses of family environment, peer groups, social support, life events, and divorce often yield moderate heritability estimates (Plomin, 1994). Genetic influence on such environmental measures might appear paradoxical: Environments and experiences have no DNA, so how can they be affected by genetic factors? A resolution to this paradox is that the environment is not independent of the individual. Individuals play an active role in creating their own environments and experiences. Thus, to the extent that the environment reflects genetically influenced characteristics of the individual, we can expect to find genetic influence on environmental measures.

What personal characteristics might mediate genetic contributions to environmental measures? Researchers examining the mechanisms through which individuals are exposed to certain situations have found that individuals tend to choose situations or activities that reflect their personality. Therefore, personality is a good candidate for explaining genetic influences on environmental measures. That is, genetically influenced personality traits could affect how people select, construct, or perceive their environments.

Multivariate genetic analyses have been used to explore the extent to which genetic effects on environmental measures overlap with genetic effects on personality. Such studies suggest that personality traits can account for a portion of genetic effects on some environmental measures. For example, genetic effects on neuroticism and extraversion accounted for approximately 20% of the genetic variance in a measure of

* Not included in his publication.

current family environment in a sample of Swedish adults (Chipuer, Plomin, Pedersen, McClearn, & Nesselroade, 1993). Personality has also been found to account for between 30% and 40% of the genetic influence on divorce risk (Jockin, McGue, & Lykken, 1996). Perhaps most surprising is one study's finding that for females in middle or late adulthood, genetic influences on life events were entirely mediated by neuroticism, extraversion, and openness to experience (Saudino, Pedersen, Lichtenstein, McClearn, & Plomin, 1997). That is, these three core dimensions of personality accounted for all of the genetic influences on life events. These results are not limited to adulthood. Genetic effects on a combined observational and interview measure of the home environment of 2-year-olds were mediated predominantly by genetic effects on tester ratings of task orientation, a temperament dimension, reflecting attention span, persistence, and the tendency to be goal oriented (Saudino & Plomin, 1997). This finding suggests that, to some extent, parents structure infants' environments in response to genetically influenced attentional characteristics of their infants.

It should be noted, however, that personality may not explain genetic influence on all environmental measures. For example, multivariate analyses of data for adoptive and nonadoptive siblings found that genetic influences on parent-report measures of the family environment in middle childhood were largely independent of genetic influence on observed temperament in infancy and early childhood (Braungart, 1994). Similarly, a recent study of young adult twin and nontwin siblings found that there was no significant genetic covariance between personality and a self-report measure of perceptions of the classroom environment (Vernon, Jang, Harris, & McCarthy, 1997). In both of these cases, however, it is possible that measures assessing other personality traits would have produced different results. It is also possible that genetic effects on some measures of the environment may not be due to genetic

effects on personality. A prudent interpretation of the research thus far suggests that genetic contributions to some measures of the environment are in part due to personality.

The finding that genetic variance in personality mediates genetic influence on environmental measures raises the question as to how the genetic effects arise. The answer depends on the extent to which the measure of the environment accurately assesses the objective environment of the individual. When the environment is measured via self-report, as was the case for the aforementioned studies of adult family environment and life events, it is possible that responses might reflect the individual's perceptions of environments or experiences, perceptions that are filtered through the individual's genetically influenced personality. Thus, personality might bias an individual's perceptions, and, consequently, the genetic covariation between personality and the environment might arise through the effects of personality on the person's perceptions, not on the environment per se. However, such perceptual processes may not tell the whole story. Genetic influences on objective, externally verifiable events such as divorce or on observations of infants' home environments provide evidence that, in some instances, environmental measures do not simply reflect genetic influences on perceptions of the environment. In these cases, the finding of significant genetic covariation between personality and environmental measures suggests a gene-environment correlation. That is, individuals are differentially exposed to environments and experiences as a function of their genetically influenced personality.

The finding that personality can explain at least some of the genetic influences on objective measures of the environment has important implications for psychologists. Traditionally, we have viewed the environment as an exogenous force that acts upon the individual. The presence of gene-environment correlations underlying the covariation between personality and environmental measures provides

evidence for what many personality psychologists have long suspected: In some instances, the environment reflects rather than affects characteristics of individuals.

Conclusions

The finding of genetic influences on personality traits is only a first step in the understanding of individual differences in personality. Behavioral geneticists are taking new directions in their approach to the study of personality, and this research is yielding exciting new findings. More researchers are assessing personality through objective behavioral measures or multiple raters. This approach not only buttresses the findings from self- and parent-report questionnaires, but also can address issues of measure-specific and situational effects. Similarly, research examining the role that personality plays in the interface between nature and nurture suggests that personality mediates genetic influences on the environment. As more researchers begin to employ objective measures of the environment, the question of genetic mediation via perceptions versus gene-environment correlation will be answered. Clearly, there is much more to be discovered about personality as researchers move beyond the rudimentary heritability question.

Recommended Readings

Eaves, L. J., Eysenck, H. J., & Martin, N. G. (1989). *Genes, culture and personality.* New York: Academic Press.

Loehlin, J. C. (1992). *Genes and environment in personality development.* Newbury Park, CA: Sage.

Plomin, R., DeFries, J. C., McClearn, G. E., & Rutter, M. (1997). (See References)

References

Braungart, J. M. (1994). Genetic influence on "environmental" measures. In J. C. DeFries, R. Plomin, & D. W. Fulker (Eds.), *Nature, nurture during middle childhood* (pp. 233–248). Cambridge, MA: Blackwell.

Braungart, J. M., Plomin, R., DeFries, J. C., & Fulker, D. W. (1992). Genetic influence on tester-rated infant temperament as assessed by Bayley's Infant Behavior Record: Nonadoptive and adoptive siblings and twins. *Developmental Psychology, 28,* 40–47.

Cherny, S. S., Fulker, D. W., Corley, R., Plomin, R., & DeFries, J. C. (1994). Continuity and change in infant shyness from 14 to 20 months. *Behavior Genetics, 24,* 365–380.

Chipuer, H. M., Plomin, R., Pedersen, N. L., McClearn, G. E., & Nesselroade, J. R. (1993). Genetic influence on family environment: The role of personality. *Developmental Psychology, 29,* 110–118.

Emde, R. (Ed.). (in press). *The transition from infancy to early childhood: Genetic and environmental influences.* New York: Cambridge University Press.

Jockin, V., McGue, M., & Lykken, D. T. (1996). Personality and divorce: A genetic analysis. *Journal of Personality and Social Psychology, 71,* 288–299.

Neale, M. C., & Stevenson, J. (1989). Rater bias in the EASI temperament scales: A twin study. *Journal of Personality and Social Psychology, 56,* 446–455.

Philips, K., & Matheny, A. P. (1997). Evidence for genetic influence on both cross-situation and situation-specific components of behavior. *Journal of Personality and Social Psychology, 73,* 129–138.

Plomin, R. (1994). *Genetics and experience: The interplay between nature and nurture.* Newbury Park, CA: Sage.

Plomin, R., Coon, H., Carey, G., DeFries, J. C., & Fulker, D. (1991). Parent-offspring and sibling adoption analyses of parental ratings of temperament in infancy and early childhood. *Journal of Personality, 59,* 705–732.

Plomin, R., DeFries, J. C., McClearn, G. E., & Rutter, M. (1997). *Behavioral genetics* (3rd ed.). New York: W. H. Freeman.

Plomin, R., & Nesselroade, J. R. (1990). Behavioral genetics and personality change. *Journal of Personality, 58,* 191–220.

Saudino, K. J., & Cherny, S. S. (in press-a). Parent ratings of temperament in twins. In R. Emde (Ed.), *The transition from infancy to early childhood: Genetic and environmental influences.* New York: Cambridge University Press.

Saudino, K. J., & Cherny, S. S. (in press-b). Sources of continuity and change in observed temperament. In R. Emde (Ed.), *The transition from infancy to early childhood: Genetic and environmental influences.* New York: Cambridge University Press.

Saudino, K. J., McGuire, S., Reiss, D., Hetherington, E. M., & Plomin, R. (1995). Parent ratings of EAS temperaments in twins, full siblings, half siblings and step siblings. *Journal of Personality and Social Psychology, 68,* 723–733.

Saudino, K. J., Pedersen, N. L., Lichtenstein, P., McClearn, G. E., & Plomin, R. (1997). Can personality explain genetic influences on life events? *Journal of Personality and Social Psychology, 72,* 196–206.

Saudino, K. J., & Plomin, R. (1997). Cognitive and temperamental mediators of genetic contributions to the home environment during infancy. *Merrill-Palmer Quarterly, 43,* 1–23.

Schmitz, S., Saudino, K. J., Plomin, R., Fulker, D. W., & DeFries, J. C. (1996). Genetic and environmental influences on temperament in middle childhood: Analyses of teacher and tester ratings. *Child Development, 67,* 409–422.

Vernon, P. A., Jang, K. L., Harris, J. A., & McCarthy, J. M. (1997). Environmental predictors of personality differences: A twin and sibling study. *Journal of Personality and Social Psychology, 72,* 177–183.

 Article Review Form at end of book.

Name two "adaptive problems" Buss identifies as differing for men and women. How might evolutionary history shape our personalities today?

Psychological Sex Differences

Origins through sexual selection

David M. Buss

University of Michigan

Men and women clearly differ in some psychological domains. A. H. Eagly (1995) shows that these differences are not artifactual or unstable. Ideally, the next scientific step is to develop a cogent explanatory framework for understanding why the sexes differ in some psychological domains and not in others and for generating accurate predictions about sex differences as yet undiscovered. This article offers a brief outline of an explanatory framework for psychological sex differences—one that is anchored in the new theoretical paradigm of evolutionary psychology. Men and women differ, in this view, in domains in which they have faced different adaptive problems over human evolutionary history. In all other domains, the sexes are predicted to be psychologically similar. Evolutionary psychology jettisons the false dichotomy between biology and environment and provides a powerful metatheory of why sex differences exist, where they exist, and in what contexts they are expressed (D. M. Buss, 1995).

Evolutionary psychology predicts that males and females will be the same or similar in all those domains in which the sexes have faced the same or similar adaptive problems.

Both sexes have sweat glands because both sexes have faced the adaptive problem of thermal regulation. Both sexes have similar (although not identical) taste preferences for fat, sugar, salt, and particular amino acids because both sexes have faced similar (although not identical) food consumption problems. Both sexes grow calluses when they experience repeated rubbing on their skin because both sexes have faced the adaptive problem of physical damage from environmental friction.

In other domains, men and women have faced substantially different adaptive problems throughout human evolutionary history. In the physical realm, for example, women have faced the problem of childbirth; men have not. Women, therefore, have evolved particular adaptations that are absent in men, such as a cervix that dilates to 10 centimeters just prior to giving birth, mechanisms for producing labor contractions, and the release of oxytocin in the blood stream during childbirth.

Men and women have also faced different information-processing problems in some adaptive domains. Because fertilization occurs internally within the woman, for example, men have faced the adaptive problem of uncertainty of paternity in putative offspring. Men who failed to solve this problem risked investing resources in children who were not their own. All people descend from a long line of ancestral men whose adaptations (i.e., psychological mechanisms) led them to behave in ways that increased their likelihood of paternity and decreased the odds of investing in children who were putatively theirs but whose genetic fathers were other men. This does not imply, of course, that men were or are consciously aware of the adaptive problem of compromised paternity.

Women faced the problem of securing a reliable or replenishable supply of resources to carry them through pregnancy and lactation, especially when food resources were scarce (e.g., during droughts or harsh winters). All people are descendants of a long and unbroken line of women who successfully solved this adaptive challenge—for example, by preferring mates who showed the ability to accrue resources and the willingness to provide them for particular women (Buss, 1994). Those women who failed to solve this problem failed to survive, imperiled the survival chances of their children, and hence failed to continue their lineage.

Evolutionary psychologists predict that the sexes will differ in precisely those domains in which women and men have faced different sorts of adaptive problems (Buss, 1994). To an evolutionary psychologist, the likelihood that the sexes are psychologically identical in domains in which they have recurrently confronted different adaptive problems over the long expanse of human evolutionary history is essentially zero (Symons, 1992). The key question, therefore, is not whether men and women differ psychologically. Rather, the key questions about sex differences, from an evolutionary psychological perspective, are (a) In what domains have women and men faced different adaptive problems? (b) What are the sex-differentiated psychological mechanisms of women and men that have evolved in response to these sex-differentiated adaptive problems? (c) Which social, cultural, and contextual inputs moderate the magnitude of expressed sex differences?

Sexual Selection Defines the Primary Domains in Which the Sexes Have Faced Different Adaptive Challenges

Although many who are not biologists equate evolution with natural selection or survival selection, Darwin (1871) sculpted what he believed to be a second theory of evolution—the theory of sexual selection. Sexual selection is the causal process of the evolution of characteristics on the basis of reproductive advantage, as opposed to survival advantage. Sexual selection occurs in two forms. First, members of one sex can successfully outcompete members of their own sex in a process of intrasexual competition. Whatever characteristics lead to success in these same-sex competitions—be they greater size, strength, cunning, or social skills—can evolve or increase in frequency by virtue of the reproductive advantage accrued by the winners through increased access to more numerous or more desirable mates.

Second, members of one sex can evolve preferences for desirable qualities in potential mates through the process of intersexual selection. If members of one sex exhibit some consensus about which qualities are desirable in the other sex, then members of the other sex who possess the desirable qualities will gain a preferential mating advantage. Hence, the desirable qualities—be they morphological features such as antlers or plumage or psychological features such as a lower threshold for risk taking to acquire resources—can evolve by virtue of the reproductive advantage attained by those who are preferentially chosen for possessing the desirable qualities. Among humans, both causal processes—preferential mate choice and same-sex competition for access to mates—are prevalent among both sexes, and probably have been throughout human evolutionary history (Buss, 1994).

Hypotheses about Psychological Sex Differences Follow from Sexual Asymmetries in Mate Selection and Intrasexual Competition

Although a detailed analysis of psychological sex differences is well beyond the scope of this article (see Buss, 1994), a few of the most obvious differences in adaptive problems include the following.

Paternity Uncertainty

Because fertilization occurs internally within women, men are always less than 100% certain (again, no conscious awareness implied) that their putative children are genetically their own. Some cultures have phrases to describe this, such as "mama's baby, papa's maybe." Women are always 100% certain that the children they bear are their own.

Identifying Reproductively Valuable Women

Because women's ovulation is concealed and there is no evidence that men can detect when women ovulate, ancestral men had the difficult adaptive challenge of identifying which women were more fertile. Although ancestral women would also have faced the problem of identifying fertile men, the problem is considerably less severe (a) because most men remain fertile throughout their life span, whereas fertility is steeply age graded among women and (b) because women invest more heavily in offspring, making them the more "valuable" sex, competed for more intensely by men seeking sexual access. Thus, there is rarely a shortage of men willing to contribute the sperm necessary for fertilization, whereas from a man's perspective, there is a pervasive shortage of fertile women.

Gaining Sexual Access to Women

Because of the large asymmetry between men and women in their minimum obligatory parental investment —nine months gestation for women versus an act of sex for men—the direct reproductive benefits of gaining sexual access to a variety of mates would have been much higher for men than for women throughout human evolutionary history (Symons, 1979; Trivers, 1972). Therefore, in social contexts in which some short-term mating or polygynous mating were possible, men who succeeded in gaining sexual access to a variety of women, other things being equal, would have experienced greater reproductive success than men who failed to gain such access (see also Greiling, 1993, for adaptive benefits to women of short-term mating).

Identifying Men Who Are Able to Invest

Because of the tremendous burdens of a nine-month pregnancy and subsequent lactation, women who selected men who were able to invest resources in them and their offspring would have been at a tremendous advantage in survival and reproductive currencies compared with women who were indifferent to the investment capabilities of the man with whom they chose to mate.

Identifying Men Who Are Willing to Invest

Having resources is not enough. Copulating with a man who had resources but who displayed a hasty postcopulatory departure would have been detrimental to the woman, particularly if she became pregnant and faced raising a child without the aid and protection of an investing father. A man with excellent resource-accruing capacities might channel resources to another woman or pursue short-term sexual opportunities with a variety of women. A woman who had the ability to detect a man's willingness to invest in her and her children would have an adaptive advantage compared with women who were oblivious to a man's willingness or unwillingness to invest.

These are just a few of the adaptive problems that women and men have confronted differently or to differing degrees. Other examples of sex-linked adaptive problems include those of coalitional warfare, coalitional defense, hunting, gathering, combating sex-linked forms of reputational damage, embodying sex-linked prestige criteria, and attracting mates by fulfilling the differing desires of the other sex—domains that all have consequences for mating but are sufficiently wide-ranging to span a great deal of social psychology (Buss, 1994). It is in these domains that evolutionary psychologists anticipate the most pronounced sex differences—differences in solutions to sex-linked adaptive problems in the form of evolved psychological mechanisms.

Psychological Sex Differences Are Well Documented Empirically in the Domains Predicted by Theories Anchored in Sexual Selection

When Maccoby and Jacklin (1974) published their classic book on the psychology of sex differences, knowledge was spotty and methods for summarizing the literature were largely subjective and interpretive (Eagly, this issue).* Since that time,

*Not included in this publication.

there has been a veritable explosion of empirical findings, along with quantitative meta-analytic procedures for evaluating them (e.g., Eagly, 1995; Feingold, 1990; Hall, 1978; Hyde, in press; Oliver & Hyde, 1993; Rosenthal, 1991). Although new domains of sex differences continue to surface, such as the recently documented female advantage in spatial location memory (Silverman & Eals, 1992), the outlines of where researchers find large, medium, small, and no sex differences are starting to emerge more clearly.

A few selected findings illustrate the heuristic power of evolutionary psychology. Cohen (1977) used the widely adopted d statistic as the index of magnitude of effect to propose a rule of thumb for evaluating effect sizes: 0.20 = "small," 0.50 = "medium," and 0.80 = "large." As Hyde (in press) has pointed out in a chapter titled "Where Are the Gender Differences? Where Are the Gender Similarities?," sex differences in the intellectual and cognitive ability domains tend to be small. Women's verbal skills tend to be slightly higher than men's (d = −0.11). Sex differences in math also tend to be small (d = 0.15). Most tests of general cognitive ability, in short, reveal small sex differences.

The primary exception to the general trend of small sex differences in the cognitive abilities domain occurs with spatial rotation. This ability is essential for successful hunting, in which the trajectory and velocity of a spear must anticipate correctly the trajectory of an animal as each moves with different speeds through space and time. For spatial rotation ability, d = 0.73. Other sorts of skills involved in hunting also show large magnitudes of sex differences, such as throwing velocity (d = 2.18), throwing distance (d = 1.98), and throwing accuracy (d = 0.96; Ashmore, 1990). Skilled hunters, as good providers, are known to be sexually attractive to women in current and traditional tribal societies (Hill & Hurtado, 1989; Symons, 1979).

Large sex differences appear reliably for precisely the aspects of sexuality and mating predicted by evolutionary theories of sexual strategies (Buss & Schmitt, 1993). Oliver and Hyde (1993), for example,

documented a large sex difference in attitudes toward casual sex (d = 0.81). Similar sex differences have been found with other measures of men's desire for casual sex partners, a psychological solution to the problem of seeking sexual access to a variety of partners (Buss & Schmitt, 1993; Symons, 1979). For example, men state that they would ideally like to have more than 18 sex partners in their lifetimes, whereas women state that they would desire only 4 or 5 (d = 0.87; Buss & Schmitt, 1993). In another study that has been replicated twice, 75% of the men but 0% of the women approached by an attractive stranger of the opposite sex consented to a request for sex (Clark & Hatfield, 1989).

Women tend to be more exacting than men, as predicted, in their standards for a short-term mate (d = 0.79). Women tend to place greater value on good financial prospects in a mate—a finding confirmed in a study of 10,047 individuals residing in 37 cultures located on six continents and five islands from around the world (Buss, 1989a). More so than men, women especially disdain qualities in a potential mate that signal inability to accrue resources, such as lack of ambition (d = 1.38) and lack of education (d = 1.06). Women desire physical protection abilities more than men, both in short-term mating (d = 0.94) and in long-term mating (d = 0.66).

Men and women also differ in the weighting given to cues that trigger sexual jealousy. Buss, Larsen, Westen, and Semmelroth (1992) presented men and women with the following dilemma: "What would upset or distress you more: (a) imagining your partner forming a deep emotional attachment to someone else or (b) imagining your partner enjoying passionate sexual intercourse with that other person" (p. 252). Men expressed greater distress about sexual than emotional infidelity, whereas women showed the opposite pattern. The difference between the sexes in which scenario was more distressing was 43% (d = 0.98). These sex differences have been replicated by different investigators (Wiederman & Allgeier, 1993) with physiological recording devices (Buss et al., 1992) and have been replicated in other cultures (Buunk, Angleitner, Oubaid, & Buss, 1994).

These sex differences are precisely those predicted by evolutionary psychological theories based on sexual selection. They represent only a sampling from a larger body of supporting evidence. The sexes also differ substantially in a wide variety of other ways that are predicted by sexual selection theory, such as in thresholds for physical risk taking (Wilson & Daly, 1985), in frequency of perpetrating homicides (Daly & Wilson, 1988), in thresholds for inferring sexual intent in others (Abby, 1982), in perceptions of the magnitude of upset people experience as the victims of sexual aggression (Buss, 1989b), and in the frequency of committing violent crimes of all sorts (Daly & Wilson, 1988). As noted by Donald Brown (1991), "it will be irresponsible to continue shunting these [findings] aside, fraud to deny that they exist" (p. 156). Evolutionary psychology sheds light on why these differences exist.

Conclusions

Strong sex differences occur reliably in domains closely linked with sex and mating, precisely as predicted by psychological theories based on sexual selection (Buss, 1994). Within these domains, the psychological sex differences are patterned in a manner that maps precisely onto the adaptive problems men and women have faced over human evolutionary history. Indeed, in most cases, the evolutionary hypotheses about sex differences were generated a decade or more before the empirical tests of them were conducted and the sex differences discovered. These models thus have heuristic and predictive power.

The evolutionary psychology perspective also offers several insights into the broader discourse on sex differences. First, neither women nor men can be considered "superior" or "inferior" to the other, any more than a bird's wings can be considered superior or inferior to a fish's fins or a kangaroo's legs. Each sex possesses mechanisms designed to deal with its own adaptive challenges—some similar and some different—and so notions of superiority or inferiority are logically incoherent from the vantage point of evolutionary psychology. The metatheory of evolutionary psychology is descriptive, not prescriptive—it carries no values in its teeth.

Second, contrary to common misconceptions about evolutionary psychology, finding that sex differences originated through a causal process of sexual selection does not imply that the differences are unchangeable or intractable. On the contrary, understanding their origins provides a powerful heuristic to the contexts in which the sex differences are most likely to be manifested (e.g., in the context of mate competition) and hence provides a guide to effective loci for intervention if change is judged to be desirable.

Third, although some worry that inquiries into the existence and evolutionary origins of sex differences will lead to justification for the status quo, it is hard to believe that attempts to change the status quo can be very effective if they are undertaken in ignorance of sex differences that actually exist. Knowledge is power, and attempts to intervene in the absence of knowledge may resemble a surgeon operating blindfolded—there may be more bloodshed than healing (Tooby & Cosmides, 1992).

The perspective of evolutionary psychology jettisons the outmoded dualistic thinking inherent in much current discourse by getting rid of the false dichotomy between biological and social. It offers a truly interactionist position that specifies the particular features of social context that are especially critical for processing by our evolved psychological mechanisms. No other theory of sex differences has been capable of predicting and explaining the large number of precise, detailed, patterned sex differences discovered by research guided by evolutionary psychology (e.g., Bailey, Gaulin, Agyei, & Gladue, 1994; Buss & Schmitt, 1993; Daly & Wilson, 1988; Ellis & Symons, 1990; Gangestad & Simpson, 1990; Greer & Buss, 1994; Kenrick & Keefe, 1992; Symons, 1979). Evolutionary psychology possesses the heuristic power to guide investigators to the particular domains in which the most pronounced sex differences, as well as similarities, will be found. People grappling with the existence and implications of psychological sex differences cannot afford to ignore their most likely evolutionary origins through sexual selection.

References

Abby, A. (1982). Sex differences in attributions for friendly behavior: Do males misperceive females' friendliness? *Journal of Personality and Social Psychology, 32,* 830–838.

Ashmore, R. D. (1990). Sex, gender, and the individual. In L. A. Pervin (Ed.), *Handbook of personality: Theory and research* (pp. 486–526). New York: Guilford Press.

Bailey, J. M., Gaulin, S., Agyei, Y., & Gladue, B. A. (1994). Effects of gender and sexual orientation on evolutionarily relevant aspects of human mating psychology. *Journal of Personality and Social Psychology, 66,* 1074–1080.

Brown, D. (1991). *Human universals.* Philadelphia: Temple University Press.

Buss, D. M. (1989a). Sex differences in human mate preferences: Evolutionary hypotheses tested in 37 cultures. *Behavioral and Brain Sciences, 12,* 1–49.

Buss, D. M. (1989b). Conflict between the sexes: Strategic interference and the evocation of anger and upset. *Journal of Personality and Social Psychology, 56,* 735–747.

Buss, D. M. (1994). *The evolution of desire: Strategies of human mating.* New York: Basic Books.

Buss, D. M. (1995). Evolutionary psychology: A new paradigm for psychological science. *Psychological Inquiry, 6,* 1–30.

Buss, D. M., Larsen, R., Westen, D., & Semmelroth, J. (1992). Sex differences in jealousy: Evolution, physiology, and psychology. *Psychological Science, 3,* 251–255.

Buss, D. M., & Schmitt, D. P. (1993). Sexual strategies theory: An evolutionary perspective on human mating. *Psychological Review, 100,* 204–232.

Buunk, B., Angleitner, A., Oubaid, V., & Buss, D. M. (1994). *Sexual and cultural differences in jealousy: Tests from the Netherlands, Germany, and the United States.* Manuscript submitted for publication.

Clark, R. D., & Hatfield, E. (1989). Gender differences in receptivity to sexual offers. *Journal of Psychology and Human Sexuality, 2,* 39–55.

Cohen, J. (1977). Statistical power analysis for the behavioral sciences. San Diego, CA: Academic Press.

Daly, M., & Wilson, M. (1988). *Homicide.* New York: Aldine de Gruyter.

Darwin, C. (1871). *The descent of man and selection in relation to sex.* London: Murray.

Eagly, A. H. (1995). The science and politics of comparing women and men. *American Psychologist, 50,* 145–158.

Ellis, B. J., & Symons, D. (1990). Sex differences in sexual fantasy: An evolutionary psychological approach. *Journal of Sex Research, 27,* 527–556.

Feingold, A. (1990). Gender differences in effects of physical attractiveness on romantic attraction: A comparison across five research paradigms. *Journal of Personality and Social Psychology, 59,* 981–993.

Gangestad, S. W., & Simpson, J. A. (1990). Toward an evolutionary history of female sociosexual variation. *Journal of Personality, 58,* 69–96.

Greer, A., & Buss, D. M. (1994). Tactics for promoting sexual encounters. *Journal of Sex Research, 5,* 185–201.

Greiling, H. (1993, June). *Women's short-term sexual strategies.* Paper presented at the Conference on Evolution and the Social Sciences, London School of Economics, London, England.

Hall, J. A. (1978). Gender effects in decoding nonverbal cues. *Psychological Bulletin, 85,* 845–852.

Hill, K., & Hurtado, M. (1989). Hunter-gatherers of the new world. *American Scientist, 77,* 437–443.

Hyde, J. S. (in press). Where are the gender differences? Where are the gender similarities? In D. M. Buss & N. Malamuth (Eds.), *Sex, power, conflict: Feminist and evolutionary perspectives.* New York: Oxford University Press.

Kenrick, D. T., & Keefe, R. C. (1992). Age preferences in mates reflect sex differences in reproductive strategies. *Behavioral and Brain Sciences, 15,* 75–133.

Maccoby, E. E., & Jacklin, C. N. (1974). *The psychology of sex differences.* Stanford, CA: Stanford University Press.

Oliver, M. B., & Hyde, J. S. (1993). Gender differences in sexuality: A meta-analysis. *Psychological Bulletin, 114,* 29–51.

Rosenthal, R. (1991). *Meta-analytic procedures for social research* (rev. ed.). Newbury Park, CA: Sage.

Silverman, I., & Eals, M. (1992). Sex differences in spatial abilities: Evolutionary theory and data. In J. Barkow, L. Cosmides, & J. Tooby (Eds.), *The adapted mind: Evolutionary psychology and the generation of culture* (pp. 539–549). New York: Oxford University Press.

Symons, D. (1979). *The evolution of human sexuality.* New York: Oxford University Press.

Symons, D. (1992). On the use and misuse of Darwinism in the study of human behavior. In J. Barkow, L. Cosmides, & J. Tooby (Eds.), *The adapted mind: Evolutionary psychology and the generation of culture* (pp. 137–159). New York: Oxford University Press.

Tooby, J., & Cosmides, L. (1992). Psychological foundations of culture. In J. Barkow, L. Cosmides, & J. Tooby (Eds.) *The adapted mind: Evolutionary psychology and the generation of culture* (pp. 119–136). New York: Oxford University Press.

Trivers, R. (1972). Parental investment and sexual selection. In B. Campbell (Ed.), *Sexual selection and the descent of man* (pp. 136–179). New York: Aldine de Gruyter.

Wiederman, M. W., & Allgeier, E. R. (1993). Gender differences in sexual jealousy: Adaptationist or social learning explanation? *Ethology and Sociobiology, 14,* 115–140.

Wilson, M., & Daly, M. (1985). Competitiveness, risk taking, and violence: The young male syndrome. *Ethology and Sociobiology, 6,* 59–73.

Article Review Form at end of book.

WiseGuide Wrap-Up

- Genes and environment work together to shape our personalities. We may inherit a gene for shyness, but, if given the right kind of supportive environment, that might be shaped into something that looks more like quietness than social anxiety. Similarly, alcoholism and drug addiction might arise from a genetic predisposition to develop compulsive behaviors combined with a history of trauma.

- Behavioral genetic research needs to become more sophisticated. In particular, behavioral geneticists need to stop relying on self-report measures of personality, understand the situational differences in personality, and focus on the ways that nature and nurture work together in the development of personality.

- Evolutionary psychologists focus on the ways the environment in which humans evolved shaped the development of certain aspects of our psyches and personalities. Buss notes that the environment of our evolutionary history presented different evolutionary tasks for men and women and, thus, may have influenced them accordingly.

R.E.A.L. Sites

This list provides a print preview of typical **coursewise** R.E.A.L. sites. There are over 100 such sites at the **courselinks**™ site. The danger in printing URLs is that web sites can change overnight. As we went to press, these sites were functional using the URLs provided. If you come across one that isn't, please let us know via email to: webmaster@coursewise.com. Use your Passport to access the most current list of R.E.A.L. sites at the **courselinks**™ site.

Site name: Human Behavior & Evolution Society
URL: http://psych.lmu.edu/hbes.htm
Why is it R.E.A.L.? This is the home web site of the Human Behavior and Evolution Society, which is interested in exploring the influence of evolutionary history on current human behavior, including such diverse topics as personality, cognition, crime, and clinical issues. The web site includes information about researchers in the area, graduate programs, and other resources.
Key topics: evolution of personality, gender

Site name: Society for Neuroscience
URL: http://www.sfn.org
Why is it R.E.A.L.? This is the primary site for those interested in the relationship between brains and behavior. The site includes information about the society, the field in general, upcoming events and conferences, and links to related societies and members.
Key topics: biological aspects of personality, genes and behavior

section 4

Personality Development and Change

Questions about how our personalities develop and the extent to which we can change aspects of our personality represent some of the most interesting and personally meaningful questions in the field of personality psychology. Everyone wants to know how his or her friends and family got to be the way they are and (sometimes) whether there is any chance they can change. You may wonder why your grandfather is always worrying about money, even though he's fairly comfortable financially, or why you and your brother seem so different, even though you're nearly the same age. Or you may wonder why many of the college students you know are trying to "find themselves" when only a few years ago they seemed to know exactly who they were. You may have noticed that your parents haven't changed much over the years, whereas your older brother seems very different from the way he was in high school, and you may wonder why. Questions such as these—about what makes people who they are and when and how they can change—permeate much of the work in the field of personality psychology. This section is dedicated to research that focuses directly on these questions and after reading these articles you will have some idea of how to answer these questions.

As you read these articles, you'll want to think about differences in the authors' ways of conceptualizing personality. You'll notice that some (e.g., McCrae and Costa) think of personality in relatively broad terms, whereas others (e.g., Stewart and Healy) focus on more specific aspects of personality. Some (e.g., Erikson) describe tasks or conflicts that are relevant to all people, whereas others (e.g., Sulloway) look at tasks and conflicts that develop out of one's specific family situation. Finally, some authors (e.g., Erikson, Stewart, and Healy) are optimistic about the potential for change throughout the lifecourse, and others (e.g., Sulloway, McCrae, and Costa) see personality as more fixed after childhood. These kinds of differences represent some of the central ways personality theories differ from one another.

Erikson's (1950) chapter "Eight Ages of Man" is a classic piece on personality development. His primary argument is that personality development follows a clear pattern which mirrors the way our lives are organized and structured over time. He describes eight stages of development: infancy, toddlerhood, preschool, middle childhood, adolescence, early adulthood, middle adulthood, and late adulthood. Each has its own central task or conflict. For example, during infancy we struggle with the task of developing trust and the conflict of trust vs. mistrust. Our experiences at this time play a large role in shaping our core sense of whether the world is a trustworthy place. Personality, in Erikson's model, is shaped by how we resolve the central conflict of each stage. If you know a preschooler, you are probably keenly aware of his or her growing desire to "Do it myself"—something that ties directly

Learning Objectives

- Name and describe the central task for each of Erikson's eight stages of development.

- Explain why Stewart and Healy argue that social changes have the most influence on our personalities when they happen during adolescence and early adulthood.

- Understand why Sulloway argues that laterborn children are the most likely to rebel.

- Learn which aspects of personality are most stable over the lifecourse.

Reading 12. Do you think the developmental stages of personality always occur in this order? What problems do you see with understanding personality development in terms of stages?

Reading 13. Do you see the effects of historical events or social changes on the personalities of people you know? What is the time of life Stewart and Healy argue in which we are most "susceptible" to the influence of social events and why?

Reading 14. What does Sulloway see as the main difference between firstborns and laterborns? How are firstborns like only children, and how are they different?

Reading 15. How does McCrae and Costa's vision of the consistency of personality match with your experience and that of those people you know well? What aspects of personality seem most open to change and which least?

into Erikson's model. He also points out that the task of identity development—making choices about what kind of person one wants to be and choosing one's professional arena—is a much more demanding task in modern societies, where we have many choices, that it is in traditional societies, where choices are fewer. Finally, Erikson broke new ground in his time for introducing the concept of adult development, providing an outline of some of the tasks and conflicts people face in adulthood. Previous theories really focused only on child development, and Erikson's model provided the seed for what is now an entire field of study.

In their 1989 article, "Linking Individual Development and Social Changes," Stewart and Healy demonstrate how our personalities can be shaped in part by the major social and historical events surrounding us. Perhaps some of you have grandparents or other relatives who lived through the Great Depression. Stewart and Healy's description of how this experience of extreme poverty and economic uncertainty helped shape the personalities of those who lived through it, even long after the economic situation had changed, might help you to better understand them. They also demonstrate that events which happen during an individual's late adolescence and early adulthood—when identities are being formed, in Erikson's model—have a larger impact on us than do those which occur at other points in our lives. Since many of you are in this developmental phase now, you might consider what social changes or historical events might be shaping whom you are becoming.

In his book, *Born to Rebel*, Sulloway returns to an age-old idea—that one's personality is shaped, at least in part, by one's place within the family structure. The introduction to that book is found here, and in it he lays out his argument that firstborn, secondborn, and laterborn children are born into essentially "different" families and, therefore, find different roles to fulfill within the family. In particular, he argues that firstborns tend to be conservative and follow parent wishes because they are the only children to hold the privileged position of having their parents' undivided attention for a period of time. Secondborns are more likely to rebel because the role of "parent pleaser" has already been taken by the firstborn. Included in this reader is a "test" that you can take to assess your own propensity for rebelliousness, given your place in your family structure and a host of other characteristics of your family. It will be interesting for you to see how well it describes you.

McCrae and Costa are some of the primary proponents of the view that personality is fairly stable throughout the lifecourse, and very stable after age 30. They conceptualize personality in terms of fairly broad traits, such as extroversion, and find that—on average—people don't show much change in these personality traits over very long periods of time. "The Stability of Personality" is a short review of some of that work, and the address to the web site for Costa's lab is included in the R.E.A.L. sites listed on page 99.

Do you think the developmental stages of personality always occur in this order? What problems do you see with understanding personality development in terms of stages?

Eight Ages of Man

Erik Erikson

Basic Trust vs. Basic Mistrust

The first demonstration of social trust in the baby is the ease of his feeding, the depth of his sleep, the relaxation of his bowels. The experience of a mutual regulation of his increasingly receptive capacities with the maternal techniques of provision gradually helps him to balance the discomfort caused by the immaturity of homeostasis with which he was born. In his gradually increasing waking hours he finds that more and more adventures of the senses arouse a feeling of familiarity, of having coincided with a feeling of inner goodness. Forms of comfort, and people associated with them, become as familiar as the gnawing discomfort of the bowels. The infant's first social achievement, then, is his willingness to let the mother out of sight without undue anxiety or rage, because she has become an inner certainty as well as an outer predictability. Such consistency, continuity, and sameness of experience provide a rudimentary sense of ego identity which depends, I think, on the recognition that there is an inner population of remembered and anticipated sensations and images which are firmly correlated with the outer population of familiar and predictable things and people.

What we here call trust coincides with what Therese Benedek has called confidence. If I prefer the word "trust," it is because there is more naïveté and more mutuality in it: an infant can be said to be trusting where it would go too far to say that he has confidence. The general state of trust, furthermore, implies not only that one has learned to rely on the sameness and continuity of the outer providers, but also that one may trust oneself and the capacity of one's own organs to cope with urges; and that one is able to consider oneself trustworthy enough so that the providers will not need to be on guard lest they be nipped.

The constant tasting and testing of the relationship between inside and outside meets its crucial test during the rages of the biting stage, when the teeth cause pain from within and when outer friends either prove of no avail or withdraw from the only action which promises relief: biting. Not that teething itself seems to cause all the dire consequences sometimes ascribed to it. As outlined earlier, the infant now is driven to "grasp" more, but he is apt to find desired presences elusive: nipple and breast, and the mother's focused attention and care. Teething seems to have a prototypal significance and may well be the model for the masochistic tendency to assure cruel comfort by enjoying one's hurt whenever one is unable to prevent a significant loss.

In psychopathology the absence of basic trust can best be studied in infantile schizophrenia, while lifelong underlying weakness of such trust is apparent in adult personalities in whom withdrawal into schizoid and depressive states is habitual. The re-establishment of a state of trust has been found to be the basic requirement for therapy in these cases. For no matter what conditions may have caused a psychotic break, the bizarreness and withdrawal in the behavior of many very sick individuals hides an attempt to recover social mutuality by a testing of the borderlines between senses and physical reality, between words and social meanings.

Psychoanalysis assumes the early process of differentiation between inside and outside to be the origin of projection and introjection which remain some of our deepest and most dangerous defense mechanisms. In introjection we feel and act as if an outer goodness had become an inner certainty. In projection, we experience an inner harm as an outer one: we endow significant people with the evil which actually is in us. These two mechanisms, then, projection and introjection, are assumed to be modeled after whatever goes on in infants when they would like to externalize pain and internalize pleasure, an intent which must yield to the testimony of the maturing senses and ultimately of reason. These mechanisms are, more or less normally, reinstated in acute crises of love, trust, and faith in adulthood and can characterize irrational attitudes toward adversaries and enemies in masses of "mature" individuals.

The firm establishment of enduring patterns for the solution of the nuclear conflict of basic trust versus basic mistrust in mere existence is the first task of the ego, and thus first of all a task for maternal care. But let it be said here that the amount of trust derived from earlier infantile experience does not seem to depend on absolute quantities of food or demonstrations of love, but rather on the quality of the maternal relationship. Mothers create a sense of trust in their children by that kind of administration which in its quality combines sensitive care of the baby's individual needs and a firm sense of personal trustworthiness within the trusted framework of their culture's life style. This forms the basis in the child for a sense of identity which will later combine a sense of being "all right," of being oneself, and of becoming what other people trust one will become. There are, therefore (within certain limits previously defined as the "musts" of child care), few frustrations in either this or the following stages which the growing child cannot endure if the frustration leads to the ever-renewed experience of greater sameness and stronger continuity of development, toward a final integration of the individual life cycle with some meaningful wider belongingness. Parents must not only have certain ways of guiding by prohibition and permission; they must also be able to represent to the child a deep, an almost somatic conviction that there is a meaning to what they are doing. Ultimately, children become neurotic not from frustrations, but from the lack or loss of societal meaning in these frustrations.

But even under the most favorable circumstances, this stage seems to introduce into psychic life (and become prototypical for) a sense of inner division and universal nostalgia for a paradise forfeited. It is against this powerful combination of a sense of having been deprived, of having been divided, and of having been abandoned—that basic trust must maintain itself throughout life.

Each successive stage and crisis has a special relation to one of the basic elements of society, and this for the simple reason that the human life cycle and man's institutions have evolved together. In this chapter we can do little more than mention, after

the description of each stage, what basic element of social organization is related to it. This relation is twofold: man brings to these institutions the remnants of his infantile mentality and his youthful fervor, and he receives from them—as long as they manage to maintain their actuality—a reinforcement of his infantile gains.

The parental faith which supports the trust emerging in the newborn, has throughout history sought its institutional safeguard (and, on occasion, found its greatest enemy) in organized religion. Trust born of care is, in fact, the touchstone of the *actuality* of a given religion. All religions have in common the periodical child-like surrender to a Provider or providers who dispense earthly fortune as well as spiritual health; some demonstration of man's smallness by way of reduced posture and humble gesture; the admission in prayer and song of misdeeds, of misthoughts, and of evil intentions; fervent appeal for inner unification by divine guidance; and finally, the insight that individual trust must become a common faith, individual mistrust a commonly formulated evil, while the individual's restoration must become part of the ritual practice of many, and must become a sign of trustworthiness in the community.* We have illustrated how tribes dealing with one segment of nature develop a collective magic which seems to treat the Supernatural Providers of food and fortune as if they were angry and must be appeased by prayer and self-torture. Primitive religions, the most primitive layer in all religions, and the religious layer in each individual, abound with efforts at atonement which try to make up for vague deeds against a maternal matrix and try to restore faith in the goodness of one's strivings and in the kindness of the powers of the universe.

Each society and each age must find the institutionalized form of reverence which derives vitality from its world-image—from predestination to indeterminacy. The clinician can only observe that many are proud to

*This is the communal and psychosocial side of religion. Its often paradoxical relation to the spirituality of the individual is a matter not to be treated briefly and in passing (see *Young Man Luther*). (E. H. E.)

be without religion whose children cannot afford their being without it. On the other hand, there are many who seem to derive a vital faith from social action or scientific pursuit. And again, there are many who profess faith, yet in practice breathe mistrust both of life and man.

Autonomy vs. Shame and Doubt

In describing the growth and the crises of the human person as a series of alternative basic attitudes such as trust vs. mistrust, we take recourse to the term a "sense of," although, like a "sense of health," or a "sense of being unwell," such "senses" pervade surface and depth, consciousness and the unconscious. They are, then, at the same time, ways of *experiencing* accessible to introspection; ways of *behaving*, observable by others; and unconscious *inner states* determinable by test and analysis. It is important to keep these three dimensions in mind, as we proceed.

Muscular maturation sets the stage for experimentation with two simultaneous sets of social modalities: holding on and letting go. As is the case with all of these modalities, their basic conflicts can lead in the end to either hostile or benign expectations and attitudes. Thus, to hold can become a destructive and cruel retaining or restraining, and it can become a pattern of care: to have and to hold. To let go, too, can turn into an inimical letting loose of destructive forces, or it can become a relaxed "to let pass" and "to let be."

Outer control at this stage, therefore, must be firmly reassuring. The infant must come to feel that the basic faith in existence, which is the lasting treasure saved from the rages of the oral stage, will not be jeopardized by this about-face of his, this sudden violent wish to have a choice, to appropriate demandingly, and to eliminate stubbornly. Firmness must protect him against the potential anarchy of his as yet untrained sense of discrimination, his inability to hold on and to let go with discretion. As his environment encourages him to "stand on his own feet," it must protect him against meaningless and arbitrary experiences in shame and of early doubt.

The latter danger is the one best known to us. For if denied the gradual and well-guided experience of the autonomy of free choice (or if, indeed, weakened by an initial loss of trust) the child will turn against himself all his urge to discriminate and to manipulate. He will overmanipulate himself, he will develop a precocious conscience. Instead of taking possession of things in order to test them by purposeful repetition, he will become obsessed by his own repetitiveness. By such obsessiveness, of course, he then learns to repossess the environment and to gain power by stubborn and minute control, where he could not find large-scale mutual regulation. Such hollow victory is the infantile model for a compulsion neurosis. It is also the infantile source of later attempts in adult life to govern by the letter, rather than by the spirit.

Shame is an emotion insufficiently studied, because in our civilization it is so early and easily absorbed by guilt. Shame supposes that one is completely exposed and conscious of being looked at: in one word, self-conscious. One is visible and not ready to be visible; which is why we dream of shame as a situation in which we are stared at in a condition of incomplete dress, in night attire, "with one's pants down." Shame is early expressed in an impulse to bury one's face, or to sink, right then and there, into the ground. But this, I think, is essentially rage turned against the self. He who is ashamed would like to force the world not to look at him, not to notice his exposure. He would like to destroy the eyes of the world. Instead he must wish for his own invisibility. This potentiality is abundantly used in the educational method of "shaming" used so exclusively by some primitive peoples. Visual shame precedes auditory guilt, which is a sense of badness to be had all by oneself when nobody watches and when everything is quiet—except the voice of the superego. Such shaming exploits an increasing sense of being small, which can develop only as the child stands up and as his awareness permits him to note the relative measures of size and power.

Too much shaming does not lead to genuine propriety but to a secret determination to try to get away with things, unseen—if, indeed, it does not result in defiant shamelessness. There is an impressive American ballad in which a murderer to be hanged on the gallows before the eyes of the community, instead of feeling duly chastened, begins to berate the onlookers, ending every salvo of defiance with the words, "God damn your eyes." Many a small child, shamed beyond endurance, may be in a chronic mood (although not in possession of either the courage or the words) to express defiance in similar terms. What I mean by this sinister reference is that there is a limit to a child's and an adult's endurance in the face of demands to consider himself, his body, and his wishes as evil and dirty, and to his belief in the infallibility of those who pass such judgment. He may be apt to turn things around, and to consider as evil only the fact that they exist: his chance will come when they are gone, or when he will go from them.

Doubt is the brother of shame. Where shame is dependent on the consciousness of being upright and exposed, doubt, so clinical observation leads me to believe, has much to do with a consciousness of having a front and a back—and especially a "behind." For this reverse area of the body, with its aggressive and libidinal focus in the sphincters and in the buttocks, cannot be seen by the child, and yet it can be dominated by the will of others. The "behind" is the small being's dark continent, an area of the body which can be magically dominated and effectively invaded by those who would attack one's power of autonomy and who would designate as evil those products of the bowels which were felt to be all right when they were being passed. This basic sense of doubt in whatever one has left behind forms a substratum for later and more verbal forms of compulsive doubting; this finds its adult expression in paranoiac fears concerning hidden persecutors and secret persecutions threatening from behind (and from within the behind).

This stage, therefore, becomes decisive for the ratio of love and hate, cooperation and willfulness, freedom of self-expression and its suppression. From a sense of self-control without loss of self-esteem comes a lasting sense of good will and pride; from a sense of loss of self-control and of foreign overcontrol comes a lasting propensity for doubt and shame.

If, to some reader, the "negative" potentialities of our stages seem overstated throughout, we must remind him that this is not only the result of a preoccupation with clinical data. Adults, and seemingly mature and unneurotic ones, display a sensitivity concerning a possible shameful "loss of face" and fear of being attacked "from behind" which is not only highly irrational and in contrast to the knowledge available to them, but can be of fateful import if related sentiments influence, for example, interracial and international policies.

We have related basic trust to the institution of religion. The lasting need of the individual to have his will reaffirmed and delineated within an adult order of things which at the same time reaffirms and delineates the will of others has an institutional safeguard in the *principle of law and order.* In daily life as well as in the high courts of law—domestic and international—this principle apportions to each his privileges and his limitations, his obligations and his rights. A sense of rightful dignity and lawful independence on the part of adults around him gives to the child of good will the confident expectation that the kind of autonomy fostered in childhood will not lead to undue doubt or shame in later life. Thus the sense of autonomy fostered in the child and modified as life progresses, serves (and is served by) the preservation in economic and political life of a sense of justice.

Initiative vs. Guilt

There is in every child at every stage a new miracle of vigorous unfolding, which constitutes a new hope and a new responsibility for all. Such is the sense and the pervading quality of initiative. The criteria for all these senses and qualities are the same: a crisis, more or less beset with fumbling and fear, is resolved, in that the child suddenly seems to "grow together" both in his person and in his body. He appears "more himself," more loving, relaxed and brighter in his judgment, more activated and activating. He is in free possession of a surplus of energy which permits him to forget failures quickly and to approach what seems desirable (even if it also seems uncertain and even dangerous) with undiminished and more accurate direction. Initiative adds to autonomy the quality of undertaking, planning and "attacking" a task for the sake of being active and on the move, where before self-will, more often than not, inspired acts of defiance or, at any rate, protested independence.

I know that the very word "initiative" to many, has an American, and industrial connotation. Yet, initiative is a necessary part of every act, and man needs a sense of initiative for whatever he learns and does, from fruit-gathering to a system of enterprise.

The ambulatory stage and that of infantile genitality add to the inventory of basic social modalities that of "making," first in the sense of "being on the make." There is no simpler, stronger word for it: it suggests pleasure in attack and conquest. In the boy, the emphasis remains on phallic-intrusive modes; in the girl it turns to modes of "catching" in more aggressive forms of snatching or in the milder form of making oneself attractive and endearing.

The danger of this stage is a sense of guilt over the goals contemplated and the acts initiated in one's exuberant enjoyment of new locomotor and mental power: acts of aggressive manipulation and coercion which soon go far beyond the executive capacity of organism and mind and therefore call for an energetic halt on one's contemplated initiative. While autonomy concentrates on keeping potential rivals out, and therefore can lead to jealous rage most often directed against encroachments by younger siblings, initiative brings with it anticipatory rivalry with those who have been there first and may, therefore, occupy with their superior equipment the field toward which one's initiative is directed. Infantile jealousy and rivalry, those often embittered and yet essentially futile attempts at demarcating a sphere of unquestioned privilege, now come to a climax in a final contest for a favored position with the mother; the unusual failure leads to resignation, guilt, and anxiety. The child indulges in fantasies of being a giant and a tiger, but in his dreams he runs in ter-

ror for dear life. This, then, is the stage of the "castration complex," the intensified fear of finding the (now energetically erotized) genitals harmed as a punishment for the fantasies attached to their excitement.

Infantile sexuality and incest taboo, castration complex and superego all unite here to bring about that specifically human crisis during which the child must turn from an exclusive, pregenital attachment to his parents to the slow process of becoming a parent, a carrier of tradition. Here the most fateful split and transformation in the emotional powerhouse occurs, a split between potential human glory and potential total destruction. For here the child becomes forever divided in himself. The instinct fragments which before had enhanced the growth of his infantile body and mind now become divided into an infantile set which perpetuates the exuberance of growth potentials, and a parental set which supports and increases self-observation, self-guidance, and self-punishment.

The problem, again, is one of mutual regulation. Where the child, now so ready to overmanipulate himself, can gradually develop a sense of moral responsibility, where he can gain some insight into the institutions, functions, and roles which will permit his responsible participation, he will find pleasurable accomplishment in wielding tools and weapons, in manipulating meaningful toys—and in caring for younger children.

Naturally, the parental set is at first infantile in nature: the fact that human conscience remains partially infantile throughout life is the core of human tragedy. For the superego of the child can be primitive, cruel, and uncompromising, as may be observed in instances where children overcontrol and overconstrict themselves to the point of self-obliteration; where they develop an over-obedience more literal than the one the parent has wished to exact; or where they develop deep regressions and lasting resentments because the parents themselves do not seem to live up to the new conscience. One of the deepest conflicts in life is the hate for a parent who served as the model and the executor of the superego, but who (in some form) was found trying

to get away with the very transgressions which the child can no longer tolerate in himself. The suspiciousness and evasiveness which is thus mixed in with the all-or-nothing quality of the superego, this organ of moral tradition, makes moral (in the sense of moralistic) man a great potential danger to his own ego—and to that of his fellow man.

In adult pathology, the residual conflict over initiative is expressed either in hysterical denial, which causes the repression of the wish or the abrogation of its executive organ by paralysis, inhibition, or impotence; or in overcompensatory showing off, in which the scared individual, so eager to "duck," instead "sticks his neck out." Then also a plunge into psychosomatic disease is now common. It is as if the culture had made a man over-advertise himself and so identify with his own advertisement that only disease can offer him escape.

But here, again, we must not think only of individual psychopathology, but of the inner powerhouse of rage which must be submerged at this stage, as some of the fondest hopes and the wildest phantasies are repressed and inhibited. The resulting self-righteousness—often the principal reward for goodness—can later be most intolerantly turned against others in the form of persistent moralistic surveillance, so that the prohibition rather than the guidance of initiative becomes the dominant endeavor. On the other hand, even moral man's initiative is apt to burst the boundaries of self-restriction, permitting him to do to others, in his or in other lands, what would neither do nor tolerate being done in his own home.

In view of the dangerous potentials of man's long childhood, it is well to look back at the blueprint of the life-stages and to the possibilities of guiding the young of the race while they are young. And here we note that according to the wisdom of the ground plan the child is at no time more ready to learn quickly and avidly, to become bigger in the sense of sharing obligation and performance than during this period of his development. He is eager and able to make things cooperatively, to combine with other children for the purpose of constructing and planning, and he is willing to profit from teachers and to emulate ideal prototypes. He remains, of course, identified with the parent of the same sex, but for the present he looks for opportunities where work-identification seems to promise a field of initiative without too much infantile conflict or oedipal guilt and a more realistic identification based on a spirit of equality experienced in doing things together. At any rate, the "oedipal" stage results not only in the oppressive establishment of a moral sense restricting the horizon of the permissible; it also sets the direction toward the possible and the tangible which permits the dreams of early childhood to be attached to the goals of an active adult life. Social institutions, therefore, offer children of this age an *economic ethos*, in the form of ideal adults recognizable by their uniforms and their functions, and fascinating enough to replace, the heroes of picture book and fairy tale.

Industry vs. Inferiority

Thus the inner stage seems all set for "entrance into life," except that life must first be school life, whether school is field or jungle or classroom. The child must forget past hopes and wishes, while his exuberant imagination is tamed and harnessed to the laws of impersonal things—even the three R's. For before the child, psychologically already a rudimentary parent, can become a biological parent, he must begin to be a worker and potential provider. With the oncoming latency period, the normally advanced child forgets, or rather sublimates, the necessity to "make" people by direct attack or to become papa and mama in a hurry: he now learns to win recognition by producing things. He has mastered the ambulatory field and the organ modes. He has experienced a sense of finality regarding the fact that there is no workable future within the womb of his family, and thus becomes ready to apply himself to given skills and tasks, which go far beyond the mere playful expression of his organ modes or the pleasure in the function of his limbs. He develops a sense of industry—i.e., he adjusts himself to the inorganic laws of the tool world. He can become an eager and absorbed unit of a productive situation. To bring a productive situation to completion is an aim which gradually supersedes the whims and wishes of play. His ego boundaries include his tools and skills: the work principle (Ives Hendrick) teaches him the pleasure of work completion by steady attention and persevering diligence. In all cultures, at this stage, children receive some *systematic instruction*, although, as we saw in the chapter on American Indians, it is by no means always in the kind of school which literate people must organize around special teachers who have learned how to teach literacy. In preliterate people and in nonliterate pursuits much is learned from adults who become teachers by dint of gift and inclination rather than by appointment, and perhaps the greatest amount is learned from older children. Thus the *fundamentals of technology* are developed, as the child becomes ready to handle the utensils, the tools, and the weapons used by the big people. Literate people, with more specialized careers, must prepare the child by teaching him things which first of all make him literate, the widest possible basic education for the greatest number of possible careers. The more confusing specialization becomes, however, the more indistinct are the eventual goals of initiative; and the more complicated social reality, the vaguer are the father's and mother's roles in it. School seems to be a culture all by itself, with its own goals and limits, its achievements and disappointment.

The child's danger, at this stage, lies in a sense of inadequacy and inferiority. If he despairs of his tools and skills or of his status among his tool partners, he may be discouraged from identification with them and with a section of the tool world. To lose the hope of such "industrial" association may pull him back to the more isolated, less tool-conscious familial rivalry of the oedipal time. The child despairs of his equipment in the tool world and in anatomy, and considers himself doomed to mediocrity or inadequacy. It is at this point that wider society becomes significant in its way of admitting the child to an understanding of meaningful roles in its technology and economy. Many a child's development is disrupted when family life has failed to prepare him for school life, or when school life fails to sustain the promises of earlier stages.

Regarding the period of a developing sense of industry, I have referred to *outer and inner hindrances* in the use of new capacities but not to aggravations of new human drives, nor to submerged rages resulting from their frustration. This stage differs from the earlier ones in that it is not a swing from an inner upheaval to a new mastery. Freud calls it the latency stage because violent drives are normally dormant. But it is only a lull before the storm of puberty, when all the earlier drives reemerge in a new combination, to be brought under the dominance of genitality.

On the other hand, this is socially a most decisive stage: since industry involves doing things beside and with others, a first sense of division of labor and of differential opportunity, that is, a sense of the *technological ethos* of a culture, develops at this time. We have pointed in the last section to the danger threatening individual and society where the schoolchild begins to feel that the color of his skin, the background of his parents, or the fashion of his clothes rather than his wish and his will to learn will decide his worth as an apprentice, and thus his sense of *identity*—to which we must now turn. But there is another, more fundamental danger, namely man's restriction of himself and constriction of his horizons to include only his work to which, so the Book says, he has been sentenced after his expulsion from paradise. If he accepts work as his only obligation, and "what works" as his only criterion of worthwhileness, he may become the conformist and thoughtless slave of his technology and of those who are in a position to exploit it.

Identity vs. Role Confusion

With the establishment of a good initial relationship, to the world of skills and tools, and with the advent of puberty, childhood proper comes to an end. Youth begins. But in puberty and adolescence all samenesses and continuities relied on earlier are more or less questioned again, because of a rapidity of body growth which equals that of early childhood and because of the new addition of genital maturity. The growing and developing youths, faced with this physiological revolution within them, and with tangible adult tasks ahead of them are now primarily concerned with what they appear to be in the eyes of others as compared with what they feel they are, and with the question of how to connect the roles and skills cultivated earlier with the occupational prototypes of the day. In their search for a new sense of continuity and sameness, adolescents have to refight many of the battles of earlier years, even though to do so they must artifically appoint perfectly well-meaning people to play the roles of adversaries; and they are ever ready to install lasting idols and ideals as guardians of a final identity.

The integration now taking place in the form of ego identity is, as pointed out, more than the sum of the childhood identifications. It is the accrued experience of the ego's ability to integrate all identifications with the vicissitudes of the libido, with the aptitudes developed out of endowment, and with the opportunities offered in social roles. The sense of ego identity, then, is the accrued confidence that the inner sameness and continuity prepared in the past are matched by the sameness and continuity of one's meaning for others, as evidenced in the tangible promise of a "career."

The danger of this stage is role confusion.* Where this is based on a strong previous doubt as to one's sexual identity, delinquent and outright psychotic episodes are not uncommon. If diagnosed and treated correctly, these incidents do not have the same fatal significance which they have at other ages. In most instances, however, it is the inability to settle on an occupational identity which disturbs individual young people. To keep themselves together they temporarily overidentify, to the point of apparent complete loss of identity, with the heroes of cliques and crowds. This initiates the stage of "falling in love," which is by no means entirely, or even primarily, a sexual matter—except where the

*See "The Problem of Ego-Identity," *J. Amer. Psa. Assoc.*, 4:56–121.

mores demand it. To a considerable extent adolescent love is an attempt to arrive at a definition of one's identity by projecting one's diffused ego image on another and by seeing it thus reflected and gradually clarified. This is why so much of young love is conversation.

Young people can also be remarkably clannish, and cruel in their exclusion of all those who are "different," in skin color or cultural background, in tastes and gifts, and often in such petty aspects of dress and gesture as have been temporarily selected as *the* signs of an in-grouper or out-grouper. It is important to understand (which does not mean condone or participate in) such intolerance as a defense against a sense of identity confusion. For adolescents not only help one another temporarily through much discomfort by forming cliques and by stereotyping themselves, their ideals, and their enemies; they also perversely test each other's capacity to pledge fidelity. The readiness for such testing also explains the appeal which simple and cruel totalitarian doctrines have on the minds of the youth of such countries and classes as have lost or are losing their group identities (feudal, agrarian, tribal, national) and face world-wide industrialization, emancipation, and wider communication.

The adolescent mind is essentially a mind of the *moratorium*, a psychosocial stage between childhood and adulthood, and between the morality learned by the child, and the ethics to be developed by the adult. It is an ideological mind—and, indeed, it is the ideological outlook of a society that speaks most clearly to the adolescent who is eager to be affirmed by his peers, and is ready to be confirmed by rituals, creeds, and programs which at the same time define what is evil, uncanny, and inimical. In searching for the social values which guide identity, one therefore confronts the problems of *ideology* and *aristocracy*, both in their widest possible sense which connotes that within a defined world image and a predestined course of history, the best people will come to rule and rule develops the best in people. In order not to become cynically or apathetically lost, young people must somehow be able to convince themselves that those who succeed in their

anticipated adult world thereby shoulder the obligation of being the best. We will discuss later the dangers which emanate from human ideals harnessed to the management of super-machines, be they guided by nationalistic or international, communist or capitalist ideologies. In the last part of this book we shall discuss the way in which the revolutions of our day attempt to solve and also to exploit the deep need of youth to redefine its identity in an industrialized world.

Intimacy vs. Isolation

The strength acquired at any stage is tested by the necessity to transcend it in such a way that the individual can take chances in the next stage with what was most vulnerably precious in the previous one. Thus, the young adult, emerging from the search for and the insistence on identity, is eager and willing to fuse his identity with that of others. He is ready for intimacy, that is, the capacity to commit himself to concrete affiliations and partnerships and to develop the ethical strength to abide by such commitments, even though they may call for significant sacrifices and compromises. Body and ego must now be masters of the organ modes and of the nuclear conflicts, in order to be able to face the fear of ego loss in situations which call for self-abandon: in the solidarity of close affiliations, in orgasms and sexual unions, in close friendships and in physical combat, in experiences of inspiration by teachers and of intuition from the recesses of the self. The avoidance of such experiences because of a fear of ego loss may lead to a deep sense of isolation and consequent self-absorption.

The counterpart of intimacy is distantiation: the readiness to isolate and, if necessary, to destroy those forces and people whose essence seems dangerous to one's own, and whose "territory" seems to encroach on the extent of one's intimate relations. Prejudices thus developed (and utilized and exploited in politics and in war) are a more mature outgrowth of the blinder repudiations which during the struggle for identity differentiate sharply and cruelly between the familiar and the foreign. The danger of this stage is that intimate, competitive, and combative relations are experienced with and against the selfsame people. But as the areas of adult duty are delineated, and as the competitive encounter, and the sexual embrace, are differentiated, they eventually become subject to that *ethical sense* which is the mark of the adult.

Strictly speaking, it is only now that *true genitality* can fully develop; for much of the sex life preceding these commitments is of the identity-searching kind, or is dominated by phallic or vaginal strivings which make of sex-life a kind of genital combat. On the other hand, genitality is all too often described as a permanent state of reciprocal sexual bliss. This then, may be the place to complete our discussion of genitality.

For a basic orientation in the matter I shall quote what has come to me as Freud's shortest saying. It has often been claimed, and bad habits of conversation seem to sustain the claim, that psychoanalysis as a treatment attempts to convince the patient that before God and man he has only one obligation: to have good orgasms, with a fitting "object," and that regularly. This, of course, is not true. Freud was once asked what he thought a normal person should be able to do well. The questioner probably expected a complicated answer. But Freud, in the curt way of his old days, is reported to have said: "Lieben und arbeiten" (to love and to work). It pays to ponder on this simple formula; it gets deeper as you think about it. For when Freud said "love" he meant *genital* love, and genital *love*; when he said love *and* work, he meant a general work-productiveness which would not preoccupy the individual to the extent that he loses his right or capacity to be a genital and a loving being. Thus we may ponder, but we cannot improve on "the professor's" formula.

Genitality, then, consists in the unobstructed capacity to develop an orgastic potency so free of pregenital interferences that genital libido (not just the sex products discharged in Kinsey's "outlets") is expressed in heterosexual mutuality, with full sensitivity of both penis and vagina, and with a convulsion-like discharge of tension from the whole body. This is a rather concrete way of saying something about a process which we really do not understand. To put it more situationally: the total fact of finding, via the climactic turmoil of the orgasm, a supreme experience of the mutual regulation of two beings in some way takes the edge off the hostilities and potential rages caused by the oppositeness of male and female, of fact and fancy, of love and hate. Satisfactory sex relations thus make sex less obsessive, overcompensation less necessary, sadistic controls superfluous.

Preoccupied as it was with curative aspects, psychoanalysis often failed to formulate the matter of genitality in a way significant for the processes of society in all classes, nations, and levels of culture. The kind of mutuality in orgasm which psychoanalysis has in mind is apparently easily obtained in classes and cultures which happen to make a leisurely institution of it. In more complex societies this mutuality is interfered with by so many factors of health, of tradition, of opportunity, and of temperament, that the proper formulation of sexual health would be rather this: A human being should be potentially able to accomplish mutuality of genital orgasm, but he should also be so constituted as to bear a certain amount of frustration in the matter without undue regression wherever emotional preference or considerations of duty and loyalty call for it.

While psychoanalysis has on occasion gone too far in its emphasis on genitality as a universal cure for society and has thus provided a new addiction and a new commodity for many who wished to so interpret its teachings, it has not always indicated all the goals that genitality actually should and must imply. In order to be of lasting social significance, the utopia of genitality should include:

1. mutuality of orgasm

2. with a loved partner

3. of the other sex

4. with whom one is able and willing to share a mutual trust

5. and with whom one is able and willing to regulate the cycles of

   a. work

   b. procreation

   c. recreation

6. so as to secure to the offspring, too, all the stages of a satisfactory development.

It is apparent that such utopian accomplishment on a large scale cannot be an individual or, indeed, a therapeutic task. Nor is it a purely sexual matter by any means. It is integral to a culture's style of sexual selection, cooperation, and competition.

The danger of this stage is isolation, that is the avoidance of contacts which commit to intimacy. In psychopathology, this disturbance can lead to severe "character-problems." On the other hand, there are partnerships which amount to an isolation à deux, protecting both partners from the necessity to face the next critical development—that of generativity.

Generativity vs. Stagnation

In this book the emphasis is on the childhood stages, otherwise the section on generativity would of necessity be the central one, for this term encompasses the evolutionary development which has made man the teaching and instituting as well as the learning animal. The fashionable insistence on dramatizing the dependence of children on adults often blinds us to the dependence of the older generation on the younger one. Mature man needs to be needed, and maturity needs guidance as well as encouragement from what has been produced and must be taken care of.

Generativity, then, is primarily the concern in establishing and guiding the next generation, although there are individuals who, through misfortune or because of special and genuine gifts in other directions, do not apply this drive to their own offspring. And indeed, the concept generativity is meant to include such more popular synonyms as *productivity* and *creativity*, which, however, cannot replace it.

It has taken psychoanalysis some time to realize that the ability to lose oneself in the meeting of bodies and minds leads to a gradual expansion of ego-interests and to a libidinal investment in that which is being generated. Generativity thus is an essential stage on the psychosexual as well as on the psychosocial schedule. Where such enrichment fails altogether, regression to an obsessive need for pseudo-intimacy takes place, often with a pervading sense of stagnation and personal impoverishment. Individuals, then, often begin to indulge themselves as if they were their own—or one another's—one and only child; and where conditions favor it, early invalidism, physical or psychological, becomes the vehicle of self-concern. The mere fact of having or even wanting children, however, does not "achieve" generativity. In fact, some young parents suffer, it seems, from the retardation of the ability to develop this stage. The reasons are often to be found in early childhood impressions; in excessive self-love based on a too strenuously self-made personality; and finally (and here we return to the beginnings) in the lack of some faith, some "belief in the species," which would make a child appear to be a welcome trust of the community.

As to the institutions which safeguard and reinforce generativity, one can only say that all institutions codify the ethics of generative succession. Even where philosophical and spiritual tradition suggests the renunciation of the right to procreate or to produce, such early turn to "ultimate concerns," wherever instituted in monastic movements, strives to settle at the same time the matter of its relationship to the Care for the creatures of this world and to the Charity which is felt to transcend it.

If this were a book on adulthood, it would be indispensable and profitable at this point to compare economic and psychological theories (beginning with the strange convergencies and divergencies of Marx and Freud) and to proceed to a discussion of man's relationship to his production as well as to his progeny.

Ego Integrity vs. Despair

Only in him who in some way has taken care of things and people and has adapted himself to the triumphs and disappointments adherent to being, the originator of others or the generator of products and ideas—only in him may gradually ripen the fruit of these seven stages. I know no better word for it than ego integrity. Lacking a clear definition, I shall point to a few constituents of this state of mind. It is the ego's accrued assurance of its proclivity for order and meaning. It is a post-narcissistic love of the human ego—not of the self—as an experience which conveys some world order and spiritual sense, no matter how dearly paid for. It is the acceptance of one's one and only life cycle as something that had to be and that, by necessity, permitted of no substitutions: it thus means a new, a different love of one's parents. It is a comradeship with the ordering ways of distant times and different pursuits, as expressed in the simple products and sayings of such times and pursuits. Although aware of the relativity of all the various life styles which have given meaning to human striving, the possessor of integrity is ready to defend the dignity of his own life style against all physical and economic threats. For he knows that an individual life is the accidental coincidence of but one life cycle with but one segment of history; and that for him all human integrity stands or falls with the one style of integrity of which he partakes. The style of integrity developed by his culture or civilization thus becomes the "patrimony of his soul," the seal of his moral paternity of himself (". . . pero el honor/Es patrimonio del alma": Calderón). In such final consolidation, death loses its sting.

The lack or loss of this accrued ego integration is signified by fear of death: the one and only life cycle is not accepted as the ultimate of life. Despair expresses the feeling that the time is now short, too short for the attempt to start another life and to try out alternate roads to integrity. Disgust hides despair, if often only in the form of "a thousand little disgusts" which do not add up to one big remorse: *mille petits dégôuts de soi, dont le total ne fait pas un remords, mais un gêne obscure."* (Rostand)

Each individual, to become a mature adult, must to a sufficient degree develop all the ego qualities mentioned, so that a wise Indian, a true gentleman, and a mature peasant share and recognize in one another the final stage of integrity. But each cultural entity, to develop the particular style of integrity suggested by its historical place, utilizes a particular combination of these conflicts, along with specific provocations and prohibitions of infantile sexuality. Infantile conflicts become creative only if sustained by the firm support of cultural institutions and of the special leader classes representing them. In order to approach or experience integrity, the individual must know how to be a follower of image bearers in religion and in politics, in the economic order and in technology, in aristocratic living and in the arts and sciences. Ego integrity, therefore, implies an emotional integration which permits participation by followership as well as acceptance of the responsibility of leadership.

Webster's Dictionary is kind enough to help us complete this outline in a circular fashion. Trust (the first of our ego values) is here defined as "the assured reliance on another's integrity," the last of our values. I suspect that Webster had business in mind rather than babies, credit rather than faith. But the formulation stands. And it seems possible to further paraphrase the relation of adult integrity and infantile trust by saying that healthy children will not fear life if their elders have integrity enough not to fear death.

An Epigenetic Chart

In this book the emphasis is on the childhood stages. The foregoing conception of the life cycle, however, awaits systematic treatment. To prepare this, I shall conclude this chapter with a diagram. In this, as in the diagram of pregenital zones and modes, the diagonal represents the normative sequence of psychosocial gains made as at each stage one more nuclear conflict adds a new ego quality, a new criterion of accruing human strength. Below the diagonal there is space for the precursors of each of these solutions, all of which begin with the beginning; above the diagonal there is space for the designation of the derivatives of these gains and their transformations in the maturing and the mature personality.

The underlying assumptions for such charting are (1) that the human personality in principle develops according to steps predetermined in the growing person's readiness to be driven toward, to be aware of, and to interact with, a widening social radius; and (2) that society, in principle, tends to be so constituted as to meet and invite this succession of potentialities for interaction and attempts to safeguard and to encourage the proper rate and the proper sequence of their enfolding. This is the "maintenance of the human world."

But a chart is only a tool to think with, and cannot aspire to be a prescription to abide by, whether in the practice of childtraining, in psychotherapy, or in the methodology of child study. In the presentation of the psychosocial stages in the form of an *epigenetic chart* analogous to the one employed in Chapter 2* for an analysis of Freud's psychosexual stages, we have definite and delimited methodological steps in mind. It is one purpose of this work to facilitate the comparison of the stages first discerned by Freud as sexual to other schedules of development (physical, cognitive). But any one chart delimits one schedule only, and it must not be imputed that our outline of the psychosocial schedule is intended to imply obscure generalities concerning other aspects of development— or, indeed, of existence. If the chart, for example, lists a series of conflicts or crises, we do not consider all development a series of crises: we claim only that psychosocial development proceeds by critical steps—"critical" being a characteristic of turning points, of moments of decision between progress and regression, integration and retardation.

*Does not appear in this publication.

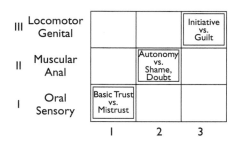

Figure II

It may be useful at this point to spell out the methodological implications of an epigenetic matrix. The more heavily-lined squares of the diagonal signify both a sequence of stages and a gradual development of component parts: in other words, the chart formalizes a progression through time of a differentiation of parts. This indicates (1) that each critical item of psychosocial strength discussed here is systematically related to all others, and that they all depend on the proper development in the proper sequence of each item; and (2) that each item exists in some form before its critical time normally arrives.

If I say, for example, that a favorable ratio of basic trust over basic mistrust is the first step in psychosocial adaptation, a favorable ratio of autonomous will over shame and doubt, the second, the corresponding diagrammatic statement expresses a number of fundamental relations that exist between the two steps, as well as some facts fundamental to each. Each comes to its ascendance, meets its crisis, and finds its lasting solution during the stage indicated. But they all must exist from the beginning in some form, for every act calls for an integration of all. Also, an infant may show something like "autonomy" from the beginning in the particular way in which he angrily tries to wriggle himself free when tightly held. However, under normal conditions, it is not until the second year that he begins to experience the whole *critical opposition of being an autonomous creature and being a dependent one*; and it is not until then that he is ready for a decisive encounter with his environment, an environment which, in turn, feels called

upon to convey to him its particular ideas and concepts of autonomy and coercion in ways decisively contributing to the character and the health of his personality in his culture. It is this encounter, together with the resulting crisis, that we have tentatively described for each stage. As to the progression from one stage to the next, the diagonal indicates the sequence to be followed. However, it also makes room for variations in tempo and intensity. An individual, or a culture, may linger excessively over trust and proceed from I 1 over I 2 to II 2, or an accelerated progression may move from I 1 over II 1 to II 2. Each such acceleration or (relative) retardation, however, is assumed to have a modifying influence on all later stages.

An epigenetic diagram thus lists a system of stages dependent on each other; and while individual stages may have been explored more or less thoroughly or named more or less fittingly, the diagram suggests that their study be pursued always with the total configuration of stages in mind. The diagram invites, then, a thinking through all of its empty boxes: if we have entered Basic Trust in I 1 and Integrity in VIII 8, we leave the question open, as to what trust might have become in a stage dominated by the need for integrity even as we have left open what it may look like and, indeed, be called in the stage dominated by a striving for autonomy (II 1). All we mean to emphasize is that trust must have developed in its own right, before it becomes something more in the critical encounter in which autonomy develops—and so on, up the vertical. If, in the last stage (VIII 1), we would expect trust to have developed into the most mature *faith* that an aging person can muster in his cultural setting and historical period, the chart permits the consideration not only of what old age can be, but also what its preparatory stages must have been. All of this should make it clear that a chart about genesis suggests a global form of thinking and rethinking which leaves details of methodology and terminology to further study.

	1	2	3	4	5	6	7	8
VIII Maturity								Ego Integrity vs. Despair
VII Adulthood							Generativity vs. Stagnation	
VI Young Adulthood						Intimacy vs. Isolation		
V Puberty and Adolescence					Identity vs. Role Confusion			
IV Latency				Industry vs. Inferiority				
III Locomotor-Gential			Initiative vs. Guilt					
II Muscular-Anal		Autonomy vs. Shame, Doubt						
I Oral Sensory	Basic trust vs. Mistrust							

Figure 12

*To leave this matter truly open, certain misuses of the whole conception would have to be avoided. Among them is the assumption that the sense of trust (and all the other "positive" senses postulated) is an *achievement*, secured once and for all at a given state. In fact, some writers are so intent on making an *achievement scale* out of these stages that they blithely omit all the "negative" senses (basic mistrust, etc.) which are and remain the dynamic counterpart of the "positive" ones throughout life. The assumption that on each stage a goodness is achieved which is impervious to new inner conflicts and to changing conditions is, I believe, a projection on child development of that success ideology which can so dangerously pervade our private and public daydreams and can make us inept in a heightened struggle for a meaningful existence in a new, industrial era of history. The personality is engaged with the hazards of existence continuously, even as the body's metabolism copes with decay. As we come to diagnose a state of relative strength and the symptoms of an impaired one, we face only more clearly the paradoxes and tragic potentials of human life.

The stripping of the stages of everything but their "achievements" has its counterpart in attempts to describe or test them as "traits" or "aspirations" without first building a systematic bridge between the conception advanced throughout this book and the favorite concepts of other investigators. If the foregoing sounds somewhat plaintive, it is not intended to gloss over the fact that in giving to these strengths the very designations by which in the past they have acquired countless connotations of superficial goodness, affected niceness, and all too strenuous virtue, I invited misunderstandings and misuses. However, I believe, that there is an intrinsic relationship between ego and language and that despite passing vicissitudes certain basic words retain essential meanings.

I have since attempted to formulate for Julian Huxley's *Humanist Frame* (Allen and Unwin, 1961; Harper and Brothers, 1962) a blueprint of essential strengths which evolution has built both into the ground plan of the life stages and into that of man's institutions (an expanded discussion is offered in Chapter IV, "Human Strength and the Cycle of Generations," of my *Insight and Responsibility* [W. W. Norton, 1964]). While I cannot discuss here the methodological problems involved (and aggravated by my use of the term "basic virtues"), I should append the list of these strengths because they are really the lasting outcome of the "favorable ratios" mentioned at every step of the chapter on psychosocial stages. Here they are:

Basic Trust vs. Basic Mistrust: Drive and *Hope*
Autonomy vs. Shame and Doubt: Self-Control and *Willpower*
Initiative vs. Guilt: Direction and *Purpose*
Industry vs. Inferiority: Method and *Competence*
Identity vs. Role Confusion: Devotion and *Fidelity*
Intimacy vs. Isolation: Affiliation and *Love*
Generativity vs. Stagnation: Production and *Care*
Ego Integrity vs. Despair: Renunciation and *Wisdom*

The italicized words are called *basic* virtues because without them, and their re-emergence from generation to generation, all other and more changeable systems of human values lose their spirit and their relevance. Of this list, I have been able so far to give a more detailed account only for Fidelity (see *Youth, Change, and Challenge*, E. H. Erikson, editor, Basic Books, 1963). But here again, the list represents a total conception within which there is much room for a discussion of terminology and methodology. (E. H. E.)

 Article Review Form at end of book.

Do you see the effects of historical events or social changes on the personalities of people you know? What is the time of life Stewart and Healy argue in which we are most "susceptible" to the influence of social events and why?

Linking Individual Development and Social Changes

Abigail J. Stewart
University of Michigan

Joseph M. Healy, Jr.
Wesleyan University

Abstract

In this article we argue for the need to develop a more adequate understanding of the connections between psychological research subjects' experience of social history and their personality development. We present the outlines of a general model according to which individuals' relative receptivity to the impact of social events is mediated by their life stage. Secondary analyses based on several data sets illustrate how women's work and family lives may be understood in terms of the general model. These analyses include data collected over the past 40 years from women in birth cohorts ranging from World War I to the baby boom.

Over the past few intensely self-critical and self-reflective decades, psychologists have understood more and more that our own historical situation influences our work (see, e.g., Buss, 1975; Gergen, 1973; Riegel, 1972; Sampson, 1977).

We have learned to accept that this influence is present both in terms of the questions we are able to think to ask, or the theoretical frameworks we adopt, and in the kinds of topics our values and experiences lead us to consider worthy of study. We know that this influence of our own historical experience is present when we can see links between developments of theory and social history (Morawski, 1982; Scarr, 1985). For example, we have come to agree that it is probably no accident that Freud's thinking about hysteria arose in turn-of-the-century Vienna (see, e.g., Schorske, 1979), whereas Kohut's theories about narcissism arose in the United States of the 1970s (Kahn, 1985). Similarly, we know it is no historical accident that national movements for the rights of Blacks and women coincided with our profession's recognition of subjects' rights and that research topics, such as androgyny, emerge and gain widespread professional interest at certain historical moments (Lewin, 1984; Morawski, 1985; Sampson, 1977). These kinds of changes in part reflect changing social norms and values that affect the culture as a whole and in part reflect the inclusion of new groups within psychology; thus, as

more women and people of color entered the discipline, new subjects were explored and legitimated (see Lykes & Stewart, 1986).

An understanding that our work is embedded in a historical context is extremely important. At the same time, though, we must also incorporate this *self*-understanding into our thinking about the people we set out to study. Participants in our research are no less influenced by social history than we are, yet we mostly continue to ignore our subjects' experience of social history. We attend a bit more often to our subjects' experience of social structure by including assessment of variables such as social class, gender, race, and ethnicity. Although we need more adequate ways to integrate these features of subjects' lives into our research and theory, our focus in this article is on our subjects' social experience *over time*. By ignoring the historical dimension of our subjects' social experience, not only do we unnecessarily impoverish our understanding of our subjects' lives, but we also ignore an important source of information to account for apparent inconsistencies in research findings, a point to which we will return further on.

Stewart, A. J., and Healy, J. (1989). "Linking Individual Development and Social Changes." *American Psychologist*, 44, 30–42. Copyright © 1989 by the American Psychological Association. Reprinted with permission.

Studies of the Influence of Social Changes on Individual Lives

There are a few important studies in which serious efforts were made to study aspects of social history. Perhaps the most significant example is Elder's (1974) study of children of the Great Depression and the related research he has published since that book (e.g., Elder, 1978; Elder, van Nguyen, & Caspi, 1985). Elder took a sample of children generally thought of as defining a "longitudinal study of child development" (the Oakland Growth study; see H. E. Jones, 1939, and Clausen, 1964, for general descriptions of the sample and data collected) and showed how that sample also defined a study of the impact of the Depression. By comparing children in families hard-hit with those in families relatively less affected by the Depression, he was able to examine how individual differences in the experience of the Depression affected children both at the time and in their later lives. In later research Elder (1979, 1981a, 1981b; Elder, Caspi, & van Nguyen, 1986) compared the children he first studied—who were young adolescents at the time of the Depression—with children from a second "longitudinal study of child development" (the Berkeley Guidance Study, Eichorn, Clausen, Haan, Honzik, & Mussen, 1981, and MacFarlane, 1938, have described the sample and data) who were born later and were therefore young children during the Depression. In this way, using a cohort comparison, Elder was able to show that the stage of development of the child at the time of a major, dislocating social experience was an important factor in determining the effects of that experience.

More recently, Elder (1986) extended this approach to an exploration of the impact of World War II experience in the military for men's later life course. He considered the different effects of military experience for young and older men. In this study, apparent *cohort* differences appeared to really reflect life course *timing* differences: Military experience provided real opportunities for upward mobility for disadvantaged *younger* men but not for their equally disadvantaged older brothers. Elder recently showed that military experience played a similar role in Japanese men's lives (Elder & Meguro, 1985).

In other studies of the psychological impact of social events on individual lives, a number of researchers explored the psychological and behavioral consequences for students' later lives of their earlier political activism in the late 1960s and early 1970s (see, e.g., Block, 1972; Mitchell & Block, 1983). More typically, though, studies of the impact of social events have been conducted within the broad framework of research on stress; thus, work on "war neurosis" (Fairbank, Langley, Jarvie, & Keane, 1981; Figley, 1978; Grinker & Spiegel, 1945; Helzer, Robins, Wish, & Hesselbrock, 1979; Rado, 1942) and on the impact of civilian bombing during World War II (e.g., Glover, 1942; Janis, 1951; Schmideberg, 1942) tended to be limited to an examination of the impact of terrible events and situations on individuals' relatively short-term mental health. Studies taking a longer or broader view—examining effects on normal personality development, or on the timing and choice of life patterns—have been quite rare. (See, however, Wilson, 1980, on the effects of the Vietnam War on long-term personality integration and psychosocial development and Elder & Meguro's 1985, data on the impact of military experience on the timing and life patterns of men.)

There is, however, another tradition in psychology that considers the impact of social history in a rather different way. Such research explores how some variables—especially social attitudes—have changed over periods that include significant social events *likely* to affect those variables (see, e.g., Lipman-Blumen & Tickamyer, 1975; Mason, Czajka, & Arber, 1976). In this research, the impact of broad social trends—such as decreasing sex role traditionality—is assessed, rather than the impact of particular events (such as the Great Depression or World War II). One example of this type of research is Veroff, Douvan and Kulka's (1981) replication in 1976 of the 1957 study (Gurin, Veroff, & Feld, 1960) of national patterns of well-being and mental health (see also Douvan, 1983; Kulka, 1982; Veroff, 1983). The replication study explicitly considered broad social trends in mental health as well as cohort differences. Thus, for example, Veroff et al. reported that although national levels of well-being were quite similar in 1957 and 1976, nevertheless there was an overall increase in feelings of uncertainty and worries about the future. This overall change, however, was most marked in the younger cohort—those people raised in affluence who found themselves in their 20s in entry-level jobs in a contracting economy. Thus, the attitude change seemed to reflect overall economic changes as well as an interaction between economic circumstances and cohort.

In a different area, patterns of help seeking showed radical change between 1957 and 1976. In 1957 most people talked over their problems with their spouses; in 1976, many more people were likely also to seek professional help with "problems in living" and to discuss those problems with friends and colleagues. However, Veroff et al. (1981) noted that the oldest cohort (those already middle-aged in 1957) did not show much change in these respects. Here the argument is that a broad, national trend toward increasing psychological preoccupation and sophistication lies behind the shift in help seeking.

This sort of account of broad social trends in mental health characteristics and behavior provides both significant information about social change directly and a context for examining data drawn from more limited, less representative samples. For example, when we consider the factors that might promote good mental health outcomes in elderly individuals, it is clearly important to attend to the cohort from which the elderly are drawn. Given the Veroff et al. (1981) findings about particular cohorts, variables and interventions that might facilitate well-being for one cohort may be expected to be quite irrelevant in another, in specific and intelligible ways.

The implications of both Elder's and Veroff et al.'s findings, then, are quite broad and should affect everyday research design and interpretation (see Riegel, 1972). There is, however, at least one good reason that we psychologists have not been incorporating an understanding of the importance of individuals' social-historical experience into our research: We do not have an adequate conceptual model of how to do it. Although Erikson argued repeatedly for the importance of considering individual development in conjunction with historical circumstances (see, e.g., Erikson, 1975), especially in accounting for the development of charismatic leaders (see, e.g., his discussion of Hitler in Erikson, 1950/1963, and of Gandhi in Erikson, 1969), he did not provide a detailed discussion of these links in the lives of most men and women. We would like to offer the beginnings of a model of how social changes and individual lives might be linked. This model is loosely based on what we know about both life-span personality development and research on the influence of social events on individual lives.

A Model Linking Individual Development and the Influence of Social Changes

Many theories that focus on the sociocultural context of personality development (Adorno, Frenkel-Brunswik, Levinson, & Sanford, 1950; Bowlby, 1969; Erikson, 1950/1963, 1968, 1980; Mannheim, 1952), and certainly Elder's data on the impact of the Depression, suggest that the likely area of impact of major social-historical events for young children is the *broad values and expectations about the world* that form during childhood (see especially Elder, 1974, and L. Y. Jones, 1980). Children's experience of social-historical events is, of course, likely to be filtered through their experience of their own families. Some families—and therefore some children—will be more directly affected by social events than others. Children whose fathers participated in—even died in—overseas combat in World War II and the Korean War fill our research literature on the effects of "father absence," though we have not understood them to be children affected by social historical events in a way different from their peers. In addition to considering the affective and relational consequences

of these experiences for children, it may be useful to note that one consequence of such absence would be the formation of background assumptions about the lack of reliability and dependability of social institutions, including families.

More generally, children raised in periods of stability and prosperity in families that are secure and economically "comfortable" should develop fairly positive and optimistic views of the world and social institutions, expecting that basic needs can and will be met. Perhaps as a result of these expectations, such secure children come to value opportunities for personal development and interpersonal relationships. Alternatively, children raised in hard times, especially if their own families suffer, develop more pessimistic views and assume that life may indeed be a struggle for subsistence (see Table 1). Values deriving from these fundamental views may also develop: Just as those raised in prosperity come to value self-development, those raised in hard times may come to value independence, hard work, and security. The worldview that forms in childhood is often later out of awareness; it is made up of a nonconscious set of background assumptions about the way the world does, and should, work.

The impact of events on late adolescents or young adults is likely to be different (see Braungart, 1975, 1976, 1980; Erikson, 1968, 1975; Mannheim, 1952; Stewart & Healy, 1986). Adolescents bring a set of experiences and already formed worldviews and values to any historical event. Events they face may or may not, then, be ones that can be assimilated into these preexisting views. The impact of events that are not radically discrepant with their life experience to date may not be large; thus, children from economically deprived families may not experience the advent of a national depression in their late adolescence as demanding revision of their values. However, if events occur that *are* radically discrepant with adolescents' life experience to date, those events may have enormous power in shaping the newly developing *personal identity* of the adolescent. Thus, young men and women raised in complacent, Edwardian England,

who were suddenly faced in 1914 with international conflict and violence on a massive scale, tended to ground their identity formation in their experience of World War I (see Wohl, 1979). Similarly, children raised in the prosperity and self-righteous moralism of the 1950s and early 1960s in this country, when faced in their late adolescence with the Vietnam War of the later 1960s, defined themselves, in substantial numbers, in terms of their experience fighting or protesting that war (see Braungart, 1975; L. Y. Jones, 1980; Wilson, 1980). Alternatively, children raised in the grim Depression and war years, who came of age in a booming postwar economy in a nation that had distinguished itself in the world community both in terms of strength and compassion, defined themselves in those new and heady terms—terms of affluence, optimism, and global responsibility (see Whyte, 1957).

"Mature adults"—defined here not in terms of age, but as individuals committed to careers and/or family lives—are likely to experience social and political events somewhat differently because the strength of these early adulthood commitments precludes the possibility of drastic self-definitional change at this time (Jacques, 1965; Levinson, 1978; Osherson, 1980; Vaillant, 1978). These events may have profound effects on options available in the job and housing markets, the educational opportunities available to their children, and so on, but they are not likely to change either basic values and expectations about life or to change an individual's self-definition—at least not at this age. Social events, then, may affect middle-aged individuals' *behavior*—what they actually do—but not how they understand or think about what they are doing. Thus, for example, historian William Chafe (1972, 1977, 1983) argued that during the booming economy after World War II many young mothers returned to the labor force while their children were still young. Many of these women had acquired their self-definitions during the postwar pressure for women to leave the labor force and provide secure homes for husbands and children, but their new labor-force participation was not accompanied by change either in

Table I Links between Individual Development and Social Events

Age When Social Event Is Experienced	Focus of Impact of Event
Childhood and early adolescence	Fundamental values and expectations (e.g., family values, assumptive frameworks)
Early adulthood	Opportunities and life choices; identity (e.g., vocational identity)
Mature adulthood	Behavior (e.g., labor force participation)
Later adulthood	New opportunities and choices: revision of identity

values or self-definition. Instead, the behavior was construed as behavior for the *family*—behavior that was undertaken not out of personal need or desire but for the sake of the children's education or family vacations. Thus, the expanding labor market of the time affected young adult women's opportunities and behavior but did not affect their personal identities or their beliefs about what was proper behavior.

This relative imperviousness of basic beliefs and identity to social experience changes some time in later adulthood (Gould, 1978; Jung, 1931/1960; Osherson, 1980). Whether due to the accumulation of life experiences that cannot be accommodated by earlier perspectives and identities or to internal developmental pressures we do not fully understand, at least some individuals do experience radical *revisions of their beliefs and identities* when faced with significant social events in later adulthood. For example, women who raised children at home during the 1950s and early 1960s were sometimes moved by the women's movement of the later 1960s and 1970s to reconsider the structure of their lives—to go back to school, abandon a marriage, or find a career. These women sometimes reconstructed their worldviews, and their personal identities, in radical ways.

Using the Model in Research

How can we use this model—however sketchy and incomplete it may be—in our research? First, on the basis of the model, we expect that the same events will have different effects on different cohorts; thus, cohort

analyses within age-heterogeneous samples will often be important. Second, we can expect that the same events will also have different effects *within* cohorts depending on the particular experience of the individual. Thus, individual differences in an experience—such as the presence or absence of family hardship—in childhood and/or adolescence will have consequences for the impact of certain events, such as the Depression, both at the time and later. Finally, the experience of psychologically significant social events at different stages of adulthood will have different consequences not only for the individual personally but also for his or her children. Thus, women who are parents may, as the model suggests, change their behavior in response to dislocating social events, but not their attitudes and values. This discrepancy in worldview and behavior may then have complex consequences for their children; it certainly will make it more difficult for researchers to decide what a parent is "modeling" (attitudes or behavior) and what a child is internalizing or learning. We will illustrate these three general points with data (drawn from several different sources) on U.S. women's life patterns in the period following World War II.

Cohort Differences in the Impact of Social Events

First let us consider the use of cohort analysis in age-heterogeneous samples. In 1963 and again in 1975, Ginzberg and Associates (1966; Yohalem, 1978) studied a group of women who had been graduate students at Columbia University during the postwar period (1945–1951). This

study of *Educated American Women* reported on the work and family lives of this unusual sample of women. It is a rich and fascinating study, but it reported on these women without regard to their birth cohorts and hence their differing experiences of social history. However, the sample is large enough to be divided into separate cohorts.

Three cohorts can be defined in terms that make social-historical sense in terms of women's changing labor-force opportunities. We know that women were offered extensive labor-force opportunities during World War II but then were expected to leave the labor force after the war to make room for returning soldiers (see Hartmann, 1982). Given the model just presented, we might expect that a woman's developmental stage at the time of those wartime labor-force opportunities—and at the time of the demand for women to stay out of the labor force postwar—would be consequential in her later career and life pattern. We can in fact divide the sample into cohorts on the basis of the women's developmental stage at the time of the war.

As may be seen in Table 2, there is a group of women who were born before World War I who were already mature adults by World War II. These women's identity formation should have taken place not during the war, but during the Depression. Extrapolating a bit from Elder's (1974) and others' (see e.g., Hartmann, 1982) conclusions about the impact of the Depression on individuals of various ages, these women should have internalized a strong sense of the importance of self-reliance and financial security in their identities; at the same time, they should have incorporated traditional family values because the family was generally experienced as the most reliable social institution during that period. Given their traditional family values, we would expect such women to view marriage and motherhood as inconsistent with career activity for women.

The second cohort of women, born between 1918 and 1922, were entering early adulthood during World War II; according to the model we have proposed, then, these women should be likely to incorporate labor-force activity for women into their

Table 2	Three Birth Cohorts' Experience of Social History		
Cohort	**Childhood and Adolescence**	**Early Adulthood**	**Mature Adulthood**
Older (born 1906–1914; N = 24)	Inter-war years	Depression	World War II
Middle (born 1918–1922; N = 49)	Depression	World War II	Postwar
Younger (born 1925–1929; N = 42)	Depression and World War II	Postwar	1950s

Note. These cohorts were drawn from the *Educated American Women* (Ginzberg & Associates, 1966; Yohalem, 1978) study.

identities, though their worldview (derived during the Depression) would include traditional family values. As a result, the antiwork, profamily values associated with the era of "feminine mystique" (see Friedan, 1963) of their adulthood might affect their behavior, *and* seem consonant with their underlying worldview, but it should not change their fundamental personal identities as workers. These women, then, should tend to experience marriage and family as demanding the sacrifice of career in the short term, but they should retain vocational identities even through relatively long periods of unemployment. In addition, they should convey to their children that there is no necessary incompatibility between femininity and employment even when they themselves give up employment in the service of their family roles.

Finally, a cohort of women did not achieve early adulthood until the postwar period. Accordingly, they should more or less wholly incorporate into their identities the profamily sex role definition for women dominant at that time. However, their childhood and early adolescence included a period in which labor-force activity of women was viewed as not only acceptable but a patriotic duty. For these women, motherhood should be more or less obligatory but perhaps not experienced as in conflict with employment at all. These three cohorts, then, may be expected to construct their adult lives rather differently and to respond to changing opportunities for women differently.

It is important to note here that the data available to explore these ideas are quite limited and reflect women's actual behaviors and *not* their beliefs or identities. Nonetheless, we may assess how well the data that do exist fit with the hypothesized internal experiences.

Table 3	Reported Impact of World War II by Birth Cohort	
Cohort	**Percentage Reporting "Some" Impact**
Older (born 1906–1914)	48
Middle (born 1918–1922)	71
Younger (born 1925–1929)	51

Note. $x^2(2, N = 115) = 4.45, p = .10$. Cohorts were drawn from the *Educated American Women* (Ginzberg & Associates, 1966; Yohalem, 1978) study.

First, the cohorts tended to differ in their reported retrospective perception of the importance of the war for their later lives. They were asked, in 1963 (Ginzberg & Associates, 1966, p. 207), whether the war had affected "your education, work, marriage, or life circumstances" and in what way. The answer to this question can only tell us, of course, about the degree to which women *viewed* the war as having an effect. It cannot tell us about effects that were either indirect or out of awareness. Thus, we predicted that the women who were late adolescents or young adults during the War and therefore in the midst of identity definition would be most likely to have felt the war to have been important in their lives. For older women, the war's significance could be great, but it should not have generally produced changes in identity. For younger females, the war should have had consequences for the formation of beliefs and values, but these consequences should be substantially out of awareness. As may be seen in Table 3, it is indeed the middle cohort—the women who "came of age" during the war—who saw it as having the biggest impact on their lives, though nearly half of the other cohorts saw it as having at least some impact. We do not know precisely what the impact was, even at a conscious level. One reason for the relatively greater persistence of

its impact for this cohort, though, may be understood in terms of the different impact of the postwar period for the three cohorts.

During the immediate postwar period, which we have identified as a time when women were pressured to remove themselves from the labor force and adopt a narrowly defined family role, only the two older cohorts could really be construed as mature adults. These two cohorts differed greatly in their life situations at that time. As may be seen in Table 4, although 22% of the total sample were mothers by 1950, only 4% of the older cohort were; whereas 41% of the middle cohort were. Thus, the middle cohort—even of these highly educated women—was apparently responding more than the older one to the pressures to provide families for returning soldiers. It is clear that this early difference in response to profamily pressure cannot be entirely accounted for by the older cohort's greater age, because a substantial number actually became mothers *after* 1950 (as will be shown). The profamily pressures were, as we would expect, strongest of all for the younger cohort. Although 15% of the total sample eventually became mothers, only 25% of the oldest cohort did and 59% of the middle cohort did; however, 88% of the youngest cohort did (see Table 5). It is clear, then, that separating the cohorts gives us a picture of these

Table 4 Postwar Motherhood by Birth Cohort

Cohort	Percentage with Children As of 1950
Older (born 1906–1914; aged 36–44 in 1950)	4
Middle (born 1916–1920; aged 28–32 in 1950)	41
Younger (born 1926–1930; aged 21–25 in 1950)	10

Note. x^2(2, N = 115) = 18.52, p < .001. Cohorts were drawn from the *Educated American Women* (Ginzberg & Associates, 1966; Yohalem, 1978) study.

Table 5 Eventual Motherhood by Birth Cohort

Cohort	Percentage with Children As of 1975
Older (born 1906–1914)	25
Middle (born 1916–1920)	59
Younger (born 1926–1930)	88

Note. x^2(2, N = 115) = 26.40, p < .001. Cohorts were drawn from the *Educated American Women* (Ginzberg & Associates, 1966; Yohalem, 1978) study.

Table 6 Correlations of Family Variables with Labor-Force Participation for Women of Childbearing Age by Birth Cohort

Cohort[a]	Correlation of Labor Force Participation With	
	Motherhood	Responsibility for Young Child[b]
Middle (born 1918–1922)	–.47*	–.52**
Younger (born 1925–1929)	–.22	–.06

Note. Cohorts were drawn from the *Educated American Women* study (Ginzberg & Associates, 1966; Yohalem, 1978).
[a]Data taken when subjects were at roughly comparable ages in terms of childbearing and childrearing: from 1963 for the older cohort (age 41–45) and from 1975 for the younger (age 46–50). [b]Defined in terms of the presence of children and the age of the youngest child: 4 = youngest is preschool age, 3 = youngest is school-age, 2 = youngest is adolescent, or 1 = no children.
* p < .01, ** p < .001.

women's family lives quite different from the one we obtain from the aggregate sample. It should also be noted that this picture—of decreasing deviation from a normative family structure across these three birth cohorts—is completely consistent with national patterns for women, regardless of race, social class, and education (see Uhlenberg, 1974).

Labor-force participation also varied by cohort. It was, of course, extremely high for the oldest cohort, which eschewed traditional family roles (96% were employed in 1963 when they were about age 50), but it was quite high for the middle cohort despite their far heavier family re-

sponsibilities (76% were employed in 1963 when they were in their mid-40s). Moreover, despite their *extremely* high commitment to motherhood, 55% of the youngest cohort were employed in 1963, and 74% were employed in 1975 when they were in their late 40s. Although these labor force participation rates are all higher than those for these women's overall birth cohorts, the three cohorts' relative rates in comparison with one another are quite consistent with national rates for their cohorts (see Figure 2 in Waite, 1981)*.

*Does not appear in this publication.

It is, moreover, fascinating to note that the middle and later cohorts differed not only in their acceptance of motherhood and their commitment to employment but also in the relationship between these two variables (assessed both in terms of the presence and age of children in women's families; see Table 6). For the middle cohort, who experienced traditional family values as children, labor-force opportunities during the period of identity formation, and the feminine mystique as adults, labor-force participation was strongly negatively correlated with motherhood even when they were in their 40s. In contrast, for the younger cohort, who experienced labor-force participation of women during their childhood and the feminine mystique during the time of identity formation, the two variables (including age of youngest child, on which there was much better variance) were uncorrelated by the time the women were in their 40s. It is as if the two activities were experienced as irrelevant to each other, and certainly not in conflict. For the middle cohort, who formed traditional family values as children but who benefited from the wartime labor-force opportunities in early adulthood, the conflict between the roles was much sharper. For some women in this cohort, the conflict was so strong it required sacrifice of one role or the other at any given moment; for others, it required permanent choice between roles. For most, simultaneous role occupancy was impossible. Those women in the middle cohort who became mothers probably provided conflicted modeling for their children because for this cohort both employment and motherhood were experienced as significant but mutually exclusive. In contrast, the younger cohort was less aware of any inconsistency between these roles (see L. Y. Jones, 1980, and Gerson, 1985, for discussions of differences among women rearing children during the 1950s).

To summarize, then, we may view the Ginzberg and Associates (1966) sample as including three cohorts of women whose separate experiences of social history are reflected—indirectly—in the course of their work and family lives. Although all of the women in this sample differed from other U.S. women in many ways, and each cohort within the sample probably differed from other U.S. women in somewhat *different* ways, nevertheless the three cohorts' patterns of family activity and labor force participation were similar in comparison with each other to national patterns for the larger cohorts (see both Uhlenberg 1974, and Waite, 1981). Overall, the older cohort of women may be viewed as having formed traditional family values and identities that could rarely accommodate both work and family roles. This particular sample included a large number of women who made a choice of the work role early on and apparently viewed it as inconsistent with a family role. These women were, of course, affected by World War II and the postwar period in that their opportunities waxed and waned. But their fundamental attitudes and identities were largely unchanged.

The middle cohort experienced much of the same environment for the formation of traditional sex role attitudes in childhood and early adolescence. But in late adolescence they were exposed to a drastically altered employment and social environment at the same time that they formed their identities. However, the postwar antiwork, profamily pressures created a long period in adulthood during which vocational and family roles were experienced as contradictory. We suggest, though, that these women did maintain vocational identities throughout their lives (which were reflected in their high level of employment in late adulthood) and that they may have communicated the acceptability of careers for women to their children along with more traditional family values.

Finally, the youngest cohort of women was exposed to the phenomenon of widespread female employment during formative years and strong profamily pressures at the transition to adulthood. For these women, the acceptability of career activity for women was, according to our model, a background belief and was therefore not experienced as inconsistent with family roles. However, marriage and motherhood should have been consciously experienced as providing central elements of the identity created in early adult-

hood. Traditional family values were incorporated into conscious identity, but nontraditional beliefs about women's working roles would coexist, with the inconsistency out of awareness. All of this discussion assumes that the women in each cohort experienced social history in some monolithic, or uniform, way. Even though each cohort may have been unified in some "average" experience, there are probably important individual differences among cohort members in their experience of social events.

Intracohort Differences in the Experience of Social Changes

The notion of individual differences among cohort members, along with the observation that baby boom daughters were exposed to mothers with very different kinds of attitudes about work and family roles for women, brings us to the second way in which we may incorporate a historical perspective in our research: by examining intracohort differences in the impact of social experiences. There are a number of ways to do this. For example, if we believe we are studying women who are, as young adults, confronted with a radically different social world than that of their mothers, then we may want to consider the degree to which those women have accepted or rejected their mothers' construction of the world. One such illustration may be found in our research on the transition to motherhood.

In the context of a study of individuals' adaptation to a wide variety of life changes (school, marriage, college, etc.), we studied a small sample of new mothers. In 1977, 40 couples expecting their first child were recruited (by newspaper advertisements) to participate in the study. Participants were White, in their late 20s, and generally college educated. Our goal was to assess the course of emotional adaptation to parenthood over the next two years or so in terms of our hypothesized sequence of emotional stances adopted in response to any major life change. According to our theory (see Stewart, 1982; Stewart, Sokol, Healy, & Chester, 1986; Stewart, Sokol, Healy, Chester, & Weinstock-Savoy, 1982, for

an account of the theory and the particular study), individuals' emotional disequilibrium in response to life changes should be reflected in their adoption of a relatively passive-receptive stance in which they experience themselves as confused, are aware of loss, and seek signs of help and support from others. Over time, this stance is hypothesized to give way to more independent, proactive stances and yields, ideally, to a stable emotional equilibrium in which the external environment has receded in saliences. We found that the new mothers, as a group, did tend to show this pattern, particularly if they did not experience additional changes (e.g., of residence, job) soon after the birth of the first child. It is clear, though, that attention to the historical context might add an important dimension to our understanding of the experience of these young women.

The White, middle-class young women in our sample were becoming mothers at a time when the possibility of combining work and family had become normative in a way that had not been so when their own mothers became mothers—at the height of the "feminine mystique." It is likely, then, that the transition to motherhood in the late 1970s might actually be more difficult for women experiencing internal and external pressure to resume paid employment if they held traditional values like those of their mothers. Although we have no direct measure of women's own values, or their mothers', we did ask women to rate themselves and their mothers on 10 personality traits, using 5-point scales. We created an overall perceived similarity to mother scale by summing the absolute differences between self and mother ratings on the 10 traits. We then divided the sample at the median, creating two groups: those who felt more and those who felt less similar to their mothers. In Table 7 we present overall emotional adaptation scores for these two groups a few months after the baby was born and 28 months later. Women who saw themselves as more like their mothers scored somewhat higher on overall adaptation in the early period (when, presumably, pressure for paid employment was relatively low). However, the women who saw them-

Table 7 Analysis of Modal Emotional Adaptation Scores for New Mothers

Group	Mean Emotional Adaptation Score[a]	
	Immediately after Birth	28 Months Later
Women who perceive themselves to be similar to their mothers (n = 16)	2.25	2.12
Women who perceive themselves to be different from their mothers (n = 13)	2.00[b]	2.85[b]

Note. Data are from Stewart et al. (1982, 1986).

[a]Scores range from 1 (for the receptive stance) to 4 (for the integrated stance). Higher scores indicate greater emotional adaptation.

[b]These means are significantly different from each other.

selves as relatively *unlike* their mothers scored much higher 28 months later (when employment pressures were probably quite high): for the interaction, $F(1, 27) = 3.29$, $p < .10$. In fact, only the group of women who saw themselves as *unlike* their mothers showed significant change in emotional stance, $F(1, 27) = 4.56$, $p < .05$, and change in the predicted sequence (from a relatively receptive stance to a more assertive one).

Obviously, this strategy ignores actual differences among these women's mothers themselves. It is also quite an indirect way of assessing individual differences in intracohort experience. In a recent follow-up of a sample of women first studied in the course of research on personality and situation as sources of women's life patterns, we adopted a more direct approach (see Stewart, 1975, 1978, 1980, and Stewart & Salt, 1981, for detailed descriptions of the sample and earlier analyses). This sample of women all graduated from college in 1964, having been born during World War II. Their immediate postcollege world—often mentioned in their questionnaire responses at earlier data-collection points—included the Peace Corps, the civil rights movement, and the women's movement. In the fall of 1986, the women were 43 years old, and we decided to ask them to rate a series of 26 social events, ranging from the Depression (occurring before they were born) to Three Mile Island, Watergate, and the oil crisis, in terms of the degree to which these events had "personal meaning" for them both at the time they occurred

and now. We then asked women to choose a single event from the list that was "*particularly* meaningful" and to explain its significance. Sixty-one of the 91 women who responded described one particularly meaningful event. Of these, 11 discussed events that had occurred during their childhood or early adolescence and 6 discussed events that had occurred during their mature adulthood. Forty-four, or 72%, of the women chose events from their late adolescence or early adulthood $x^2(2, N = 61) = 18.50$, $p < .001$ (see Table 8). It is important to note that fully 30% of the women selected the women's movement as the event that was particularly meaningful to them. It appears, then, that for this cohort, those social events that were felt to have special personal meaning did in fact cluster during the identity-formation period. However, it is impossible to be sure on the basis of these data alone—drawn from a single cohort—that the events that occurred during late adolescence for them were not simply more vivid or socially important than events as other stages of their lives (though World War II and the Cold War, for example, were events from other stages). Fortunately, Howard Schuman and Jacqueline Scott at the Survey Research Center at the University of Michigan's Institute for Social Research shared some preliminary results from their 1986 national survey exploring the "intersection of personal and national history" with us. In this survey (discussed in Schuman & Scott, 1987, p. 958) a cross-sectional probability sample of

adults (of all ages) was asked the following question:

There have been a lot of national and world events and changes over the past 50 years—say, from about 1930 right up until today. Would you mention one or two such events or changes that seem to you to have been *especially* important. There aren't any right or wrong answers to the question—just whatever national or world events or changes over the past 50 years that come to mind as important to you.

This question is, of course, very different from ours. It focuses on "importance" rather than on personal meaning, and it is entirely uncued, whereas we provided 26 specific alternative events. Schuman and Scott (1987) actually examined the impact of cuing responses and found that providing a cue was likely to increase the choice of certain kinds of rare responses to these questions (for example, "the invention of the computer"). Nevertheless, despite the difference in the question, the data from this survey can help us assess the degree to which our sample's choice of events reflects aspects of the events rather than the individual cohort's life stage at the time of the events.

Of the 1,253 individual responses Schuman and Scott (1988) obtained from Black and White men and women over 18, the largest proportion (29.3%) referred to World War II, followed by references to the Vietnam War, space exploration, the Kennedy presidency or assassination, and the civil rights movement. Four of these most frequently occurring events occurred during the relevant period in our sample's lives, suggesting that indeed that cohort may have experienced some unusually vivid or important social events during their transition to adulthood. On the other hand, of the four events mentioned most often in the Schuman and Scott survey and coinciding with our sample's young adulthood, one (space exploration) was *never* mentioned in our sample as particularly meaningful. Moreover, the most frequently mentioned event in Schuman and Scott's sample (World War II) was mentioned by only 3 women in our sample. The event mentioned *most* often by our sample (the women's movement) was mentioned by only 3.4% of the Schuman and Scott sample. (When the Schuman and Scott sample

Table 8	Ratios of "Particularly Meaningful Events" by Women Born during World War II

Era of Event	Number of 62 Subjects Selecting "Particularly Meaningful Events" from This Era
Pre-1961 (6 events)[a]	11
1961–1967 (9 events)[b]	44
1968–1979 (5 events)[c]	6

Note. Data are from the sample described in Stewart (1975, 1978, 1980; Stewart & Salt, 1981). Expected frequencies of event selection for each era were calculated from the proportion of all events falling in that era. $x^2(2, N = 61) = 18.50, p < .001$.
[a]Depression, World War II, Hiroshima, McCarthyism, Korean War, Cold War.
[b]Kennedy presidency, Cuban missile crisis, Peace Corps/Vista, War on Poverty, Martin Luther King, civil rights movement, Vietnam war, women's movement, peace movement. [c]1968 Democratic convention, Woodstock, Watergate, oil crisis, Three-Mile Island.

Table 9	Correlations between Rated Meaningfulness of the Women's Movement and Career Pattern

Career Pattern Variable	Correlations with Rated Meaningfulness of the Women's Movement[a]
Total labor force participation since college[b]	-.12
Nontraditionality of occupation[c]	.24*
Work-family role combination[d]	.27*
Occupational course[e]	.33**

*$p < .05$. **$p < .01$.

Note. $N = 87$. Data are from the sample described in Stewart (1975, 1978, 1980; Stewart & Salt, 1981). [a]Personal meaningfulness of the event rated 1 = not at all to 3 = very. [b]Amount of time in part- and full-time employment. [c]4 = field of full-time occupation is nontraditional for women; 3 = field of full-time occupation is traditional for women; 2 = part-time or inconsistent employment; 1 = no employment. [d]2 = combines employment and family; 1 = no role combination. [e]5 = traditional masculine career trajectory since college; 4 = same career trajectory as 5, but in traditionally female field; 3 = full-time employment in 1986, but no trajectory; 2 = part-time employment in 1986, but no trajectory; 1 = continuously unemployed since college (adapted from Helson, Mitchell, & Moane, 1984).

is disaggregated by race, cohort, and sex, it turns out that within the cohort that was age 40–49 in 1986, no men mentioned the women's movement at all, whereas 5% of White and 14% of Black women did. Even the figures for women are, however, much lower than those for our highly educated, privileged sample).

Finally, Schuman found a striking relationship between age at the time of the event and mention of both World War II and the Vietnam War. For both wars, individuals who were under 25 at the time of the event were much more likely to mention it than those who were older. There is, then, reason to suspect that social events do vary in their broad impact and that a number of broadly

significant events occurred during the transition to adulthood of our sample. However, the events most meaningful to our sample were not widely cited as important by a national sample in general or by a comparable age cohort in particular, and the event most often mentioned by the national sample was only infrequently mentioned by our sample.

Overall our cohort of women may be differentiated from cohorts before and after in terms of the broad social events that shaped their identity and also from other men and women of their age in terms of which events meant the most to them. In fact, within this sample itself, women differed from each other in terms of which events had the greatest impact

and whether social events had much impact at all. Although we are dealing here with a retrospective statement of the impact of social events, we can consider whether there is any evidence for any concrete effect of these events on our sample of women's lives.

A straightforward approach is to consider whether those women who claimed to have been affected by the women's movement in fact led lives that might be said to reflect the values and goals of that movement. Broadly speaking, the women's movement can be construed as advocating women's right to equal opportunity in the workplace and to an expanded range of personal sex role definitions. Thus, it provided encouragement for women's vocational self-definition as well as for women's consideration of alternative role structures. As may be seen in Table 9, a high level of felt meaning associated with the women's movement was significantly correlated with combining employment and family roles in midlife, nontraditional occupational choice, and pursuit of a career in a traditionally male career pattern (continuous or continuously advancing education or employment after college), but not with total labor-force participation after college. Of course, it is possible that women whose lives end up including careers view the women's movement as meaningful only after the fact. This possibility seems relatively unlikely, but even if it is true it suggests that certain social experiences at one point in time remain available for use in self-definition later. In general, then, these analyses suggest that within a single cohort we can assess the differential impact of social events for individuals during identity-formative years; obviously, this analysis strategy could be employed to study probable consequences of other events of importance to other groups or cohorts, or of the same event in other groups or cohorts.

Consequences of Social Changes for Parenting

The final aspect of the impact of social experiences on individual lives that we want to consider is their impact on the parenting of individuals who experience changes at various

Table 10	Mothers Employment Orientation over Time and Daughters' Role Combination	
Mothers' Employment Orientation over Time		**Percentage of Daughters Combining Motherhood and Employment**
Glad to leave employment at time of motherhood or no later employment (N = 24)		21
Sorry to leave employment at time of motherhood; later employment (N = 14)		57

Note. Data are from mothers who participated in the *Patterns of Child Rearing* (Sears, Maccoby, & Levin, 1957) study and from daughters who participated in a 1978 follow-up of the (now adult) children from this study (McClelland & Pilon, 1983).

stages of adulthood. We have already seen in the data on transition to motherhood that women's identification with their mothers may have a cost if they are operating in a social environment radically different from their mothers'. This finding and our model point to a more general set of principles that might be useful in making sense of the literature on the effect of maternal employment. We have argued that some young mothers who stayed at home in the era of the feminine mystique had already formed strong vocational identities before they became mothers, whereas others had not. Among those with strong vocational identities, many had formed traditional values at an early age that led them to view employment and motherhood as fundamentally in conflict. In contrast, some women held background views of the legitimacy of work roles for women while forming their identities around marriage and motherhood roles. These variables may complicate the picture when we try to understand the impact of mothers' employment behavior for their daughters. By directly examining them, we can be clearer than we have been about when maternal employment has straightforward consequences for daughters and when it does not.

Sears, Maccoby, and Levin's (1957) classic study, *Patterns of Child Rearing*, involved collection of data from young mothers of kindergartners in 1951. In 1978 McClelland and Pilon (1983) followed up the now-adult sons and daughters of those women, thus unintentionally affording us a cross-generational sample with which to consider this issue. In the original study, mothers were asked how they felt about giving up paid employment in order to be mothers. (The question was put this way because nearly all of the women *did* give up paid employment when they became mothers.) In 1978, the daughters—then in *their* early 30s—were asked both about their own lives and about whether their mothers were *ever* employed during the daughters' lives. Two groups of mothers can be compared: mothers who regretted giving up employment, and later resumed employment versus mothers who were happy to give up employment at the time of motherhood or who never resumed employment (see Table 10). Daughters of mothers who regretted giving up employment and later resumed it were significantly more likely to combine roles themselves than other daughters, $x^2(1, N = 48) = 5.18$, $p < .05$. These regretting and resuming mothers may have maintained vocational identities throughout their motherhood regardless of their lack of actual employment; they may also have been able eventually to enact that identity when the women's movement arose in their mature adulthood (they were in their late 40s at the height of the movement). Despite the fact that these women were not employed outside the home during their daughters' childhood, nevertheless they may have modeled the possibility of simultaneously performing the mother role and retaining a vocational identity.

Finally, aspects of *daughters'* young adult lives may themselves importantly affect the ways in which mothers' experiences are transmitted to the next generation. Returning for a moment to the class of 1964 sample (Stewart, 1975, 1978, 1980; Stewart & Salt, 1981), we would expect that mothers' employment history may be a particularly significant predictor of women's own employment among those women relatively unaffected by the women's movement (thus perhaps accounting for some of the inconsistencies in the literature on the impact of maternal employment). As may be seen in Table 11, there is a strong positive correlation between maternal employment and several daughter employment variables among women who did *not* find much personal meaning in the women's movement; there is virtually no correlation among those women who were influenced by the women's movement. These results suggest that identification with cohort-defining events and parental identification are both important variables conditioning the transgression of social historical events.

Conclusions

The data discussed in this article are largely based in samples of educated White women and focus on the consequences for these women of social-historical changes in labor-force opportunities and sex role definitions affecting such women. Most narrowly, these data suggest that even among this limited group of women, the impact of the expanded work role for women in World War II and the impact of the contracted one in the postwar period were quite different depending on the age and life stage of the women at the time. Conceptually related analyses within a later cohort indicate that events occurring during the transition to adulthood were more meaningful than those in other periods and that the single most often-cited event— the women's movement—had consequences for women's later lives. Finally, exposure to a female role model whose presumed vocational identity and work behavior were inconsistent seemed to result in identification with the identity rather than the behavior.

There may be some fairly general lessons here, lessons that are worth exploring in other data. Most broadly, we have argued that social

Table 11	Correlation of Mother's Employment with Daughters' Work Orientation		
		Correlation with Mother's Employment among Those for Whom Meaning of Women's Movement Was	
Daughter's Work Orientation Variable		**Major (N = 49–51)**	**Minor (N = 31–32)**
Total labor force participation[a]		−.12	.46*
Nontraditionality of occupation[b]		.10	.61**
Family–employment combination[c]		−.16	.32
Occupational course[d]		−.01	.52*

Note. Data are from the sample described in Stewart (1975, 1978, 1980; Stewart & Salt, 1981). [a]Amount of time in part- and full-time employment. [b]4 = field of full-time occupation is nontraditional for women; 3 = field of full-time occupation is traditional for women; 2 = part-time or inconsistent employment; 1 = no employment. [c]2 combines employment and family; 1 = no role combination. [d]5 = traditional masculine career trajectory since college; 4 = same career trajectory as 5, but in traditionally female field; 3 = full-time employment in 1986, but no trajectory; 2 = part-time employment in 1986, but no trajectory; 1 = continuously unemployed since college (adapted from Helson, Mitchell, & Moane, 1984).
* $p < .01$. ** $p < .001$.

experiences, in interaction with individual development, have consequences for individuals' worldviews when they are experienced in childhood, for their identities when they are experienced in later adolescence and the transition to adulthood, and for their behavior when they are experienced in mature adulthood. We have little data with which to explore the conditions under which later adults do or do not experience major revisions of identity in response to social changes. Perhaps, though, if particularly powerful life changes (such as divorce or bereavement) happen to coincide with this life stage, then individuals may be more open to the effects of social change. Similarly, the accident of particularly powerful *social* events coinciding with this life stage may result in higher average rates of impact for one cohort than for another. Another possibility is that a given individual or cohort may have, throughout adulthood, experienced an accumulation of hard-to-assimilate social changes that simply reach some threshold demanding radical revision in outlook at this age. Finally, for some people, intergenerational influences may reverse at this stage of the life cycle, with one predictor of late adult change before simultaneous freedom from day-to-day parenting

responsibilities and exposure to one's late-adolescent children's responses to social events.

It is clear that these general hypotheses need to be explored with other data, but on the strength of the data examined here we believe some rather more specific hypotheses can now be generated. First, it seems that parental models are especially powerful when cohort experiences around the transition to adulthood are *not* very powerful for either individual or social historical reasons. This was the case for daughters who were relatively unaffected by the women's movement, but was not the case with the young mothers who identified with their mothers but were subject to new sex role pressures. In these cases, identity-formation may be susceptible to parental influence directly, or indirectly by extension of basic values formed earlier. In contrast, if the social world changes in ways that do not fit parents' own early adult experience, parents' behavior in response to changed opportunities may be inconsistent with their identities. This was, we think, a widespread experience for women who participated as young adults in the labor force during World War II and then became mothers during the feminine mystique years. Parental models will be

least powerful in their influence if children experience major cohort-defining events in early adulthood. Thus, in general, those women who were influenced by the women's movement ignored their mothers' pattern of giving up employment in favor of motherhood, or alternating roles, and instead relied on evolving cohort norms for role combination.

Some experiences are cohort defining and also likely to produce major internal conflict for adults defined in earlier eras. In fact, cohort-defining social events probably are precisely those social events that create unanticipated conditions for the transition to adulthood for a particular cohort, conditions that are different both from those that came before and those that came after in terms of those aspects of life that are most relevant to identity formation (ideology, occupational identity, family roles). World War II was cohort defining for young adult women able to participate in the labor market but relatively confusing for older women who expected work and family roles to be incompatible. Similarly, women who experienced the women's movement as *adults* found it difficult to assimilate into their earlier sex role learning. For adult women burdened with responsibility for small children, the women's movement was often experienced, at least at the time, as irrelevant and threatening. But for late adolescents and some older women, it offered opportunities for self-definition and personal development. A social event like the Vietnam War was cohort defining in very different senses for those who fought in it and for those who fought against it, but it was—for those who made the transition to adulthood during it—cohort defining because issues of ideology and work and family roles were transformed during it and by its occurrence.

Using these general principles, we can make predictions for any given cohort about individuals' likely overall cohort identification as well as their reliance on parental teaching and modeling. We can also estimate the degree of internal conflict a given cohort will experience as adults about central roles in their lives, as a result of disjunctive later events. Similarly, we can begin to specify what types of events are likely to be cohort defining and productive of internal conflict. Identification of important cohort-defining events, and meaningful cohorts, in our recent social history will permit us to elaborate the initial conceptualization presented here of the links between individual development and social changes in our research participants' lives.

References

Adorno, T. W., Frenkel-Brunswik, E., Levinson, D. J., & Sanford, R. N. (1950). *The authoritarian personality.* New York: Harper.

Block, J. H. (1972). Generational continuity and discontinuity in the understanding of societal rejection. *Journal of Personality and Social Psychology, 2,* 333–345.

Bowlby, J. (1969). *Attachment and loss: Vol. 1. Attachment.* London: Hogarth.

Braungart, R. G. (1975). Youth and social movements. In S. Dragastin & G. Elder (Eds.), *Adolescence in the life cycle* (pp. 255–290). Washington, DC: Hemisphere.

Braungart, R. G. (1976). College and noncollege youth politics in 1972: An application of Mannheim's generation unit model. *Journal of Youth and Adolescence, 5,* 325–347.

Braungart, R. G. (1980). Youth movements. In J. Adelson (Ed.), *Handbook of adolescent psychology* (pp. 560–597). New York: Wiley.

Buss, A. R. (1975). The emerging field of the sociology of psychological knowledge. *American Psychologist, 30,* 988–1002.

Chafe, W. H. (1972). *The American woman: Her changing social, political, and economic roles, 1920–1970.* New York: Oxford University Press.

Chafe, W. H. (1977). *Women and equality: Changing patterns in American culture.* New York: Oxford University Press.

Chafe, W. H. (1983). The challenge of sex equality: Old values revisited or a new culture? In M. Horner, C. C. Nadelson, & M. Notman (Eds.), *The challenge of change: Perspectives on family, work, and education* (pp. 23–38). New York: Plenum.

Clausen, J. A. (1964). Personality measurement in the Oakland Growth Study. In J. E. Birren (Ed.), *Relations of development and aging* (pp. 165–175). Springfield, IL: Charles C. Thomas.

Douvan, E. (1983). Family roles in a twenty-year perspective. In M. Horner, C. C. Nadelson, & M. Notman (Eds.), *The challenge of change: Perspectives on family, work, and education* (pp. 199–217). New York: Plenum.

Eichorn, D. H., Clausen, J. A., Haan, N., Honzik, M. P., & Mussen, P. H. (Eds.). (1981). *Present and past in middle life.* New York: Academic Press.

Elder, G. (1974). *Children of the Great Depression.* Chicago: University of Chicago Press.

Elder, G. H. (1978). Family history and the life course. In T. Hareven (Ed.), *Transitions: The family and the life course in historical perspective* (pp. 17–64). New York: Academic Press.

Elder, G. H. (1979). Historical change in life patterns and personality. In P. B. Baltes & O. G. Brim, Jr. (Eds.), *Life-span development and behavior* (Vol. 2, pp. 117–159). New York: Academic Press.

Elder, G. H. (1981a). History and the life course. In D. Bertaux (Ed.), *Biography and society* (pp. 77–115). Beverly Hills, CA: Sage.

Elder, G. H. (1981b). Social history and life experience. In D. H. Eichorn, J. A. Clausen, N. Haan, M. P. Honzik, & P. H. Mussen (Eds.), *Present and past in middle life* (pp. 3–31). New York: Academic Press.

Elder, G. H. (1986). Military times and turning points in men's lives. *Developmental Psychology, 22,* 233–245.

Elder, G. H., Caspi, A., & van Nguyen, T. (1986). Resourceful and vulnerable children: Family influences in hard times. In R. K. Silbereisen et al. (Eds.), *Development as action in context* (pp. 167–186). Berlin: Springer-Verlag.

Elder, G. H., & Meguro, Y. (1985, August). *Wartime in men's lives: A comparative study of American and Japanese cohorts.* Paper presented at the meeting of the American Sociological Association, Washington, DC.

Elder, G. H., van Nguyen, T., & Caspi, A. (1985). Linking family hardship to children's lives. *Child Development, 56,* 361–375.

Erikson, E. (1963). *Childhood and society.* New York: Norton. (Original work published 1950)

Erikson, E. (1968). *Identity: Youth and crisis.* New York: Norton.

Erikson, E. (1969). *Gandhi's truth.* New York: Norton.

Erikson, E. (1975). *Life history and the historical moment.* New York: Norton.

Erikson, E. (1980). *Identity and the life cycle.* New York: Norton.

Fairbank, J. A., Langley, K., Jarvie, G. J., & Keane, T. M. (1981). A selected bibliography on posttraumatic stress disorders in Viet Nam veterans. *Professional Psychology, 12,* 578–586.

Figley, C. (Ed.). (1978). *Stress disorders among Viet Nam veterans.* New York: Brunner/Mazel.

Friedan, B. (1963). *The feminine mystique.* New York: Dell.

Gergen, K. J. (1973). Social psychology as history. *Journal of Personality and Social Psychology, 26,* 309–320.

Gerson, K. (1985). *Hard choices: How women decide about work, career and motherhood.* Berkeley, CA: University of California Press.

Ginzberg, E., & Associates. (1966). *Educated American women: Life styles and self-portraits.* New York: Columbia University Press.

Glover, E. (1942). Notes on the psychological effects of war conditions on the civilian population: Part III: The Blitz. *International Journal of Psychoanalysis, 23,* 17–37.

Gould, R. (1978). *Transformations.* New York: Simon & Schuster.

Grinker, R. R., & Spiegel, J. P. (1945). *Men under stress.* Philadelphia: Blakiston.

Gurin, G., Veroff, J., & Feld, S. (1960). *Americans view their mental health.* New York: Basic Books.

Hartmann, S. M. (1982). *The home front and beyond: American women in the 1940s.* Boston: Twayne.

Helson, R., Mitchell, V., & Moane, G. (1984). Personality and patterns of adherence and nonadherence to the social clock. *Journal of Personality and Social Psychology, 46,* 1079–1096.

Helzer, J. E., Robins, L. N., Wish, E., & Hesselbrock, M. (1979). Depression in Viet Nam veterans and civilian controls. *American Journal of Psychiatry, 136,* 526–529.

Jacques, E. (1965). Death and the midlife crisis. *International Journal of Psychiatry, 46,* 502–513.

Janis, I. L. (1951). *Air war and emotional stress.* New York: McGraw-Hill.

Jones, H. E. (1939). Procedures of the Adolescence Growth Study. *Journal of Consulting Psychology, 3,* 177–180.

Jones, L. Y. (1980). *Great expectations: America and the baby boom generation.* New York: Coward, McCann & Geoghegan.

Jung, C. G. (1960). The stages of life. In *Collected works* (Vol. 8). Princeton, NJ: Princeton University Press. (Original work published 1931)

Kahn, E. (1985). Heinz Kohut and Carl Rogers: A timely comparison. *American Psychologist, 40,* 893–904.

Kulka, R. A. (1982). Monitoring social change via survey replication: Prospects and pitfalls from a replication survey of social roles and mental health. *Journal of Social Issues, 38,* 17–38.

Levinson, D. (1978). *The seasons of a man's life.* New York: Ballantine.

Lewin, M. (1984). (Ed.). *In the shadow of the past: Psychology portrays the sexes.* New York: Columbia University Press.

Lipman-Blumen, J., & Tickamyer, A. R. (1975). Sex roles in transition: A ten-year perspective. In A. Inkeles, J. Coleman, & N. Smelser (Eds.), *Annual review of sociology 1975.* Palo Alto, CA: Annual Reviews.

Lykes, M. B., & Stewart, A. J. (1986). Evaluating the feminist challenge to research in personality and social psychology. *Psychology of Women Quarterly, 10*(4), 393–410.

MacFarlane, J. W. (1938). Studies in child guidance I: Methodology of data collection and organization. *Monographs of the Society for Research in Child Development, 3* (Serial No. 6).

Mannheim, K. (1952). The problem of generations. In *Essays on the sociology of knowledge* (pp. 276–322). London: Routledge & Kegan Paul. (Original work published 1928)

Mason, K. O., Czajka, J. L., & Arber, S. (1976). Change in U.S. women's sex-role attitudes: 1964–1974. *American Sociological Review, 41,* 573–596.

McClelland, D. C., & Pilon, D. A. (1983). Sources of adult motives in patterns of parent behavior in early childhood. *Journal of Personality and Social Psychology, 44,* 564–574.

Mitchell, V., & Block, J. H. (1983). Assessing personal and social change in two generations. In M. Horner, C. C. Nadelson, & M. H. Notman (Eds.), *The challenge of change: Perspectives on family, work, and education* (pp. 223–262). New York: Plenum.

Morawski, J. G. (1982). On thinking about history as social psychology. *Personality and Social Psychology Bulletin, 8,* 393–401.

Morawski, J. G. (1985). The measurement of masculinity and femininity: Engendering categorical realities. *Journal of Personality, 53*(2), 196–223.

Osherson, S. D. (1980). *Holding on or letting go.* New York: Free Press.

Rado, S. (1942). Pathodynamics and treatment of traumatic war neurosis (traumatophobia). *Psychosomatic Medicine, 4*(1), 362–368.

Riegel, K. (1972). Influence of economic and political ideologies on the development of developmental psychology. *Psychological Bulletin, 78,* 129–141.

Sampson, E. E. (1977). Psychology and the American ideal. *Journal of Personality and Social Psychology, 35,* 767–782.

Scarr, S. (1985). Constructing psychology: Making facts and fables for our times. *American Psychologist, 40,* 499–512.

Schmideberg, M. (1942). Some observations on individual reactions to air raids. *International Journal of Psychoanalysis, 23,* 146–176.

Schorske, C. (1979). *Fin-de-siècle Vienna: Politics and culture.* New York: Knopf.

Schuman, H., & Scott, J. (1987). Problems in the use of survey questions to measure public opinion. *Science, 236,* 957–959.

Schuman, H., & Scott, J. (1988, August). *The intersection of personal and national history.* Paper presented at the American Sociological Association meeting, Atlanta, GA.

Sears, R. R., Maccoby, E. E., & Levin, H. (1957). *Patterns of child rearing.* Evanston, IL: Row, Peterson.

Stewart, A. J. (1975). *Longitudinal prediction from personality to life outcomes among college-educated women.* Unpublished doctoral dissertation. Harvard University.

Stewart, A. J. (1978). A longitudinal study of coping styles in self-defining and socially defined women. *Journal of Consulting and Clinical Psychology, 46,* 1079–1084.

Stewart, A. J. (1980). Personality and situation in the prediction of women's life patterns. *Psychology of Women Quarterly, 5*(2), 195–206.

Stewart, A. J. (1982). The course of individual adaptation to life changes. *Journal of Personality and Social Psychology, 42,* 1100–1113.

Stewart, A. J., & Healy, J. M., Jr. (1986). The role of personality development and experience in shaping political commitment: An illustrative case. *Journal of Social Issues, 42*(2), 11–31.

Stewart, A. J., & Salt, P. (1981). Life stress, life-styles, depression and illness in adult women. *Journal of Personality and Social Psychology, 40,* 1063–1069.

Stewart, A. J., Sokol, M., Healy, J. M., Jr., & Chester, N. L. (1986). Longitudinal studies of psychological consequences of life changes in children and adults. *Journal of Personality and Social Psychology, 50,* 143–151.

Stewart, A. J., Sokol, M., Healy, J. M., Jr., Chester, N. L., & Weinstock-Savoy, D. (1982). Adaptation to life changes in children and adults: Cross-sectional studies. *Journal of Personality and Social Psychology, 43,* 1270–1281.

Uhlenberg, P. (1974, May). Cohort variations in family life cycle experiences of U.S. females. *Journal of Marriage and the Family,* 284–291.

Vaillant, G. (1978). *Adaptation to life.* Boston: Little, Brown.

Veroff, J. (1984). Psychological orientations to the work role: 1957–1976. In M. Horner, C. C. Nadelson, & M. H. Notman (Eds.), *The challenge of change: Perspectives on family, work, and education* (pp. 123–180). New York: Plenum.

Veroff, J., Douvan, E., & Kulka, R. A. (1981). *The inner American: A self-portrait from 1957–1976.* New York: Basic.

Waite, L. (1981). U.S. women at work. *Population Bulletin, 36*(2), 1–43.

Whyte, W. H. (1957). *The organization man.* Garden City, NY: Doubleday.

Wilson, J. P. (1980). Conflict, stress, and growth: The effects of war on psychosocial development among Vietnam veterans. In C. R. Figley & S. Leventman (Eds.), *Strangers at home: Vietnam veterans since the war.* New York: Praeger.

Wohl, R. (1979). *The generation of 1914.* Cambridge, MA: Harvard University Press.

Yohalem, A. M. (1978). *The careers of professional women: Commitment and conflict.* Montclair, NJ: Allanheld, Osmun.

 Article Review Form at end of book.

What does Sulloway see as the main difference between firstborns and laterborns? How are firstborns like only children, and how are they different?

Introduction and How to Test Your Own Propensity to Rebel

F. J. Sulloway

This book is inspired by a perplexing puzzle. Why do some people have the genius to reject the conventional wisdom of their day and to revolutionize the way we think? Copernicus, Newton, and Darwin are just three of the bold visionaries who have radically transformed our understanding of the world. No matter how radical the idea, and no matter how fierce the opposition, some people have quickly recognized the brilliance of the innovation and come to its defense.

When Darwin proposed his theory of evolution by natural selection, he plunged the scientific community into acrimonious debate that has continued even to this day. In spite of intense opposition to Darwin's ideas, some scientists quickly recognized Darwin as the greatest scientific revolutionary since Isaac Newton. Others, deeply disturbed by the possibility of humankind's descent from apes, branded him as a misguided atheist who had forsaken the true methods of scientific inference. Eventually the minority viewpoint prevailed over the majority, and Darwin lies buried in Westminster Abbey, not far from Isaac Newton.

Darwin's success as a revolutionary thinker raises a second criti-cal question. Why, during radical revolutions, do some people rapidly discard their old, erroneous ways of thinking whereas others hold tenaciously to the prevailing dogma? Historians, sociologists, philosophers, and psychologists have all proposed answers to the questions I am raising. In spite of numerous hypotheses, and considerable empirical research, there is no satisfactory answer to the question of why some people rebel and why others, just as zealously, defend the status quo.

In the case of Darwin's theory of evolution, religious convictions clearly played a part in the reception. But many revolutions in science have been fiercely contested on technical rather than ideological grounds. For example, Alfred Wegener's theory of continental drift was resisted for half a century before finally gaining acceptance among geologists.

Age has sometimes been suggested as a relevant factor, but this influence cannot explain why parents have sometimes championed new ideas and why their own offspring have sometimes opposed the same innovation.[1] The great naturalist, Étienne Geoffroy Saint-Hilaire believed in evolution a quarter of a century before Darwin announced his theory of natural selection. Yet Étienne's son Isidore, who was also a naturalist, opposed these heterodox ideas. In the political domain, Benjamin Franklin's eldest son, William, op-posed the American Revolution and was expelled from the country as a Loyalist. Many further examples could be given to show that age is surprisingly independent of revolutionary proclivities.

Another fashionable hypothesis about radical thinking involves Freud's notion of oedipal rivalry. Revolutionary thinkers are often said to have experienced a difficult relationship with a parent.[2] Using a case history approach, it is not hard to find corroborative evidence for this thesis. Using the same approach, it is just as easy to find evidence to the contrary. It is true that young Darwin experienced somewhat greater conflict with his father than most scientists. But Alfred Russel Wallace, who codiscovered the theory of natural selection, had excellent relationships with both parents. Other famous scientists who have managed to revolutionize the thinking of their disciplines without having experienced appreciable oedipal conflict include Francis Bacon, René Descartes, Louis Pasteur, and Max Planck. Even Sigmund Freud had a better relationship with his parents than most scientists.

Wealth and social status have frequently been called upon to explain differences in revolutionary allegiances.[3] Appeals to social class fail to elucidate one of the most puzzling features about revolutionary controversies. More often than not, major revolutions tend to polarize family members, including siblings who have grown up together. As one witness to the French Revolution commented during the Reign of Terror, "The worst part of this deplorable revolution is the discord sown by it in private circles, among families and friends and even between lovers. Nothing is free from the contagion."[4] Consistent with this verdict, historians have repeatedly failed to find meaningful socioeconomic differences among the members of the French National Convention (1792–94). Yet bitter feuding among these predominantly middle-class deputies led to the harsh policies of the Terror and also caused these politicians to send more than fifty of their colleagues to the guillotine. For compelling evidence on this score, one need look no further than the sixteen brothers who were elected to the convention. More often than not, these brothers affiliated themselves with *rival* political factions. The Protestant Reformation had a similar impact on family members, turning husbands against their wives, parents against their offspring, and siblings fratricidally against one another.[5]

What is missing from these and other attempts to explain radical thought is a simple but startling observation about human behavior: most individual differences in personality, including those that underlie the propensity to rebel, arise *within* the family. The question of why some people rebel, including why a few particularly far-sighted individuals initiate radical revolutions, is synonymous with the question of why siblings are so different.

Born to Rebel is organized into four parts, each of which adds a new layer to the basic argument. Part One sets forth a central problem: Why do some scientists, but not others, readily accept radical ideas? The story of Charles Darwin's conversion to the theory of evolution illustrates a frequent feature about revolutionary ideas. Most people, including scientists, *resist radical innovations.* Faced with the same biological evidence that caused Darwin to accept evolution, his closest colleagues refused to abandon their creationist convictions. Far more than evidence was required to transform Darwin into a radical

revolutionary. The biographical circumstances that paved Darwin's way exemplify some of the insights I have garnered from the study of 6,000 lives in Western history. Some people, it seems, are born to rebel.

The crux of my argument stems from a remarkable discovery. Siblings raised together are almost as different in their personalities as people from different families.[6] This finding, firmly established by studies in personality psychology, raises the question of how the family experience can be so different for each child. Do siblings differ because of random influences and experiences within the family, or are some of these influences systematically linked to variables that partition the family environment? Certainly gender is a relevant consideration, but is gender the only one or even the most important?

What about birth order, which is different for each sibling? Although a review of the birth-order literature strongly underscores the relevance of this variable, these findings have generally been dismissed because they are often contradictory. As it turns out, these inconsistencies are largely methodological. In addition to methodological problems, the voluminous birth-order literature has lacked an adequate theoretical perspective to make sense out of the results. Properly reinterpreted, the literature on birth order reveals striking trends and allows a crucial first step toward resolving the problem of why siblings are so different.

Darwinian theory, and the nascent field of evolutionary psychology, provide useful guidelines for understanding family life, including the question of why siblings are so different. One particularly important source of sibling differences is competition over family resources. Disputes over these resources, especially over parental affection, create rivalries. In nature, any recurring cause of conflict tends to promote adaptations that increase the odds of coming out on top. In their efforts to gain a competitive edge, siblings use physical advantages in size and strength. These disparities dictate many of the tactics that siblings employ in mutual competition. A crucial factor for measuring these physical differences, as well as for determin-

ing status within the family, is order of birth. Over time, the strategies perfected by firstborns have spawned counterstrategies by laterborns. The result has been an evolutionary arms race played out within the family. Even the Bible concurs with evolutionary theory regarding the primacy of sibling strife: the first biblical murder—that of Abel by his elder brother, Cain—was fratricidal.

It is natural for firstborns to identify more strongly with power and authority. They arrive first within the family and employ their superior size and strength to defend their special status. Relative to their younger siblings, firstborns are more assertive, socially dominant, ambitious, jealous of their status, and defensive. As underdogs within the family system, younger siblings are inclined to question the status quo and in some cases to develop a "revolutionary personality." In the name of revolution, laterborns have repeatedly challenged the time-honored assumptions of their day. From their ranks have come the bold explorers, the iconoclasts, and the heretics of history.

The influence of birth order, like that of gender, can be traced throughout history with clear and dramatic consequences. For most of recorded history, birth order has often determined who lived and who died, who possessed political power and who lacked it, and who was successful in efforts to find a mate and to reproduce. In prior centuries, parents often invested more heavily in firstborns to guarantee that at least one offspring would successfully perpetuate the family lineage. Historically, firstborns have tended to have more offspring. Even before the advent of primogeniture, scarce resources exerted a constant restraining influence on family size, causing the incidence of infanticide, as well as parental neglect, to be most frequent among younger siblings. In their efforts to survive childhood, and to pass on their genes to the next generation, laterborns have perennially been in conflict with their elder siblings.[7]

The evolution of behavior is a separate issue from how behaviors are individually learned. Children do not inherit special genes for being firstborns or laterborns, only genes for engaging successfully in competition for parental investment. The family environment determines how these competitive tendencies are expressed. In terms of personality, every firstborn is a potential laterborn, and vice versa. The psychological consequences of birth order provide compelling evidence for the role of the family environment.

This book is not so much about birth order as it is about family dynamics. Part Two explores a variety of influences, besides birth order, that affect personality. Siblings become different for the same reason that species do over time: divergence minimizes competition for scarce resources. For example, children can increase the amount of nurturing and attention they receive from parents if they avoid direct competition and instead appeal to whichever parent is unencumbered. The story of sibling differences is the story of family structure and how niches are partitioned within it. It is also the story of parental investment and any perceived biases in it. In spite of their best efforts to the contrary, parents occasionally exhibit favoritism toward some of their children. No social injustice is felt more deeply than that suffered within one's own family. When unassuaged, such feelings undermine respect for authority, laying the foundations for a revolutionary personality.

Particular factors such as gender, temperament, parent-offspring conflict, and parental loss add to our ability to predict revolutionary personality. Together these and other variables shape *sibling strategies* that are aimed at maximizing parental investment. Even only children employ sibling strategies. This seeming paradox is explained by the threat of unborn siblings, whose Darwinian influence on family life is as real as the ova and sperm in which they reside.

Some readers may consider this theory of personality development to be overly deterministic. It should be borne in mind, however, that sibling strategies are largely *self*-determined as a result of voluntary choices. If siblings wished to do so, they could easily pursue strategies differing from the ones they typically employ. Siblings behave in predictable ways because some responses to family life are more efficacious than others. It should also be appreciated that fam-

ily life shapes general trends in personality, not the fine details, leaving much about individual behavior that cannot be explained even by the most complex theories or models. The debate over whether human behavior is "determined" is largely sterile: Some of it is, and some of it is not.

Sibling strategies typically entail *emergent* properties. Birth order, gender, and temperament all interact to produce personality characteristics that could not be anticipated based on a simple aggregate of these influences. A theory of sibling strategies serves to highlight these emergent features of personality and also seeks to delineate their links with family structure and dynamics.

Part Three considers the role of social influences, especially social attitudes and social class. To a significant extent, social influences encompass *between*-family differences. Although such disparities exert little direct effect on personality, they do shape social attitudes and values, which have substantial influence on behavior. A variety of biographical paradoxes are resolved by understanding the relative independence of personality and social attitudes. A person with a "conforming" personality may espouse liberal attitudes that have been learned from parents or other authority figures. Social attitudes also reflect sibling differences, not only among offspring but also among their immediate forebears. The social attitudes of mates are highly correlated. Over the generations, sibling differences in worldviews become compounded by the process of assortative mating, or "like marrying like." The worldviews endorsed by families are substantially sibling differences in another guise. To explain radical thinking, much of what we need to know are, or once were, sibling differences.

Much of Part Three is devoted to general history. Neither birth order nor family dynamics are responsible for the emergence of radical revolutions in history. But once such social and political upheavals have been set in motion, the family provides a crucial source for the individual differences that fuel them. Distinguishing between behavior that is attributable to personality differences and behavior that arises from other causes, such as sociological or situational influ-

ences, is often difficult. Without the application of scientific criteria, the correct and incorrect hunches of historians cannot easily be differentiated. Methods heretofore employed by historians are excellent for hypothesis generation, but they are inadequate for hypothesis testing. In connection with this study I have computerized more than half a million biographical data points, culled from tens of thousands of biographies. To integrate and analyze so much information, I have availed myself of computer technologies and hypothesis testing. Most people think of science as a subject, such as physics or chemistry. Science is not a subject but a *method*. Much of history can be studied scientifically.[8]

Are the principal sources of rebelliousness the same in social life as they are in science? As an arena for the expression of sibling strategies, politics is complicated by violence. Left-wing terrorism and egalitarianism are very different political inclinations. Historically, such movements reveal correspondingly different characteristics of siblings.

To elucidate the role of family dynamics in political life, I have studied the Protestant Reformation and the French Revolution. These two radical social revolutions provide both a check on my general thesis and a further illumination of it. The best predictors of attitudes toward social change during these two radical events are differences between siblings. The French Revolution is the story of Cain and Abel writ large. To the extent that social class helps to explain the Reign of Terror, it illustrates how and why the shared family background forges such disparate political opinions among siblings.

Conflict between spouses reflects the rules of sibling strife. Most spouses have grown up with siblings and have learned adaptive strategies in their efforts to establish a family niche of their own. Social revolutions bring these sibling differences to the fore. Not every Reformation spouse had the good fortune to marry someone with the same birth order. As a result, Reformation couples often became embroiled over religious and political issues. Henry VIII is not the only husband whose authority was tested by a discontented spouse.

Having embraced the Protestant heresy, some of these royal wives were imprisoned by their husbands. Others met with the executioner's blade. Birth order is an excellent predictor of these marital conflicts, including those experienced by Henry VIII and his six wives.

In the fourth and last part of the book I synthesize my findings about the propensity to rebel. In doing so I wrestle with the highly contingent nature of history. What is unique about history is the diversity of the situations it presents. Human behavior is predictable, but only when the context has been adequately specified. The detection of recurring patterns requires that we give historical context just as much explanatory weight as individual biographical influences. Although historians have rightly appreciated the role of historical context, they have failed to investigate this issue scientifically. Owing to the plethora of interactions between individual dispositions and behavioral contexts, this problem is too complex to be resolved by narrative methods.

Using independent criteria, innovations can be analyzed and classified. Once innovations have been properly classified, they exhibit remarkable cross-revolution consistency in the type of supporters they recruit. In science, firstborns are sympathetic to conservative innovations, which laterborns generally oppose. "Vitalist" doctrines in biology have provided repeated examples of this firstborn predilection. In contrast to conservative innovations, the proposals of radical revolutionaries have typically clashed with accepted social beliefs, especially with prevailing religious dogma. Copernican theory and Darwinism were both radical revolutions, led by laterborns and strenuously opposed by firstborns.

Because different types of revolutions inspire different individual responses by the same person, no single episode of historical change will suffice to explain who will play a leadership role in history. It is essential to study many historical events and to classify these events in terms of their defining features. Once historical events are properly categorized, consistency in human behavior can often be demonstrated.

At the onset of this study, my goal was to explain just one aspect of human behavior—the propensity to rebel. Nothing prepared me for what I encountered. Behavioral solutions to the dilemmas of family life preadapt people to the merits of change. To accept or reject the status quo is a fundamental decision that we must all sometimes make. We first learn to make such decisions within the family. As the great forge of individual tendencies toward revolution and counterrevolution, the family is one of the foremost engines of historical change. In ways that I did not suspect when I began, the causes of rebellion reside within every family. This story is about us all.

Appendix II

How to Test Your Own Propensity to Rebel

The final appendix outlines a formula that can be used to predict any individual's likelihood of supporting radical innovations. The formula builds on the base-rate probabilities given in Table 10. These predicted probabilities are derived from a logistic regression model for the 28 scientific debates in my study. The table specifies the likelihood that an individual will support a radical revolution such as Copernican theory or Darwinism. These probabilities are stratified by age, social attitudes, and birth order.[1]

To determine an individual's base-rate probability, find the applicable category in Table 10. For example, a firstborn who is over the age of sixty and socially conservative has a 3 percent likelihood of endorsing a radical innovation such as Darwinism. A lastborn who is under the age of thirty and who is socially liberal, has a likelihood of acceptance of 96 percent.

These base-rate probabilities may be adjusted to take into account seven additional biographical influences. To the appropriate predicted probability in Table 10, add or subtract the following percentages, depending on an individual's attributes:

1. **Pronounced parent-offspring conflict.** In the case of firstborns who have experienced pronounced conflict with a parent, add 30 percent to the relevant base-rate probability in Table 10. "Pronounced parent-offspring conflict" may be defined as more conflict than is found in four-fifths of the general population. For laterborns who have experienced pronounced parent-offspring conflict, add 10 percent to appropriate base-rate probability in Table 10. For cases in which parent-offspring conflict (or deidentification) is less extreme, but exceeds that observed in two-thirds of the general population, these two adjustments may be halved.

2. **Pronounced shyness.** For firstborns who are shyer than four-fifths of the general population, add 20 percent to the relevant probability in Table 10. For shy lastborns, subtract 15 percent from the appropriate probability in Table 10. Make no adjustment for middle children.

3. **Age gaps between adjacent siblings.** For firstborns whose age gap with their closest sibling is less than 2.0 years or more than 5.0 years, add 5 percent to the base rate probability in Table 10. Only children may consider themselves to be large-age-gap firstborns. For laterborns who are less than 2.0 years younger than their next older sibling, or more than 5.0 years younger, subtract 5 percent from the base-rate probability.

4. **Parental loss and surrogate parenting by older siblings.** If a firstborn has lost a parent before the age of ten and has acted as a surrogate parent toward younger siblings, subtract 15 percent from the base-rate probability in Table 10. If a laterborn has lost a parent before the age of ten and has experienced surrogate parenting by older siblings, add 10 percent to the base-rate probability in Table 10.

5. **Gender.** For females born prior to 1900, add 10 percent to the base-rate probability in Table 10. Recent studies do not show consistent gender differences on openness to ideas.[2] Still, women are more politically liberal than men, and a modest upward adjustment—perhaps 5 percent—seems warranted for women in contemporary populations.

Table 10 Predicted Probabilities of Supporting Radical Conceptual Innovations

A. Base-Rate Probabilities

	Firstborns (Including Only Children)	Middle Children	Lastborns
Individuals under the age of 30			
Social conservatives[a]	14	40	49
Social moderates[a]	48	77	84
Social liberals[a]	75	92	96
Individuals aged 30 to 59			
Social conservatives	6	22	26
Social moderates	25	58	66
Social liberals	52	82	86
Individuals aged 60 and over			
Social conservatives	3	12	15
Social moderates	15	44	50
Social liberals	36	72	76

Enter relevant base rate (A) here: _____ %

B. Adjustments to Base-Rate Probabilities

1. **Pronounced parent-offspring conflict**
   (add 30 percent for firstborns and 10 percent for laterborns)   + _____ %

2. **Pronounced shyness**
   (add 20 percent for firstborns; subtract 15 percent for lastborns)   ± _____ %

3. **Age spacing**
   (add 5 percent for firstborns, for close [0–2.0 years] or distant [more than 5.0 years]
   spacing; subtract 5 percent for laterborns, for close or distant spacing)   ± _____ %

4. **Early parental loss and surrogate parenting**
   (subtract 15 percent for firstborns; add 10 percent for laterborns)   ± _____ %

5. **Gender**
   (for women born before 1900, add 10 percent; for women born after 1900, add 5 percent)   + _____ %

6. **Race and ethnicity**
   (add 10 percent for minorities)   + _____ %

7. **Friendship**
   (add 10 percent for being a close personal friend of a radical innovator)   + _____ %

8. . . . . *Total adjustments from Section B (preliminary)*   _____ %[b]

C. Calculate the absolute difference between 50 percent and the applicable base-rate percentage (from Section A)   _____ %

D. Subtract line C from 50 and divide the result by 50   _____ %

E. Multiply line B.8 by the fraction on line D   _____ %

F. If line E is positive, add line E to Line A
If line E is negative, subtract line E from line A

This is the applicable predicted probability   _____ %

a. For the purposes of this table, social *conservatives* rank in the first quartile of the general population; social *moderates* are in the middle half of the population; and social *liberals* are in the last quartile of the population.

b. No predicted probability can be lower than 0 or higher than 100, so adjustments in Section B need to be modified as Section A base-rate probabilities depart from 50 percent. Suppose that the base-rate probability in Section A is 92 percent, as it is for a young and socially liberal middle child. Suppose also that the total adjustments in Section B sum to +10 percent. The formula for determining the *corrected* adjustment would be line C (92 − 50 = 42), modified by line D, which is (50 − 42)/50, or 8/50, or .16. When the line B.8 adjustment (+10 percent) is multiplied by .16, the corrected adjustment becomes 1.6 percent rather than 10 percent. When this modified adjustment is added to line A (92 percent), the correct predicted probability becomes 93.6 percent.

6. **Race and ethnicity.** For individuals from minority races or ethnic groups—especially those subject to discrimination (for example, blacks and Jews)—add 10 percent to the base-rate probability in Table 10.

7. **Friendship.** If an individual is particularly good friends with the leader of a radical revolution, add 10 percent to the predicted probability in Table 10.

This ten-variable formula for openness to radical innovation mimics the results of a multivariate logistic regression model. One should use common sense in applying this model within any particular behavioral context. For example, during pre-Darwinian debates over evolution, less than a third of the scientific community endorsed this controversial idea. For the scientific population as a whole, the mean rate of acceptance for pre-Darwinian theories of evolution was 30 percent, not 50 percent, as Table 10 assumes.

Applied to the participants of a radical controversy, the formula presented in this appendix will do a good job of rank ordering participants according to their likelihood of acceptance. On average, the base-rate formula in Table 10, Section A, should be 75 percent correct in classifying individuals as supporters or opponents of innovation, as long as the innovation is truly a Radical Ideological Revolution.[3] After making appropriate adjustments to this base-rate prediction in sections B–F, the formula's accuracy should approach 85 percent. Fudging on details will decrease the formula's accuracy.

If you, or someone else, is a clear-cut exception to the formula's prediction, ask yourself *why*. The most likely causes of exceptions will involve some of the influences, including *situational factors*, that are discussed throughout this book. No formula can do complete justice to all of the contingencies that affect human behavior, although formulas can include appropriate adjustments for some of these contingencies.

Addendum to the paperback edition: A few reviewers have noted that I did not divulge my own birth order in the hardback edition of this book. Given that my findings are based on

extensive hypothesis testing conducted over twenty-six years, and given that birth order is only one of the many significant predictors of human behavior that I document in this book, I did not consider this information worth mentioning. Still, to satisfy curiosity, I report here that I am the third of four sons (but a functional lastborn owing to a large gap between myself and my youngest brother). Based on this and other pertinent biographical predictors of radical thinking listed in Table 10, my own propensity to rebel was 96 percent when I began research on this book in 1970.

Notes

1. On age and scientific innovation, see, for example, Hull, Tessner, and Diamond 1978; Blackmore 1978.
2. On Oedipal conflict and radicalism, see Erikson 1958; Wolfenstein 1967; Rejai and Phillips 1979: 175-78; Rejai and Phillips 1983: 151-52.
3. For claims about socioeconomic factors in political change, see Lefebvre 1962-64, 1: 214, 266; Martin 1973: 95; Rejai and Phillips 1979: 97-99; Rejai and Phillips 1983: 75; Soboul 1980:8. On the Protestant Reformation, see Hillerbrand 1973: 38; Spitz 1985: 184; Ozment 1992: 20. On social class and revolutionary tendencies in science, see Shapin 1979b; Cooter 1984: 43-44; Desmond 1989; Desmond and Moore 1992.
4. Quoted in Loomis 1964: 55.
5. Dickens 1989: 51, 220. See also Scarisbrick 1968: 508; Kelley 1981:78.
6. For useful reviews of the research on sibling differences, see Plomin and Daniels 1987; Dunn and Plomin 1990.
7. On birth order and reproductive success, see Duby 1978; Boone 1986: 869; MacDonald 1991. On birth order and infanticide, see Scrimshaw 1978, 1984; Hrdy 1987. On sibling conflict in history, see Daly and Wilson 1988a: 30, who note that feudal royalty supplies "a seemingly endless tale of fraternal bloodletting."
8. One reason why historians have been able to dispense with formal hypothesis testing is that people do not generally die as a result of bad history. In the medical sciences, untested assertions about the benefits of a new drug, leading to its premature use on patients, would constitute malpractice. Still, it does not take a loss of life to demonstrate that, as a method of testing hypotheses, objective procedures are preferable to narrative modes of evalution (Faust 1984).

Notes to Appendix II

1. The predicted probabilities listed in Table 10 are based on a logistic regression

model that includes complete biographical data on 1,436 participants in 28 scientific controversies (1543–1967). The model includes four significant main effects: age, social attitudes, relative birth rank, and ideological implications of the innovation. The model also includes three significant two-way interaction effects: ideological implications by age; ideological implications by social attitudes; and ideological implications by relative birth rank. All main effects are statistically significant at $p < .0001$, and the interaction effects are statistically significant at $p < .005$. The two-way interaction effects reflect the fact that age, social attitudes, and relative birth are all significantly better predictors of receptivity in proportion to the radicalism of the innovation.

Predicted probabilities in Table 10 are listed only for those scientific controversies that involved radical ideological implications. For this class of controversies, the model's predictors yield a multiple correlation with observed radicalism of .50 ($df = 1/582$, $t = 13.46$, $p < 1$ in a billion; 75.2 percent correct classifications, based on the 2×2 table of observed versus predicted outcomes). For participants in Technical Revolutions and Controversial Innovations, the multiple correlation is .31 ($df = 1/482$, $t = 6.38$, $p < 1$ in a billion; 69.0 percent correct classifications). For scientists who debated Conservative Theories, the multiple correlation is: .10 ($df = 1/366$; $t = 1.88$, $p < .06$; 59.2 percent correct classifications). The chance rate for correct classifications is 50.4 percent.

2. On studies of gender and openness to ideas, see Feingold 1994.
3. For Technical Revolutions and Controversial Innovations, approximate probabilities derived from the model may be calculated as follows. For conservative firstborns, multiply the base-rate probability in Table 10 by 5.0. For socially moderate firstborns, multiply the base-rate probability by 1.8. For radical firstborns, multiply the base-rate probability by 1.2. For middleborns and lastborns who are social conservatives, multiply the base-rate probability by 1.8. For middleborns and lastborns who are social moderates or liberals, multiply the base-rate probability by 1.1. In debates over Conservative Theories, firstborns and social conservatives are more likely than their counterparts to endorse new ideas. Although young people are more likely to endorse Conservative Theories, the role of age is significantly less predictive than it is during liberal innovations.

 Article Review Form at end of book.

How does their vision of the consistency of personality match with your experience and that of those people you know well? What aspects of personality seem most open to change and which least?

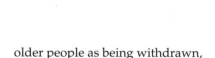

The Stability of Personality

Observations and evaluations

**Robert R. McCrae
and Paul T. Costa, Jr.**

"There is an optical illusion about every person we meet," Ralph Waldo Emerson wrote in his essay on "Experience":

In truth, they are all creatures of given temperament, which will appear in a given character, whose boundaries they will never pass: but we look at them, they seem alive, and we presume there is impulse in them. In the moment it seems impulse; in the year, in the lifetime, it turns out to be a certain uniform tune which the revolving barrel of the music-box must play.[1]

In his brief passage, Emerson anticipated modern findings about the stability of personality and pointed out an illusion to which both laypersons and psychologists are prone. He was also perhaps the first to decry personality stability as the enemy of freedom, creativity, and growth, objecting that "temperament puts all divinity to rout." In this article, we summarize evidence in support of Emerson's observations but offer arguments against his evaluation of them.[2]

Evidence for the Stability of Adult Personality

Emerson used the term *temperament* to refer to the basic tendencies of the individual, dispositions that we call *personality traits*. It is these traits, measured by such instruments as the Minnesota Multiphasic Personality Inventory and the NEO Personality Inventory, that have been investigated in a score of longitudinal studies over the past 20 years. Despite a wide variety of samples, instruments, and designs, the results of these studies have been remarkably consistent, and they are easily summarized.

1. The mean levels of personality traits change with development, but each final adult levels at about age 30. Between 20 and 30, both men and women become somewhat less emotional and thrill-seeking and somewhat more cooperative and self-disciplined—changes we might interpret as evidence of increased maturity. After age 30, there are few and subtle changes, of which the most consistent is a small decline in activity level with advancing age. Except among individuals with dementia, stereotypes that depict older people as being withdrawn, depressed, or rigid are unfounded.

2. Individual differences in personality traits, which show at least some continuity from early childhood on, are also essentially fixed by age 30. Stability coefficients (test-retest correlations over substantial time intervals) are typically in the range of .60 to .80, even over intervals of as long as 30 years, although there is some decline in magnitude with increasing retest interval. Given that most personality scales have short-term retest reliabilities in the range from .70 to .90, it is clear that by far the greatest part of the reliable variance (i.e., variance not due to measurement error) in personality traits is stable.

3. Stability appears to characterize all five of the major domains of personality—neuroticism, extraversion, openness to experience, agreeableness, and conscientiousness. This finding suggests that an adult's personality profile as a whole will change little over time, and studies of the stability of configural measures of personality support that view.

American Psychological Society (This article was written by government employees. The U.S. government holds copyright.)

McCrae, R.R., and Costa, Jr., P.T. (1994). "The Stability of Personality: Observations and Evaluations." *Current Directions in Psychological Science*, 3, 173–175.

4. Generalizations about stability apply to virtually everyone. Men and women, healthy and sick people, blacks and whites all show the same pattern. When asked, most adults will say that their personality has not changed much in adulthood, but even those who claim to have had major changes show little objective evidence of change on repeated administrations of personality questionnaires. Important exceptions to this generalization include people suffering from dementia and certain categories of psychiatric patients who respond to therapy, but no moderators of stability among healthy adults have yet been identified.[3]

When researchers first began to publish these conclusions, they were greeted with considerable skepticism—"I distrust the facts and the inferences" Emerson had written—and many studies were designed to test alternative hypotheses. For example, some researchers contended that consistent responses to personality questionnaires were due to memory of past responses, but retrospective studies showed that people could not accurately recall how they had previously responded even when instructed to do so. Other researchers argued that temporal consistency in self-reports merely meant that individuals had a fixed idea of themselves, a crystallized self-concept that failed to keep pace with real changes in personality. But studies using spouse and peer raters showed equally high levels of stability.[4]

The general conclusion that personality traits are stable is now widely accepted. Some researchers continue to look for change in special circumstances and populations; some attempt to account for stability by examining genetic and environmental influences on personality. Finally, others take the view that there is much more to personality than traits, and seek to trace the adult developmental course of personality perceptions or identify formation or life narratives.

These latter studies are worthwhile, because people undoubtedly do change across the life span. Marriages end in divorce, professional careers are started in mid-life, fashions and attitudes change with the times. Yet often the same traits can be seen in new guises: Intellectual curiosity merely shifts from one field to another, avid gardening replaces avid tennis, one abusive relationship is followed by another. Many of these changes are best regarded as variations on the "uniform tune" played by individuals' enduring dispositions.

Illusory Attributions in Temporal Perspective

Social and personality psychologists have debated for some time the accuracy of attributions of the causes of behavior to persons or situations. The "optical illusion" in person perception that Emerson pointed to was somewhat different. He felt that people attribute behavior to the live and spontaneous person who freely creates responses to the situation, when in fact behavior reveals only the mechanical operation of lifeless and static temperament. We may (and we will!) take exception to this disparaging, if common, view of traits, but we must first concur with the basic observation that personality processes often appear different when viewed in longitudinal perspective: "The years teach much which the days never know."

Consider happiness. If one asks individuals why they are happy or unhappy, they are almost certain to point to environmental circumstances of the moment: a rewarding job, a difficult relationship, a threat to health, a new car. It would seem that levels of happiness ought to mirror quality of life, and that changes in circumstances would result in changes in subjective well-being. It would be easy to demonstrate this pattern in a controlled laboratory experiment: Give subjects $1,000 each and ask how they feel!

But survey researchers who have measured the objective quality of life by such indicators as wealth, education, and health find precious little association with subjective well-being, and longitudinal researchers have found surprising stability in individual differences in happiness, even among people whose life circumstances have changed markedly. The explanation is simple: People adapt to their circumstances rapidly, getting used to the bad and taking for granted the good. In the long run, happiness is largely a matter of enduring personality traits:[5] "Temper prevails over everything of time, place, and condition, and . . . fix[es] the measure of activity and of enjoyment."

A few years ago, William Swann and Craig Hill provided an ingenious demonstration of the errors to which too narrow a temporal perspective can lead. A number of experiments had shown that it was relatively easy to induce changes in the self-concept by providing self-discrepant feedback. Introverts told that they were really extraverts rated themselves higher in extraversion than they had before. Such studies supported the view that the self-concept is highly malleable, a mirror of the evolution of the immediate environment.

Swann and Hill replicated this finding, but extended it by inviting subjects back a few days later. By that time, the effects of the manipulation had disappeared, and subjects had returned to their initial self-concepts. The implication is that any one-shot experiment may give a seriously misleading view of personality processes.[6]

The relations between coping and adaptation provide a final example. Cross-sectional studies show that individuals who use such coping mechanisms as self-blame, wishful thinking, and hostile reactions toward other people score lower on measures of well-being than people who do not use these mechanisms. It would be easy to infer that these coping mechanisms detract from adaptation, and in fact the very people who use them admit that they are ineffective. But the correlations vanish when the effects of prior neuroticism scores are removed; an alternative interpretation of the data is thus that individuals who score high on this personality factor use poor coping strategies and also have low well-being: The association between coping and well-being may be entirely attributable to this third variable.[7]

Psychologists have long been aware of the problems of inferring causes from correlational data, but they have not recognized the pervasiveness of the bias that Emerson warned about. People tend to understand behavior and experience as the result of the immediate context, whether intrapsychic or environmental. Only by looking over time can one see the persistent effects of personality traits.

The Evaluation of Stability

If few findings in psychology are more robust than the stability of personality, even fewer are more unpopular. Gerontologists often see stability as an affront to their commitment to continuing adult development; psychotherapists sometimes view it as an alarming challenge to their ability to help patients;[8] humanistic psychologists and transcendental philosophers think it degrades human nature. A popular account in *The Idaho Statesman* ran under the disheartening headline "Your Personality—You're Stuck With It."

In our view, these evaluations are based on misunderstandings: At worst, stability is a mixed blessing. Those individuals who are anxious, quarrelsome, and lazy might be understandably distressed to think that they are likely to stay that way, but surely those who are imaginative, affectionate, and carefree at age 30 should be glad to hear that they will probably be imaginative, affectionate, and carefree at age 90.

Because personality is stable, life is to some extent predictable. People can make vocational and retirement choices with some confidence that their current interests and enthusiasms will not desert them. They can choose friends and mates with whom they are likely to remain compatible. They can vote on the basis of candidates' records, with some assurance that future policies will resemble past ones. They can learn which co-workers they can depend on, and which they cannot. The personal and social utility of personality stability is enormous.

But it is precisely this predictability that so offends many critics. ("I had fancied that the value of life lay in its inscrutable possibilities," Emerson complained.) These critics view traits as mechanical and static habits and believe that the stability of personality traits dooms human beings to lifeless monotony as puppets controlled by inexorable forces. This is a misunderstanding on several levels.

First, personality traits are not repetitive habits, but inherently dynamic dispositions that interact with the opportunities and challenges of the moment.[9] Antagonistic people do not yell at everyone; some people they flatter, some they scorn, some they threaten. Just as the same intelligence is applied to a lifetime of changing problems, so the same personality traits can be expressed in an infinite variety of ways, each suited to the situation.

Second, there are such things as spontaneity and impulse in human life, but they are stable traits. Individuals who are open to experience actively seek out new places to go, provocative ideas to ponder, and exotic sights, sounds, and tastes to experience. Extraverts show a different kind of spontaneity, making friends, seeking thrills, and jumping at every chance to have a good time. People who are introverted and closed to experience have more measured and monotonous lives, but this is the kind of life they choose.

Finally, personality traits are not inexorable forces that control our fate, nor are they, in psychodynamic language, ego alien. Our traits characterize us; they are our very selves;[10] we act most freely when we express our enduring dispositions. Individuals sometimes fight against their own tendencies, trying perhaps to overcome shyness or curb a bad temper. But most people acknowledge even these feelings as their own, and it is well that they do. A person's recognition of the inevitability of his or her one and only personality is a large part of what Erik Erikson called ego *integrity*, the culminating wisdom of a lifetime.

Notes

1. All quotations are from "Experience," in *Essays: First and Second Series*, R. W. Emerson (Vintage, New York, 1990) (original work published 1844).
2. For recent and sometimes divergent treatments of this topic, see R. R. McCrae and P. T. Costa, Jr., *Personality in Adulthood* (Guilford, New York, 1990); D. C. Funder, R. D. Parke, C. Tomlinson-Keasey, and K. Widaman, Eds., *Studying Lives Through Time: Personality and Development* (American Psychological Association, Washington, DC, 1993); T. Heatherton and J. Weinberger, *Can Personality Change?* (American Psychological Association, Washington, DC, 1994).
3. I. C. Siegler, K. A. Welsh, D. V. Dawson, G. G. Fillenbaum, N. L. Earl, E. B. Kaplan, and C. M. Clark, Ratings of personality change in patients being evaluated for memory disorders, *Alzheimer Disease and Associated Disorders, 5,* 240–250 (1991); R. M. A. Hirschfeld, G. L. Klerman, P. Clayton, M. B. Keller, P. McDonald-Scott, and B. Larkin, Assessing personality: Effects of depressive state on trait measurement, *American Journal of Psychiatry, 140,* 695–699 (1983); R. R. McCrae, Moderated analyses of longitudinal personality stability, *Journal of Personality and Social Psychology, 65,* 577–585 (1993).
4. D. Woodruff, The role of memory in personality continuity: A 25 year follow-up, *Experimental Aging Research, 9,* 31–34 (1983); P. T. Costa, Jr., and R. R. McCrae, Trait psychology comes of age, in *Nebraska Symposium on Motivation: Psychology and Aging,* T. B. Sonderegger, Ed. (University of Nebraska Press, Lincoln, 1992).
5. P. T. Costa, Jr., and R. R. McCrae, Influence of extraversion and neuroticism on subjective well-being: Happy and unhappy people, *Journal of Personality and Social Psychology, 38,* 668–678 (1980).
6. The study is summarized in W. B. Swann, Jr., and C. A. Hill, When our identities are mistaken: Reaffirming self-conceptions through social interactions, *Journal of Personality and Social Psychology, 43,* 59–66 (1982). Dangers of single-occasion research are also discussed in J. R. Council, Context effects in personality research, *Current Directions in Psychological Science, 2,* 31–34 (1993).
7. R. R. McCrae and P. T. Costa, Jr., Personality, coping, and coping effectiveness in an adult-sample, *Journal of Personality, 54,* 385–405 (1986).
8. Observations in nonpatient samples show what happens over time under typical life circumstances; they do not rule out the possibility that psychotherapeutic interventions can change personality. Whether or not such change is possible, in practice much of psychotherapy consists of helping people learn to live with their limitations, and this may be a more realistic goal than "cure" for many patients. See P. T. Costa, Jr., and R. R. McCrae, Personality stability and its implications for clinical psychology, *Clinical Psychology Review, 6,* 407–423 (1986).
9. A. Tellegen, Personality traits: Issues of definition, evidence and assessment, in *Thinking Clearly About Psychology: Essays in Honor of Paul E. Meehl,* Vol. 2, W. Grove and D. Cicchetti, Eds. (University of Minnesota Press, Minneapolis, 1991).
10. R. R. McCrae and P. T. Costa, Jr., Age, personality, and the spontaneous self-concept, *Journals of Gerontology: Social Sciences, 43,* S177–S185 (1988).

 Article Review Form at end of book.

WiseGuide Wrap-Up

- People change and develop over the course of their lives as they face new challenges and tasks. Erikson and others suggest this development has a typical pattern within each culture.

- Major social changes can have an impact on the personalities of those who live through them. Life-altering events include negative historical events, such as the Great Depression and World War II, and positive social changes, such as the Civil Rights and Women's Movements.

- Our propensity to rebel against authority may be shaped by our place in the family structure. Each child in a family needs to define his or her "niche" in the family, and the niches we find tend to fall into patterns depending on whether we were firstborns, secondborns, later-borns, or the "baby" of the family.

- Some aspects of personality show considerable consistency across the lifecourse and show enormous consistency after age 30 for most people. Such consistency is most likely found in broadly defined characteristics, such as our sociability or tendency to be nervous or stressed.

R.E.A.L. Sites

This list provides a print preview of typical coursewise R.E.A.L. sites. There are over 100 such sites at the courselinks™ site.) The danger in printing URLs is that web sites can change overnight. As we went to press, these sites were functional using the URLs provided. If you come across one that isn't, please let us know via email to: webmaster@coursewise.com. Use your Passport to access the most current list of R.E.A.L. sites at the courselinks™ site.

Site name: The Personality Project

URL: http://fas.psych.nwu.edu/personality.html

Why is it R.E.A.L.? This is a primary web site in personality psychology. In provides an overview of theories, recent key articles, and links to just about everything in personality. You'll find links to web sites of individual researchers and labs around the country, as well as information and links to personality-related societies and graduate programs. It offers useful advice to students on a number of topics.

Key topics: personality theories

Site name: Laboratory of Personality and Cognition

URL: http://lpcwww.grc.nia.nih.gov/

Why is it R.E.A.L.? This is the home web site of Paul Costa's lab at the National Institutes of Health. It provides lots of information on his team's research in the areas of personality and adult development, aging, health and well-being, and predictors of intellectual competence and decline. This is a good resource for work in this area.

Key topics: personality consistency, personality change, adult development

section

5

Learning Objectives

- Learn how and why some personality psychologists find it useful to describe people's personalities in terms of the goals that motivate their behavior rather than the behavior itself.

- Describe how political leaders' personalities shape their approach to world crises.

- Understand how—for some people—thinking negatively can be an effective strategy for doing well.

Personality and Motivation

 **WiseGuide Intro**

What motivates people to behave as they do? This is one of the central questions asked by personality psychologists. Many believe that, if you look for the motivation(s) underlying someone's behavior, rather than simply paying attention to the behavior itself, you will have a better understanding of the person. Looking at what people are trying to accomplish through their behavior can provide a means of making sense of the contradictions in their personalities or behavior. However, you don't have to be a personality psychologist to want to understand why people behave the way they do. All of us have been puzzled at one time or another by the behavior of another person—why does this person always see the things that can go wrong in any situation? Why does that person alienate everyone? Why is this other person always trying to help everyone she meets—even virtual strangers? The articles in this section provide a sampling of some of the work done by personality psychologists whose focus is making sense of behavior that doesn't always seem to make sense. They do this by trying to understand the underlying motivations for people's behavior and how people strategically plan how to best achieve their goals.

Winter's article, "Power, Affiliation, and War," introduces an approach to understanding personality that focuses on discerning the central, or "core," motivations that influence one's behavior and the choices one makes. He then reports how one can measure these central motivation themes in the public statements, writings, and speeches of political leaders. In particular, he assesses whether political leaders are more motivated by a desire to control and have power over others or to have others like him or her. Finally, he demonstrates how we can see these underlying motivational themes of power or affiliation needs guiding the behavior of political leaders. We often assume that political leaders are making choices based on some political ideals or on their conceptions of what is best for the country. Winter proposes that we can understand the outcomes of historical crises, such as the Cuban Missile Crisis or World War II, in terms of the motivation themes in the personalities of the political leaders at the time. Currently, debates are raging about the role that "character" should play in the choosing of political leaders, and this article may provide you with a new way of thinking about the "character" issues in politics. As this book is being written, a committee in the House of Representatives is meeting to decide whether to start impeachment hearings for President Clinton. As you read Winter's article, reflect on how you would characterize President Clinton's "core," or central, motivational themes, using the ideas described in the article. Then, you might speculate about how such motivations can be seen in the actions he has taken as president.

This section of the reader also includes an interview with Dr. Julie Norem, entitled "The Power of Negative Thinking." Norem has studied the strategies people use to motivate themselves to perform well in situations that they deem important. In this interview, she outlines two successful strategies—called defensive pessimism and strategic optimism—that people use to manage their anxiety before an important performance, such as an exam, a date, or a race. With one strategy, people think about all the things that can possibly go wrong in a given situation and systematically work to eliminate each one. In fact, they actually exacerbate their fears and use this fear to energize themselves in order to overprepare, and in this overpreparation they ensure their success. Interfering with their ability to think about all that can go wrong can actually impair their performance! Other people—called strategic optimists—spend considerable effort avoiding having to think about any possible problems that could arise. If you make strategic optimists think about all that could go wrong, they end up worrying too much and then don't perform well. See if you recognize yourself and your friends in Dr. Norem's descriptions.

Questions

Reading 16. How can Kennedy's actions in the Cuban Missile Crisis be understood in terms of his personality? How would you characterize the personality of the current president in terms of the motivational themes Winter noted here?

Reading 17. How can negative thinking motivate some people? What might be a cost of using such a strategy to motivate yourself over the long run?

How can Kennedy's actions in the Cuban Missile Crisis be understood in terms of his personality? How would you characterize the personality of the current president in terms of the motivational themes Winter noted here?

Power, Affiliation, and War

Three tests of a motivational model

David G. Winter

From previous research, a model relating war outbreak to a pattern of high power motivation and low affiliation motivation is developed and tested by content analysis of (a) historical materials from over 300 years of British history (b) British-German communications at the outbreak of World War I, and (c) United States-Soviet communications during the Cuban Missile Crisis. In all 3 studies, observed motive patterns in relation to war-versus-peace outcomes support the essential features of the model. Furthermore, wars once underway end only after power motivation drops and not after affiliation increases. Finally, ending of wars is followed by declines in power and achievement motivation. Alternative interpretations of the results are discussed and further, multivariate research is outlined.

What are the psychological dynamics of war and peace? Why do some crises lead to war, whereas others are peacefully resolved? This article outlines a model, first introduced by McClelland (1975, chap. 9), that specifies the power and affiliation motives as psychological causes of war and peace. The model is then tested in three ways: (a) with content analysis of historical documents over almost 4 centuries of British history, then with a comparative content analysis of government-to-government communications in (b) a crisis that led to war and (c) a crisis that was peacefully resolved.

Explaining War

Of course in answering these questions one must not overstate the case for the effects of psychological factors. History is an interactive game with many players, with rules and even the shape of the game table set by forces beyond individual political actors: geography, history, economics, political structures, culture, perhaps even biology (Groebel & Hinde, 1989; Nelson & Olin, 1979). For all of their power, however, these forces do not operate in a psychological vacuum. The historian Joll (1968) stressed the importance of studying people's "unspoken assumptions" or "mentalities," because "it is only by studying the minds of men that we shall understand the causes of anything" (p. 24). Given the many proximal and distal "causes" of war, there

is surely blame enough to go around. If psychology cannot discover every cause of war, it can at least explain some of the variance.

Comparing Two Crises

To set the stage for the research reported in this article, it is useful to recall some basic facts about two 20th-century crises, one that led to a world war and one that was peacefully resolved. Looking backward from the present time, these results may seem inevitable; looking forward from the time of these crises, however, they were not.

1914

On June 28, 1914, Archduke Franz Ferdinand, heir to the Habsburg throne, and his wife Sophie were shot and killed while touring the Bosnian city of Sarajevo. For a few weeks thereafter, nothing much seemed to happen. Assassinations—even of royalty and heads of state—have become a familiar story by 1914, and so after dutiful coverage of the funeral, newspapers in London and Berlin focused on more traditional news. Only a few years before, Norman Angell's (1910)

Winter, David G., "Power, Affiliation, and War: Three Tests of a Motivational Model." *Journal of Personality and Social Psychology*, 65, 532–545.

The Great Illusion had "proved" that a major European War was economically impossible.

Yet within 6 weeks, almost all of Europe was at war, caught up in a mood of exhilaration that did not spare even the most marginalized and alienated intellectual (Morton, 1989).[1] The endless carnage lasted more than 4 years, leading eventually to a second world war and even (through the breakup of the Ottoman Empire) reverberating today in the Balkans and in the Persian Gulf.

Why? At the time, few participants seemed to have any understanding of how the war came about. In his memoirs, Prince von Bülow (1932) recorded a conversation with German Chancellor Theobald von Bethmann-Hollweg in early August 1914:

> Bethmann stood in the centre of the room. Shall I ever forget his face, the look in his eyes! . . . At last I said to him: "Well, tell me, at least, how it all happened." He raised his long, thin arms to heaven and answered in a dull, exhausted voice: "Oh—if I only knew! [*Ja, wer das wüsst!*]." (pp. 165–166)

1962

At 7 p.m. on October 22, 1962, United States President John F. Kennedy announced to a nationwide television audience that Soviet offensive missiles had been detected in Cuba. He proclaimed a blockade (or "quarantine") of Cuba, demanded immediate removal of the missiles, and concluded with a chilling threat:

> It shall be the policy of this nation to regard any nuclear missile launched from Cuba against any nation in the Western hemisphere as an attack by the Soviet Union on the United States, requiring a full retaliatory response upon the Soviet Union. (Sorenson, 1965, p. 700)

During the next few days, the Soviet Embassy in Washington began burning its archives, United States Secretary of Defense Robert McNamara wondered whether October 27 might be the last Saturday he would ever see (Blight & Welch,

1989, pp. 75, 88), and President Kennedy estimated the chances of nuclear war as "somewhere between one out of three and even" (Sorenson, 1965, p. 705).[2] Yet for all the dangers, on this occasion World War III did not begin. Why not?

Psychological Explanations of War

A survey of the personality and social psychology research literature suggests several variables that might lead to conflict escalation and war: motives such as the aggressive or death instincts (Freud, 1930/1961), pride (Frank, 1986), and relative deprivation (Crosby, 1976; Davies, 1969); perceptions and misperceptions of one's enemy, one's own mortality, the balance of power, and the consequences of actions (Jervis, 1976; Lebow, 1981; White, 1984); oversimplified cognitive processing (Suedfeld & Tetlock, 1977; Suedfeld, Tetlock, & Ramirez, 1977); false heuristics (Jervis, 1976; Kahneman & Tversky, 1973; Neustadt & May, 1986); deleterious effects of stress on judgment (Holsti, 1972); certain influence and bargaining strategies (Leng & Walker, 1982; Leng & Wheeler, 1979); and the "social trap" phenomenon (Brockner & Rubin, 1985; Teger, Cary, Katcher, & Hillis, 1980), when leaders feel they have "too much invested to quit."

This article focuses on the power and affiliation motives as two personality characteristics that may be related to the social outcomes of war and peace. After a brief review of the relevant personality and political psychology research literature, I present a model based on studies by McClelland (1975, chap. 9) relating motives to social outcomes. I then use data drawn from the content analysis of historical documents, in which motives are measured "at a

distance," to carry out three tests of the model.

Power and Affiliation Motives

The strivings for power and affiliation consistently emerge as two major dimensions of human motivation, from the speculation of the pre-Socratic philosopher Empedocles, who saw history as a battle between forces of strife and forces of love, down to the modern motive catalogue of Murray (1938), who included several aspects of power (dominance, exhibition, aggression, and perhaps nurturance) along with affiliation in his catalogue of human motives. Recent studies using circumplex models (Conte & Plutchik, 1981; Freedman, Leary, Ossorio, & Coffey, 1951; Wiggins, 1980), hierarchical cluster analysis (Wicker, Lambert, Richardson, & Kohler, 1984), as well as ethnopsychology analysis (Kornadt, Eckensberger, & Emminghaus, 1980) confirm the near universal importance of these two dimensions of human motivation.

Using the McClelland–Atkinson method of experimental arousal (see Atkinson, 1958; Smith, 1992), Veroff (1957), along with Uleman (1972), and finally Winter (1973), developed and refined a system for scoring power motivation in thematic apperception. Atkinson, Heyns, and Veroff (1954) developed a similar measure of affiliation motivation to which McAdams (1982) has since added a related measure of the intimacy motive. Recently, Winter (1991a) adapted these systems (along with that for scoring the achievement motive) for use with fiction, speeches, interview transcripts, and in fact almost any other kind of imaginative verbal material.

Laboratory Studies of Power and Affiliation

Several years of laboratory research give a detailed portrait of people who score high in the power motive (Winter, 1973; Winter & Stewart, 1978; see also McClelland, 1985, chap. 8). They are concerned about having impact on other people. They seek and

---

[1]Thus, in the first weeks of the war, Freud wrote to his disciple Ferenczi that "all my libido is given to Austria-Hungary" (Jones, 1953–1957, Vol. 2, p. 192).

[2]This estimate is supported by recent revelations of accidental complications and misperceptions that could well have triggered a nuclear exchange; for example, the presence of undetected short-range nuclear missiles that the local Soviet commander in Cuba was authorized to use (Allyn & Blight, 1992; Allyn et al., 1989; Blight & Welch, 1989; Garthoff, 1989, Oberdorfer, 1992).

get formal social power. They are concerned about prestige. As leaders and managers, they are able to create an inspirational work climate, or charisma, that motivates subordinates (McClelland & Burnham, 1976) so that they are often successful managers (McClelland & Boyatzis, 1982; Winter, 1991b). Of course power-seeking people also have their negative side. In negotiating and bargaining they are confrontational and exploitative (Schnackers & Kleinbeck, 1975; Terhune, 1968). When they lack a sense of responsibility, especially, they engage in a variety of "profligate," impulsive actions such as drinking and drug use, risk taking, sexual exploitation, and verbal and physical aggression. (This is true for both women and men; see Winter, 1988; Winter & Barenbaum, 1985). At the physiological level, the power motive is linked to sympathetic nervous system arousal (McClelland, 1982), which suggests that it may be the cognitive-motivational superstructure of the body's fight-or-flight behavior system, with roots in human primordial adaptive tendencies.

The affiliation and intimacy motives involve a concern for warm and close relations with other people. They are associated with cooperative and friendly behavior, at least when the situation is perceived as "safe." McAdams (1985) suggested that these two motives can act as a check on power motivation by channeling concerns for control and influence into more prosocial, nurturant directions. (For convenience, the affiliation-intimacy motives are referred to simply as the *affiliation motive*).

Power and Affiliation Motives and Theories About War

There are many grounds for believing that the power and affiliation motives may be associated with the social outcomes of violence, aggression, and war. Many of the aggressive, profligate behaviors of power-motivated people (discussed above) are either individual analogues to war or else concomitants of war, whereas the friendly and cooperative behavior of affiliation-

motivated people is an individual analogue to peace seeking.

In theoretical terms, the power motive seems closely related to many classical motivelike concepts invoked to explain war (see Nelson & Olin, 1979, pp. 17–23). Clausewitz's (1831/1962) famous definition of *war* as "an act of force to compel our adversary to do our will" (p. 63) is practically a paraphrase of the scoring definition for power motivation. Other cognate concepts include "destructive" or "death instincts" (Freud, 1933/1964, pp. 210–211), "honor" (Frank, 1986), the "ways of power" (Schmookler, 1984, chap. 1), and "symbolic commitment" (Sullivan, 1979). Even more "cognitive" motives such as the desire for justice or the feeling of relative deprivation (Crosby, 1976; Davies, 1969) may involve an implicit power motive, which increases the sense of deservingness or entitlement, hence feelings of resentment and envy, and consequently concerns for "justice" (see Grupp, 1975; Winter & Stewart, 1978, p. 415).[3]

Political Psychology Studies

Given these theoretical considerations, it is not surprising that at-a-distance empirical studies of political leaders have found direct links between power motivation and war, on the one hand, and affiliation motivation and peace, on the other. In a study of American presidents, using motive scores from first inaugural addresses, Winter (1973, 1991a)

[3]For example, one long-term cause of World War I was clearly Germany's rapid economic growth in the last decades of the 19th century and the difficulties of achieving a commensurate colonial empire and political influence in Europe—or, as German chancellor Bethmann-Hollweg put it, that "today [Germany] needs a place in the sun" (quoted in Jarausch, 1973, p. 145). For such economic-political comparisons to lead to war, however, one must further assume a widespread feeling among the Germans that such imperial influence was "deserved" (as well as feelings among the French, British, and Russians that it was not). Economic growth may stimulate a desire for power, but it does not always do so. Thus, the Dutch and Swiss were content to use money to make more money rather than to expand their territories (cf. Schama, 1987).

found a significant correlation between presidential power motivation and United States entry into war during that president's administration. Presidential affiliation motivation, in contrast, predicted arms control agreements. Among a heterogeneous group of 22 southern Africa political leaders, power motivation was related to expert judges' ratings of "warlike disposition" or the "propensity to resort to violence" (Winter, 1980).

Among 45 heads of state, Hermann (1980b) found significant relationships between power motivation and pursuit of an independent (rather than interdependent) foreign policy and between affiliation motivation and an interdependent foreign policy. In a study of members of the Soviet Politburo during the mid-1970s, Hermann (1980a) found that those members favoring detente scored high in affiliation and low in power.

At the collective level, McClelland (1975, pp. 325–328) found that internal violence and political instability flourished in countries where affiliation was low and power high.

Taken together, all of these laboratory and at-a-distance findings suggest the hypothesis that war is positively related to power motivation and (with somewhat less confidence) negatively related to affiliation motivation. The rest of this article is devoted to a systematic exploration of this hypothesis using motives measured at a distance.

A Model of Motivation and Social Outcomes

McClelland's Historical Studies

Over the past 3 decades, McClelland (1961, 1975) has pioneered the application of motivation measures to cultural documents—stories in childrens' readers, popular fiction, or diaries—to estimate motive levels of groups, nations, or other collectivities (see Inkeles & Levinson, 1969, for a review of this and other methods of measuring collective personality or national character). In two research

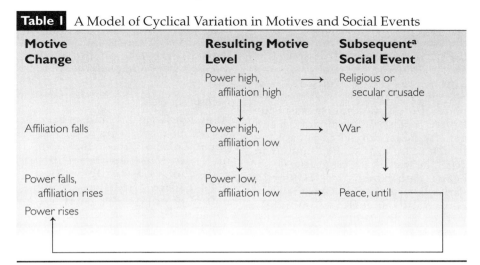

Table 1 A Model of Cyclical Variation in Motives and Social Events

Motive Change	Resulting Motive Level	Subsequent[a] Social Event
	Power high, affiliation high	Religious or secular crusade
Affiliation falls	Power high, affiliation low	War
Power falls, affiliation rises	Power low, affiliation low	Peace, until
Power rises		

Note. Table is based on studies by McClelland (1975, chap. 9).
[a]After a lag of 10–20 years.

studies using these methods, McClelland (1975, chap. 9) suggested some complex psychohistorical links between levels of motivation as measured in popular literature and two kinds of subsequent social events: secular "crusades" and war. Both studies involved a rather crude, macrocosmic focus. A study of British history from 1550 through 1800 used the half century as the unit of measurement and analysis, whereas a study of the United States from 1780 through 1969, used the decade. Table 1 shows a more formal model constructed from these suggested links. In the figure, the solid arrows represent autonomous development of the motivation levels and the social trends, and the dashed arrows represent hypothetized causal connections form motivation to social events.

In explicating this model, we begin at Step 1 in the resulting-motive-level column, with both power and affiliation motives at high levels. McClelland (1975) observed that such a motive pattern, involving as it does both a desire to have impact (power) and a concern with others' welfare and friendship (affiliation), leads after a decade or so to movements of social reform, such as Jacksonian populism, the New Deal, the Civil Rights movement in the United States, or the Puritan and Methodist movements in Great Britain. What happens next? McClelland (1975) suggested that affiliation motivation typically declines, whereas power re-

mains high (Step 2). At the social level, this pattern typically leads to war a decade or so later. After a war, McClelland suggested that affiliation rises and power declines (1975, p. 348). This leads to peace (Step 3), which lasts until power again rises; then the cycle starts again.

Perhaps the most essential feature of this model is that war follows from a motivational pattern of high power and low affiliation. In this article I carry out three tests of this feature, using historical data of different kinds from different nations and historical eras and with different units of time (ranging from a year down to a few days). In its original form, the model used long, imprecise, and variable units of time (a half century or a decade), nonsystematic definitions of *social reform* and *war,* and imprecise changing lags from the time at which motives were measured to the time when social outcomes occurred. The present research uses more precise definitions and smaller, more systematic units of time. Metaphorically, it can be thought of as a series of increasingly precise examinations of the model, through a series of "lenses" of increasing sharpness of focus and resolving power.

In the first test, motive levels from a series of British government documents—the Sovereign's Speech from the Throne spanning the years from 1603 to 1988—are related to occurrences of war in British history. The other two tests involve analysis

of government-to-government communications during two crises—Great Britain and Germany during the outbreak of World War I in 1914 and the United States and the Soviet Union during the Cuban Missile Crisis in 1962. Because the latter crisis did not lead to war, it is an especially important discriminant test of the model.

"Motives" of Collectivities

Because all three studies involve scoring motive imagery in documents produced by collectivities, some discussion of the nature and meaning of these scores is appropriate. Individual persons are said to have motives, but what do researchers mean by the motives of collectivities or groups? Individuals' motives are usually conceptualized as stable dispositions or propensities for becoming aroused by certain classes of stimuli or incentives (e.g., power, affiliation, and achievement); thus, in particular situations, motives may be variably aroused (see Atkinson, 1982; Winter, 1973, chap. 2).

When the techniques used to measure motives in individuals—content analysis of thematic apperceptive or other verbal material (see Smith, 1992)—are applied to the verbal productions of collectivities, institutions, or groups (see Winter, 1991a, 1992), the resulting scores predict the same kinds of actions or outcomes as they do among individuals. But what does a collectivity-based score mean? It can be thought of as a proxy for an aggregation of the scores of those individuals who make up the group or control the institution (i.e., an aggregation of different dispositions, each at a different level of arousal). (This would be analogous to the procedure of Kock, 1965, who obtained overall motive scores for a series of factories by combining the scores of the individual managers of each factory, each weighted by that person's level of power.) Short-term fluctuations in collectivity-based scores, of the sort to be described below, would then be thought of as changes in aggregated levels of aroused motivation. As McClelland (1985) suggested,

On the whole it seems preferable to think of collective motive scores as more analogous to aroused motivational states, which can shift quite rapidly as a result of [short-term] influences. . . . These aroused motivational states may create effects on group behavior much like the effects produced in individuals by the chronic states of arousal that we have labeled motive dispositions. (p. 470)

Whether scores from collective documents are true proxies (rather than metaphors) for aggregated individual scores can only be determined by systematic research comparing the two along the lines of Kock's (1965) study. For the present, the predictive convergence of the two measures suggests that it may be useful to think of collectivity-based scores in this way.

On the other hand, collective scores can also be thought of as reflecting nonmotivational concepts (e.g., ideological or psychological climate, values, or even short-term "mood") that some may find more appropriate in making attributions to collectivities (see McClelland, 1985, pp. 422, 470). Thus, in an introduction to a new edition of *The Achieving Society*, McClelland (1976) wrote that a motive score derived from popular literature

should be thought of as an ideological climate variable which can affect child-rearing but also many other things in the environment of an individual in the society. It shapes his ideas about what is important; it affects the sanctions that a society imposes for various types of behavior; it sets the norms that he accepts. Thus I find no real difficulty in . . . renaming [achievement motivation] "the social pressure to achieve" . . . when thinking of it as a societal ideology. (p. E)

In the long run, researchers may be able to decide between these two alternative conceptions through systematic archival studies analyzing verbal products of both collectivities (e.g., government statements) and also individuals (e.g., transcripts of remarks, memos, or diaries) drawn from the same extended episodes of political decision making.

Testing the Model: Wars in British History, 1603–1988

The Sovereign's Speech

At the opening of each session of Parliament in Great Britain, the queen or king gives a speech that outlines the reasons for summoning Parliament, reviews events since the last parliamentary session, and mentions legislation to be introduced in the current session. (This speech is also called the "Speech from the Throne," or the "Queen's [King's] Speech." It is analogous to the annual State of the Union messages in the United States, although shorter and usually more eloquent.) Since King James I summoned Parliament in 1603, the texts of these speeches have been published in *Hansard's Parliamentary Debates.* Nowadays, of course, this speech is completely written by the Prime Minister and Cabinet; Wilding and Laundy (1972) suggested that this has actually been the case since the rise of the cabinet system in the late 17th century. Thus, the Sovereign's Speech is really the product of that loosely defined but important group called the British government, so that motive imagery scores based on these speeches can therefore be taken as a rough measure of changing levels of motivation within that British government.

Method

Scoring Sovereign's Speeches

In line with standard procedures, texts of these speeches were randomly mixed together and scored for power, affiliation, and achievement imagery according to the running text scoring system (Winter, 1991a), outlined in Table 2, by a trained scorer who had previously demonstrated high reliability (category agreement above .90 on materials prescored by experts, which is the standard for research of this kind; see Winter, 1991a, p. 67) and who was unaware of the purposes and hypotheses of the study. In years when there were two or more speeches, motive imagery scores and number of words were aggregated across those speeches. Raw scores were then converted into images per 1,000 words and then standardized ($M = 50$, $SD = 10$) separately for each motive. The result is a time series of motive levels of the British government from 1603 through 1988. During the early part of this period, Parliament did not meet every year; thus, motive scores are only available for 255 years instead of 386. Beginning in Shakespeare's time,

these scores span Civil War and Restoration, the Industrial Revolution, the rise and fall of the British Empire, and the birth of atomic energy and computers.

Measuring Wars

Although Great Britain has been involved in many wars since the beginning of the 17th century, there is no single consensus list. Different war scholars use different definitions (e.g., by number of casualties, nature of opponents, duration, or consequentiality of results). Some scholars count massacres, raids, and major mutinies (so frequent in the history of the British Empire) as wars, whereas others do not. For present purposes, it seemed important to include such incidents because they were a natural consequence of expanding British imperialism, itself an important social consequence of power motivation. Furthermore, war scholars do not agree on how to divide long and complex periods of strife, such as the era of the Napoleonic Wars, into individual wars.

A single integrated list of British wars between 1601 and 1988 was developed as follows: All wars mentioned by Kende (1978), Kohn (1987), Modelski (1972), Richardson (1960), Small and Singer (1982), Wilkinson (1980), and Wright (1962) were combined into an initial list. Incidents that did not actually involve British military forces or that were more in the nature of personal (rather than collective) rebellions were excluded. The years in which each war (or British participation in the war) began and ended were established on the basis of the most specific account of above sources. The result was a list of 169 wars.[4] Great Britain was involved in at least 1 war during 325 of the 386 years in question, or about 84% of the time. In terms of war entry, Great Britain entered at least 1 war during 127 years; during 97 of these years, there was another ongoing war, whereas 30 years would otherwise have been peaceful. Finally, during 62 years, Great Britain was at peace and stayed at peace. (Depending on speech

[4] A copy of this list, together with the definitional criteria for *war*, can be obtained from David G. Winter.

Table 2	Brief Outline of Motive Imagery Scoring in Verbal Material
Imagery Type	**Definition**
Achievement	Someone is concerned about a standard of excellence
	Directly, by words indicating the quality of performance, or indirectly, by actions clearly suggesting a concern for excellence, or by success in competition.
	By negative emotions or counter-striving in response to failure.
	By carrying out some unique, unprecedented accomplishment.
Affiliation	Someone is concerned about establishing, maintaining or restoring friendship or friendly relations among persons, groups, etc.
	By expression of positive, friendly, or intimate feelings toward other characters, nations, etc.
	By expression of sadness or other negative feeling about separation or disruption of a friendly relationship, or wanting to restore it.
	By affiliative, companionate activities.
	By friendly, nurturant acts.
Power	Someone is concerned about having impact, control, or influence on another person, group, or the world at large.
	By taking strong, forceful actions that inherently have impact on other people or the world at large.
	By controlling or regulating others.
	By attempting to influence, persuade, convince, make or prove a point, argue.
	By giving unsolicited help or advice.
	By impressing others or the world at large; prestige or reputation.
	By eliciting a strong emotional reaction in someone else.

Note. Adapted from Winter (1989); see also Winter (1991, p. 63). This outline is not adequate for scoring purposes. A complete manual, together with instructions, practice materials, expert scoring, and calibration materials, is available at cost from David G. Winter.

availability, the actual samples range downward from these numbers.)

Results

Entering a War

Considering only years in which a speech from the Throne was delivered, power motivation was significantly higher in the 221 years when Great Britain was at war than in the 34 completely peaceful years (Ms = 51.24 and 46.94, respectively; t = 2.22, p < .03). Affiliation motivation showed a nonsignificant tendency to be lower during war (Ms = 49.77 and 52.12, respectively). A combined measure of (standardized) power minus (standardized) affiliation also significantly differentiated war-entry years from peace years (Ms = 1.58 and −5.18; t = 1.97, p < .06). Although these results are consistent with the most essential feature of the model, they are not a very powerful causal test, because being in a war undoubtedly increases power motive imagery in the speeches. The most critical compari-

son, therefore, involves the 30 years when Great Britain started the year at peace but then entered a war with the 62 completely peaceful years. As a further test of causal direction, motive scores during the preceding 5 years were also examined. The results are shown in Tables 3 and 4.

As shown in Table 3, the power-minus-affiliation scores tended to be higher in war-entry years, but the difference was more significant for the first year before war entry. (The differences were also significant for each motive separately.) For the second year before war entry, the power-minus-affiliation difference was only a trend, and this disappeared completely by 5 years before war entry.

Because of the complex way in which the dependent variable was defined (war entry from peace vs. peace), which led to a good deal of missing data, trend analysis was not appropriate for these data. However, when the dependent variable was regressed on power-minus-affiliation

scores for the 3 years before war entry, as shown in Table 4, essentially the same results were obtained.[5] Thus, the initial test supports one of the most important features of the model: During the time just before Great Britain entered a war from an otherwise peaceful state, power motivation was relatively high and affiliation motivation was relatively low.

[5]One further possible confound is that the years before any particular year in which Great Britain was at peace or entered a war may also be years in which Great Britain was at war. Because power was higher and affiliation was lower in at-war years, how might this affect the present analysis? It would work against the present hypothesis for at-peace years. For war-entry years, it would support the hypothesis, but the overall sequence—that war raises power motivation, which in turn leads to additional wars—would represent a further elaboration of the hypothesis rather than a spurious relationship.

Table 3 Motive Patterns and War Entry in British History, 1603–1988

	Power Motive Imagery Minus Affiliation Motive Imagery in Sovereign's Speeches						
	Years in Which Great Britain Entered a War			Years in Which Great Britain Did Not Enter a War			
Year of Speech	n	M	SD	n	M	SD	p of Difference
Same year	19	1.58	10.58	34	−5.18	12.33	.055
1 year prior	18	4.78	10.73	36	−6.83	13.10	<.003
2 years prior	20	0.50	14.98	39	−5.15	14.29	.17
3 years prior	18	−8.50	12.24	42	−5.14	12.72	
4 years prior	16	−0.69	9.59	43	−4.54	13.85	
5 years prior	21	−2.14	13.53	39	−1.31	14.76	

Note. Data are for years in which Great Britain entered or did not enter a war while at peace. Power and affiliation motive scores are each standardized separately.

Table 4 Regression of War Entry from Peace on Motive Pattern in Previous Years

Power Motive Imagery Minus Affiliation Motive Imagery in Sovereign's Speeches	War Entry			
	r	β	t	p
1 year prior	.30	.30	2.13	.038
2 years prior	.21	.17	1.19	.238
3 years prior	−.05	−.19	1.40	.166

Note. n = 58, R = .37, p < .05 when scores for all 3 years are entered into the regression.

Ending a War

Can a motivational analysis predict when wars will end? This question can be answered by comparing the 90 years in which Great Britain ended a war with the 131 years in which wars were going on but did not end. (Again the actual sample sizes vary downward because of years without speeches.) In years when a war ended, as well as for the 2 preceding years, power-minus-affiliation scores were lower than in years when wars continued, but the difference was not significant.

When power and affiliation scores are considered separately, as in Table 5, however, it appears that power motivation was indeed lower during the year or 2 before wars ended, whereas affiliation scores showed no differences. The first effect (declining power) is consistent with the model, but the second (affiliation noneffect) is not. That is, wars end when the power motive declines, but not when affiliation rises. Thus, although wars might bring about affiliative bonding among soldiers or heightened affiliative concerns due to personal loss and generalized horror at the carnage of war, the present analysis suggests that such heightened affiliative concerns do not affect the ending of wars. Perhaps when a war is going on, affiliation motives can be "captured" by power, arousing desires for revenge or at least a reluctance to write off sunken costs—in Lincoln's words at Gettysburg, "that we here highly resolve that these dead shall not have died in vain."

Motivational Effects of War

What are the motivational effects of a war after it is over? Using the same groupings as above (years in which a war ended vs. years in which a war was going on but did not end). Table 6 shows that the decline in power motivation that precedes the end of wars continues for a few years afterward, just as McClelland's (1975) original model suggests it would. Because elevated power motivation precedes war entry, this postwar motivational trend may constitute a "refractory period" in which the conclusion of one war makes it less likely that another war will begin. However, war endings had no significant effects on affiliation motivation levels, contrary to the suggestion of McClelland's (1975) original model (refer back to Table 1).[6]

Because the nature of war did change dramatically in the 19th century, one may wonder whether these effects are consistent across the entire 385 years. When the data are divided into the years before 1800 and the years after 1800, the results are in the same direction in both cases, but the significance of the post-1800 results is usually greater, in part because of the larger number of cases.

Testing the Model: The Outbreak of World War I Between Britain and Germany

The outbreak of World War I offers a more sharply focused test of the motivational model of war over a much shorter time span. Suddenly and without warning, the assassination of Austrian Archduke Franz Ferdinand at Sarajevo turned into general war, although no one wanted, expected, or even understood this escalation. The July 1914 crisis has become a classic example for scholars seeking to explain wars (see, for example Holsti, 1972).

[6]A result unrelated to the model is also worth noting: Achievement motivation also dropped after the end of wars. Because the achievement motive is related to entrepreneurial success and economic development (see McClelland, 1961), could this be a motivational reason why wars are often followed by periods of economic stagnation and depression?

Table 5 Power Motivation and Ending of Wars in British History, 1603–1988

| | Standardized Power Motive Imagery in Sovereign's Speeches | | | | | | |
| | Years in Which Great Britain Ended a War | | | Years in Which Great Britain, at War, Did Not End a War | | | |
Year of Speech	n	M	SD	n	M	SD	p of Difference
Same year	90	49.71	9.86	131	52.30	11.12	.079
1 year prior	96	49.87	9.31	123	52.69	11.51	.053
2 years prior	94	50.05	10.22	121	52.32	10.50	.115
3 years prior	90	51.87	10.35	121	50.97	10.17	
4 years prior	84	51.16	10.82	125	51.26	9.62	
5 years prior	90	51.10	10.99	122	50.54	9.29	

Table 6 Postwar Power Motivation in British History, 1603–1988

| | Standardized Power Motive Imagery in Sovereign's Speeches | | | | | | |
| | Years in Which Great Britain Ended a War | | | Years in Which Great Britain, at War, Did Not End a War | | | |
Year of Speech	n	M	SD	n	M	SD	p of Difference
Same year	90	49.71	9.86	131	52.30	11.12	.072
1 year prior	87	50.10	9.51	131	51.89	11.62	
2 years prior	92	49.35	9.65	128	51.97	11.42	.069
3 years prior	93	48.33	10.15	121	52.99	11.09	.002
4 years prior	91	49.35	10.90	126	51.68	10.92	
5 years prior	95	49.41	9.79	123	51.54	11.15	

In this article I focus on the outbreak of war between Great Britain and Germany in 1914. Of all the separate conflicts involved in the July 1914 crisis, this conflict (along with that between Germany and Russia) converted a Balkan war between Austria-Hungary and Serbia into a world war (see Remak, 1984). Yet the German-British conflict was in many respects the most surprising and least "necessary" of the conflicts. Britain and Germany were not members of opposed alliances. They shared cultural and dynastic roots and a protestant religious orientation. Although the two nations had been economic, colonial, and naval rivals since the latter decades of the 19th century and although they harbored mutual suspicions, many leaders in each country wanted to strengthen ties with the other. Relations had actually improved during the 2 or 3 years before mid-1914. Only 2 years before, in 1912, Britain and Germany successfully worked together to prevent the First Balkan War from turning into a general European war. Thus, for example, 12 days before Sarajevo,

Bethmann-Hollweg cabled to Lichnowsky, the German ambassador to Britain that

Whether in such a case [Russian intervention in a Balkan crisis] it would come to a general European conflagration, would depend exclusively on the attitude of Germany and England. If we should both stand forth with determination as the guarantors of European peace . . . on the basis of a common plan . . . war could be avoided. . . . Otherwise any number of secondary conflicts of interest between Russia and Austria might light the torch of war. (June 16, 1914; quoted in Montgelas & Schücking, 1924, p. 55; see also Bethmann-Hollweg, 1919/1920, pp. 115, 166)

(See Fischer, 1964, pp. 286–292; Joll, 1984, p. 172; and Kennedy, 1980, chaps. 19 and 22 for a detailed account of British-German relations during this period.) Thus, an analysis of British and German motive levels during the July crisis may help to explain this surprising escalation of the conflict.

Method

Much of the communication and maneuvering during the 1914 crisis took place between heads of governments and foreign ambassadors. For these conversations there is no objective record, although reports produced by each side may be of value in analyzing misperceptions and distortions (see Winter, 1987). For the 12 days from July 24 through August 4, however, there were 16 direct communications from the British to the German government and 19 direct communications from Germany to Great Britain. Most of these are written communications handed by an ambassador to the head of state or foreign ministry of the host country; some are draft cables to an ambassador that were transmitted verbatim to a host government. On a few occasions, Kaiser William and Prince Henry of Prussia even corresponded directly with King George V. These communications and their sources in the published collections of diplomatic documents are listed in the appendix. They are the kinds of documents analyzed by Holsti (1972, see p. 96 especially) and Suedfeld and Tetlock (1977) in their comparative-crisis studies.

| Table 7 | Motive Patterns in British and German Government-to-Government Communications in 1914 | | | | | | |

| Government | Standardized Power Motive Imagery Minus Standardized Affiliation Imagery[a] | | | | | | |
| | Early in Crisis[b] | | | Late in Crisis[c] | | | |
	n	M	SD	n	M	SD	Change
German	5	−10.20	17.64	5	5.10	8.64	15.30
British	4	−6.00	5.94	4	1.13	6.28	7.13
British and German	9	−8.33	13.18	9	3.33	7.51	11.66

Note. All communications for each day are aggregated to give a single score for that communication day. t for change in combined British and German from early to late = 2.31, p < .05.
[a]Standardization carried out separately for British and German documents. [b]First half of each country's communication days. [c]Second half of each country's communication days.

The 35 documents were randomly mixed together and scored by a trained scorer (category agreement above .90 on materials prescored by experts) who was unaware of the purposes and hypotheses of the study. When a country made more than one communication in a single day, these were aggregated for that day. Imagery scores were then divided by text length to produce motive images per 1,000 words and then standardized in the usual way. (British and German documents were each standardized separately.) To see whether motive levels changed in the course of the crisis, the entire series of "communication days" was divided at the middle for each country. This yielded 5 "early" and 5 "late" days for Germany and 4 each for Great Britain. The dividing points were between July 30–31 for Germany and between July 31–August 1 for Great Britain. (The German declaration of war on Russia, which was the first formal "internationalization" of what started out as a crisis between Austria-Hungary and Serbia, occurred on the evening of August 1.)

Results

Table 7 presents the results. The government-to-government exchanges between Great Britain and Germany show, for both sides, a significant increase in power-minus-affiliation motive imagery from the early to the late parts of the crisis. Even in the short space of 12 days, then, motive

levels can change dramatically in the directions specified by the model, before the outbreak of war that had been unexpected.

Testing the Model: The Cuban Missile Crisis

Because the United States and the Soviet Union did not go to war in October 1962, the Cuban Missile Crisis offers an excellent comparison with 1914 and has been so used by many scholars (e.g., Holsti, 1972; Lebow, 1981; Suedfeld & Tetlock, 1977). In recent years, American and Soviet scholars have held joint discussions and disclosed new material (Allyn, Blight, & Welch, 1989; Blight & Welch, 1989), so that researchers' understanding of the crisis continues to change and deepen.

Method

At least three sets of direct personal talks—between United States Attorney General Robert Kennedy and Soviet Ambassador Anatoly Dobrinin, between news correspondent Joseph Scali and KGB official Aleksandr Fomin, and between Soviet Premier Nikita Khrushchev and American businessman William Knox—played important parts in the resolution of the crisis, but in each case there is no objective, verbatim record of who said what to whom. There are, however, complete versions of several direct government-to-government communica-

tions for the whole period of the crisis. These include President Kennedy's speech of October 22, 1962, that disclosed the existence of the missiles and demanded their removal, an official Soviet reply transmitted the next day by TASS (the Soviet official news agency), and 10 letters exchanged between President Kennedy and Premier Khrushchev during October 22–28, at which time a Soviet pledge to remove the missiles and a United States pledge not to invade Cuba effectively brought the crisis to an end. (Only 4 of these 10 letters were publicized at the time. Texts of several additional, post-October 28 Kennedy–Khrushchev letters have recently been declassified, but they really belong to the post-crisis period.)

For the present analysis, texts of the two public statements were taken from The New York Times and texts of the letters were taken from the United States Department of State Bulletin (U.S. Department of State, 1973). Documents were randomly mixed together and scored for motive imagery by a trained scorer (category agreement above .90 on materials prescored by experts) unaware of the purposes and hypotheses of this study. The entire series was divided in the middle (between October 24–25) to give three early and three late documents for each side. Recent interviews with Soviet officials reported by Blight and Welch (1989) suggest that this dividing point slightly preceded a critical watershed (October 25 or 26) in Soviet policy formulation during the crisis.

Results

Table 8 presents the results of the Cuban Missile Crisis analysis. In this case there was a significant decrease in power-minus-affiliation scores for both sides from the early to the late phase of the crisis. Thus, in a crisis where war was possible but avoided, there was a significant shift away from the war motivational pattern: Power motive levels decreased and affiliation increased. One detail of the Kennedy–Khrushchev correspondence deserves elaboration in light of the results. On October 26, Premier Khrushchev sent a long, rambling conciliatory letter proposing the

Table 8	Motive Patterns in Cuban Missile Crisis Government-to-Government Communications

	Standardized Power Motive Imagery Minus Standardized Affiliation Imagery[a]						
	Early in Crisis[b]			Late in Crisis[c]			
Government	n	M	SD	n	M	SD	Change
American	3	11.00	22.52	3	−10.67	7.02	−21.67
Soviet	3	10.33	14.01	3	−10.33	3.52	−20.66
American and Soviet	6	10.67	16.78	6	−10.50	4.97	−21.17

Note. t for change in combined American and Soviet from early to late = 2.91, p < .02.
[a]Standardization carried out separately for American and Soviet documents. [b]First half of the series of communications. [c]Second half of the series of communications.

Table 9	Comparison of Motive Pattern Changes in 1914 and the Cuban Missile Crisis

	Standardized Power Motive Imagery Minus Standardized Affiliation Imagery[a]					
	Early in Crisis[b]			Late in Crisis[c]		
Conflict	n	M	SD	n	M	SD
World War I (Germany and Great Britain)	9	−5.79	17.75	9	6.77	11.31
Cuban Missile Crisis (United States and Soviet Union)	6	5.21	8.40	6	−6.70	3.88

[a]Standardization carried out on all documents pooled. [b]Phase (early vs. late) defined as in Tables 7 and 8; see text for details.

mutual pledges that eventually constituted the basis of the final resolution of the crisis. The next day, however, he sent a so-called "second letter" that, by adding on to these pledges a demand for removal of United States missiles from Turkey, suggested (at the manifest level) a more aggressive stance and seemed to increase tension. In fact, however, this second letter had a much lower power-minus-affiliation score (difference score of −14.90, each component score standardized, with M = 50 and SD = 10) than did its predecessor (difference score of −7.80). In motivational terms, that is, the second letter was bellicose. Perhaps this helps to explain the repeated hints of President Kennedy's (perhaps uncon-

scious) positive response to this letter, as recorded in the published transcript of the October 27 meeting of the Executive Committee of the National Security Council (ExComm), convened by President Kennedy to handle the crisis:

To any man at the United Nations or any other rational man it will look like a very fair trade. . . . Most people will regard this as not an unreasonable proposal, I'll just tell you that. . . . Everybody's going to think that this is very reasonable. (Kennedy, 1962, pp. 3, 13)

In fact, Allyn et al. (1989) suggested that President Kennedy actually (albeit secretly) accepted—perhaps even initiated—a missiles-in-Cuba trade. If this is true, perhaps the increasingly pacific

motive levels of Premier Khrushchev's letters played a subtle, even unconscious part.

Tables 9 and 10 combine the World War I and Cuban Missile Crisis data into a two-way analysis of variance, showing a highly significant interaction effect between crisis and phase. (The means and standard deviations vary slightly from those in Tables 7 and 8 because in Table 9 standardization was carried out on the entire combined pool of documents. This does not affect the results.)

General Discussion

Why Was the Cuban Missile Crisis Different from 1914?

What caused this dramatic motivational shift on both sides in 1962, so different in nature and consequences from that of 1914? What was the psychological mechanism? Was it a sudden, stark realization of the consequences of nuclear war? United States Secretary of Defense McNamara, for example, recalled the fear that October 27 might be the last Saturday he saw and concluded that "there was enough fear of the consequences of a nuclear war in the American Administration to be deterred" (Blight & Welch, 1989, pp. 88, 199; see also the statement of State Department Legal Counsel Abram Chayes on p. 26). Premier Khrushchev expressed this concern even more vividly: "What good would it have done me in the last hour of my life to know that though our great nation and the United States were in complete ruins, the national honor of the Soviet Union was intact?" (interview with Norman Cousins, quoted in Blight & Welch, 1989, p. 221).

Plausible as this explanation may seem, one must still remember that in 1914 many leaders accurately foresaw that what they were doing would bring about the end of civilization as they knew it. British Foreign Minister Grey's words are a famous example: "The lamps are going out all over Europe; we shall not see them lit again in our lifetime" (Grey, 1925, p. 20). In July 1914, Kurt Riezler, the close confidant of

Table 10	Variance of Power-Minus-Affiliation Scores in 1914 and the Cuban Missile Crisis				
Source	**Sum of Squares**	**df**	**MS**	**F**	**Significance**
Crisis (1719 vs. Cuban Missile Crisis)	11.07	1	11.07	0.07	ns
Phase (early vs. late)[a]	0.75	1	0.75	0.01	ns
Crisis × Phase	1,078.42	1	1,078.42	7.06	.014
Within cell	3,972.56	26	152.79		

[a]Phase (early vs. late) defined as in Tables 7 and 8; see text for details.

Bethmann-Hollweg, observed that "the chancellor expects from a war, however it ends, a revolution of all existing order," while recording Bethmann-Hollweg's prophecy that "a doom greater than human power [ein Fatum grösser als Menschenmacht] is hanging over the European situation and our people" (Erdmann, 1972, pp. 158, 183).

To explain the peaceful resolution of the Cuban Missile Crisis, Blight and Welch (1989) invoked special, perhaps unprecedented mechanisms such as "the look and feel of nuclear danger," "nuclear learning," and the "burden of responsibility" (see also Blight, 1989). If on further analysis these mechanisms are related to more psychological concepts of responsibility, then the scoring system developed by Winter and Barenbaum (1985) could be used to explore more precisely the role of responsibility during this and other crises.

Issues and Alternative Interpretations of the Results

Although most of the results of the present studies are in line with predictions from the model outlined in Table 1, several issues and alternative interpretations need to be considered.

Inferring Causality

First, there is one issue of correlation versus causality. There was a difference in motive level trends associated with a difference in crisis outcome. From this, one could conclude (a) that the motive trends are a cause of crisis outcome, (b) that motive trends are the result of crisis out-come, or (c) that motive trends are an epiphenomenon of crisis outcome. One way to increase confidence in causal inferences would be to study the day-by-day correlations between the motive levels in a country's documents and the hostility or intensity of threat of its actions, using different forward and backward lags. For the two crises in the present research, however, this would be difficult. Holsti (1972, p. 242) presented day-by-day scaled estimates of the level of threat in each country's actions in 1914, but because the data for Germany aggregate German actions directed toward all other countries, the intensity of threatening German actions toward Britain cannot be separated from intensity of threatening German actions toward other nations (e.g., Russia, France, or Belgium). Holsti also presented, for each country, day-by-day estimates of perceived hostility (1972, p. 243). Clearly, such perceptions should also be included in a sophisticated causal model (see Zinnes, 1968), but, again, the aggregation of data across all other nations as sources makes this impossible in the 1914 case. One would have to begin by redoing much of the original Holsti study.

In the case of the Cuban Missile Crisis, the brevity of the period between President Kennedy's first speech (October 22) and the resolution (October 28) gives too few data points for a lagged analysis using Holsti's (1972) data on United States and Soviet actions and perceptions (pp. 190–191). As more documents and taperecorded transcripts of the meetings of the ExComm become available, however, it might be possible to do lagged analysis using shorter time units. Meanwhile, a day-by-day lagged analysis of motivation, perception, and action could be carried out on a crisis that lasted a long time, such as the 1990–1991 buildup to the Gulf War.

Motives, or Other Psychological Characteristics?

The observed relationship between motive trends and crisis outcomes might really be due to their mutual correlation with a third variable, for example, some other psychological factor known to predict war.

Thus, Suedfeld and his associates (Raphael, 1982; Suedfeld & Bluck, 1988; Suedfeld & Tetlock, 1977; Suedfeld et al., 1977) have shown that levels of integrative complexity go down in crises that lead to war, whereas they remain high during peacefully resolved crises. Do motives and integrative complexity both exert independent causal effects or is one an epiphenomenon of the other? Further comparative longitudinal studies of crises, incorporating both sets of variables, are now under way in an effort to resolve such questions.

Similarly, the observed motive levels might be an epiphenomenon of some other associated psychological state, such as the emotions of anger or excitement associated with sympathetic nervous system arousal. On the other hand, McClelland's (1982, 1987) research linking power motivation, sympathetic nervous system arousal, and emotions argues that such associations are intrinsic rather than spurious.

Finally, the observed differences in motive level change might be an epiphenomenon of other, "nonpsychological" (or nonmotivational) factors such as a government's conscious and deliberate decision for war (after which its rhetoric may be expected to show higher power motivation); calculated attempts to threaten, bluff, or deter; the residues of previous policy; or rational reactions to the actions of the other country.

Changing Units of Time

Although the results of all three studies are consistent, it should be noted that the time units involved vary from years in the first study to days and even hours in the second and third studies. Do changes in motive levels have the same psychological and political function and meaning for both intervals? In the narrow sense of predicting outcome, perhaps they do, but further studies with crises of different duration would be a useful confirmation.

For all these reasons, then, the present analysis can only be suggestive. As discussed earlier, further research that takes account of these and other variables, that considers the joint effects of motivational and situational factors (in Murray's 1938, terms *need* and *press*), and that considers many different kinds of crises, will be necessary to make confident causal inferences about the psychological dynamics of war and peace.

Still, the present results may have value in terms of practical prediction as well as theoretical heuristics. The present measures of motivation and integrative complexity could be elaborated into an online early warning system for monitoring government statements and communications, even as further research explores the why and how of the observed relationships.

Summary and Implications

Three tests of a model relating high power motivation and low affiliation motivation to war, derived from McClelland's (1975) early work, have confirmed the essential feature of the model, that a motive profile of high power and low affiliation is associated with subsequent war. The British historical data further suggest that wars come to an end when power decreases rather than when affiliation rises and, finally, that wars have the short-term effect of lowering levels of power and achievement motivation.

In the present research, motives were measured in official speeches and secret government-to-government communications. Time spans ranged from almost 400 years of British history down to a few anxious days. Wars ranged from small colonial incidents in remote regions, to World War I, to the thermonuclear World War III that did not happen. Taken together, the results suggest that power motivation may be one

important psychological cause of war: When it rises, war is likely; when it falls, war is less likely and ongoing wars are likely to end. The affiliation motive works in an opposite fashion, at least with respect to the beginnings of wars. These results are consistent with previous at-a-distance studies of individual political leaders as well as an extensive body of laboratory research.

Judgment of Historians

Such a conclusion fits well with recent historians' accounts of the mentalities or unspoken assumptions of leaders and peoples in 1914. Taylor (1967) described those times:

Men's minds seem to have been on edge in the last two or three years before the war in a way they had not been before, as though they had become unconsciously weary of peace and security. . . . Men wanted violence for its own sake; they welcomed war as a relief from materialism. (p. 185)

More systematically, Joll (1968) traced the influence of oversimplified versions of Nietzsche and pseudo-Darwinian ideas of a perpetual struggle for survival on popular mentalities during the years before World War I. For example, Austrian Chief of Staff Conrad von Hötzendorf (one of the strongest proponents of crushing Serbia in July 1914) vividly expressed the struggle-for-survival theme in his memoirs:

Mankind's struggle for existence [is] . . . a driving motive in the world. . . . It is in accordance with this great principle that the catastrophe of the world war came about inevitably and irresistibly as the result of the motive forces in the lives of states and peoples, like a thunderstorm which must by its nature discharge itself. (quoted in Joll, 1968, p. 18)

In a recent discussion of the controversy between Fritz Fischer and his critics about the origins of World War I, Janssen (1984, pp. 296–298) suggested that the major competing origin explanations can be characterized as involving power, prestige, and risk—in his view, separate concepts but, from the perspective of the present theory and research, actually reflecting different aspects of the power motive.

Reflections of the Participants

The conclusions of this article also fit with the reflections of the political leaders themselves. Writing his memoirs in 1919, after Germany's defeat and the harsh Versailles Treaty, German Chancellor Bethmann-Hollweg answered his own question about how it all happened: "Germany also has fallen under the spell of the ideal of power then dominating the world" (1919/1920, p. 114). In his memoirs, written 6 years later, British Foreign Secretary Grey (1925) also identified power concerns as a major cause of the war—though he differentiated power into separate components of domination (Germany) and honor (Britain):

Germany was deliberately aiming at world predominance. . . . Germans felt German Kultur to be a superior thing that ought to dominate the world. (Grey, 1925, Vol. 2, p. 29)
Did Bethmann-Hollweg not understand, could he not see, that he was making an offer that would dishonour us if we agreed to it? (Grey, 1925, Vol. 1, p. 317)

Implications for Personality Research

From the perspective of personality psychology, these studies suggest that personality theory and variables can be translated into objective measures that can be applied at a distance to individuals and groups. As a result, rigorous personality research can now be extended to include history, biography, political science, and related fields, and the personality "laboratory" can be expanded to include libraries and archives, the past as well as the present, the White House Cabinet Room, the House of Commons floor, and even—in an era of stunning political reconstructions—the inner recesses of the Kremlin.

From the perspective of those concerned with peace, these results suggest some key motivational factors related to war that can be measured and thereby monitored. If future archival and laboratory research can discover ways of tempering the power motive—perhaps through responsibility, self-control, or affiliation—these warlike motivational factors could even be diverted or "tamed" in the interest of securing and preserving peace.

References

Allyn, B. J., & Blight, J. G. (1992, November 2). Closer than we knew [Letter to the editor]. *The New York Times*, p. A16.

Allyn, B. J., Blight, J. G., & Welch, D. A. (1989). Essence of revision: Moscow, Havana, and the Cuban missile crisis. *International Security, 14*, 136–172.

Angell, N. (1910). *The great illusion: A study of the relation of military power in nations to their economic and social advantage*. London: Heinemann.

Atkinson, J. W. (Ed.). (1958). *Motives in fantasy, action and society*. Princeton, NJ: Van Nostrand.

Atkinson, J. W. (1982). Motivational determinants of thematic apperception. In A. J. Stewart (Ed.), *Motivation and society* (pp. 3–40). San Francisco: Jossey-Bass.

Atkinson, J. W., Heyns, R. W., & Veroff, J. (1954). The effect of experimental arousal of the affiliation motive on thematic apperception. *Journal of Abnormal and Social Psychology, 49*, 405–410.

Bethmann-Hollweg, Th. von. (1920). *Reflections on the World War*. London: Thornton Butterworth. (Original work published 1919)

Blight, J. G. (1989). *The shattered crystal ball: Fear and learning in the Cuban Missile Crisis*. Savage, MD: Rowman & Littlefield.

Blight, J. G., & Welch, D. A. (1989). *On the brink: Americans and Soviets reexamine the Cuban Missile Crisis*. New York: Hill & Wang.

Brockner, J., & Rubin, J. Z. (1985). *Entrapment in escalating conflicts: A social psychological analysis*. New York: Springer-Verlag.

Bülow, B. von. (1932). *Memoirs of Prince von Bülow: Vol. 3. The World War and Germany's collapse 1909–1919*. Boston: Little, Brown.

Clausewitz, K. von. (1962). *War, politics, and power* (E. M. Collins Ed.). New York: Henry Regnery (Gateway editions). (Original work published 1831)

Conte, H. R., & Plutchik, R. (1981). A circumplex model for interpersonal personality traits. *Journal of Personality and Social Psychology, 40*, 701–711.

Crosby, F. (1976). A model of egoistic relative deprivation. *Psychological Review, 83*, 85–113.

Davies, J. C. (1969). The J-curve of rising and declining satisfactions as a cause of some great revolutions and a contained rebellion. In H. D. Graham & T. R. Gurr (Eds.), *The history of violence in America* (pp. 690–729). New York: Bantam Books.

Erdmann, K. D. (Ed.). (1972). *Kurt Riezler: Tagebücher, Aufsätze, Dokumente [Kurt Riezler: Diary, articles, documents]*. Göttingen, Germany: Vandenhoeck & Ruprecht.

Fischer, F. (1964). Weltpolitik, Weltmachtstreben, und deutsche Kriegziele [World policy, the striving for world power, and German war aims]. *Historische Zeitschrift, 199*, 265–346.

Frank, J. D. (1986). The role of pride. In R. K. White (Ed.), *Psychology and the prevention of nuclear war* (pp. 220–226). New York: New York University Press.

Freedman, M. B., Leary, T. F., Ossorio, A. G., & Coffey, H. S. (1951). The interpersonal dimension of personality. *Journal of Personality, 20*, 143–161.

Freud, S. (1961). Civilization and its discontents. In J. Strachey (Ed. and Trans.), *The standard edition of the complete psychological works of Sigmund Freud* (Vol. 21, pp. 57–145). London: Hogarth Press. (Original work published 1930)

Freud, S. (1964). On war. In J. Strachey (Ed. and Trans.), *The standard edition of the complete psychological works of Sigmund Freud* (Vol. 22, pp. 197–215). London: Hogarth Press. (Original work published 1933)

Garthoff, R. L. (1989). *Reflections on the Cuban Missile Crisis*. Washington, DC: Brookings Institution.

Gooch, G. P., & Temperley, H. (Eds.). (1926). *British documents on the origins of the war 1898–1914: Volume II. The outbreak of war: Foreign Office documents, June 28th–August 4th 1914*. London: His Majesty's Stationery Office.

Grey, E. (1935). *Twenty-five years* (2 vols.) New York: Frederick A. Stokes.

Groebel, J., & Hinde, R. A. (Eds.). (1989). *Aggression and war: Their biological and social bases*. Cambridge, England: Cambridge University Press.

Grupp, F. (1975, March). *The power motive in the American state bureaucracy*. Paper presented at the Yale University Conference on Psychology and Politics. New Haven, CT.

Hermann, M. G. (1980a). Assessing the personalities of Soviet Politburo members. *Personality and Social Psychology Bulletin, 6*, 332–352.

Hermann, M. G. (1980b). Explaining foreign policy behavior using personal characteristics of political leaders. *International Studies Quarterly, 24*, 7–46.

Holsti, O. (1972). *Crisis escalation war*. Montreal, Quebec, Canada: McGill University Press.

Inkeles, A., & Levinson, D. J. (1969). National character: The study of modal personality and sociocultural systems. In G. Lindzey & E. Aronson (Eds.), *Handbook of social psychology* (rev. ed.; Vol. 4, pp. 418–506). Reading, MA: Addison-Wesley.

Janssen, K. -H. (1984). Gerhard Ritter: A patriotic historian's justification. In H. W. Koch (Ed.), *The origins of the First World War: Great power rivalry and German war aims* (pp. 292–318). London: Macmillan.

Jarausch, K. H. (1973). *The enigmatic chancellor: Bethmann-Hollweg and the hubris of imperial Germany*. New Haven, CT: Yale University Press.

Jervis, R. (1976). *Perception and misperception in international relations*. Princeton, NJ: Princeton University Press.

Joll, J. (1968). *1914: The unspoken assumptions*. London: Weidenfeld & Nicolson.

Joll, J. (1984). *The origins of the First World War*. London & New York: Longman.

Jones, E. (1953–1957). *The life and work of Sigmund Freud*. London: Hogarth Press.

Kahneman, D., & Tversky, A. (1973). On the psychology of prediction. *Psychological Review, 80*, 237–251.

Kende, I. (1978). Wars of ten years (1967–1976). *Journal of Peace Research, 3*, 227–241.

Kennedy, J. F. (Speaker). (1962). *Presidential Recordings: Cuban Missile Crisis Meetings, October 27, 1962*. Transcript published by the John F. Kennedy Library, Boston.

Kennedy, P. M. (1980). *The rise of the Anglo-German antagonism 1860–1914*. Winchester, MA: Allen & Unwin.

Kock, S. W. (1965). *Foretagsledning och motivation [Management and motivation]*. Unpublished doctoral dissertation, Swedish School of Economics, Helsinki, Finland.

Kohn, G. C. (1987). *Dictionary of wars*. Garden City, NY: Doubleday-Anchor.

Kornadt, H. -J., Eckensberger, L. H., & Emminghaus, W. B. (1980). Cross-cultural research on motivation and its contribution to a general theory of motivation. In H. Triandis & W. Lonner (Eds.), *Handbook of cross-cultural psychology* (Vol. 3, pp. 223–321). Boston: Allyn & Bacon.

Lebow, R. N. (1981). *Between peace and war: The nature of international crisis.* Baltimore, MD: Johns Hopkins University Press.

Leng, R. J., & Walker, S. G. (1982). Comparing two studies of crisis bargaining: Confrontation, coercion, and reciprocity. *Journal of Conflict Resolution, 26,* 571–591.

Leng, R. J., & Wheeler, H. G. (1979). Influence strategies, success, and war. *Journal of Conflict Resolution, 23,* 655–684.

McAdams, D. P. (1982). Intimacy motivation. In A. J. Stewart (Ed.), *Motivation and society* (pp. 133–171). San Francisco: Jossey-Bass.

McAdams, D. P. (1985). *Power, intimacy and the life story.* Homewood, IL: Dorsey Press.

McClelland, D. C. (1961). *The achieving society.* Princeton, NJ: Van Nostrand.

McClelland, D. C. (1975). *Power: The inner experience.* New York: Irvington.

McClelland, D. C. (1976). *The achieving society* (with a new introduction). New York: Irvington.

McClelland, D. C. (1982). The need for power, sympathetic activation and illness. *Motivation and Emotion, 6,* 31–41.

McClelland, D. C. (1985). *Human motivation.* Glenview, IL: Scott, Foresman.

McClelland, D. C. (1987). Biological aspects of human motivation. In F. Halisch & J. Kuhl (Eds.), *Motivation, intention, and volition* (pp. 11–19). Berlin: Springer-Verlag.

McClelland, D. C., & Boyatzis, R. E. (1982). The leadership motive pattern and long term success in management. *Journal of Applied Psychology, 67,* 737–743.

McClelland, D. C., & Burnham, D. H. (1976, March–April). Power is the great motivator. *Harvard Business Review,* pp. 100–110, 159–166.

Modelski, G. (1972). War and the Great Powers. *Peace Research Society Papers, 18,* 45–59.

Montgelas, M., & Schücking, W. (Eds.). (1924). *Outbreak of the World War: German documents collected by Karl Kautsky.* New York: Oxford University Press.

Morton, F. (1989). *Thunder at twilight: Vienna 1913–1914.* New York: Scribner.

Murray, H. A. (1938). *Explorations in personality.* New York: Oxford University Press.

Nelson, K. L., & Olin, S. C. (1979). *Why war? Ideology, theory, and history.* Berkeley, CA: University of California Press.

Neustadt, R. E., & May, E. R. (1986). *Thinking in time: The uses of history for decision-makers.* New York: Free Press.

Oberdorfer, D. (1992, January 14). Cuban Missile Crisis more volatile than thought. *Washington Post,* pp. A1, A14.

Raphael, T. D. (1982). Integrative complexity theory and forecasting international crises: Berlin 1946–1962. *Journal of Conflict Resolution, 26,* 423–450.

Remak, J. (1984). 1914—The third Balkan War: Origins reconsidered. In H. W. Koch, (Ed.), *The origins of the First World War* (pp. 86–100). London: Macmillan.

Richardson, L. F. (1960) *Statistics of deadly quarrels.* Pittsburgh and Chicago: Boxwood.

Schama, S. (1987). *The embarrassment of riches: An interpretation of Dutch culture in the golden age.* New York: Knopf.

Schmookler, A. B. (1984). *The parable of the tribes: The problem of power in the social evolution.* Berkeley, CA: University of California Press.

Schnackers, U., & Kleinbeck, U. (1975). Machmotiv und machtthematisches Verhalten in einem Verhandlungsspiel [Power motivation and power-related behavior in a bargaining game]. *Archiv für Psychologie, 127,* 300–319.

Small, M., & Singer, J. D. (1982). *Resort to arms.* Beverly Hills, CA: Sage.

Smith, C. P. (Ed.). (1992). *Motivation and personality: Handbook of thematic content analysis.* New York: Cambridge University Press.

Sorenson, T. C. (1965). *Kennedy.* New York: Harper & Row.

Suedfeld, P., & Bluck, S. (1988). Changes in integrative complexity prior to surprise attacks. *Journal of Conflict Resolution, 32,* 626–635.

Suedfeld, P., & Tetlock, P. (1977). Integrative complexity of communications in international crises. *Journal of Conflict Resolution, 21,* 169–184.

Suedfeld, P., Tetlock, P., & Ramirez, C. (1977). War, peace, and integrative complexity: UN speeches on the Middle East problem, 1947–1976. *Journal of Conflict Resolution, 21,* 427–442.

Sullivan, M. P. (1979). Foreign policy articulations and U.S. conflict behavior. In J. D. Singer & M. D. Wallace (Eds.), *To auger well* (pp. 215–235). Beverly Hills, CA: Sage.

Taylor, A. J. P. (1967). The outbreak of the First World War. In *Europe: Grandeur and decline.* Harmonsworth, Middlesex, England: Penguin.

Teger, A., Cary, M., Katcher, A., & Hillis, J. (1980). *Too much invested to quit.* Elmsford, NY: Pergamon Press.

Terhune, K. W. (1968). Motives, situation, and interpersonal conflict within prisoners' dilemma. *Journal of Personality and Social Psychology Monograph Supplement, 8*(3, Pt. 2).

Uleman, J. S. (1972). The need for influence: Development and validation of a measure, and comparison with the need for power. *Genetic Psychology Monographs, 85,* 157–214.

U.S. Department of State. (1973, November 19). *Department of State Bulletin, 69,* 635–655.

Veroff, J. (1957). Development and validation of a projective measure of power motivation. *Journal of Abnormal and Social Psychology, 54,* 1–8.

White, R. K. (1984). *Fearful warriors: A psychological profile of U.S.–Soviet relations.* New York: Free Press.

Wicker, F. W., Lambert, F. B., Richardson, F. C., & Kohler, J. (1984). Categorical goal hierarchies and classification of human motives. *Journal of Personality, 52,* 285–305.

Wiggins, J. S. (1980). Circumplex models of interpersonal behavior. In L. Wheeler (Ed.), *Review of personality and social psychology* (Vol. 1, pp. 265–294). Beverly Hills, CA: Sage.

Wilding, N., & Laundy, P. (1972). *An encyclopaedia of Parliament* (4th ed.). London: Collier-Macmillan.

Wilkinson, D. (1980). *Deadly quarrels: Lewis Richardson and the statistical study of war.* Berkeley, CA: University of California Press.

Winter, D. G. (1973). *The power motive.* New York: Free Press.

Winter, D. G. (1980). Measuring the motive patterns of southern Africa political leaders at a distance. *Political Psychology, 2*(2), 75–85.

Winter, D. G. (1987, April). *Power motive distortion in British and German* newspapers and diplomatic dispatches at the outbreak of World War I. Paper presented at the annual meeting of the Eastern Psychological Association, Arlington, VA.

Winter, D. G. (1988). The power motive in women—and men. *Journal of Personality and Social Psychology, 54,* 510–519.

Winter, D. G. (1989). *Manual for scoring motive imagery in running text.* Department of Psychology, University of Michigan, Ann Arbor: Author.

Winter, D. G. (1991a). Measuring personality at a distance: Development of an integrated system for scoring motives in running text. In A. J. Stewart, J. M. Healy, Jr., & D. J. Ozer (Eds.),

Perspectives in personality: Approaches to understanding lives (pp. 59–89). London: Jessica Kingsley.

Winter, D. G. (1991b). A motivational model of leadership: Predicting long-term management success from TAT measures of power motivation and responsibility. *Leadership Quarterly, 2(2),* 67–80.

Winter, D. G. (1992). Content analysis of archival productions, personal documents, and everyday verbal productions. In C. P. Smith (Ed.), *Motivation and personality: Handbook of thematic content analysis* (pp. 110–125). Cambridge, England: Cambridge University Press.

Winter, D. G., & Barenbaum, N. B. (1985). Responsibility and the power motive in women and men. *Journal of Personality, 53,* 335–355.

Winter, D. G., & Stewart, A. J. (1978). The power motive. In H. London & J. Exner (Eds.), *Dimensions of personality* (pp. 391–447). New York: Wiley.

Wright, Q. (1962). *A study of war* (rev. ed.). Chicago: University of Chicago Press.

Zinnes, D. A. (1968). The expression and perception of hostility in prewar crisis: 1914. In J. D. Singer (Ed.), *Quantitative international politics: Insights and evidence* (pp. 85–119). New York: Free Press.

 Article Review Form at end of book.

Appendix

List of July–August 1914 British and German Government-to-Government Communications

Date	Communication	Source
	From Great Britain to Germany	
7/25	From British foreign secretary to German ambassador	GD 186, 191A
	From British foreign secretary to German ambassador	BD 114, 115
7/27	From British ambassador to German Foreign Ministry	GD 304
	From British ambassador to German Foreign Ministry	GD 353
7/30	From King George V to Prince Henry	GD 452
7/31	From British ambassador to German Foreign Ministry	GD 497
8/1	From King George V to Kaiser William	GD 574
	Text from Foreign Secretary submitted verbatim	GD 595, BD 411
	From the British embassy to German Foreign Ministry	GD 610
	From King George V to Kaiser William	GD 612
8/3	From British foreign secretary to German ambassador	BD 542
8/4	From British foreign secretary to German ambassador	BD 643
	From British ambassador to German Foreign Ministry	GD 823
	From British ambassador to German Foreign Ministry	GD 824
	From British ambassador to German Foreign Ministry	GD 839
8/5	From British ambassador to German Foreign Ministry	GD 863
	From Germany to Great Britain	
7/24	From German ambassador to British Foreign Office	BD 100
7/26	From German ambassador to British Foreign Office	BD 145
7/28	From German ambassador to British Foreign Office	BD 236
7/29	From German chancellor to British ambassador	GD 373
7/30	From Prince Henry to King George V	GD 417
7/31	Text from German chancellor submitted verbatim to British Foreign Office	GD 488
	From the German embassy to British Foreign Office	GD 513, BD 372
	From Kaiser William to King George V	GD 477
8/1	From German embassy to British Foreign Office	BD 397
	From Kaiser William to King George V	GD 575
8/2	From German embassy to British Foreign Office	BD 471, GD 677
	Text from German chancellor submitted verbatim to British Foreign Office	BD 472, GD 643
	Text from German foreign minister submitted verbatim to British Foreign Office	GD 667
	From German embassy to British Foreign Office	BD 539
8/3	From German chancellor to British ambassador	BD 553
	From German embassy to British Foreign Office	BD 577
8/4	Text from German foreign minister submitted verbatim to British Foreign Office	BD 587, GD 810
	From German embassy to British Foreign Office	BD 608
	Text from German foreign minister submitted verbatim to British Foreign Office	GD 829, BD 612

Note. GD = document from Montgelas and Schücking (1924); BD = document from Gooch and Temperley (1926).

How can negative thinking motivate some people? What might be a cost of using such a strategy to motivate yourself over the long run?

The Power of Negative Thinking

Cut yourself some slack. You don't have to look on the bright side all the time, says a surprisingly upbeat psychologist.

Julie K. Norem

We live in a nation full of sopping-wet optimists. If you hadn't noticed, take a look at the self-empowerment books crowding B. Dalton's. Or turn on the TV. Talk shows and religious programs extol the benefits of wearing a happy face to keep the bummage away, yeah, even when the plant manager tells you your job is being eliminated by a machine.

Doesn't all this upbeat, smiley-faced crapola just make you want to hurl?

It does, sometimes, admits Julie K. Norem, Ph.D., a psychology professor at Wellesley College. "To say everyone should be optimistic, to say that pessimism is always bad is a gross oversimplification," she says. "A lot of people out there do very, very well but are nevertheless quite pessimistic."

Norem calls them "defensive pessimists," highly successful people who use anxiety and fear of disaster to help manage their stress and improve their performance. We talked with Norem about optimism, pessimism and the power that comes from the dark side.

It's refreshing to hear that we don't have to be gung-ho optimists to be successful and happy. Kind of makes us want to read Dostoyevsky.

It's not only okay to be pessimistic; it's healthy for some people, especially those who are anxious. You're suppressing a part of your personality if you avoid worry. In fact, a lot of people out there can't perform any other way. They are at their best when they dwell on the negative.

You call them "defensive pessimists." Would you give us a thumbnail sketch?

Okay. Simple example. A guy has to give a speech. (You see, defensive pessimism is usually tied to a particular kind of performance.) Anyway, this guy has given dozens of speeches in the past and they've all gone really well. Nevertheless, he's terribly anxious and he's convinced he's going to make a fool of himself. So he works hard on that speech. He switches the jokes around 10 times. He rehearses and rehearses. He has the suit picked out two weeks in advance and brings a spare tie in his briefcase just in case he gets mustard on it. Speech time comes and he's great.

What a neurotic worrywart. He had nothing to fear.

Not at all. I mean it's possible that his anxiety, in some objective sense, seems unjustified. But my point is he *needed* to

bellyache over that speech. It was therapeutic. One characteristic of defensive pessimists is that they usually go into situations with very low expectations and tend to look at the worst-case scenario. By reflecting on what's ahead and working through ways to keep the worst case from happening, they actually harness that anxiety as motivation to do their best.

But isn't worry distracting? Doesn't it interfere with action?

That's the difference between pessimists and defensive pessimists. Pessimists don't feel they have control. They freeze up, withdraw. Defensive pessimists use that thinking-through process to figure out how to deal with any scenario. It's a highly effective coping strategy.

What about when it comes to health? You have to root for optimism there, don't you? Studies show that a positive attitude can be a powerful healer.

Most of those studies looked at recovery after some sort of health problem, like heart surgery. I'd like to argue that defensive pessimists may be better at preventive health than optimists. They know what can go wrong and they have a plan to avoid it. A study by a student of mine on HIV awareness found that defensive pessimists were better informed on AIDS risks than optimists were. That suggests they might be more careful.

What can we learn from defensive pessimists?

I think anyone who thinks he has trouble with anxiety can see it as a positive process. By thinking through something constructively, you become more in control, and your performance is less likely to be disrupted by worry.

Is there a downside to defensive pessimism?

Sure. Nobody likes being around negative people. They're not much fun. And they tend to get on your nerves. But that's easy to fix. If you are a pessimist who's really vocal when working through your anxiety, and you are starting to annoy your friends, just shut up about it.

 **Article Review Form at end of book.**

WiseGuide Wrap-Up

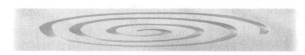

- Personality can be understood in terms of the major themes or motivations that can be seen in our behavior and choices. Winter demonstrates how we can see such motivations in the behavior of political leaders and their responses to world crises.

- Typically, we think of pessimistic or negative thinking as damaging to our performance—"Think positively!" we say. Norem notes that, for some people, negative thinking can be very motivating and can help them achieve important goals.

R.E.A.L. Sites

This list provides a print preview of typical **coursewise** R.E.A.L. sites. There are over 100 such sites at the **courselinks**™ site. The danger in printing URLs is that web sites can change overnight. As we went to press, these sites were functional using the URLs provided. If you come across one that isn't, please let us know via email to: webmaster@coursewise.com. Use your Passport to access the most current list of R.E.A.L. sites at the **courselinks**™ site.

Site name: The International Society for Political Psychology

URL: http://ispp.org/

Why is it R.E.A.L.? This is the site for The International Society for Political Psychology. The organization is for people who are interested in the relationship of psychological research to understanding politics and political leaders. This is an excellent web site, offering many links to other organizations, conference organizers, graduate programs, and general psychology search engines and web links.

Key topics: personality and motivation, political psychology

section

6

Learning Objectives

- Learn what temperament is and how it might be shaped by environment.

- Learn about how attachment relationships are formed between infants and caregivers.

- Describe how early attachment relationships influence later friendships and eventually romantic relationships.

- Discuss differences in the way introverts and extroverts respond to a situation in which they are meeting a new person.

- Note several strategies shy people can use to help overcome their shyness.

Personality and Social Relationships

WiseGuide Intro

Personality psychology can be a powerful tool for use in understanding personal relationships. The articles in this section all deal with the relationship between one's personality and one's pattern in forming and maintaining both friendships and romantic relationships. As we think about our own relationships or those of people we know, we can frequently see patterns in the kinds of bonds we form and the ease with which we are able to develop new relationships. There are a number of ways to approach the connection between personality and social relationships. These articles focus on three ways of looking at this connection: (1) temperament, or one's tendency toward boldness or timidity; (2) introversion and extroversion, or the extent to which one enjoys meeting new people and interacting with people, and (3) attachment styles, or the core patterns of relationships formed in infancy and reformed throughout life as one encounters new relationships.

In "Babies, Bonds and Brains," Wright explores current research into the role that environment plays in shaping one's temperament. Temperament is one's overall emotional orientation—some people are relatively bold, loud, and aggressive, whereas others are more timid, quiet, and reserved. Although temperament has been long thought to be a biologically determined, prewired part of our personalities because of the differences infants show right from the start, researchers are returning to an exploration of the role that early environments play in shaping different temperaments. Wright reviews work conducted by several researchers, with both monkeys and human infants, showing a strong link between the social environment of one's early history and important social functioning later in life.

Thorne reports an interesting and simple study: what happens when introverts and extroverts are left alone with and instructed to get to know a stranger? How do they do it? She videotaped three sets of one-on-one meetings—introverts meeting introverts, introverts meeting extroverts, and extroverts meeting extroverts—and then analyzed what happened in these interactions. Her findings are very interesting, in that they show how introverts can perpetuate feelings of social failure in each new situation, whereas extroverts can perpetuate feelings of social success in the same settings. She also ties the behaviors seen in the videos back to differences in the basic assumptions introverts and extroverts make about themselves and others. This article represents an interesting and exciting way to understand the fear and dread or excitement and enthusiasm felt by introverts and extroverts, respectively, as they anticipate social situations. The ideas also provide excellent hints about how one might behave "more like an extrovert" in situations warranting that. Stocker's article, "Don't Be Shy," offers more direct advice for becoming more outgoing. Most people feel some

Questions

Reading 18. What is a temperament? How does a monkey's "home life" affect its temperament?

Reading 19. What is one strategy introverts use to start a conversation with someone they have never met before? What are some of the assumptions extroverts make that help them start a conversation with a stranger?

Reading 20. What percentage of people consider themselves persistently personable and outgoing? What are three strategies suggested by the author to combat shyness?

Reading 21. What is one difference between securely and insecurely attached children? What is one technique to help parents form better attachments with their children?

Reading 22. How do early attachment styles relate to the way children develop friendships in middle childhood? What are some of the characteristics of avoidant children that make it difficult for them to make friends?

anxiety, and many people feel a great deal of anxiety, in social situations—and most people would prefer not to feel this way. This article reports a set of strategies for helping to overcome shyness.

In "The Loving Ties That Bond," Greenberg reports on research indicating that infants form an attachment to their primary caregiver, regardless of the care they receive. The *nature* of this attachment, however, will vary, depending on the dependability of this caregiver and the quality of that relationship. The article reviews the ways that researchers study and understand the nature of this relationship. The attachment history formed through this "first" relationship forms a model through which we develop our expectations about the understandings of how relationships work. A burgeoning area of research in personality concerns the implications that this early relationship has for understanding friendships and romantic relationships later in life.

The next article, "Stages of Friendship Growth in Preadolescence As Related to Attachment History," demonstrates the relationship between this early attachment relationship with a caregiver and children's patterns of forming friendships with their peers. We all can think back to our childhoods and remember how easy it was for some to make friends, how difficult it was for others, and how still others made sure that no one wanted to be their friends. This article ties these patterns back to children's first relationships—did they learn to think of relationships as safe and loving? scary and unreliable? just plain disappointing? Check out the Adult Attachment Lab R.E.A.L. web site listed on page 154 for the reviews of research indicating that this attachment history also plays a large role in how we enact our romantic relationships in adulthood—you might find it helps you to finally understand something mysterious about your own or your friends' relationships.

What is a temperament? How does a monkey's "home life" affect its temperament?

Babies, Bonds and Brains

The relationship between love and development

Karen Wright

In terms of behavioral development, I was something of a late bloomer. My mother reports that I slept away most of my infancy and toddlerhood, and even my adolescence was unremarkable. I didn't enter my angst-and-experimentation phase until my mid-20s, when, like a tortured teen, I blamed my parents for everything. Several years and several thousand dollars in psychotherapy later, I let my parents off the hook. I realized it couldn't all be their doing—my faults, my fears, my penchant for salty, cheese-flavored snack foods. I am not, after all, the simple product of my upbringing.

This healthy outlook threatened to come undone one recent afternoon as I stood outside the cages at the National Institutes of Health Animal Center in Poolesville, Maryland, watching Stephen Suomi's monkeys. Suomi, a primatologist at the National Institute of Child Health and Human Development, studies the effects of rearing environments on the behavior of young rhesus macaques. Fifty graduates of his program live in the center's five-acre enclosure; at the moment, they are gathered in a large chain-link cell with sawdust on the floor and mon-

key toys dangling from the ceiling. The arrival of human visitors stirs this cohort like dry leaves in a whirlwind, and its members quickly segregate into three factions. The boldest rush to get a cage-front view of the newcomers; a second phalanx hovers behind them, cautious but curious; and at the far end of the cage a third group forms a simian huddle of abject fear.

These monkeys are most definitely the products of their respective upbringings. The three groups were raised in three distinct settings. The bold monkeys spent the first six months of life being shuttled between monkey play groups and individual cages (and so were used to human handling); the sensibly cautious ones were reared by their natural families with mothers, fathers, and siblings; and the fearful monkeys grew up parentless among same-age peers, to whom they retain an abnormally strong attachment.

Suomi is keenly interested in the spectrum of behavior among his macaques—from bold and aggressive to anxious and withdrawn—for it parallels the human trait known as temperament, the fundamental cast of personality that governs our propensity for hobnobbing, taking risks, or seeking thrills. He and other researchers have found that temperament is reflected in biology as well as

behavior: heart rate, immune response, stress-hormone levels, and other physiological measures can be correlated with temperamental styles in humans and monkeys alike. And despite some investigators' assertions to the contrary, Suomi's experiments imply that temperament may be largely the result of a young monkey's home life.

"The patterns have some genetic heritability," says Suomi, jangling his car keys in front of the cage to get an even more exaggerated response. "But our work shows that you can modify these tendencies quite dramatically with certain types of early experiences."

Suomi belongs to the league of scientists who are studying the role that early childhood environment plays in determining adult behavior. He and his colleagues are working a bit beyond the pale, as late-twentieth-century science seems to savor the notion of genetic determinism. But the effects of childhood environment—specifically, the "environment" supplied by parenting—are coming under renewed scrutiny now, in large part because recent neurological studies have revealed that the structure of a child's brain remains surprisingly malleable months and even years after birth. The number of connections between nerve cells in an infant's brain grows more than 20-fold in the first few months of life, for example; a two-year-old's brain contains twice as many of these connections, called synapses, as an adult's brain. Throughout early childhood, synapses multiply and are pruned away at a furious pace. Something directs this dynamic rewiring, and researchers have concluded that that something is experience.

Of course, "experience" can come in all shapes and sizes. Childhood illness and diet, for example, count as experiences, too. But there's reason to believe that a child's experience of his parents is an especially potent sculptor of the parts of the brain involved in emotion, personality, and behavior. Some studies indicate that the strength of a child's bonding with his caregivers may increase his ability to learn and to cope with stress. Others show that childhood abuse and neglect can prime the brain for a lifetime of inappropriate aggression and scattered attention.

As the twentieth century draws to a close, more than half of America's one-year-olds are spending their days with someone other than their mothers. This historic surge in day care has coincided with a rush of reports showing that early experiences may be more critical to brain development than anyone had previously imagined. Naturally, each new bulletin tweaks the guilty fears of working parents. So far, however, the news about kids and day care is pretty good. Children in day care appear to do just fine—provided the quality of the interactions between caregiver and child is high—and good day care may even enhance their social skills and performance in school. Low-quality day care, on the other hand, may compromise a child's adjustment and academic performance.

These results are not surprising to behavioral researchers, who have long appreciated the importance of bonds between caregivers and children. "We know that little kids don't hop up and run away from lions—they don't deal directly with the world much," says Megan Gunnar, a developmental psychologist at the University of Minnesota in Minneapolis. "Their survival depends on their relationships." Hence, children are keenly attuned to the cues they receive from parents, says Gunnar, and they are especially sensitive to signs of indifference. Responsive, sensitive parents inspire trust in their children, giving rise to what behavioral scientists call secure attachment; insensitive or withdrawn parents can foster insecure attachment.

Nearly four decades of behavioral research has painted a dramatic picture of how important this attachment is to a child's emotional health. University of Wisconsin psychologist Harry Harlow's pioneering studies in the late fifties and early sixties found that monkeys reared in total isolation developed aberrant feeding, mating, parenting, and socializing behaviors. Developmental psychologists now believe that bonding with a parent or other caregiver is as essential to a normal childhood as learning to walk and talk. In the absence of a "good mother," children will attach as best they can to whatever figure presents itself—just as Harlow's infant monkeys became virtually inseparable from the cloth-and-wire surrogates in their cages.

Stephen Suomi's simian charges are another example of how behavior can be warped by bonding with a maladroit mom. The timid peer-reared monkeys at the NH center are the victims of insecure attachment; their peers didn't provide the stability and sensitivity that make for a secure bond. (Imagine what a wreck you'd be if you were raised by a twin sister.) These monkeys are anxious and inhibited, and their temperaments are reflected in their reluctance to explore strange objects, their shyness with unfamiliar peers, their low status in monkey communities, and their distress on being separated from their companions. Some peer-reared monkeys, mostly males, also have self-destructive tendencies toward impulsive behavior and aggression. They're the playground bullies, and they're often shunned by, or even kicked out of, their play groups.

Clearly, peer-rearing has unhappy consequences for an individual's social skills and ability to cope with stress. It has at least one other embarrassing side effect as well. "Every animal that's reared without a mother, no matter what its other social experience may be, turns out to be hyperoral," says Suomi. "They all suck their thumbs a lot."

Peer-rearing also leaves a distinctive stamp on the monkey's physiology. Samples of cerebrospinal fluid from Suomi's impulsive monkeys show that they grow up with lower levels of serotonin, a mood-regulating biochemical that has been linked with aggression, antisocial behavior, and depression in human beings. At the same time, turnover of norepinephrine, a chemical messenger associated with fearfulness, is unusually rapid in peer-reared monkeys. The monkeys' immune systems tend to be suppressed, while their levels of stress hormones are higher and their heart rates faster than those of mother-reared monkeys. Might these be the fruits of insecure attachment?

Megan Gunnar thinks so. Gunnar studies the relationship between attachment security and reactions to stress in human infants and toddlers. She's found that stressful circumstances such as vaccinations, the presence of strangers, and separation from mom produce elevations of the stress hormone cortisol in infants. By age two, however, children with secure attachments to their mothers don't get these cortisol rushes, even when they act stressed out. Children with insecure attachments, on the other hand, continue to show elevations of cortisol. It's as if secure attachment comforts the body more than the mind.

"In the animal literature, the contact with adult conspecifics—it doesn't have to be the mom, but it needs to be somebody who acts like a mom and that the baby is familiar with—has powerful effects at blocking the activity of stress-response systems," says Gunnar. "If the attachment figure is present, and the relationship has been reliable, then some aspect of the stress response just doesn't happen."

That's a good thing, says Gunnar, because a hyperactive stress-response system can wreak havoc on the body. The racing heartbeats and suppressed immune systems that Suomi sees in peer-reared monkeys, for example, are responses that would normally occur to help the young animal cope with a transient stress—such as being left alone while mom goes out and mates. But in peer-reared monkeys, the stress response is cranked up day in, day out, and that super-responsiveness persists into adolescence—long past the age of primate attachment. Gunnar proposes that such a skewed stress-response system can promote lasting behavioral changes by interfering with brain development. In rat pups, she points out, chronic stress is known to disturb the development of the limbic system, frontal lobes, and hippocampus, parts of the brain that are involved in fearfulness and vigilance, attention focusing, learning, and memory. Gunnar suggests that secure attachment serves as a buffer against these disturbances, while insecure attachment leaves the brain open to insults that can result in lifelong anxiety, timidity, and learning difficulties.

Of course, anxious, inhibited, or impulsive behavior isn't necessarily the result of early attachment problems. The extensive work of Harvard psychologist Jerome Kagan certainly suggests that such traits can be inborn. Kagan finds that 20 percent of human infants have the behavioral and physiological signs of an inhibited temperament at just four months of age—presumably, in Kagan's view, before a child's environment would have exerted its effects. He has also found that up to 40 percent of four-month-olds have signs of a bold or fearless nature. These tendencies often mellow with time, however, so that by age four only 10 percent of children are either fearful or reckless.

Suomi finds virtually the same proportions of bold and fearful monkeys in his mother-reared troops—a fact that seems to argue for the genetic conservation of temperament. But Kagan contends that the rich inner life of the child may limit the relevance of animal studies, despite the seeming parallels in primate personalities. "It's not just what happens to you that counts— it's what you think happens to you," says Kagan. "And it is inordinately difficult to figure out what a child is thinking. Until we devise ways to measure what is in a child's head, we're not going to understand the child's environment."

The inner life of the child may help explain the phenomenon of so-called resilient children, those who somehow manage to rise above difficult home environments and live normal, even accomplished, lives. But these children are exceptional; it's clear that abusive or negligent parenting can have devastating effects on a child's emotional development. All the evidence suggests that physical abuse in childhood, for example, leads to a higher risk of drug use, mood disorders, violence, and criminality in adulthood. Girls who are sexually abused are more prone to depression, panic attacks, eating disorders, drug abuse, and suicide. And children reared in orphanages, without any parenting at all, often develop a disturbing array of social and behavioral problems. Researchers are beginning to explore the biological mechanisms for these associations, but it's not hard to imagine the psychological ones.

"I think there are people who, for genetic reasons, are more susceptible to certain kinds of stressful stimulation," says Bruce Perry, who studies physiology of abused and neglected children at the Baylor College of Medicine in Houston. "But even with the optimum genetic organization, trauma will create the problems we're talking about."

Many of the kids Perry sees have been exposed to domestic violence, and their unpredictable and threatening home lives, he says, can be read in both their physiology and their behavior. They seem to be in a perpetual state of arousal: their "fight or flight" response has somehow been permanently activated, and they have tense muscles, rapid heart rates, and trouble sleeping. Their stress-response system may be irreparably altered. "These kids grow up with a neurophysiology that is perfectly adapted to survive in a chaotic, distressing environment," says Perry. "They develop this extreme hypervigilance because they never know what is going to happen next."

But the children of domestic violence are poorly adapted to life in a nonviolent world. Their vigilance can lead them to misinterpret other people's behavior and intentions, says Perry. Boys, for example, will per- ceive hostility and aggression in a look or an offhand remark and respond too readily in kind (think Robert DeNiro in Taxi Driver). Girls are more likely to shut down or withdraw completely from even mildly threatening circumstances. In school, both boys and girls tend to tune out verbal information and become hypersensitive to nonverbal cues. They might focus more on a teacher's hand gestures, for example, than the subject he's lecturing on.

Perhaps it's not surprising that severe stress in childhood leaves both biological and behavioral scars. But researchers are learning that even less extreme emotional stressors, such as parental conflict or depression, can also have an impact on kids' behavior and biology. The children of depressed mothers, for example, are at increased risk for depression themselves, and most psychologists think the risk cannot be ascribed entirely to genetics. EEG studies by psychologist Geraldine Dawson of the University of Washington in Seattle show that babies whose mothers are depressed have reduced activity in the left frontal region of the brain—the area implicated in joy, interest, and other positive emotions.

Growing up in even a mildly bad environment appears to affect your biology. The question, of course, is whether those changes can be reversed. Several findings of research suggest that they can be. Suomi, for example, has shown that even monkeys who are born anxious and inhibited can overcome their temperamental handicap—and even rise to the top of the dominance hierarchy in their troop—if they are raised by ultranurturing supermoms. Kagan's work confirms that mothering can alter the course of an inhibited child's development. A pioneering day-care program at the University of North Carolina at Chapel Hill has cut the incidence of mental retardation by as much as 80 percent among kids whose unstimulating home environment put them at high risk for low IQ. Dawson, too, has found that psychologically depressed mothers who manage to stay positive and engaged in caregiving can minimize the impact of their depression on their babies' brain waves.

And her follow-up work revealed that, at age three, children's EEGs will return to normal if their mothers' depression lifts.

"So I wonder, how plastic is the brain?" says Dawson. "At what point in development do we start to see enduring effects as opposed to transient effects?"

The answer may be never. The new model of neural development holds that the primitive areas of the brain mature first: in the first three years of life, the regions in the cortex that govern our sensory and motor skills undergo the most dramatic restructuring and these perceptual centers, along with instinctual ones such as the limbic system, will be strongly affected by early childhood experiences. This vulnerability is nothing to scoff at, says Robert Thatcher, a neuroscientist at the University of South Florida College of Medicine in Tampa. "The limbic system is where we live, and the cortex is basically a slave to that," he explains.

But the frontal cortex, which governs planning and decision making, and the cerebellum, a center for motor skills, are also involved in emotional development. And those parts of the brain don't get rewired until a person is five to seven years old. What's more, another major restructuring of the brain occurs between ages nine and eleven, says Thatcher. Suddenly, the brain is looking less like a sculpture in stone and more like a work in progress.

In fact, Thatcher's readings of the EEGs of adolescents and adults have revealed that some reorganization of the brain may occur about every two years from birth to death. He proposes that these reorganizations happen in response to waves of nerve growth factor that sweep across the cerebral hemispheres in two-year cycles, revamping up to one-fifth of the brain's synaptic connections at the leading edge of the wave. The idea of the traveling waves is just a theory now but it's a theory that's making more sense to more scientists.

"The brain doesn't stop changing after three years," says Megan Gunnar. "For some things, the windows of influence are only beginning to close at that age, and for others they're only beginning to open." If Thatcher is right, the brain is, in fact, under lifelong renovation. Long-term studies are just now beginning to demonstrate that experiences later in life can redirect emotional and behavioral development, even in adulthood. Some of us—our parents—are greatly relieved by the news.

 Article Review Form at end of book.

What is one strategy introverts use to start a conversation with someone they have never met before? What are some of the assumptions extroverts make that help them start a conversation with a stranger?

The Press of Personality

A study of conversations between introverts and extraverts

Avril Thorne

Wellesley College

In a study of the transactional impact of personality, 52 women were grouped in pairs to get acquainted in two conversations, one with an introvert and one with an extravert. The women were selected from their scores on the Myers–Briggs Type Indicator and were asked to provide accounts of their conversations as they listened to playbacks of their interactions. The conversations were analyzed by a system informed by interactants' accounts. *The most distinctive conversational styles occurred in dispositionally matched dyads, with more moderate patterns in mixed dyads: Introverts with introverts engaged in focused problem talk, whereas extraverts with extraverts showed a wider range of topics and more claims of common ground. A qualitative analysis of the accounts suggested that differing assumptions and strategies generated the styles. The findings are discussed in terms of the power of dispositions to create situations—and evocativeness referred to by Murray (1938) as "press"—and for transactional conceptions of introversion and extraversion.*

A neglected assumption of personality psychology is that personality influences other people. Henry Murray's (1938) concept of *press*, which he defined as the directional force of an environment, object, or person, was an early recognition of this impact. Murray highlighted the evocative nature of dispositions in an unusual discussion of the process by which personality gets named:

The [experimenter]. . . . becoming as open and sensitive as possible, feels how the subject's attitude is affecting him (the E). In this way he apprehends the press (as it 'hits' him). If he feels excluded he imagines Rejection in the S; if he feels that he is being swayed to do something he imagines Dominance; if he feels anxious or irritated he infers Aggression, and so forth. (1938, p. 248)

The considerable consensus that is often obtained with personality descriptions demonstrates that individuals often make distinctive impressions on observers. The transactional impact of personality, however, has only begun to be conceptualized and explored empirically (Kiesler, 1983; Wiggins, 1974).

An impact approach to personality offers a dynamic and more realistic alternative to the assumption that dispositions and situations are independent from each other (cf. Olweus, 1977). In this alternative view, the expression of a disposition is conceived as creating a situation for (the generalized) other by eliciting particular kinds of responses. A sociable person, for example, might elicit sociable conduct from the other, or a competitive person might evoke competition. The approach also helps to account for apparent inconsistencies in personality. A sociable individual, for example, might behave more sociably when speaking with an extravert than with an introvert. This waxing and waning of conduct, rather than indicating an inconsistency in personality, indicates the compellingness of personality, the necessity of taking the other's disposition into account.

The study presented in this article examines the press of extraverts and introverts as manifested in conversations between strangers. The study of conversational style, if somewhat unusual in personality research, seems an important way of detecting dispositional press because speech is a common vehicle for expressing and responding to personality. Encounters between strangers are selected because such relations are the primary social context of extraversion–introversion theory and research. The concepts of extraversion and introversion, however, present a special challenge for an impact approach to personality because introverts would seem to have little social force and extraverts, a surfeit. Carl Jung (1923/1976), often credited with formulating the constructs, described the public appearance of extraverts as outgoing and sociable and that of introverts as reserved, inscrutable, and shy. Self-report measures score as extraverted someone who says he or she likes to meet strangers, to mix socially, and so forth, and as introverted, someone who does not (Eysenck & Eysenck, 1975; Myers, 1962). This image of extraverts as voluble with strangers and of introverts as silent has often been pursued but, interestingly, not well supported in behavioral research. Extraverts have been found to be more talkative in triads or in groups (Bem & Allen, 1974; Shaw, 1976), but not necessarily in dyads, where findings have been inconsistent (Campbell & Rushton, 1978; Cheek & Buss, 1981; Gifford, 1981; Patterson & Holmes, 1966; Ramsay, 1968; Rutter, Morley, & Graham, 1972; Siegman & Pope, 1965).

There has been little attempt in extraversion–introversion theory and research to understand the particular kinds of talk that introverts and extraverts promote. Jung (1923/1976) posited a cognitive difference in direction of attention, describing extraverts as being guided by and directed toward the outer, public world, and introverts as directed toward the inner, subjective world. Eysenck (1967) proposed a biological difference in level of cortical arousal: He posited that extraverts' relatively low arousability leads them to seek external stimulation and that introverts' higher arousability leads them to shy away from external stimulation. These theories have focused on cognitive or biological phenomena and do not seem to have facilitated transactional research.

Studies in speech of extraverts and introverts have generally ignored conversational content and style. In addition, the research has often involved confederates who are urged to behave the same way with all subjects and has not reported the behavior and personality of the confederate (Patterson & Holmes, 1966; Ramsay, 1968; Siegman & Pope, 1965). This practice has precluded the study of more spontaneous interactions and obscured the mutual influence of personalities. The only study (Cheek & Buss, 1981) that used naive subjects throughout did not focus on conversational style and was cross-sectional rather than longitudinal; consequently, the waxing and waning of conduct depending on with whom one was speaking could not be assessed directly.

My study offers methodological alternatives and provides a relatively novel approach to the conceptualization of extraversion and introversion: Interactants were asked to provide accounts (Cacioppo & Petty, 1981; Harré & Secord, 1972) of their conversations with other introverts and extraverts as they listened to playbacks of their interactions. The accounts were used to inform the development of a coding scheme for the conversations and to interpret the patterns that emerged. Because of the dearth of transactional personality research, the general hypothesis of the study was derived from interpersonal theory (e.g., Kiesler, 1983) and from nontransactional research. Numerous studies, including research that has used Thematic Apperception Test (TAT) stories, recall of prose passages, and observers' trait descriptions, have found that extraverts produce more cheerful and upbeat material than do introverts (Costa & McCrae, 1980; Lishman, 1972; Shapiro & Alexander, 1975; Thorne, 1981). If such expressions are contagious, the most upbeat conversations should come from extraverts/extravert dyads, the most serious from introvert/introvert dyads. The operationalization of extraversion–introversion in terms of particular speech acts, however, was inductively informed by speakers' accounts.

Method

Subjects

Subjects were 52 college women from a large west coast university for whom participation in research fulfilled a course requirement. The average age was 19 years, ranging from 18 to 25 years. The 26 women who tested as extraverts did not differ statistically from the 26 introverts in age, year in school, reported grade point average, or distribution of academic interests. College majors were about equally represented across the fields of political science, business, the humanities, and the natural and social sciences.

Measure of Extraversion–Introversion

Subjects were selected as a result of their scores on the Extraversion and Introversion scales of the Myers–Briggs Type Indicator, Form F (Myers, 1962; Myers & McCaulley, 1985). The two scales share a substantial number of items and correlate approximately –.95. The scale items mostly refer to conduct in general social context or in unspecified gatherings of people (e.g., talking easily to almost anyone or only under certain circumstances, and being a good mixer or being rather quiet and reserved). The highest reported correlates for this Extraversion scale are the Extroversion scale of the Eysenck Personality Questionnaire and the Sociability scale of the California Psychological Inventory, $r = .74, .67$, respectively (Steele & Kelly, 1976; Stricker & Ross, 1964).

Procedures

Pretest

Participants were part of a pretest group ($n = 150$ women) recruited from large introductory psychology courses. They were told that the purpose of the testing was to provide information about a general sample of students. Introversion (I) and Extraversion (E) items constitute only one eighth of the test, but the entire inventory was used to provide more extensive feedback to those who so desired once the research concluded. The E minus 1 difference scores were compiled into a distribution ($M = 3.3$, $SD = 12.9$) and people scoring in the upper and lower quartiles were selected as candidates.

Recruitment

Approximately 1 week after completing the questionnaire, candidates were telephoned and asked to participate in a second study, which they were told, "will not be described until your arrival." This precaution was taken because it was felt that revealing the nature of the study would discourage introverts from participating. Acceptance rates did not differ between introverts (26/30) and extraverts (26/32). The E–I difference scores for the final sample averaged +15 (range = 9 to 24) for extraverts and –13 (range = –5 to –21) for introverts.

Collection of Conversations and of Trait and Comfort Ratings

Schedules were arranged so that two extraverts and two introverts arrived for the same session. The research was introduced as an exploratory study of conversations. The researcher determined that the women were not previously acquainted and asked them to participate in two randomly paired conversations with each other. Participants were actually paired according to a prearranged schedule so that each would converse with a dispositionally similar (I/I or E/E) as well as dissimilar (I/E) other. The order of conversations was randomized. The women were seated at a 45° angle about 3 ft apart from each other. An operating videotape camera was visible across the room. Each conversation was 10 min long, being terminated by a knock on the door. The pairings produced a total of 52 conversations (13 I/I, 13 E/E, and 26 I/E). To validate the method of subject selection, the researcher subsequently asked interactants to rate each partner on a list of trait descriptions. Interactants were also asked to rate their degree of comfort with each partner.

Collection of Accounts

To help develop indexes of conversational style, the researchers scheduled as many interactants as possible for individual playback sessions. More than three fourths of the subjects could be scheduled, with a few more introverts than extraverts participating (22/26 I; 18/26 E). Each session occurred 1 to 2 weeks following the conversations, lasted about 1 hr, and was audio recorded. The session was conducted by the author or by one of several undergraduate women assistants. In explaining the purpose of the session, we likened our role to that of an outsider who can best understand the meaning of an encounter through the eyes of its participants (Harré & Secord, 1972). We told the informant that we were interested in anything that she could tell us about her conversations, from the most mundane proceedings to the most striking events that may have happened. An audio recording[1] of her conversations was then played back, and the informant was asked to stop the tape whenever she wished to comment on the action. Such questions as "What led (you/her) to say that? and "What's happening here?" were among the most directive forms of questioning used.

Debriefing

At no time were participants informed that extraversion–introversion was the focus of the research. The decision to withhold this information was made when we found, during a pilot study, that informing the subjects of this fact typically enhanced their tendency to remember each other as types instead of as persons.

Measures

Trait and Comfort Ratings

The list of trait descriptors included relevant as well as buffer items. The relevant items had been found to correlate significantly with Myers–Briggs Extraversion–Introversion across pooled observers and various samples (cheerful, enthusiastic, outgoing, talkative, sociable; aloof, serious, reserved, shy). The buffer items had been found to be independent of extraversion–introversion (mature, intelligent, conventional, boastful, artistic, sincere, obnoxious, and worrying; Thorne, 1981). Subjects were also asked to rate their degree of comfort in each conversation. For each descriptor, ratings could range from *very uncharacteristic* (1) to *very characteristic* (5).

Speech Acts

The conceptualization of speech acts was informed by the accounts and refined through a pilot study. Eight kinds of utterances appeared to meet the criteria of meaningfulness and codability. Compliments, agreements, reaches for similarity, stories, and pleasure talk were expected to be more characteristic of extraverts. Hedges and problem talk were expected to be more characteristic of introverts. A final category, disagree/criticize, was included because the women, in their accounts, seemed to regard such utterances as potent acts of rudeness that occurred occasionally.

In the first category, a *compliment* ("I like your blouse," "Your job is impressive!") was defined as an expression of admiration for the other's activities, given that the other had not already expressed that enthusiasm. The initiatory nature of a compliment distinguishes it from the next speech act, agreement, which is conditional on the other's having first offered a definite opinion or evaluation. Compliments were sometimes described in the accounts as devices for perking things up (e.g., to get the other to shift from problem talk to pleasure talk).

In the next category of speech acts, *agree* was defined as direct acknowledgement of sharing the other's opinion, for example, "I think so, too," in response to "Teaching assistants are more energetic than a lot of professors," and "Yeah, me too," in response to "I hate looking for

[1]The decision to replay audio dubs of the audiovisual recording was due to the inaccessibility of videotape facilities during the overlapping hours in which playback sessions were scheduled.

work." In applying the category, coders were instructed to exclude noninterruptive overlay (e.g., "yeah," "mmm-hmmm") because, according to the accounts, overlay was a conventional way of saying "I am listening" rather than "I definitely agree."

The category *reach for similarity* was defined as the claiming of common ground, in which a connection with the other, at least once removed, is announced; in this case, a third person would be brought in to connect with the other's experience. Examples included "You're from Los Angeles? I have an aunt who used to live down there," and "One of my roommates is taking foreign languages, like you." The most unusual reach in the study came from an extravert who said, "You have a turtle? A friend of mine has a kitty!"

Another speech act, the *story*, was defined as a recounting of a specific sequence of events; it had characters, was located in time and space, and bore the semblance of a plot. Sometimes a story was signaled by "Let me tell you this story"; other times it was not. Generic recountings of events (e.g., "I used to always go to matinee movies and they had great popcorn") were to be excluded. Unlike the other categories, a story could span as many utterances as deemed to be included therein.

The category *pleasure talk* was defined as an expression of satisfaction or enjoyment of one's own activities. Examples included "I like jogging" and "Steinbeck is wonderful." To qualify in this category, an utterance had to be a definite statement of satisfaction unweakened by a qualifier or tag hedge; that is, statements such as, "I sorta like her," and "I like it a lot, well, not really" qualified as hedges, not pleasure talk.

The speech act *problem talk* was defined as an expression of dissatisfaction with one's own activities. Examples included, "Whenever I take an English class it really messes me up," and "I've got to look for an apartment because my roommates are driving me nuts." As with the previous category, hedged evaluations were to be excluded.

The *hedge* was defined as an expression of a qualification, or an ambivalent evaluation, as in "The exam was kind of hard," or "I sort of like

her." Instances of the category were signaled by qualifiers such as "kind of," "sort of," and "not too much." Such hedges seemed to serve the function of avoiding commitment. Even such apparently factual hedges as "It stays light in Denmark the whole time, well, not the whole time, maybe except for about 15 minutes" seemed to serve a protective function by averting the possibility of a factual challenge and the eventuality that one might appear unknowledgeable.

The final category, termed *disagree/criticize* in this article, tended to be called "dump" in the accounts, for it denoted direct disagreement or an expression of utter distaste for the other's activities. For example, a person says, "I'm studying microbiology," to which the other dumps, "Oh yuck! I can't stand that stuff!"

With the exception of the story category, the coding unit for all categories was an utterance, a sentence containing at least a subject (or implied subject), a verb, and often a predicate. A key event coding system was used; that is, utterances judged not to exemplify one of the categories were not coded. Categories were to be mutually exclusive. The coders worked independently and directly from the videotape, writing down and categorizing each key event as it occurred. The protocols functioned both as a summary of the content of each conversation, as well as the basis for checking exactly what was coded (the specific utterance) and into what category. The coding required about 1½ hr per 10-min conversation.

Twenty-one of the conversations were randomly selected and independently coded a second time to assess interjudge agreement. The reliability of each speech act category was assessed by dividing the total number of agreements across instances of the category by the total number of agreements plus disagreements. Interjudge reliabilities for the categories ranged from 54% to 87% (Table 1). The disagree/criticize and story categories were the least reliable and least frequently applied, emerging no more than once per conversation on the average. The story category yielded the least consensus, apparently due to different perceptions of where a story began and ended and of what constituted generic versus specific events. Due to relative infrequency and unreliability, the story and disagree/criticize categories were dropped, bringing the median reliability to 81% for the remaining categories (range = 74% to 87%).

Topic Categories

Topic categories were developed to construct a measure of topic focus and to elaborate differences in what extraverts and introverts talked about. Two speech acts, pleasure talk and problem talk, were chosen as topic carriers because the utterances, by definition, directly declared the speaker's own interests and concerns. All such utterances were copied from the coding records and given to a panel of judges to develop a list of topics. The panel settled on nine categories: school, current living

Table 1 Reliability of Judgments of Speech Act Categories

Speech Act Category	Interjudge Reliability[a]	Agreed-on Frequency
Compliment	.81	62
Agree	.80	164
Reach for similarity	.84	80
Story	.54	21
Pleasure talk	.87	196
Problem talk	.87	316
Hedge	.74	119
Disagree/criticize	.67	4

Note: N = 21 conversations.
[a]Percentages (agreements over agreements plus disagreements).

Table 2 Reliability of Judgments of Topic Categories

Topic Category	Interjudge Reliability[a]	Agreed-on Frequency
School	.95	212
Current living situation	.92	79
Roots (family, hometown)	.94	34
Extracurricular activities	.90	71
Health	.93	13
Miscellaneous people	.79	58
Employment	.88	21
Psychological research	.95	20
Self-characterizations	.71	24

Note: N = 21 conversations.
[a]Percentages (agreements over agreements plus disagreements).

situation, roots (family, hometown), extracurricular activities (hobbies, travel, etc.), health, employment, miscellaneous people (not relatives, housemates, or teachers), psychological research, and self-characterizations (e.g., "I'm rowdy," "I'm shy"). Interjudge reliabilities for each category (agreements over agreements plus disagreements across a random sample of 21 conversations) were adequate, ranging from 95% for school and psychological research to 71% for self-characterizations. A breakdown is presented in Table 2. It is interesting to note that the most ambiguous topic category concerned what constituted a self-characterization, or personality description, and what did not. Statements of attitudes and interests (e.g., school, hobbies, living situation) were sometimes difficult to separate from dispositional statements.

Talking Time

Two measures of talking time were obtained: a summary rating and an ongoing tally. The summary rating was made immediately after coding a conversation; coders were asked to assign an integer of speaking time to each participant so that the integers summed to 10, the length in minutes of the conversation. To ensure that coders were assessing talk time and not the number of utterances they had just coded, a second set of judges obtained an ongoing tally. The judges used two-channel Rusttrack event recorders, on which a stylus was manually triggered for the duration of each person's speech. Judges were instructed not to count time spent laughing or time associated with single-word affirmations of the other's statements. Interjudge reliabilities, assessed by Pearson correlations, were .92 for the ongoing method and .80 for the summary method. The two measures correlated (.89), uncorrected for attenuation. The magnitude of the correlation attests to the validity of the more efficient summary ratings of talking time.

Results

Design of Analyses

Each woman spoke in two conversations, with a dispositionally similar and dissimilar other. The arrangement approximates a 2 (subject disposition) × 2 (partner disposition) factorial design with repeated measures on the second factor. However, the factors are not strictly independent because subjects also serve as partners in matched cells (E/E, I/I), whereas the roles are separated in mixed cells. For the conversational measures, independent *t* tests were conducted between the I/I and E/E dyads, the only independent cells. The extent to which styles changed in mixed dyads was assessed by separate repeated measures *t* tests for introverted speakers (I with I, I with E) and for extraverted speakers (E with I, E with E). For the questionnaire data, repeated measures analyses of variance were used to assess the influence of rater and target disposition on trait ratings.

Trait and Comfort Ratings

Cell means and results for analyses of variance on the trait and comfort ratings are presented in Table 3. Seven of the nine trait ratings showed significant partner effects and nonsignificant rater and interaction effects. Regardless of the disposition of the rater, Myers–Briggs extraverts were viewed as relatively outgoing, cheerful, enthusiastic, and talkative, and introverts were seen as reserved, serious, and shy. The findings presented here validate the method of subject selection. In addition, the findings suggest that the customary neglect of the influence that observer dispositions have on trait ratings is of little consequence, at least in the domain of extraversion–introversion (e.g., Thorne, 1981).

Effects for rater disposition, although rare, occurred for judgments of sociability and comfort. Introverts rated introverted partners as less sociable and less comfortable to be with, than they rated extraverted partners. Extraverts, on the other hand, reported feeling comfortable with both extraverted and introverted partners, and reported that both partners were sociable. This discrepancy may indicate that extraverts are simply more likely to attribute a sociable attitude to any interaction partner, or that an actual change existed in introverts' behavior in the direction of greater sociability with extraverts. Introverts' reports of greater comfort with extraverts than with introverts seem to indicate that extraverts were not merely attributing sociability to introverts but were also eliciting it. This possibility will be explored in the analysis of speech acts.

No significant differences were obtained for ratings of aloofness. Mean ratings were highest, however, for the I/I cell. In the context of conversations between strangers, it apparently takes two introverts to feel uncomfortable, appear unsociable, and, to some extent, seem aloof. The significant findings for aloofness in the prior research (Thorne, 1981) may have been due to a prevalence of introverted observers in those assessments.

Table 3 Means and Analyses of Variance for Trait and Comfort Descriptions

| | Cell Means[a] | | | | F ratios | | |
| | Rater Introvert | | Rater Extravert | | | | |
Variable	Partner Introvert	Partner Extravert	Partner Introvert	Partner Extravert	Rater	Partner	Rater × Partner
Cheerful	3.0	3.8	3.4	4.1	3.16	18.64***	0.42
Enthusiastic	2.7	3.6	3.3	3.7	2.76	11.00**	2.02
Outgoing	2.6	3.7	3.1	3.9	2.34	19.95***	0.31
Talkative	2.9	3.9	3.4	3.9	1.40	14.42***	1.15
Sociable	3.2	4.1	3.9	4.1	5.38*	9.87**	4.24*
Aloof	2.7	2.2	2.0	2.2	2.12	0.51	3.00
Serious	3.6	3.0	3.3	2.9	0.98	6.00*	0.38
Reserved	3.6	2.8	3.4	2.7	0.54	9.95**	0.05
Shy	3.1	2.4	2.7	2.0	3.63	9.49**	0.01
Comfort[b]	2.9	3.7	3.9	3.8	8.31**	3.99*	4.78*

Note. N = 26 per cell.
[a]Ratings ranged from *very uncharacteristic* (1) to *very characteristic* (5).
[b]Self-rating.
* $p < .05$, two-tailed. ** $p < .01$, two-tailed. *** $p < .001$, two-tailed.

Results for the buffer items were wholly consistent with previous findings (Thorne, 1981). No significant partner, rater, or interaction effects were obtained for ratings of artistic, boastful, conventional, intelligent, mature, obnoxious, sincere, or worrying: Fs (1, 50) ranged from .01 to 2.51, $p > .10$.

Talking Time

Results for the summary and ongoing measures of talking time were similar, but findings are reported for the ongoing method because it calibrates minutes instead of relative percentages. Average minutes time by type of speaker are shown in the first row of Table 4. The results of independent t tests between introverted and extraverted dyads and of repeated measures t tests for introverted and extraverted individuals, are presented in the last three columns of the table.

Table 4 shows that mean amounts of talking time were equal for introverted and extraverted dyads, with no significant changes in dispositionally mixed dyads. The finding of equal talking time, although not particularly surprising in light of the inconsistent results of previous research, does seem incon-

sistent with interactants' ratings of extraverts as more talkative than introverts (see Table 3). In the accounts, the term *talkative* appeared to refer to the relative ease with which talk unfolded, rather than the amount of talk per se; extraverts generally were perceived as more skilled at getting and keeping a conversation going. Measures of talking time that are sensitive to instances of the intuition of speech, and to volume and other paralinguistic features, may be more appropriate criteria for talkativeness (Scherer, 1979).

Speech Acts[2]

A breakdown of speech act frequencies by type of speaker is shown in Table 4. Also shown are the results of independent and repeated measures t tests. No significant differences were obtained for total number of utterances coded, a finding that parallels the results for talking time. Significant differences were obtained, however, for type of utterance. Contrasts of introverted and ex-

[2]Results for speech acts and topics are reported for frequencies normalized by square root transformations, although the results did not differ when raw frequencies were used.

traverted dyads showed significantly more hedges and problem talk for introverts and significantly more pleasure talk, agreements, compliments, and to some extent, reaches for similarity ($p < .08$) for extraverts. In addition, means for dispositional act frequencies were more extreme in dispositionally similar than in mixed dyads. Extraverts showed more pleasure talk, reaches for similarity, compliments, and agreements with extraverts than with introverts. Introverts showed more hedges and problem talk with introverts than with extraverts. Thus, as expected, expressions of extraversion and introversion were accentuated by a dispositionally similar partner.

The last two columns of Table 4 assess the extent to which styles changed significantly from one situation to the next. Introverts showed significantly more problem talk when conversing with an introvert than with an extravert. Extraverts showed significantly more pleasure talk when conversing with an extravert than with an introvert. Repeated measures t tests for the other speech act categories, although tending to show changes in the expected direction, were not statistically significant. The strength of the findings for pleasure and problem

Table 4 Means and *t* Tests for Speech Act Categories and Talking Time

Variable	Mean Frequency				t^b		
	II[a]	IE	EI	EE	II-EE	II-IE	EI-EE
Total talking time (minutes)	4.7	4.5	4.7	4.7	0.01	0.71	0.35
Speech act category (frequencies)							
Pleasure talk	3.7	4.1	5.1	7.6	−3.48**	−0.22	−2.15*
Agree	3.0	3.8	4.1	4.8	−2.62*	−0.90	−1.08
Reach for similarity	1.0	.9	1.5	1.7	−1.83	0.18	−0.62
Compliment	1.2	1.1	1.6	2.0	−2.09*	0.05	−1.06
Hedge	3.5	2.4	1.8	1.9	2.11*	1.81	−0.13
Problem talk	9.2	7.0	7.1	5.8	3.48**	2.56*	0.61
Total speech acts	21.5	19.1	21.2	23.8	−1.40	1.41	−1.42

Note. I = introvert; E = extravert.
[a]First letter of each cell designates speaker disposition and the second letter designates partner disposition.
[b]First column gives *t* values for independent *t* tests between I/I and E/E dyads ($df = 50$). Second and third columns give repeated measures *t* tests for introverted and extraverted speakers ($df = 25$).
* $p < .05$, two-tailed. ** $p < .01$, two-tailed.

talk indicates that the accommodations that did occur entailed shifts in the expression of satisfaction with the world at large, rather than changes in tendencies to specifically connect self with other (i.e., agree, compliment, reach for similarity).

Topic Focus and Content

Topic focus was measured by converting the number of utterances in each topic category into ipsative percentages and by summing the squares of the percentages. Higher numbers on the index indicated greater topic focus. Results for this measure are shown in the first row of Table 5. The remainder of the table presents a breakdown by topic category.

A *t* test between matched dyads showed significantly greater topic focus for introverts than for extraverts. The difference was due largely to introverts' focusing on the most obvious similarity, school. School was the only topic on which introverted pairs tended to exceed extraverted pairs ($p < .07$). Extraverted dyads, on the other hand, extended beyond school talk to talk about extracurricular activities ($p < .01$) and to some extent, roots (family matters and hometown; $p < .08$).

Topic focus was more moderate for speakers in mixed dyads. However, the accommodation approached statistical significance only for extraverts ($p < .12$). When talking with introverts, extraverts narrowed their focus by talking significantly less about extracurricular activities and roots than they had with extraverts. Introverts, on the other hand, talked significantly less about school and somewhat more about miscellaneous people ($p < .20$) with extraverts than they did with introverts. Talk about the research was more frequent in mixed dyads than it was in matched dyads, although this trend was only significant for extraverted speakers. The increase in research talk in mixed dyads may have been caused by extraverts' attempts to elicit or respond to the introverts' apparent discomfort about the camera and the situation in general. For introverts, this discomfort was perhaps easier to admit to a comfortable extravert than to an equally uncomfortable introvert.

Across all conversations, self-characterizations ("I'm outgoing") were relatively rare. The infrequent use of trait descriptors to characterize oneself concurs with earlier findings for written personality descriptions (Bromley, 1977). In light of the significant findings for other aspects of conversational style, it appears that personality does not have to be named to be an important aspect of communication.

Accounts

The accounts were not analyzed systematically because of base-rate problems in the frequency with which observations were volunteered. The nondirective method by which the accounts were obtained, although not optimal from the standpoint of verification, was deemed necessary in this context of discovery. Many of the most interesting observations concerned constraints and strategies because such concepts moved beyond act frequencies to more generative conceptions of conversation style.

Cited in the accounts were descriptions of what seemed to be two kinds of constraints, context press and dispositional press, and of the strategies underlying dispositional press. Observations about *context press* tended to be phrased in terms of basic obligations or rules of politeness. For example, one woman, in response to a query about why she pretended to agree with her partner when she felt otherwise, said, "Oh, it isn't nice to disagree!" It appeared that the woman in the study, regardless of disposition, shared an understanding of what was appropriate for getting acquainted: to find common ground, to share equally in talk, and to maintain the appearance of common ground regardless of whether such avowals were less than genuine.

Table 5 Means and *t* Tests for Topic Focus and Content

Variable	Mean Frequency				t^b		
	II[a]	IE	EI	EE	II-EE	II-IE	EI-EE
Topic focus[c]	0.53	0.47	0.49	0.40	2.53*	0.94	1.63
Topic content (frequencies)							
Extracurricular activities	0.9	1.7	1.5	3.5	−3.02**	−1.00	−2.34*
Roots (family, hometown)	0.6	0.6	0.7	1.3	−1.81	0.10	−2.40*
Miscellaneous people	0.5	1.0	0.8	1.5	−1.63	−1.35	−0.94
Health	0.1	0.3	0.2	0.3	−0.65	−0.88	−0.30
Self-characterizations	0.4	0.5	0.4	0.4	−0.11	−0.46	0.17
Psychological research	0.5	0.8	0.8	0.2	1.21	−0.30	2.43*
Employment	0.6	0.3	0.2	0.6	−0.17	0.74	−1.49
Current living situation	3.2	2.5	1.8	1.8	1.21	0.57	0.63
School	6.5	3.6	6.0	4.4	1.88	2.60*	1.01
Total	12.8	11.0	12.2	13.5	−0.43	1.62	−0.86

Note. I = introvert; E = extravert.
[a]First letter of each cell designates speaker disposition and second letter designates partner disposition.
[b]First column gives *t* values for independent *t* tests between I/I and E/E dyads (*df* = 50). Second and third columns give repeated measures *t* tests for introverted and extraverted speakers *df* = 25).
[c]See text for metric.
* *p* < .05, two-tailed. ** *p* < .01, two-tailed.

These context rules seem to explain two quantitative findings: that introverts talked as much as did extraverts and that overt disagreement was seldom expressed by introverts or extraverts.

Accounts of *dispositional press* highlighted the constraints on mood and topic imposed by each partner. For example, Karen, an introvert, described her sedentary secretarial job to both partners. The introverted partner merely nodded, and Karen continued to describe the drudgery of her job. The conversation then spiraled into what both introverts perceived as a solemn rut. The extraverted partner, on the other hand, responded to Karen's description of her job with a joke by saying, "You sit all day at your job? That sounds real interesting!" Karen confessed that she did not pursue the job topic any further because, "I thought if I told her right out that I hate my work, she would think I was a negative person." Many of the introverts felt that the conversation with the extravert was a breath of fresh air. Some extraverts, on the other hand, said they did not feel so pressed to say nice things and to refrain from complaining about problems when talking with an introvert, as opposed to an extravert. In general, introverts seemed more relieved by the conversation with an extravert than did extraverts; the latter were about evenly divided in their preferences for talking with one partner or the other.

How did subjects account for their own particular press? The situation was less comfortable for introverts, many of whom said they disliked talking with strangers and avoided it whenever possible. Given such a predicament, introverts tended to describe themselves as falling back on roles with which they felt comfortable. One frequently noted introverted strategy was to take the role of interviewer. By so doing, one could get a background on the other and avoid having to express one's own interests and concerns. Another introvert role, that of adviser, sometimes was mentioned by introverts as used with other introverts. The prevalence of problem talk in introverted conversations was perhaps partly constituted by speakers alternating the role of adviser as each took her turn at elaborating difficulties.

Instead of describing a strategy geared toward establishing a division of labor, some extraverts perfunctorily characterized their style as pursuing a mutual and general background of interests, with the basic assumption that there were a number of possible interests in common (i.e., everyone has hobbies, goes to school, lives somewhere, and comes from somewhere). Unlike introverts, who did not seem to assume much common ground was possible, extraverts assumed a considerable amount of similarity; their main concern was to explore its extent. For example, some extraverts described reaches for similarity as natural ways of finding common ground in what to them was a relatively small, pleasant world that is shared easily. Introverts who described this tactic, on the other hand, were more attuned to the hazards of reaches for similarity and were less inclined to make a reach in the absence of information about the possibility of shared ground. These differences in perceptions of reaches are merely suggestive, because the means for this act did not differ significantly. However, the accounts are interesting in light of literature on self-presentational approaches to social anxiety (e.g., Arkin, Lake, & Baumgardner, 1986; Schlenker & Leary, 1982).

Discussion

In this study, I sought to examine the mutual impact of extraverts and introverts on conversational style. As expected, the most extreme conversational patterns occurred for dispositionally matched pairs, with more moderate patterns occurring for mixed pairs. Extraverts promoted upbeat and expansive conversations, whereas introverts promoted more serious and focused discourse. This overall finding supports the view that the expression of a disposition creates a situation for the person who encounters it. The findings also help to explain apparent inconsistencies in personality: Changes in conduct from one conversation to the next were due to the interacting press of personalities.

Although extraverted and introverted dyads differed across numerous measures of conversational content and style, the acts showing significant accommodations in dispositionally mixed dyads were pleasure and problem talk, expressions of affect. The tendency to match each partner's predisposed emotional tone is perhaps not surprising, for it would seem difficult to have a conversation if one speaker were insistently upbeat and the other serious.

Although the expression of affect may be an especially evocative aspect of personality, the link between extraversion–introversion and affect requires conceptual clarification. Extraversion–introversion theory cannot readily account for why extraverts, when left to their own devices, showed more positive affect than did introverts, both in this study and in previous, nontransactional, research (Costa & McCrae, 1980; Lishman, 1972; Shapiro & Alexander, 1975). The differences in affective content of the conversations may relate to the tension that is presumed to accompany social anxiety or shyness (Cheek & Buss, 1981). Other concepts that seem relevant to the affective and attentional differences obtained in the study presented here are the notions of obsessive and hysterical style, particularly in their more recent formulations (e.g., Shapiro, 1965). Jung (1981/1969) showed an early interest in these styles, and his subsequent formulations of introversion and extraversion were somewhat derivative of his earlier work. The connection between extraversion–introversion and affect cannot, of course, be readily understood by invoking yet another set of distinctions. However, future research might profitably integrate extraversion–introversion theories with theories about affect and emotional experience. Psychodynamic theories, for example, generally hold that early affective experience importantly shapes character and that dispositions in adult life have the important function of management, control, and expression of affective life.

My results not only highlight an important gap in extraversion–introversion theory, but also help to fill in another gap, by elaborating the social niche and phenomenology of extraverts and of introverts. Extraverts' claims of similarity and esteem, and their promotion of comfortable social relations, suggest the niche of catalyst of sociability. The assumption of this social role seems to express an underlying expectation that experience can and should be shared. Introverts, on the other hand, reported that they fell back on their roles of interviewer or, in some cases, that of adviser. These roles require the elicitation of the other's world more so than the mutual construction and endorsement of shared worlds. The mutual discomfort of introverts appeared to be caused by the situated incompatibility of their role preferences. Both members of a dyad cannot be interviewers unless the role is alternated, and such alternations would seem difficult to achieve within the confines of a brief conversation. The interviewer role in particular seems to express an underlying expectation that experience cannot be shared so much as appreciated as different. A similar notion of introversion was proposed by Shapiro & Alexander (1975) in a study of TAT responses.

A conception of extraversion–introversion as differing assumptions of commonality and as differing social niches or roles helps to account for the different kinds of demands that introverts and extraverts make and for the particular quality of their rapport. The framework is particularly useful for elaborating introversion, which until the present study has been primarily conceived as an asocial, and sometimes antisocial, disposition.[3] The formulation may not, however, generalize to more intimate social relations. Although studies of the quality of long-term relations between extraverts and introverts have yet to be done, it seems unlikely that introverts presume that they are different from all others. In addition, introverts do not always dislike each others' company; in fact, studies of assortative mating suggest the opposite (Cattell & Nesselroade, 1967). It is possible that the concepts of extraversion and introversion have a limited focus of convenience. The concepts may be most useful to understand how people characteristically influence general social encounters, whereas other dispositional concepts may be more useful to understand individual differences in more intimate relationships.

From the perspective of past studies of extraversion and introversion, the most relevant contribution of this study is an account of the nonsignificant differences for talking time. The finding appeared to be due to the press of the dyadic context, which seemed to obligate each speaker in the pair to assume an equal share of the load. This obligation would presumably not have been felt in triads or larger groups. For example, one of the introverts said, "I was hoping you would put us in a group so I could just sit back and take it easy." The few subjects who spoke a large amount of the time were described in the accounts as impolite, as violating what appeared to be a generally perceived rule to share equally in talk. The equal talk imperative, as well as the apparent taboo on disagreement, may have been accentuated by the

[3] The distinction Cheek & Buss (1981) proposed between nonshyness and sociability essentially separates the *ability* to be sociable (nonshyness) from the *preference* to be sociable (sociability). The present conception of extraversion as an assumption that experience can and should be shared combines the ability aspect (can) and the preference aspect (should). The conception is thus consistent with Cheek & Buss's view that extraversion is a superordinate construct that includes nonshyness as well as sociability.

fact that all of the speakers were women (Maltz & Borker, 1983; Miell & Le Voi, 1985).

The apparent imperative to share equally in talk and to submerge difference, however, was achieved differently by extraverts and introverts. Extraverts actively claimed common ground and used compliments and agreements to pry it loose. Introverts maintained common ground by sticking to the most obvious similarity—the problems of studenthood—and by hedging their assertions with phrases such as "kind of" and "sort of." Future research could profit from a more systematic examination of context press and of the alternative ways by which its imperatives can be met. Such research would entail examining relations between context press and dispositional press, the ways in which similarities and differences are achieved.

A final comment concerns implications for transactional research, specifically for the conception and measurement of personality as expressed through acts. First, the finding that *talkative* did not refer transparently to the duration of speech dictates caution in translating dispositional terminology into behavioral acts (cf. Block, 1968, Craik, 1979). Second, the high correlation found between ongoing tallies and summary ratings of talking time ($r = .89$, uncorrected for attenuation) suggests that future behavioral research could be less time-consuming. Ongoing tallies were used because of an existing controversy, at the time the study was conceived, about the relevance of summary behavioral ratings for what people "actually do" (e.g., Block, Weiss, & Thorne, 1979; Shweder, 1975). However, the findings presented here, as well as those of previous research on activity level (Buss, Block, & Block, 1980) and those on expressions of disapproval and assertiveness (Wish, D'Andrade, & Goodnow, 1980), indicate that summary behavior ratings do not necessarily sacrifice accuracy for efficiency. Finally, transactional studies can benefit from the collection and from more systematic analysis of interactants' accounts (Carlson, 1984; Ickes, Robertson, Tooke, & Teng, 1986; Peterson, 1979; Thorne, 1985). The value of these naive commentaries for conceptualizing the press of personality, the press of the general context, and the niches or role possibilities within it, was unanticipated. Although there is reason to believe that people sometimes tell us more than they can possibly know (Nisbitt & Wilson, 1977), another maxim seems true for studies of human interaction: People know more than they have customarily been asked to tell.

References

Arkin, R. M., Lake, E. A., & Baumgardner, A. H. (1986). Shyness and self-presentation. In W. H. Jones, J. M. Cheek, & S. R. Briggs (Eds.), *Shyness: Perspectives on research and treatment* (pp. 189–203). New York: Plenum Press.

Bem, D. J., & Allen, A. (1974). On predicting some of the people some of the time: The search for cross-situational consistencies in behavior. *Psychological Review, 81,* 506–520.

Block, J. (1968). Some reasons for the apparent inconsistency of personality. *Psychological Bulletin, 70,* 210–212.

Block, J., Weiss, D. S., & Thorne, A. (1979). How relevant is a semantic similarity interpretation of personality ratings? *Journal of Personality and Social Psychology, 37,* 1055–1074. New York: Wiley.

Bromley, D. B. (1977). *Personality description in ordinary language.* New York: Wiley.

Buss, D. S., Block, J. H., & Block, J. (1980). Preschool activity level: Personality correlates and developmental implications. *Child Development, 51,* 401–408.

Cacioppo, J. T., & Petty, R. E. (1981). Social psychological procedures for cognitive response assessment: The thought-listing technique. In T. V. Merluzzi, C. R. Glass, & M. Genest (Eds.), *Cognitive assessment* (pp. 309–342). New York: Guilford Press.

Campbell, A., & Rushton, J. P. (1978). Bodily communication and personality. *British Journal of Social and Clinical Psychology, 17,* 31–36.

Carlson, R. (1984). What's social about social psychology? Where's the person in personality research? *Journal of Personality and Social Psychology, 47,* 1304–1309.

Cattell, R. B., & Nesselroade, J. R. (1967). Likeness and completeness theories examined by 16 PF measures on stably and unstably married couples. *Journal of Personality and Social Psychology, 7,* 351–361.

Cheek, J. M., & Buss, A. H. (1981). Shyness and sociability. *Journal of Personality and Social Psychology, 41,* 330–339.

Costa, P. T., Jr., & McCrae, R. R. (1980). Influence of extraversion and neuroticism on subjective well-being: Happy and unhappy people. *Journal of Personality and Social Psychology, 38,* 668–678.

Craik, K. H. (1979). The smile or friendliness? The speaking turn or talkativeness? [Review of *Strategies for personality research: The observation versus interpretation of behavior*]. *Contemporary Psychology, 24,* 374–375.

Eysenck, H. J. (1967). *The biological bases of personality.* Springfield, IL: Charles C Thomas.

Eysenck, H. J., & Eysenck, S. B. (1975). *Manual of the Eysenck Personality Questionnaire.* San Diego, CA: Educational and Industrial Testing Service.

Gifford, R. (1981). Sociability: Traits, settings, and interactions. *Journal of Personality and Social Psychology, 41,* 340–347.

Harré, R., & Secord, P. F. (1972). *The explanation of social behavior.* Oxford, England: Blackwell.

Ickes, W., Robertson, E., Tooke, W., & Teng, G. (1986). Naturalistic social cognition: Methodology, assessment, and validation. *Journal of Personality and Social Psychology, 51,* 66–82.

Jung, C. G. (1969). *Studies in word association.* New York: Russell & Russell. (Original work published 1918)

Jung, C. G. (1976). *Psychological types* (H. G. Baynes & R. F. C. Hull, Trans.). Princeton, NJ: Princeton University Press. (First English translation 1923)

Kiesler, D. J. (1983). The 1982 interpersonal circle: A taxonomy for complementarity in human transactions. *Psychological Review, 90,* 185–214.

Lishman, W. A. (1972). Selective factors in memory: Part 1. Age, sex and personality attributes. *Psychological Medicine, 2,* 121–138.

Maltz, D. N., & Borker, R. A. (1983). A cultural approach to male-female miscommunication. In J. J. Gumperz (Ed.), *Language and social identity* (pp. 196–216). New York: Cambridge University Press.

Miell, D., & Le Voi, M. (1985). Self-monitoring and control in dyadic interactions. *Journal of Personality and Social Psychology, 49,* 1652–1661.

Murray, H. A. (1938). *Explorations in personality.* New York: Oxford University Press.

Myers, I. B. (1962). *Manual of the Myers–Briggs Type Indicator.* Palo Alto, CA: Consulting Psychologist Press.

Myers, I. B., & McCaulley, M. H. (1985). *Manual: A guide to the development and use of the Myers–Briggs Type Indicator.* Palo Alto, CA: Consulting Psychologists Press.

Nisbett, R. E., & Wilson, T. F. (1977). Telling more than we know: Verbal reports on mental processes. *Psychological Review, 84,* 231–259.

Olweus, D. (1977). The "modern" interactionist position. In D. Magnussion & N. S. Endler (Eds.), *Personality at the crossroads: Current issues in interactional psychology* (pp. 221–233). Hillsdale, NJ: Erlbaum.

Patterson, M., & Holmes, D. S. (1966). Social interaction correlates of the Maudsley Personality Inventory Extraversion–Introversion Scale. *American Psychologist, 21,* 724–725.

Peterson, D. R. (1979). Assessing interpersonal relationships in natural settings. *New Directions for Methodology of Behavioral Science, 2,* 33–54.

Ramsay, R. W. (1968). Speech patterns and personality. *Language and Speech, 11,* 54–63.

Rutter, T. R., Morley, I. E., & Graham, J. C. (1972). Visual interaction in a group of introverts and extraverts. *European Journal of Social Psychology, 2,* 371–384.

Scherer, K. R. (1979). Personality markers in speech. In K. R. Scherer & H. Giles (Eds.), *Social markers in speech* (pp. 147–209). New York: Cambridge University Press.

Schlenker, B. R., & Leary, M. R. (1982). Social anxiety and self-presentation: A conceptualization and model. *Psychological Bulletin, 92,* 641–669.

Shapiro, D. (1965). *Neurotic styles.* New York: Basic Books.

Shapiro, K. J., & Alexander, I. E. (1975). *The experience of introversion: An integration of phenomenological, empirical, and Jungian perspectives.* Durham, NC: Duke University Press.

Shaw, M. E. (1976). *Group dynamics: The psychology of small group behavior.* New York: McGraw-Hill.

Shweder, R. A. (1975). How relevant is an individual difference theory of personality? *Journal of Personality, 43,* 455–484.

Siegman, A. W., & Pope, B. (1965). Personality variables associated with productivity and verbal fluency in the initial interview. *Proceedings of the 73rd Annual Convention of the American Psychological Association, 73,* 273–274.

Steele, R. S., & Kelly, T. J. (1976). Eysenck Personality Questionnaire and Jungian Myers–Briggs Type Indicator correlation of extraversion–introversion. *Journal of Consulting and Clinical Psychology, 44,* 690–691.

Stricker, L. J., & Ross, J. (1964). Some correlates of a Jungian personality inventory. *Psychological Reports, 14,* 623–643.

Thorne, A. (1981). *Variations among psychological types in a social context.* Unpublished manuscript, University of California, Institute of Personality Assessment and Research, Berkeley.

Thorne, A. (1985, August). Using interactants' accounts to interpersonalize personality theory. In P. F. Secord (Chair), *Uses of interactants' accounts in interpersonal research.* Symposium conducted at the meeting of the American Psychological Association, Los Angeles.

Wiggins, J. S. (1974, February). *In defense of traits.* Invited address to the Ninth Annual Symposium on Recent Developments in the Use of the MMPI, Los Angeles.

Wish, M., D'Andrade, R. G., & Goodnow II, J. E. (1980). Dimensions of interpersonal communication: Correspondences between structures for speech acts and bipolar scales. *Journal of Personality and Social Psychology, 39,* 848–860.

Article Review Form at end of book..

What percentage of people consider themselves persistently personable and outgoing? What are three strategies suggested by the author to combat shyness?

Don't Be Shy

Advice for becoming more outgoing

Sharon Stocker

Everybody's shy some of the time, but that doesn't have to dwarf the rest of your personality. Here's how to be more outgoing in 7 easy steps.

The world's most outspoken advocate for shy people, folksy humorist Garrison Keillor, describes shyness as next to invisibility. The shy person does not shine in conversation and lacks the confidence to self-promote, so others "have only a vague impression of us as a Nice Person," he says. "People smile and look over our shoulders, looking for someone else to meet." In part, this gets it wrong by confusing being shy with being dull.

Plenty of interesting and impressively accomplished people also shrink from the spotlight, avoid speaking to others, or feel insecure about what they do—writer J. D. Salinger, painter Andrew Wyeth, and singer Barbra Streisand, to name a few. Still, there's a difference between achieving greatness but not wanting to bother with the side effects, and actively yearning for more from friendships, careers, and personal interests but being held back by wallflower tendencies.

Feeling stymied by shyness is a problem that virtually everybody faces at one time or another. In fact, only 5% to 7% of Americans consider themselves persistently personable and outgoing. The rest of us are shrinking violets at least some of the

time, often around unfamiliar people, potential romantic partners, or daunting authority figures (a response that's not only natural but often prudent). What's surprising is that so many people go a step further, actually identifying shyness as an integral part of their character—something that 40% to 50% of us do in personality surveys. And shyness appears to be on the rise. Experts explain this by noting that, while people are communicating more than ever via e-mail, voice mail, cell phones, and faxes, we're interacting less than ever face-to-face. Social skills, and the comfort that goes with practicing them, are waning.

This is not good news, because even the most expressive of late-night Internet chat-room devotees will someday have to—or at least want to—interview for a job, suggest a date for dinner, raise a hand in class, or make a cold call for business. That's not easy to do when we're thinking anxious thoughts, fearing what others will think of us, worrying that we have nothing worthwhile to say, and (when we do say something) chastising ourselves for sounding stupid—symptoms that make the inward experience of a shy person different from that of others.

At the root of shyness is self-doubt, leading to chronic, self-defeating withdrawal. Afraid to express our needs and goals to a supervisor, we miss a promotion. Feeling self-conscious in a social setting, we appear aloof and keep others at a dis-

tance. A shy person is different from an introvert, who prefers solitude. Shyness means wanting contact with others but being too uncomfortable or unskilled to achieve it.

Where does shyness come from? In some cases, genes contribute. Studies by Jerome Kagan, PhD, and colleagues at Harvard University in Boston reveal that about 15% to 20% of infants show signs of social distress at just four months—jerking their arms and legs, and crying when confronted with unfamiliar people or objects. Several years later, these same children cling more to their parents in play situations.

Experts agree, however, that an inborn predisposition to shyness pales in importance next to the social and cultural experiences of life. In people who are genetically primed for shyness, factors such as positive affirmation can build confidence, ease self-doubt, and make shyness all but disappear—something that happens in as many as a quarter of such cases. Just as important, people who initially show no signs of withdrawal can develop shy traits. Contributing factors can be unreliable attention from parents, a bullying older sibling, or a particularly stressful experience in school. Social problems in identity-forming adolescent years, and even traumatic events in adulthood, such as job loss or divorce, can foster social anxiety later in life.

The bottom line is that no matter where you fall on the shyness scale, mobility is possible, and shyness can almost always be overcome. "If you're willing to try things differently and to persist, you can make great strides," says Lynn Alden, PhD, shyness therapist and professor of psychology at the University of British Columbia, Vancouver.

We asked researchers and psychologists who have studied or treated shyness to share their techniques for successfully breaking through social inhibitions, reducing self-doubt, and drawing out latent social talent. Here are the most important steps to take:

1. SHOW UP It's natural to avoid situations that make you feel awkward, but it's not helpful if your goal is overcoming shyness. "Avoidance makes anxiety worse," says Dr. Alden. Research shows that feeling shy makes us overpredict how much anxiety we'll experience in an upcoming social situation. When asked "How uncomfortable will you feel?" before meeting someone new, shy people rate their apprehension very high. Afterward, asked how uncomfortable they actually were, most admit it wasn't as bad as they'd expected.

   "Nothing succeeds in overcoming shyness as much as experiencing social successes. But in order to succeed, you must be willing to go out and practice," says psychologist Lynne Henderson, PhD, director of the Palo Alto Shyness Clinic, and Visiting Scholar at Stanford University, Palo Alto.

2. GIVE YOURSELF CREDIT One way to improve on your success when dealing with others is to stop being your own worst critic. When you're shy, scorn for your own social performance is almost always greater than that of the people you interact with, as shown in a number of studies. "A shy person may focus on one misstep and blow it out of proportion to the exclusion of all that went well," says Dr. Alden. Take the case of Tom, a client of Dr. Alden's who was in search of romance. After attending a singles dance, Tom told Dr. Alden it had gone

miserably because he had not been as smooth as he wanted to be. She asked him to explain what happened. "Well, I was dancing with this woman," he began.

"Wait," Dr. Alden interrupted. "You were able to ask a woman to dance? And she said yes?" "Right," he said.

"Well, that's really good," she told him. Further prodding revealed Tom had been able to strike up a conversation with the woman. In fact, the woman had given Tom her phone number. But because he judged his performance poorly, Tom saw only failure. As Dr. Alden added up all the positives, Tom's confidence rose, he later gave the woman a call and they went on several dates. The romance fizzled, but not because anything was wrong with Tom—an important fact Tom was now ready to believe.

In the aftermath of what seems a less-than-perfect encounter, experts advise that you carefully review exactly what you said and did. Make no generalizations about yourself or your character. Narrow the focus to specific behaviors that didn't work for you, and pat yourself on the back for everything that went well. "If you can say. 'I didn't like this particular thing I did, and I will change it next time,' that's empowering," says Dr. Henderson. "It puts you in control."

3. TAKE BABY STEPS It's a touchstone of motivational training that big goals—whether losing 15 pounds, training for a 10K race, or becoming more outgoing—consist of small goals systematically added up. Regularly established, modest ambitions bring a steady flow of minor successes, which raise confidence and increase the desire to do more. "Self-confidence is based on keeping commitments to yourself," says Dr. Henderson. "When you do what you say you're going to do, you build trust in yourself and self-respect." The key is to break the larger goal down into small, manageable objectives, and then meet them one by one.

Let's say you'd like to join a local organization. The big goal is to become involved, meet new people, become part of a group or cause—maybe even get elected to a leadership position. But for now, all you need to think about is a single immediate objective: Go to one meeting. You don't have to accomplish anything there. Just sit. Don't say anything. While you're at it, check out who the most approachable person seems to be—perhaps someone of the same sex who has an easy smile or even looks a bit tentative, like you. Next objective: Go to another meeting. Again, just quietly observe. But this time, when the meeting is over, go up to the approachable person you identified before and say something to her—acknowledging something she said, offering an innocuous compliment. Keep it brief, no big deal.

At each subsequent meeting, try to do something new, to insert yourself further into the scene. Ask a question during the group discussion. Have a longer conversation with the person you've spoken with before. Introduce yourself to someone else, perhaps of the opposite sex. State an opinion (riskier than asking a question). Invite someone with whom you've established a rapport to coffee. Continue setting small, specific goals for every meeting, proceeding at a pace that puts you at—but not over—the edge of your discomfort.

4. GIVE UNTO OTHERS Shy people are sensitive sorts, naturally empathic toward others. But much of this empathy does not come across. Why? Because when your own nervousness consumes all your available attention, there's little left for anybody else. In one test, shy people spent 40% to 50% of a conversation focused on their own discomfort and self-doubt, while more outgoing folks concentrated on themselves only 20% of the time. "It's hard to know what somebody else wants when you're consumed by a racing heart and a dozen self-doubts," says Dr. Henderson.

Increasing our attention to others boosts the intensity of engagement in a conversation and thereby makes us more socially appealing. It may sound vaguely callous, but the better you give, the better you get. "Altruism is an antidote to shyness," Dr. Henderson says. "Helping, giving, sharing—all these things take you out of yourself, and make social interactions more pleasant." Fine, but how do you do it? It's largely a mental discipline. First, notice that you're feeling anxious and uncomfortable. Second, consciously redirect your attention to the person you're interacting with. Look at them. Listen carefully. What do you like? What's interesting about what they're saying? Try giving them a compliment or a word of support for something they've just said, such as, "Yes, that makes sense."

5. EXUDE WARMTH Shyness may be a mental state, but it can help create a physical one. The pounding heart, the perspiration, the flushed face—all can feel like a small-scale natural disaster.

"When I ask shy people how they appear to others, they initially assume the other person could see they were anxious, and was judging them negatively," says Dr. Alden. "But then we'll talk about how it really looked, that the trembling or blushing was far less noticeable than they believe. However, avoiding others by breaking eye contact, not talking, or stepping away conveys a powerful message to go away." Remember, warmth is largely communicated physically. "Eighty percent of your message is nonverbal," says Dr. Alden. "If you want that message to be positive, opening up your body language by looking friendly, making eye contact, saying hello, smiling, and nodding all go a long way."

6. ANTICIPATE FAILURE Failure is difficult, but inevitable. The more you accept it as part of the natural order, the better you'll deal with it. Think of yourself as building "social fitness," as Dr. Henderson calls it—a learning process that calls for skill-building and practice. "If I'm learning a sport, I don't expect myself to perform perfectly the first time out, and if I haven't played it in 20 years, it's going to take me a while to get back into it," she says. "I have to let myself risk some failure if I'm going to improve."

"Nobody in the world handles everything perfectly all the time," says Dr. Alden. "I have a 10% write-off rate. I just accept that 10% of the things I do will be crummy or not well received and that's life. Another 10% will go well no matter what I do. The rest is somewhere in between."

7. JOIN THE CROWD There will be times when these tips don't seem to make much difference—when everything has gone wrong, there's no basis for self-congratulation, your giving has only led to taking, you feel all the warmth of an eel, and you cannot find comfort in failure. At those times, take a look around. Try to find one person who hasn't shared this stage at one point or another. If that doesn't help, allow yourself to turn a critical eye on those around you. They're certainly not stunning conversationalists. "Shy people often think small talk is big," says Jonathan Cheek, PhD, psychology professor at Wellesley College and author of Conquering Shyness (Dell, 1989). "But if you really listen to what others are saying at a cocktail party, you'll realize they're not saying all that much."

 Article Review Form at end of book.

What is one difference between securely and insecurely attached children? What is one technique to help parents form better attachments with their children?

The Loving Ties That Bond

A baby needs to form a secure 'attachment' to the mother or another caring adult. How do these early relationships develop trust—and why do some of them fail?

Susan H. Greenberg

When goslings hatch, they will immediately become attached to the first moving object they see, whether it's their mother or the Energizer bunny. Human babies are smarter. Even in utero, they begin to recognize the muffled voices of those who will care for them. By 10 days of age, they can distinguish the smell of their mother's breast milk from that of another woman. Around 5 weeks, babies demonstrate a preference for their primary caretakers by smiling or vocalizing. They follow them intently, first with their eyes, then later on hands and knees. By 9 months, many infants scream when their parents try to leave, as if to say, "I can't bear being without you!"

And so it is that babies fall in love with their parents. Psychologists, of course, have a less romantic name for it: attachment. First postulated by British psychiatrist John Bowlby in the 1950s, attachment remains one of this century's more enduring theories of human development. Research has far outlived the particular and unfounded notion of bonding popularized in the 1970s that mothers and babies need prolonged skin-to-skin contact immediately after delivery to form a proper love connection.

Attachment holds that infants and their parents are biologically wired to forge a close emotional tie, which develops slowly over the baby's first year of life through an ongoing dialogue of coos, gazes and smiles. How it unfolds may influence everything from how we perform in school to what kind of partners and parents we become. Says Alicia Lieberman, a psychology professor at the University of California, San Francisco: "The foundation for how a child feels about himself and the world is how he feels in his relationship with the primary caregiver."

For most infants that is their mother, simply because she's usually around them the most. But young babies will become attached to anyone who is consistently available and responsive to them. "If you handed a newborn to a male cousin and he acted like the typical mother, it wouldn't matter to the baby," says Jay Belsky, professor of human development at Penn State. In fact, most babies form multiple attachments. It's nature's way of protecting them against the loss of their primary caretaker.

Yet not all attachments are good attachments. Parents who respond sensitively to their child's needs—to eat, to play, to feel safe, to be left alone—will likely build strong, nurturing relationships, which some

psychologists call "secure." Parents who don't are more likely to establish "insecure" or "anxious" attachments. "Children are prewired to fall madly in love with their caregivers," says clinical psychologist Robert Karen, author of "Becoming Attached." "The sense that love is returned, that they're valued and that they can count on their mother and father, is secure attachment." Karen estimates that two thirds of 1-year-olds in middle-class American homes are securely attached; the percentage is lower in households that face hardships such as poverty.

This notion of secure versus insecure attachment is probably the most controversial aspect of attachment theory. Bowlby's colleague Mary Ainsworth first made the distinction in the 1960s, when she devised an experiment called the "strange situation." Over several months she studied mothers and infants in their homes. When the babies turned 1, she invited each pair into the lab and placed them with a stranger in a toy-filled room. Then she observed how the baby responded when his mother left the room and when she returned. As Ainsworth expected, the mother's departure distressed some of the babies and not others. But what defined their quality of attachment was how they greeted her return. The babies whose mothers were considered responsive all rushed to them—whether for comfort or to play as if to say, "I know you're there for me!" Ainsworth labeled those children "securely attached." The infants of those deemed less responsive in the home study either ignored or rebuffed their mothers when they returned. Ainsworth concluded that these "anxiously attached" babies had no confidence that their mothers would give them what they wanted.

Such labels make many people uncomfortable. "The 'attachment people' decided incorrectly that the most important aspects of that relationship is security/insecurity," says Harvard psychologist Jerome Kagan.

"The 'strange situation' is not an accurate measure, because the child's behavior in that situation is a function of its temperament and how it's been treated." Even proponents of attachment theory acknowledge its limitations. "Attachment hasn't left enough room for what any mother of two has noticed: that children are different," says psychologist Arietta Slade of the City University of New York.

To be sure, some children find it harder to form attachments than others. Children who suffer from autism and other developmental disorders, abused children, even colicky babies, all present special challenges. But most psychologists believe that with enough sensitivity and perseverance, every caretaker can form a secure attachment with almost any child. "There is such a thing as a poor fit," says Robert Karen. "But you hope parents will find a way to connect."

They needn't do it alone. Counselors can help parents overcome their own obstacles to bonding, such as depression or substance abuse. One of the most common sources of insecure attachment is what child psychiatrist Selma Fraiberg called "the ghost in the nursery," a parent's unresolved mourning for a loved one. Psychotherapy can be extremely effective in helping mothers learn how to be more sensitive to their babies. In 1985 Alicia Lieberman proved that with a group of mothers from Latin America, many of whom had recently immigrated to the United States. She performed "strange situation" assessments on their children. Of those deemed anxiously attached—about 65 percent—she offered psychotherapy to half. "After a year, these mothers were significantly more empathic, responsive and interactive" than the control group, Lieberman says.

And what if, despite everyone's best efforts, an infant fails to form a close bond with a caring adult? "Kids who were secure as infants or toddlers in general function better in ways we value in this culture," says Belsky. "But it would be a mistake to draw the conclusion that how you end up after the first year of life determines how you'll be in later life." Indeed, few people could look at a room full of teenagers and guess accurately who was securely attached at age 1. And adults who failed to bond with their own parents are not destined to revisit that fate upon their children; plenty of them transcend their early experience—whether through attachment to another caring adult, a fulfilling marriage or psychotherapy—and raise perfectly secure kids. By the same token, a secure attachment is only a beginning. "Being secure is an asset, not a guarantee," says Belsky. In this life, that's about as good as it gets.

 Article Review Form at end of book.

How do early attachment styles relate to the way children develop friendships in middle childhood? What are some of the characteristics of avoidant children that make it difficult for them to make friends?

Stages of Friendship Growth in Preadolescence As Related to Attachment History

Shmuel Shulman

Bar-Ilan University

James Elicker & L. Alan Sroufe

University of Minnesota

A process model of friendship formation in preadolescence is proposed in this article, and the continuity of early parent–child relationships (quality and attachment) with later friendship processes and peer competence is explored. Thirty-two preadolescents, subjects in a longitudinal study of attachment and subsequent social development, were observed in 4-week summer day camps. Those who had been securely attached with their caregivers as infants revealed a higher level of peer competence than did those with anxious attachment histories. However, preadolescents of both types of attachment re-ported and were observed to form friendships. In-depth case studies of four friendship pairs of preadolescents with different attachment histories suggested that there are corresponding differences in the quality and growth processes of those pairs of friendships. A three-stage model of preadolescent friendship growth is proposed, based on relationship dimensions and reflective of earlier relational patterns.

Friendships between individuals are found throughout the life span and are considered by both individuals and scholars to have a central role in adaptation. Despite this acknowledged importance, there is still much to learn about friendships—their origins, development and functional significance for the individual. In this article three aspects of friendship will be of concern, focusing on the preadolescent period: first, early developmental history and the capacity to form friendships; second, the assess-ment of individual differences in the nature of friendships; and, third, sequences or stages in the emergence of friendships. In particular, we will ex-amine the emergence and progres-sion of friendships in children with different attachment relationship his-tories.

According to Ginsburg et al. (1986) friendship serves several func-tions. Friendship provides a partner or a playmate with whom time is spent and interesting activities are pursued (Howes, 1981). Friends are willing to help each other, investing personal time and resources (Wright, 1984). An additional form of help be-tween friends is ego support (Bigelow, 1977; Duck, 1984; Wright, 1984). Friends also support percep-tions of oneself as attractive and competent, and enhance one's self-esteem. The exchange of ideas within a secure and accepting environment is an additional provision of friendship (Duck, 1984). The individual is allowed to test ideas and notions that might be criticized in a larger group. Intimate and affective feelings are the hallmark of friendship and distinguish between 'common' friends and 'close' friends.

Selman (1980) presents an elaborated description of sequential stages in the conception of friendship. At the initial stage (characteristic of the young child), friends are chosen for momentary and concrete reasons: a partner to play with, to have fun. Later, a friend is perceived as a source of help, whose characteristics are important and considered beyond the immediate encounter. In the most advanced states, friendship is conceived in terms of requirements for mutuality, intimacy, and trust.

During preadolescence, changes in the patterns of relationships that children form can be observed. Interest in particular same-sex friends becomes more focused, and close friendships or chumships are established. Children express real interest and concern for these close friends and become aware of and sensitive to their feelings. According to Sullivan (1953), this new kind of friendship is a reflection of the emerging need for interpersonal intimacy. Studies have validated this new potential for intimacy in preadolescence, in which friends are willing to disclose and compare personal information with trust and confidentiality (Berndt, 1982; Tesch, 1983).

The various functions of friendship may also reflect the different qualities or stages of a relationship. According to Levinger & Snoek (1972) a relationship starts with a surface contact. Later, nondisclosing matters are communicated and discussed. Finally, partners may reach a unique interpersonal depth. Buhrmester et al. (1988) found that new acquaintances tend to emphasize initiation behaviors, like common interests or party going, as important during the establishment of friendship. Close friends claim that emotional support, conflict management and self-disclosure contribute to a satisfying relationship.

A friendship is a dynamic process, and achievement of higher stages of friendship may bring with it

some risks. Once a relationship is intimate, it is emotionally laden. Subsequently, the emergence of differing ideas or feelings between friends may arouse ambivalence, or even a sense of betrayal. According to Wright (1984) maintenance of friendship may demand profound social and emotional skills. Thus, it is not only the establishment of an intimate relationship that reflects an advanced level of friendship. In addition, management and resolution of emergent conflicts in thinking and feeling are crucial for friendship maintenance (Selman, 1980). We suggest, therefore, that friends do not simply feel closer to each other over time. In addition to maintaining closeness and interest, they must also overcome difficulties that may lead to the dissolution of their friendship (Hartup, 1989).

How do preadolescents cope with the challenges of forming and maintaining the friendships that are characteristic of this developmental period? Are there earlier social experiences that support them in dealing with this developmental task?

Though many preadolescents may experience new and deeper forms of friendships with age-mates, the experience of a social relationship is not new to a human being of this age. Preadolescents normally have had friends in former years, at school or in their neighborhood. Furthermore, each child has in the past established close relationships with family members, especially primary caregivers.

Sroufe & Fleeson (1986) contend that through participating in salient relationships with caregivers, the child internalizes basic expectations and attitudes concerning social partners' behavior. In addition, the individual may come to anticipate the implication of his or her expectations on the other's behavior. Assuming a coherent organizational perspective, the individual projects his/her representation of relationships onto future social contacts, leading to a repetition and confirmation of expected cycles of behavior. All in all, this process leads to the carry-over of basic relationship styles into future relationships.

The core of this theory lies in the development of the infant's ini-

tial attachment to his/her mother. Bowlby (1969, 1973, 1980) argued that there are individual differences in the quality of attachment that result from differences in the quality of early care, especially the psychological availability and responsiveness of the primary caregiver. Moreover, these early relationship experiences provide the foundation for 'inner working models' of self, other and relationships. The research of Ainsworth and colleagues (Ainsworth, et al., 1978) confirmed the link between quality of care and attachment security and provided a laboratory method for assessing the quality of the infant—caregiver relationship, resulting in classifications of secure, anxious-resistant and anxious-avoidant mother-child relationships at 12 and 18 months.

During the preschool years, children who had histories of secure attachment have been observed to have more stable play partners, were more capable of reciprocity, were more socially oriented and showed more empathy (Kestenbaum et al., in press; Sroufe, 1983; Sroufe, et al., 1986). Children with a history of anxious-resistant attachment as infants (wary, unable to be settled by their mothers) showed low peer competence in nursery school. When paired with other children, those with avoidant attachment histories (refusal of contact with their mothers) were either distant or hostile (Pastor, 1981; Troy & Sroufe, 1987).

Preadolescence is the stage when important changes take place in the domain of relationships. As outlined earlier, peer relationships and friendships also undergo important changes, and peers start to play a dominant role. Following Bowlby's (1973) theory of internal working models of self and others, and Sroufe & Fleeson's (1986) theory on the coherence of relationships, it can be assumed that preadolescents with different early relationship histories will display different patterns of peer relations and friendships.

Examination of preadolescent friendship (Bukowski et al., 1987) reveals several factors which may conceptually cluster into two qualitative dimensions. The first is the *sense of closeness* to the other—including support, affection and intimacy. The second is the *level of shared activities* with age-mates.

Similar conceptual dimensions are reflective of mother–infant attachment patterns first described by Ainsworth et al. (1978). The first is the *proximity and contact* between the infant and the mother. The second is the infant's *level of exploration and competence* while knowing that the mother is available. Secure attachment results in a functional balance between proximity and exploration (Ainsworth et al., 1978). In anxious patterns, the child is either preoccupied with the mother and unable to explore (resistant attachment) or fails to seek contact with the mother even when such contact is required for settling or reassurance (avoidant attachment). The same balance or imbalance is later seen with preschool children. Children with a secure attachment history are highly involved and competent with age-mates, using teachers for instrumental assistance only when their own resources are exhausted. Children with insecure relationship histories are usually less competent. Some are preoccupied with teachers. Others are isolated, impulsive or highly aggressive, the result being that teachers give them much attention. Children showing the latter patterns are not effectively involved with peers (Sroufe & Fleeson, 1988).

It would be reasonable to assume that Sroufe & Fleeson's (1986) theory that preadolescents with a history of secure attachment would tend to manifest relational patterns of a higher level of competence and affection (unless, of course, there have been profound changes in the child's experience in the intervening years). Children with insecure attachment histories will be less competent and will be either emotionally distant or hostile toward age-mates, or simply lacking in the necessary skills and attitudes for effective engagement.

However, as suggested earlier, relationships are not just composed of dimensions; relationships are processes. Considering the newly emerging potential for intimacy, it is important to investigate how preadolescents with different relationship histories develop friendships. Are the friendships of children with anxious relationship histories developed in a manner that will lead to a sense of intimacy at some later stage? Or could it be that due to insecurities in previous relationships, these preadolescents will be unable to develop relationships which have the potential for intimacy?

This paper has two objectives. The first is to investigate the level of social competence and friendship formation in preadolescents with different attachment histories. The second objective is to sketch a preliminary model of processes characterizing the growth of friendship in preadolescence. Initially, findings on peer competence and friendship formation in preadolescence as related to attachment history will be presented. Next, assuming the different *pathways* of developing friendships among children may reflect different attachment histories, processes of friendship development among several children with different attachment histories will be described. Finally, a general model of the processes of preadolescent friendship development will be outlined.

Method

Two summer day camps, held during consecutive summers, provided opportunities for observation of friendship formation and social competence in preadolescence. For each camp, 16 children were selected (total *n* = 32) from the larger Egeland-Sroufe longitudinal sample. (See Sroufe, 1983, for a description of the larger sample and summary of studies from infancy through early childhood.) Mean age at the time of participation in camp was 10 years 8 months (SD = 7 months). Children for each camp were selected on the basis of several criteria: attachment history (approximately equal numbers secure and anxious children); participation in the Preschool Project at age 4 (see Sroufe, 1983); and gender (equal numbers of boys and girls in each camp).

In the first camp there were nine children with secure (*B*) attachment histories (five girls, four boys), four with anxious-resistant (*C*) histories (two girls, two boys) and three with anxious-avoidant (*A*) histories (one girl, two boys). In the second camp there were eight children with *B* histories (four girls, four boys), two with *C* histories (one girl, one boy), and six with *A* histories (three girls and three boys). Attachment groups did not differ in terms of age, IQ, SES, or sex. Of the children with secure histories, nine were Caucasian and eight were non-white. Of those with anxious histories, nine were Caucasian and six were non-white.

Children were transported daily between home and camp for 4 weeks. Attendance was consistent (*M* = 18.7 days; SD = 1.7). The 4-hour daily program of activities was varied, including group meetings, singing, snacks and lunch, swimming, art and craft projects, outdoor games and sports. Weekly field trips were taken, and one overnight campout was held at the camp facility, located on the university campus. The staff consisted of graduate student camp counselors and advanced undergraduate assistants, all trained and experienced in working with preadolescents.

Nine cameras were installed in the room where indoor camp activities took place. Events were sampled and recorded on a rotating schedule by switching from one camera to the next. During outdoor activities, swimming and field trips, campers were followed by one camera operator, recording according to an event-sampling procedure.

Besides videotaping of campers' activities, in keeping with the integrative approach underlying this research and the assessment strategy taken in the earlier preschool studies (Sroufe, 1983), a wide variety of data at various levels of abstraction were collected. At the broadest, most integrative level, camp counselors made qualitative ratings, rankings and friendship nominations at the end of each camp, based on their experience with the children throughout the 4-week camp session. At a more discreet level, child-child and child-adult associations were time-sampled by observers. Sociometric interviews were also conducted with each child during the last week of each camp. All the counselors and observers contributing these data were blind to attachment histories, or any other information about the children prior to the camp. Using these three sources of information: counselors, observers and the children themselves, the following measures were obtained.

Counselor data. After 4 weeks of interaction with and observation of all camp children, counselors were asked to rate each child's level of social skills with peers on a 7-point scale (1 = very low; 7 = very high). Counselor rating scores were highly correlated (r = .76) and were averaged to produce a social skills score (four counselor scores in the first camp, five scores in the second camp). Range of mean social skills score was 1.8 to 6.5.

Observational data. Children's associations with others throughout the camp were observed using a child-sampling procedure. Children were observed in a sequential order from a randomly determined schedule. The mean number of observations per child was 127 in the first camp and 175 in the second camp. The following proportions were computed: time spent with peers and with adults in proportion of time the child was observed to be isolated. Ranges of proportions of time spent with the three alternative associates were as follows: time spent with peers, .10 to .99; time spent with adults, 0 to .52; and time being alone, 0 to .54. Percent agreement between two observers based on 2800 observations was .83.

Friendship formation. Three assessments of friendship were completed. First, at the conclusion of the camp, counselors were asked to independently list all of the stable, reciprocated friendship pairs that had formed during the 4-week camp session. Each pair receiving nominations from 50 percent or more of the counselors was considered to be a friendship.

Second, children were asked to nominate 'special friends' and 'friends' during individual sociometric interviews. Nominations of 'special friends' that were reciprocated with either a 'special friend' or 'friend' nomination by the other child were considered to be a measure of friendship. Number of nominations for 'special friends' ranged from none to three children and for 'friends', from one to ten children.

The third assessment of friendship is based on Ladd's (1983) measure of *social network affinity.* This measure combines observation of children's most frequent play partners with sociometric nominations. Play associations were determined by observing each child and those with whom he or she was interacting over the 4-week camp session. Friendships were then determined using the network affinity method by selecting those who: (1) were frequent play partners of the child (20 percent or more of total play associations); *and* (2) also nominated the child as a 'special friend' or 'friend', in the sociometric interviews.

Case studies of friendship pairs. In order to provide a richer picture of the process of preadolescent friendship growth and to clarify qualitative differences in friendship, pairs were selected for extensive descriptive observation. The selection of pairs for these case studies was accomplished by: (1) determining which friendship pairs in both camps had the highest levels of observed play associations with each other, nominated each other as friends and were listed by counselors as friends and (2) from that list selecting two pairs in which both children had secure attachments in infancy (B), a pair in which both had anxious-resistant attachments (C) and a pair in which both had anxious-avoidant attachment (A). The four pairs were then observed using videotapes recorded throughout the 4-week camp sessions, and a descriptive account of the process of friendship growth was constructed for each pair.

Assuming possible differences exist between male and female friendship pairs, a separate description of friendship growth in a secure-attachment (B type) pair for boys and girls is presented. An additional pair to be described consisted of two girls with a history of anxious-avoidant attachment history (A type), the only such friendship meeting the above criteria. Another pair of two boys consisting of partners with histories of anxious-resistant attachment (C type) is also described. This also was the only friendship of this type in the two camps.

Results

Before the analysis of friendship development in children with different attachment histories, the children's level of peer competence and capacity for friendship formation were compared using the measures described earlier.

In order to test the association of security of attachment in infancy and peer competence in middle childhood, the mean social skills rating for all 32 children were subjected to 3 × 2 ANOVA (attachment classification × sex). Means and standard deviations for the three attachment groups were as follows: secure attachment (B): 4.40 (.27); anxious-resistant attachment (C): 3.19 (.42) and anxious-avoidant attachment (A): 3.19 (.41).

Children with secure attachment in infancy were seen by camp counselors as showing higher levels of social skills than were children with anxious attachments. There was a main effect for attachment ($F(2,30)$ = 4.57, $p < .02$). There were no significant differences between the social skills of boys and girls, and *post hoc* tests showed that the two groups with anxious attachment did not differ. Thus it can be seen that counselors without prior information perceived children with secure attachment histories as more socially competent.

ANOVA with repeated measures on the proportion of time children spent with the three alternative associates (peers, adults, oneself) revealed a significant interaction effect of attachment group × alternative associate ($F(4,52) = 3.43$, $p < .05$). No significant interaction effects of sex × alternative associate and of sex × alternative associate × attachment group were found. Means and standard deviations are presented in Table 1. Further simple main effects analyses revealed that children with secure attachment histories (B), as well as children with anxious-resistant histories (C), spent different proportions of their time with peers, adults or by themselves ($F(2,52)$ = 27.54, $p < .001$ and $F(2,52) = 6.99$, $p < .01$, respectively). *Post hoc* tests showed that the B and C type children spent more time with peers than with adults or by themselves. Regarding children with anxious-avoidant attachment histories (A), no significant difference was found between the proportion of time spent with peers, adults or alone ($F(2,52)$ = .71). The A type children did not

Table I Social Participation Proportions (Means and SDs) as a Function of Attachment Classification

	Peers	Adults Only	Isolated
Secure (B)	.63	.19	.17
(n = 17)	(.22)	(.14)	(.14)
Anxious-resistant (C)	.59	.19	.22
(n = 7)	(.23)	(.13)	(.13)
Anxious-avoidant (A)	.41	.28	.32
(n = 8)	(.24)	(.13)	(.12)

show a preference for spending their time with peers as did their B and C type counterparts.

In addition to social skills with peers, another important task of preadolescence is the formation of a close friendship with a child of similar age and the same gender. It was expected that children with secure attachments in infancy would be more likely to establish a close friendship in the summer camp than would children with anxious attachments. Due to the low expected frequencies in the anxious-resistant and the anxious-avoidant groups the two anxious attachment groups were combined.

Results of the first assessment of close friendship, based on counselor nominations of stable/reciprocal friendships after 4 weeks of camp, were as follows: thirteen of 17 children with secure attachment histories were perceived to have a stable-reciprocal relationship with a peer. Concerning the children with anxious attachment histories, eight out of 15 were perceived to have a stable-reciprocal relationship, although most of these were with secure partners. While a greater proportion of the children with secure attachment histories formed close frienships, the relationship between attachment and close friendship was not significant ($x^2 = 1.80$, d.f. = 1, $p > .20$).

Results of the second assessment of close friendships, reciprocated 'special friend' nominations, also did not yield a significant difference between secure and anxious attachment groups ($x^2 = 2.46$, d.f. = 1, $p > .05$). Fifteen out of 17 children with secure attachment histories nominated a 'special friend', but nine out of 15 children with anxious attachment histories also nominated a

'special friend'. Though a high proportion of children with secure attachment histories report having had special friends, this phenomenon is also found with more than half of the children with anxious attachment histories.

The third measure of close friendship, based on social network affinity revealed a significant relationship between attachment history of close friendship ($x^2 = 4.68$, d.f. = 1, $p > .03$). Thirteen out of 17 children with secure attachment histories met the 'social network affinity' criterion for close friendship. Concerning the children with anxious attachment histories only six out of 15 met this criterion. Thus, close friendship as assessed both in terms of actual play associations *and* children's own claims about friendship is more strongly related to early relationship history than is close friendship as perceived by adults or by the preadolescents themselves. One possible implication is that the sense of having formed a close friendship is a relatively common occurrence in preadolescence. Some preadolescents may think that their associate is their close friend though there is no objective basis for their impression. Also, as discussed earlier, association between preadolescents is quite common which may bring counselors to assume that a certain dyad has a bond of close friendship. However, it is only the combination of high association, namely common activities, and the sense of closeness reflecting intimacy that represent a true close friendship. Based on this definition, preadolescents with various attachment histories differed.

Inspection of the results presented so far reveals findings that may seem contradictory. Secure at-

tachment is related to higher level of peer and social competence. Also the secure preadolescents establish more close friendships. However, preadolescents with an anxious-resistant attachment history, though revealing a lower level of peer and social competence, spend more than 50 percent of their time with peers as secure preadolescents do. Moreover, preadolescents with insecure attachments (both C and A types) have the sense of having a close friend. Their inner notion of having a close friend is also perceived by counselors.

It can be suggested that some of the preadolescents with insecure attachment histories establish friendships. However, as with the case of observed child associations, the quality of their friendship may be different from the friendships established by preadolescents with secure attachment histories. A closer inspection of friendship growth processes in adolescents with different attachment histories may highlight qualitative differences existing between friendships consisting of pairs of children with different attachment histories.

Observations on processes of friendship development in pairs with different attachment histories will now be described. Considering the different features that may reflect girls' and boys' friendships in this age group, vignettes of secure attachment pairs will be presented for both sexes. We do not have available friendships of both sexes for pairs where both partners had the same type of anxious attachment. Using an orthogenetic perspective, vignettes of pairs' behavior and interaction from Day One in summer camp until their departure on the last day of camp are presented.

Friendship development in girls with a secure attachment history. AS and CT are both attractive 10–11-year-old girls. They both have a history of secure attachment. They did not know each other before the beginning of the summer camp. In her first hour at the camp, AS was observed to communicate with other girls. She walked around the classroom and led a few girls in exploring the new environment. She explained to some girls how to use the lockers. In her actions, she displayed confidence and positive affect. Later, she was seen playing with two other girls. When, during play, she wanted to show something to another girl, AS touched the other girl gently.

On the first day, no interaction or any exchange between AS and CT was observed. CT was actively playing with another girl. She drew and wrote. At lunchtime she took the initiative to bring the food to the table where the other child was sitting.

From these representative descriptions drawn from video records, it can be seen that these two girls are instrumentally competent, and both received quite high ratings by the counselors at the end of the camp. They explored the new environment and were able to engage in activities shortly after arriving. They were capable of interacting with others, and positive mood and affect were conveyed in their social exchanges.

On the second day, these competent and friendly girls found each other. AS and CT stood close together in the swimming pool, face to face and talking. AS turned in circles and CT followed her. CT jumped into the water and AS followed her. Their interaction and play were subsequently observed in different activities. Exchanges of smiles and laughs accompanying their interaction and physical contact were observed.

Although it was evident that a relationship between the girls was emerging, they did not exclude other children. They played with other girls as well. When playing as a dyad, they were out in the open, so other girls could see them and might consider joining them.

Before the end of the first week, AS and CT moved from shared simple activities to active joint planning of what to draw, how to dance and what kinds of games to play. Later, a project to create a macramé shop emerged. Other girls joined them in this elaborated play, where each partner had a different role.

Becoming part of a larger group of girls did not diminish CT and AS's friendship. They easily moved between dyadic interactions and group activities. A real sense of closeness was portrayed in their interaction, and from time to time, in their mutual looks and touching. In one instance when AS and CT had a conflict over something, AS gently approached CT shortly afterwards and appeased her. On another occa-

sion following a prolonged interaction between AS and another girl (KS), CT seemed to feel left out or even betrayed. Full of disappointment and anger, she took AS aside and asked her, 'Are you still my friend or KS's friend?' They argued, they exchanged points of view, each directly expressing emotion. AS showed considerable kindness toward CT, and assured her she was her close friend but that KS could also be their friend. This conflict over loyalty ended with smiles, and a new sense of closeness was conveyed. Following the resolution of this loyalty conflict, AS and CT's friendship was solidified for the rest of the camp.

Thus, these two girls with secure attachment histories were able to jointly plan and perform elaborated tasks and games. As mentioned before, their mutual interaction did not preclude participation in group activities. On the emotional level, they shared a sense of closeness which appeared to be stable despite conflicts that occurred from time to time.

Friendship development in girls with anxious-avoidant attachment history. AL and IB, 11 years old, look a little bit older than their age. Pubertal changes have already started. AL is somewhat overweight. Both girls have a history of anxious-avoidant attachment.

The two girls were slightly acquainted before camp began so it was expected that they would approach each other at the camp. On the first day, they sat close to each other, but hardly communicated. They were quiet, appeared sad and in a low mood. They cautiously observed the classroom and other children from where they were sitting. Later on, they took some cards and played together with little display of affect.

When IB tried to start a conversation with another girl, AL stood behind her and watched cautiously. Later they examined the lockers, but only after the other girls had left the area. When another girl approached the lockers, AL retreated.

Although they knew each other, verbal interaction was minimal. They worked in close proximity, but hardly exchanged a word. Their affective tone appeared depressed. Very occasionally they shared a smile. The impression was that their comfort resulted from merely being together

and not from any common accomplishment of a task or in a game. It should be emphasized that, though they stayed close together most of the time, no physical contact between AL and IB was observed throughout the 4 weeks.

From the beginning, it was clear that some kind of relationship had been established between these two girls. They preferred to play in a hidden place where they could not be easily seen or reached by the others. They were untouched by the group activities developed by other girls. At most, they passively watched what other girls were doing.

AL and IB's play was simple. They usually engaged in some structured game like cards or in functional play. They enjoyed being on the swings next to each other. On one field trip when the other children toured the park and played in various playground activities, AL and IB just sat in a sand box and threw pebbles in different directions.

Not until the third week did they let other girls join them in a very simple play sequence, taking turns operating a simple toy. Later on, more interaction with others was observed. Other girls were 'permitted' to play in their hidden place. IB, and especially AL, behaved like passive followers in those group activities. However, some contact between this closed unit of the two girls and the other girls was established.

An important point should be emphasized. Though AL and IB were close, the affective tone between them was often deflated. No elaborated play developed. No conflict appeared between the two. In some instances, during the second part of the camp, we had the impression that IB would have liked to leave AL and join other girls. However, she returned to AL right away. Only later on, as described, did both girls, as a dyad, approach the group.

Friendship development in boys with a secure attachment history. YT and TN are two attractive, athletic boys, aged 11. They were not previously acquainted with each other. Both have a history of secure attachment.

A few minutes after arriving at the camp, TN was already playing a table game with other children. YT joined this group of children and left after a short while. Later, both boys were seen to be active, but working separately at the same table. TN brought some paper to the table and after a few minutes YT took some. This act of sharing took place between the two boys without their exchanging a word. It was evident that both were interested and curious about their new environment. When TN went to watch the TV camera, YT followed him.

In the days following, they were seen together more and more frequently. They shared and exchanged taking turns jumping into the water at the swimming pool. They played together on the swings, and when YT fell from the swing, TN showed sympathy. (Another boy, who had an *A* type history, laughed at YT's fall.) A conflict over an object occurred once, but they were able to resolve it. Later physical closeness was observed between them, both tender touching each other's belly buttons and, more commonly, active rough and tumble play.

YT and TN's play did not exclude others, and two other boys joined them. They played as a group of four in the swimming pool. At this stage, the third week, it was observed that YT started to establish a closeness with another boy. TN appeared to feel rejected and looked sad. However, when YT ignored him, TN was able to play actively by himself and then start to play with another boy. By the end of the camp session it could be seen that TN had been able to restore his relationship with YT in a different form. A group of four competent boys emerged. Thus, YT and TN were able to resolve the conflict between them and to re-establish their relationship within the context of a foursome.

Friendship development in boys with anxious-resistant attachment history. KD is a good-looking boy with an ever-smiling face. He is quite active and somewhat impulsive. As he stated: 'When it gets noisy and a lot is going on, I just can't control myself.' TS is somewhat shorter and more slender than KD, and his expression is worried and preoccupied. Both boys have a history of resistant attachment (*C* type).

On the first day of camp TS looked somewhat insecure, cautiously watching the environment. KD, in contrast, was very busy,

watching everything around him. KD's level of activity imparted the impression that he was roaming the room more than he was exploring. Neither joined in other boys' play for sustained periods. KD would occasionally join a table but leave again shortly.

Physical aggression toward others boys by KD and TS, separately, was observed from time to time. Sometimes the impression was that their aggressive behavior was not in response to some external obstacle or frustration, but was engaged in for its own sake. For example, when one boy bent over to go through a low door, his back was within TS's reach. TS pushed him for no apparent reason. Similar behaviors were seen with KD. These behaviors were judged to be more impulsive than hostile.

KD and TS did not interact consistently. However, they sat near each other while eating at the table. KD would occasionally suggest some common activity to TS. He would approach TS, touch him very tenderly and in a friendly way, but after a few moments their interaction would fade away.

The two boys were observed together many times at the swimming pool. They began to swim together. They sometimes moved together alongside the pool, as if to measure its depth. TS was less competent in swimming and KD helped him in a considerate manner.

Although the two spent significant amounts of time together, on some occasions KD would roam in the classroom alone and TS would sit by himself. They would join together in engaging in disobedient behavior, such as hitting the table and making noise, or refusing to leave the swimming pool on time.

TS and KD were not able to play together for sustained periods of time, nor were they able to join others' play. KD moved around a great deal, and conflict between him and other boys occurred from time to time. TS was more solitary and, on many occasions, wrapped himself in his towel by the pool (as though the towel was a transitional object). However, there were a number of occasions when the two boys chose to be together. At those times, they were very kind and tender toward one another and it was evident that they

were fond of each other. However, their closeness did not persist for very long and would dissipate with no precipitating event, such as a disagreement or conflict. Their friendship seemed to lack the commitment required for sustained interaction and growth.

A proposed model of friendship development in preadolescence. Inspection of these vignettes of four pairs of friends showed that their relationships were dynamic and developed over time. From the initial moment at camp, the behavior of the individuals conveyed the potential for developing interaction with others. Whether acting separately or in an accidental group, behavior of each was oriented toward the other (in *either a positive* or a *negative manner*). We termed this initial stage *pre-togetherness orientations*. As can be seen in Table 2, regardless of the history of attachment affiliation, individuals revealed their level of competency as if to announce their capability of being a playmate. Such behaviors may be analogous to social releasers described by observers of greeting and contact-maintaining behavior in animals (Eibl-Eibesfeldt, 1970). These orientation behaviors connoted an *affective* tone which may be an integral part of a developing relationship (Sroufe et al, 1984). Physical proximity also plays a determining role in establishing an interaction (Hartup, 1983). It was observed that prospective friends could be seen commonly in the same vicinity.

After a short period of time, sometimes as early as the second day at camp, it became evident that some children were forming pairs. At this second stage, termed *connectedness*, friends engaged in many activities together. They ate at the same lunch table and played together in the classroom, outside and in the swimming pool. They participated together in most of the available activities at the camp. This sharing of activities has been described as an important factor in friendship formation (Gottman, 1983). Furthermore, in general, friendship generally was manifested by comfort with physical contact. Friends allowed themselves to touch each other.

As two campers began to spend more and more time together, changes were observed in the quality of their *connectedness*. It was appar-

	Table 2	Major Process and Features of Developmental Course of Friendship in Preadolescents with Different Attachment Histories	

Secure Attachment	Avoidant Attachment	Resistant Attachment
Pre-togetherness orientations		
Instrumental competence	Instrumental incompetence	Varying level of competence
Positive affect	Self-preoccupation	Detachment/aggressive behavior
Active proximity	Flat affect	Unstable proximity
	Passive closeness	
	Stable proximity	
Connectedness		
High proximity	High proximity	Unstable proximity
Coordinated activities	Coordinated activities	Well-coordinated activities combined
Wide range of activities	Narrow range of activities	with no interaction
Wide range of locations	Restricted area	Sometimes clear preference of others
Non-exclusive toward others	Exclusive toward others	Physical comfort, closeness, no rough
Physical comfort, including rough	No sign of physical comfort, touch	and tumble play
and tumble play		
Creative relatedness		
Joint creative play	Simple structured play	On-off relatedness
Sociodramatic and elaborated play	Parallel play	Almost no common play
Complementary roles	Structured games	No conflict
Coping with emerging conflicts	Refrain from conflicts	

ent, at least in the pairs with secure attachment history, that the quality of their play became more elaborate, as had also been found during the preschool years. In addition, partners were better able to deal with and resolve emerging conflicts. We call this third stage *creative relatedness*.

Especially at this stage, the differences between the pairs with different attachment histories became more distinctive. In order to further illustrate the model, we will show distinctive pathways of friendship development in pairs with different attachment histories.

Friendship development in preadolescents with a secure attachment history. During the preschool years when a child wants to play with another child, he/she may approach the other directly saying something like, 'Come on, let's climb'. With this action, two important messages are conveyed— that there is an interesting activity which can be shared, and that it will be fun to be together. Preschool children convey their needs and mes-

sages directly. According to Gottman (1983), children tend to give up this high-risk strategy as they get older and begin to disclose their intentions less overtly.

Before the initiation of interaction, during *pre-together orientation*, the securely-attached pairs were able to display their resourcefulness and positive affect. They communicated their willingness and ability to play through a high level of exploration and by joining other children to play simple structured group games. Furthermore, they revealed their ability to share objects. These messages of instrumental and affective competence were probably perceived by other campers. Taking an organizational, systemic approach, it can be assumed that a competent preadolescent anticipates that in order to develop elaborated play in a context of positive affect a partner with similar capabilities must be chosen. Studies on acquaintances reveal similar trends. Potential friends are attracted by the perception of

possible rewarding of the other (Altman & Taylor, 1973). According to Berscheid & Walster (1978) perception of the other as similar and competent is the basis for initial attraction and interaction.

Following the *pre-togetherness orientation*, securely attached partners were observed to be close and active in shared activities. At this stage their activities were simple in nature, like swimming together or simple games. However, a wide range of such activities was observed. Congruent with their initial inclination for exploration of the environment their play was not restricted to a certain area. *Connectedness* was also observed in their shared explorations.

Although a clear sense of closeness between partners was evident, their *connectedness* did not isolate them from other campers. From time to time they were seen to play with other campers as a twosome or separately.

Thus, *connectedness* in the pairs with secure attachment was combined with an ongoing exploration of the wider physical and social surround.

A point may be added concerning a difference that was seen between the securely attached male and female pairs. In boys, and not in girls, rough and tumble play was also observed. It was clear that the physical 'fighting' between boys was playful. Usually a shared smile followed the termination of a fight between the friends.

It is suggested that the variety of activities, the openness of others and the ability to 'fight' playfully are probably markers of an active and growing expanding friendship, in which partners let themselves explore a wide range of togetherness.

The confidence in each other that secure partners shared was reflected in the next stage of the developing friendship, *creative relatedness*. Shared connectedness transformed into organized and planned play. Play was elaborated and rich in content. Roles were shared or exchanged by partners. The nature of the play often called for interaction with other campers. In a variety of play experiences, partners were jointly able to pursue play and to perform roles as demanded by the situation.

Exposure to different activities and other campers brought with it the possibility of conflicts arising between friends. It was interesting to observe how secure partners used different conflict resolution strategies to settle disputes. The girls would approach each other gently to appease each other and verbally expressed their feelings. Boys were seen to work out a plan (or game) which enabled them to maintain their relationship when involved in a larger group of boys. Thus, a well-established and explored friendship is not terminated when, on one occasion, reciprocity (as described by Hays, 1985; Youniss, 1980) is not practised. Children find ways to remedy the situation.

Examination of friendship in secure pairs reveals a further important phenomenon. It was not only the affective relationship between partners that developed and matured. Children jointly pursued challenging activities like dismantling and constructing a radio apparatus and setting up a macramé shop. Thus, closeness was combined with in-

creasingly rich and interesting activities. The instrumental and affective competence that characterized each partner with a secure attachment history was further developed and elaborated in the mutual interaction.

Friendship development in preadolescents with anxious-avoidant attachment history. The two girls with avoidant attachment histories clearly exhibited a low level of competence. They were very cautious and hardly explored the environment. At best, they were 'onlookers' (Parten, 1932) of the things happening around them. They chose to sit next to each other on the first day, probably due to their previous acquaintance; yet, they exchanged few words. Compared to the sense of positive affect that characterized the secure partners, these girls appeared to feel very insecure about being alone. Closeness to another probably gave them some sense of shared confidence.

It is understandable that the avoidant girls did not establish relationships with secure girls. Secure girls were probably not interested in an incompetent partner. In addition, the secure girls' activity and exploration may have overwhelmed the incompetent girls. The fact that the avoidant girls started a relationship with each other at all may have to do with friendship formation as an age-related task. During preadolescence, the need for a close and intimate friend emerges (Sullivan, 1953). Secure preadolescents use their interaction skills in incorporating their need for intimacy. However, with the insecure preadolescents we envision a 'raw', less sophisticated need for intimacy drawing the two socially incompetent partners together.

This 'raw' deep-rooted need for closeness was increasingly evident in the nature of the friendship that developed between the two avoidant partners. Their interaction was restricted on the number and variety of activities in which they engaged, and was also spatially constricted. They were not open to others joining them. It was as if the pair closed itself off as a protection from external interference. However, they were closed off from each other as well. They did not allow themselves to explore or expand their relationship. Activities were well structured, with specific roles. Their interactions were such

that closeness was not expressed. The girls were never seen touching each other. This kind of protected closeness was probably their best means of preventing the emergence of conflicts.

Thus, it is suggested that these girls established closeness for the purpose of not being left alone. The relationship did not allow the partners optimal opportunities to grow, to explore themselves and to explore the environment. Using the terms suggested by our model, it seems that a strong need for closeness and a relatively low level of competence led to the establishment of this friendship. The mutual incompetence and strong need for intimacy were the *pre-togetherness* signals. When interaction occurred, *connectedness* was overemphasized by the nature of activities and exclusion of others, thus preventing the friendship from developing to the higher level of *creative relatedness*.

Friendship development in preadolescents with anxious-resistant attachment history. Initial observation of the resistant boys' behavior at the camp could not lead to a clear conclusion concerning their instrumental competence. At times they were observed to play quite competently with others; on other occasions they roamed the classroom aimlessly. Inconsistency was evident also in their affective gestures. Sometimes they looked confident, and at other times insecure. Most importantly, right from the first days at camp they occasionally acted in a pointlessly aggressive way toward other campers.

Thus, it is suggested that unclear signals concerning competence, combined with early aggressive behavior, do not evoke the interest of the consistently competent child. It is only a preadolescent with similar tendencies who might be interested in befriending such a child. In essence, the friendship these two boys developed was inconsistent, better defined using Howes' (1983) term 'sporadic friendships'. The two boys revealed a real concern for one another. Sincere closeness was evident. However, this *connectedness* was not sustained, 'fading away' without reason. Later the friendship would resume as if no break had occurred.

Though both boys exhibited aggressive behavior toward other campers, they never quarreled with each other, and therefore did not gain experience with conflict resolution and the emotional closeness which follows it. Like the avoidant pair, this pair experienced closeness that evaporated, leading to a sense of distance between the two. They did not arrive at a *creative relatedness*, and they did not let their *connectedness* be in danger of conflict. They worked out some kind of *modus vivendi* that allowed them to be both close and apart, and thus sharing the feeling of having a friend.

General Discussion and Conclusion

Results have shown children with secure attachment histories to have higher levels of social skills with peers, compared to children with anxious attachment histories. This finding supports the notion that patterns of relationships are carried forward (Sroufe & Fleeson, 1986). Former studies have shown the continuity of adaptation to be stable into the preschool years (Kestenbaum et al., in press; Sroufe, 1983). These findings suggest the role former relational patterns play in preadolescence, when new dimensions of friendship may emerge.

Furthermore, the existence of special friendships in preadolescence was also found to be related to attachment history. A large majority (15 out of 17) of secure preadolescents reported having a close friend, and their report was validated by their friends. Thus, preadolescents with a secure attachment history are not only more competent in their social skills but they are also capable of establishing close and intimate relationships with their peers.

However, assessing the occurrence of close friendships in preadolescents with anxious attachment histories via three methods revealed that while these children are less socially competent, about 60 percent of them have a close friend. This finding led us to a more thorough inspection of friendship developmental processes in preadolescence, which is the main goal of this article. The proposed model, which concentrates on relational developmental processes, suggests different qualities of close and intimate relation-

ships in preadolescents with different attachment histories.

The model of friendship growth in preadolescence suggested in this paper encompasses two main process characteristics, which are interrelated. First, relationships are processes following an orthogenetic principle. They develop from a global state, a surface contact, into more differentiated and integrated relational patterns. Secondly, during each interaction between partners, and with each stage of friendship, two main dimensions contribute to the nature of the continuous relationship. These two dimensions are, *the affective tone and degree of closeness* between partners, and the challenging *nature of tasks friends jointly pursue*. The balance between these two determinants of closeness and competence will determine the quality of the relationship and contribute to the nature of its developmental course.

The model suggested resembles the organizational model of the initial human relationship—attachment. The infant-caregiver attachment relationship follows a similar pattern of development from undifferentiation to interdependency (Ainsworth, 1973). In addition, the *balance* between: (1) the infant's level of exploration and mastery of the environment; and (2) proximity, contact and interaction with the caregiver determines the quality of the attachment (Ainsworth et al., 1978).

Patterns of friendships developing in preadolescence not only generally resembled patterns of early caregiver–infant relationships; in addition, partners who had a history of secure attachment with their initial caregiver developed a highly *interdependent* relationship with a friend. In their relationships they were able to establish a balance between competent mastery of the environment and closeness and intimacy to the other. Thus, as suggested by Sroufe & Fleeson (1986), the basic pattern of the early relationship with the caregiver was carried over into an intimate relationship with a peer in preadolescence.

Observation of the pair with the anxious-avoidant attachment history raises the question of whether the early pattern of remoteness and avoidance is carried forward. Both avoidant girls spent most of their

time together. It is suggested that the need for human contact is probably not eliminated in avoidant infants, but rather is suppressed. In early childhood, when infants have experienced maternal rejection or unavailability, they tend to avoid their mothers. This relational pattern affects the child's mastery and security in further exploration of the world. However, when they meet another adult, a teacher, for example, they may try to seek closeness with this adult especially in times of low stress (Sroufe et al., 1983). In preadolescence, following the emergence of the need for a close friend, such a youngster may form an association with another age-mate. However, since their relational pattern lacks the elaboration of an interdependent experience, what is observed is a dependent clinging to or hovering by an age-mate, rather than the experience of a creatively related friendship.

Preadolescents with an anxious attachment history, and especially an avoidant history, often did not develop any longstanding meaningful relationships in the camp. They exhibited their relational pattern of unrelatedness and lack of interdependence. The one avoidant pair, who was closely engaged, displayed the other form of immature relationships—pure fusion where intimacy was achieved at the expense of autonomy (Selman, 1990). Their low sense of personal agency was quite pronounced, as was their inability to explore their relationship.

In summary, review of relational patterns and developmental courses in infancy, childhood and preadolescence reveal similar major dilemmas of how to be close and how to develop and to grow. Optimally, close relationships support individual self-growth. Individual self-growth, mastery and competence contribute to the further development and renewal of supportive relationships. Prospective longitudinal studies have shown that the primary relational patterns of attachment are carried over into relationships with peers in preadolescence. We suggest that these relational patterns will likely also be carried over into emerging relationships with the opposite sex during adolescence. The components of those relationships will probably represent patterns that uniquely characterize adolescent interactions. However, at a deeper level, they will resemble the basic relational patterns carried over from the earliest relational experiences.

References

Ainsworth, M. D. S. (1973) 'The Development of Infant-Mother Attachment', in B. M. Caldwell & N. H. Ricciuti (eds) *Review of Child Developmental Research*, Vol. 3. Chicago, IL: University of Chicago Press.

Ainsworth, M. D. S., Blehar, M., Waters, E., & Wall, S. (1978) *Patterns of Attachment*. Hillsdale, NJ: Erlbaum.

Altman, I. & Taylor, D. A. (1973) *Social Penetration: The Development of Interpersonal Relationships*. New York: Holt, Rinehart & Winston.

Berndt, T. J. (1982) 'The Features and Effects of Friendships in Early Adolescence', *Child Development* 53: 1447–60.

Berscheid, E. & Walster, E. H. (1978) *Interpersonal Attraction*, 2nd edn. Reading, MA: Addison-Wesley.

Bigelow, B. J. (1977) 'Children's Friendship Expectations: A Cognitive Developmental Approach', *Child Development* 48: 246–53.

Bowlby, J. (1969) *Attachment and Loss: Vol. 1. Attachment*. New York: Basic Books.

Bowlby, J. (1973) *Attachment and Loss: Vol. 2. Separation*. New York: Basic Books.

Bowlby, J. (1980) *Attachment and Loss: Vol. 3. Loss*. New York: Basic Books.

Bukowski, W. M., Newcomb, A. F. & Hoza, B. (1987) 'Friendship Conceptions among Early Adolescents: A Longitudinal Study of Stability and Change', *Journal of Early Adolescence* 7: 143–52.

Buhrmester, D., Furman, W., Wittenberg, M. T. & Reis, H. T. (1988) 'Five Domains of Interpersonal Competence in Peer Relationships', *Journal of Personality and Social Psychology* 55: 991–1008.

Duck, S. W. (1984) 'A Perspective on the Repair of Personal Relationships', in S. W. Duck (ed.) *Personal Relationships: Vol. 5. Repairing Personal Relationships*. New York: Academic Press.

Eibl-Eibesfeldt, I. (1970) *Ethology: The Biology of Behavior*. New York: Holt, Rinehart & Winston.

Ginsburg, D., Gottman, J. M. & Parker, J. G. (1986) 'The Importance of Friendship', in J. M. Gottman & J. G. Parker (eds) *Conversations with Friends*. Cambridge: Cambridge University Press.

Gottman, J. M. (1983) 'How Children Become Friends', *Monographs of the Society for Research in Child Development*, 48 (3, Serial No. 201).

Hartup, W. W. (1983) 'Peer Relations', in E. M. Hetherington (ed.) *Handbook of Child Psychology: Socialization, Personality, and Social Development*, Vol. 4. New York: Wiley.

Hartup, W. W. (1989) 'Behavioral Manifestations of Children's Friendships', in T. J. Berndt & G. W. Ladd (eds) *Peer Relationships in Child Development*. New York: Wiley.

Hays, R. B. (1985) 'A Longitudinal Study of Friendship Development', *Journal of Personality and Social Psychology* 50: 305–13.

Howes, C. (1981) 'Patterns of Friendship', paper presented at the biennial meeting of the Society for Research in Child Development, Boston, April.

Howes, C. (1983) 'Patterns of Friendship', *Child Development* 54: 1041–53.

Kestenbaum, R., Farber, E. & Sroufe, L. A. (in press) 'Individual Differences in Empathy among Preschoolers' Concurrent and Predictive Validity' in R. Eisenberg (ed.) *New Directions for Child Development*. San Francisco: Jossey-Bass.

Ladd, G. W. (1983) 'Social Networks of Popular, Average, and Rejected Children in School Setting', *Merrill-Palmer Quarterly* 29: 283–307.

Levinger, G. & Snoek, J. D. (1972) *Attractions in Relationships: A New Look at Interpersonal Attraction*. Cambridge, MA: General Learning Press.

Parten, M. B. (1932) 'Social Participation among Pre-school Children', *Journal of Abnormal Psychology* 22: 243–69.

Pastor, D. (1981) 'The Quality of Mother-Infant Attachment and its Relationship to Toddlers' Initial Sociability with Peers', *Developmental Psychology* 17: 326–35.

Selman, R. L. (1980) *The Growth of Interpersonal Understanding: Development and Clinical Analyses*. New York: Academic Press.

Selman, R. (1990) 'Fostering Intimacy and Autonomy', in W. Damon (ed.) *Child Development Today and Tomorrow*. San Francisco: Jossey-Bass.

Sroufe, L. A. (1983) 'Infant-Caregiver Attachment and Patterns of Adaptation in Preschool: The Roots of Maladaptation and Competence', in M. Perlmutter (ed.) *Development of Policy Concerning Children with Special Needs. The Minnesota Symposia on Child Psychology*, Vol. 16.

Sroufe, L. A. & Fleeson, J. (1986) 'Attachment and the Construction of Relationships', in W. W. Hartup & Z. Rubin (eds) *Relationships and Development*. Hillsdale, NJ: Erlbaum.

Sroufe, L. A. & Fleeson, J. (1988) 'Relationships within Families: Mutual Influences', in R. Hinde & J. Stevenson-Hinde (eds) *The Coherence of Family Relations*. Oxford: Oxford University Press.

Sroufe, L. A., Fox, N. & Pancake, V. (1983) 'Attachment and Dependency in Developmental Perspective', *Child Development* 54: 1614–27.

Sroufe, L. A., Schork, E., Motti, F., Lawroski, N. & LaFreniere, P. (1986) 'The Role of Affect in Social Competence', in C. Izard, J. Kagan & R. Zajonc (eds) *Affect, Cognition and Behavior*. New York: Plenum.

Sullivan, H. S. (1953) *The Interpersonal Theory of Psychiatry*. New York: Norton.

Tesch, S. A. (1983) 'Review of Friendship across the Life Span', *Human Development* 26: 266–76.

Troy, M. & Sroufe, L. A. (1987) 'Victimization among Preschoolers: The Role of Attachment Relationship History', *Journal of the American Academy of Child Psychiatry* 26: 166–72.

Wright, P. H. (1984) 'Self-referent Motivation and the Intrinsic Quality of Friendship', *Journal of Social and Personal Relationships* 1: 115–30.

Youniss, J. (1980) *Parents and Peers in Social Development*. Chicago: University of Chicago Press.

Article Review Form at end of book.

WiseGuide Wrap-Up

- The term temperament refers to a person's overall emotional tendencies or patterns. In research with monkeys, Suomi has shown that something that looks like human temperament is shaped in important ways by the environment in which monkeys are raised.

- In early development, we form attachments with caregivers that can usually be characterized in one of three ways: secure, in which we are comfortable and confident we will be cared for; anxious, in which we feel anxious because we are not certain whether we will be cared for; and avoidant, in which we are largely angry and distant, because we feel certain we will not be cared for.

- Increasingly, many of our relationships are being understood in terms of the attachment patterns we learned in infancy. Secure, anxious, and avoidant patterns are learned in infancy and— uncorrected—continue to affect our relationships with peers in later childhood and then our romantic relationships in adolescence and adulthood.

- Introverts often cope with difficult interpersonal situations in which they are meeting someone new by asking a lot of questions. This is one of several strategies you can use for overcoming shyness. Others include forcing yourself to participate in social events, working to show the warmth you feel, and taking small steps toward your social goals.

R.E.A.L. Sites

Site name: Adult Attachment Lab at UC Davis

URL: http://psychology.ucdavis.edu/Shaver/lab.html

Why is it R.E.A.L.? This site is created and maintained by the UC–Davis lab in Adult Attachment. Phil Shaver, director, is a leading researcher on the role attachment plays in adult romantic relationships. The web site contains the latest research produced by this lab and other researchers in the field, has links to other relationship- and attachment-oriented web sites, and includes key readings in the field.

Key topics: attachment, adult development, relationships

Site name: Resources for Shy People

URL: http://www.base.com/shy/

Why is it R.E.A.L.? This site has a wealth of information on shyness and resources for those who suffer from shyness. The site provides information on newsgroups and instructions for signing up, key books in the area, ideas for how to find a therapist or help in the area in which you live, poems, song lyrics, and more. It provides many links to relevant sites, and an excellent overview on the topic.

Key topics: shyness, relationships, mental health

section 7

- Understand how psychologists today are approaching the study of vulnerability and resilience.

- Learn how Freud sees one's personality as defined by one's characteristic methods of defending against unpleasant information.

- Discuss the relationship between keeping secrets and health.

- Describe what Freud saw as Mary Fields' primary conflicts, as evidenced in her dream.

Resilience and Psychological Defense

The field of personality has its roots in understanding everyday human functioning. How do people cope with adversity? What differences do individuals show in their responses both to trauma and to the everyday stresses and strains of life? Freud, as one of the early theorists in personality, saw personality primarily in terms of people's characteristic ways of coping with difficulties in life, that is, in their defense mechanisms. Today, we typically think of personality as consisting of more than defense mechanisms, but much of what we focus our attention on still concerns the characteristic ways in which people respond to situations in their environments. The articles in this section provide a range of views on personality and its relevance to understanding the way people respond to adversity and cope with difficulties.

The report of the Basic Behavioral Science Task Force, entitled "Basic Behavioral Science Research for Mental Health," is an overview of research demonstrating the links between personality research and our understanding of people's coping mechanisms and their response to life's small and large stresses. The article discusses work indicating a link between early personality patterns and later drug abuse or depression; how certain personality styles can indicate a vulnerability to stress; the relationship between personality characteristics and our ability to function well in relation to others; and the role of self-concept and self-esteem in psychological development, vulnerability, and resilience. This article highlights the view that personality has much to say about our functioning in the major spheres of human activity.

Undoubtedly, you will spend some time in your personality course covering some aspects of Freud's theories and ideas. However, many of you will not have the opportunity to read what Freud had to say in his own words. The chapter "Resistance and Repression" is included here to provide you with this chance. Freud is, at first glance, a little difficult to read. However, soon you'll find yourself in the swing of his sardonic sense of humor, and his vivid descriptions of patients may even make you laugh out loud. In this chapter, Freud writes about how patients who go to psychotherapy to relieve some problem will—surprisingly— go to great lengths to sabotage that treatment. This discussion then moves on to a review of his concept of repression. This is one of Freud's central ideas. In simple terms, he argues that when we have an idea or a memory that is extremely painful or about which we have such strong feelings that we feel we cannot cope, we repress the idea or memory. This concept has received a lot of attention in the recent debates about recovered memories of childhood sexual abuse. However, repression is a much broader concept than that, and Freud saw it as one of our primary, if fairly primitive, defense mechanisms. Read this chapter to understand Freud's ideas, but also read it just for the fun of reading Freud.

Questions

Reading 23. What are two ways in which understanding personality can contribute to understanding mental health? What are two contributors to low self-esteem?

Reading 24. Why would a patient seeking treatment put up resistance to that treatment? What is repression as Freud describes it?

Reading 25. What is the connection between keeping secrets and health? What is the effect of telling secrets?

Reading 26. What aspects of Mary's dream did Freud find important or interesting? What do you think of his interpretation of the dream?

In recent years, Pennebaker and others have come back to the idea of repression and have focused on it in a new way. Repression is a double-edged sword. On the one hand, it protects us from having to think about unpleasant or painful things. On the other, it takes mental energy to repress information, and too much repression can leave us exhausted and somewhat "overloaded." Think of the "watchman" in Freud's description of repression. Pennebaker's research highlights how "costly" this watchman can be. In "Confession and Inhibition," Pennebaker begins to unpack some of the health costs of repressing memories—or even of just keeping dark secrets that are still conscious. His work is very exciting. In study after study, he has demonstrated the mental and physical benefits of "telling" secrets or unloading stories about traumas that we typically do not share with others. We've all probably felt the relief of finally telling the truth about something, or of telling someone about a terrible experience. He goes even further with this research, highlighting how "keeping it in" places extreme stresses on the body *and* mind that can result in decreased health and general well-being.

Finally, in "Dream Analysis by Mail," Benjamin and Dixon report on a young woman who seeks Freud's advice in interpreting a recurring dream. A young woman in a different point in history, her story of a young love of whom her parents do not approve is one that rings true even today. This article provides you with an opportunity to see exactly what information Freud had when he interpreted this dream. See what you think of Freud's interpretation of the dream and of the story of this bold young woman's request for help.

What are two ways in which understanding personality can contribute to understanding mental health? What are two contributors to low self-esteem?

Basic Behavioral Science Research for Mental Health

Vulnerability and resilience

Basic Behavioral Science Task Force of the National Advisory Mental Health Council

Rockville, MD

Why do some people collapse under life stresses while others seem unscathed by traumatic circumstances such as severe illness, the death of loved ones, and extreme poverty, or even by major catastrophes such as natural disasters and war? Surprisingly large numbers of people mature into normal successful adults despite stressful, disadvantaged, or even abusive childhoods. Yet other people are so emotionally vulnerable that seemingly minor losses and rebuffs can be devastating—sometimes even precipitating severe mental disorder. Most people's coping capacities lie somewhere between these extremes.

Author's note: To obtain the full report "Basic Behavioral Science Research for Mental Health: A National Investment," write to the Behavioral, Cognitive and Social Sciences Research Branch, National Institute of Mental Health, Room IIC-16, 5600 Fishers Lane, Rockville, MD 20857. Electronic mail should be addressed to BEHAVSCI@HELIX.NIMH.GOV.

Basic behavioral science research on the nature of and variations in personality is illuminating the sources of these differences and revealing ways to bolster people's ability to deal with life's difficult and painful aspects. Studies to date suggest that there is no single source of resilience or vulnerability, Rather, many interacting factors come into play. They include not only individual genetic predispositions, which express themselves in enduring aspects of temperament, personality, and intelligence, but also qualities such as social skills and self-esteem. These, in turn, are shaped by a variety of environmental influences. For example, through their early experience and bonding with parents or other caregivers, children form expectations that shape later social experiences. These processes of social learning often influence self-esteem and behavior. Advances in behavioral science research are revealing sources of vulnerability and strength in several areas of investigation. Some key findings are described in this chapter.

Personality Psychology

Some people are shy, others extroverted; some are chronically anxious, others confident. These relatively stable personality traits set people apart as individuals and are the focus of fundamental questions being explored by personality researchers. Such questions include: How, and to what degree, are people psychologically different from one another? To what extent are those differences rooted in genetics, early experience, or current situational factors? What is the basic nature of those differences—that is, how do people differ in perceiving, constructing, and responding to their social environments? How do those differences affect mental health? How modifiable are personality traits? To what extent do these traits override the situation in determining a person's actions?

Personality, Psychopathology, and Resilience

Basic research on personality differences and their long-term behavioral expression is shedding light on important public health issues such as drug abuse and depression. One prospective longitudinal study, for example, revealed that some adolescent drug abusers had a distinctive personality pattern that often was identifiable in early childhood. In research more than a decade earlier, these troubled adolescents had been described as restless, fidgety, emotionally changeable, disobedient, nervous, domineering, immature under stress, and overreactive to frustration.

The same study revealed that the personalities of boys and girls who became severely depressed in late adolescence differed considerably during childhood. The boys had been described as undercontrolled, unsocialized, and aggressive; by contrast, the girls were seen as overcontrolled, oversocialized, shy, and introspective. Findings such as these suggest not only that depression has deep roots in early life, but that early personality patterns associated with later depression differ in important ways for males and females.

These differences may reflect the interaction of personality variables with the contrasting pressures society imposes upon males and females; it encourages males to be assertive risk takers but discourages such behavior in females. As a result, the undercontrolled young man and the overcontrolled young woman may be most at risk for later depression. When an already undercontrolled young man is encouraged to engage in risky behavior, his impulsivity may result in many negative experiences that contribute to depression. When an already overcontrolled young woman is cautioned to avoid risk, she may withdraw so much from the social world and its rewards that she, too, eventually experiences depression.

Understanding what can go wrong in personality development is essential; equally important is discovering what can go right—which personality traits contribute to psychological resilience. Research suggests, not surprisingly, that young girls who have been sexually abused usually suffer from lowered self-esteem, an impaired sense of control and competence, and increased negative emotions—all indicative of poor mental health. However, certain personality traits serve to lessen the ravages of abuse. An abused girl who can rationalize, explain, and comprehend what has happened to her and what she can do about it may thereby be able to maintain her feelings of competence. She may even take steps to end the abuse. While researchers continue to seek ways to understand and prevent child abuse, other research on "resilient" children is now focusing on ways to foster and strengthen those personality traits that help children grow up to be psychologically well adjusted, even after the severe trauma of rape.

An important conclusion from recent research is that personality patterns can change for the better under certain circumstances. For example, although patterns of antisocial, deviant, and even criminal behavior have been found to be remarkably stable from childhood through adult life, entering into a satisfying occupation and enriching personal relationships during early adulthood can break this pattern and greatly decrease the chances that deviant behavior will continue. Intervention programs are needed that build on these encouraging findings.

Personality research is helping us understand and prevent both physical and mental disorders. Increasingly, behavioral scientists are finding relationships between certain personality traits and particular diseases. The linkage between heart disease and the "Type A" personality—characterized by hostility, time urgency, impatience, anxiety, and sense of stress—has received extensive study. One well-established finding is that people who are hostile (the "lethal" component of Type A behavior) are especially prone to develop heart disease. Most important, even when more conventional risk factors, such as heredity, obesity, diet, and smoking are accounted for, hostility is demonstrably a risk factor for heart disease.

Moreover, an additional link between hostility and heart disease seems to be through a behavioral pathway. Hostile people are particularly prone to behave in ways that jeopardize their health, such as smoking, drinking, and general risk taking.

However, results of an intervention study for Type A people recovering from a heart attack suggest that their destructive personality traits can be changed. In that study, the effects of standard cardiac counseling alone were compared with a combination of cardiac counseling and counseling focused on reducing hostility and other components of Type A behavior. Compared with the control group, those receiving the combined counseling showed reductions in Type A behavior and an almost 50% reduction in subsequent heart attacks during a 4 ½-year period.

Personality as Traits

Many researchers regard personality as a relatively stable collection of individual traits. In recent years, behavioral scientists have come to agree that most variation in personality across individuals can be accounted for by differences in five broad factors, sometimes called the "Big Five" personality traits:

- EXTRAVERSION: Gregarious, daring, and enthusiastic

- AGREEABLENESS: Affectionate, empathic, and cooperative

- CONSCIENTIOUSNESS: Organized, dependable, and prompt

- EMOTIONAL STABILITY (vs. NEUROTICISM): Unexcitable, without envy or nervousness

- INTELLECT: Intelligent, imaginative, and worldly

Research on personality shows that a given individual's overall profile on the Big Five traits is relatively stable, consistent, and predictable over many years. However, many individual characteristics change over time and social settings.

Emotional Inhibition: Repression

One well-studied personality trait (the inverse of extraversion) is known as *emotional inhibition.* It includes both suppression (the conscious inhibition of emotion and thought) and repression (the unconscious inhibition of emotion and thought). At the turn of the century, Freud proposed that inappropriate repression was one of the most important contributors to mental illness. Only within the past 15 years have the measurement techniques become available to examine this phenomenon scientifically.

Through such advances, it is now possible to identify and study systematically the mental health of people who characteristically and unconsciously inhibit their emotions. These individuals, termed *repressors*, have been found to score low on personality test measures of distress but high on measures of defensiveness (i.e., unconscious self-protection). Although repressors do not seem anxious, their high defensiveness scores suggest that they experience distress but are either unaware of it or are denying it.

When repressors are exposed experimentally to a variety of emotion-producing situations, such as reading threatening phrases, they report feeling very little emotion, yet they display large physiological reactions, such as changes in heart rate, blood pressure, and skin conductance. People who are not repressors have similar physiological responses when they are exposed to emotion-provoking situations and told to inhibit any overt display of emotion. Thus, the very act of suppressing overt emotional expression—whether done unconsciously or consciously—apparently causes a sharp rise in cardiac reactions.

Research clearly demonstrates that habitually inhibiting emotions can pose a threat to physical and mental health. For example, repressors have an increased risk for impaired immune system functioning and a wide variety of health problems, including atherosclerotic disease in men, cancer, and psychologically linked symptoms such as headaches and abdominal pain. Experimental studies have also shown that writing or talking about traumatic experiences and expressing one's emotional reactions may enhance physical health and immune function and lessen use of medical services.

Emotional Inhibition: Shyness

The roots of individual personality and physiological reactivity can be seen very early in development in the characteristic patterns of sociability, activity, and emotionality known as *temperament.* These patterns include being active and outgoing or shy and inhibited. Researchers have discovered that 15% to 20% of all infants are shy. When faced with novel or moderately challenging situations, these inhibited infants and children typically escape rapidly, cover, and hide. If forced to remain in the situation, they reveal higher levels of stress hormones and sympathetic nervous system activity than do uninhibited children.

Although some people who are shy as children spontaneously become less inhibited as they grow up (and others seek change through counseling), others seem to retain this temperamental trait throughout their life span. Most shy individuals appear to lead relatively normal lives, but severely inhibited children have an increased risk of developing various childhood and adolescent anxiety and depressive disorders. They are also more likely to have close relatives who have been diagnosed as clinically anxious or depressed, suggesting that there may be a familial basis for shyness.

Dramatic individual differences in temperament have been found among monkeys and apes as well as among humans; these differences may be a general characteristic of many animal species. Rhesus monkeys exhibit many of the physiological and behavioral patterns seen in humans, and as with human children, 15% to 20% of monkey infants are shy. These patterns, which are seen in the first weeks of life, appear to be relatively stable from infancy to old age.

Animal studies using selective breeding and biological parent/foster parent comparisons indicate that although shyness is partly heritable, it can be modified substantially by early social experiences. In monkeys, inadequate mothering, for example, seems to exaggerate both behavioral and physiological features of shyness. Rearing by especially nurturant "foster mothers" encourages the infants to overcome their natural shyness. Not only do they cope with the usual stressors more effectively than do inhibited peers raised by their own mothers (demonstrating more exploration away from their foster mothers and less behavioral disturbance during weaning), they even surpass their uninhibited peers! Moreover, inhibited female monkey infants who receive this increased nurturance later develop into especially nurturant mothers themselves.

Sources of Personality Variation

Behavioral Genetics

What is the source of individual differences in personality traits? Are they determined solely by genes, or are they molded solely by the environment? During the past two decades, behavioral genetics research on the heritability of personality traits has shown that neither extreme is correct. Studies of twins, adoptees,

Personality Processes

The Big Five personality taxonomy makes it possible to categorize people into a small number of types. It also helps to summarize broad differences among individuals in their overall behavioral tendencies. However, current personality research is also identifying the psychological factors that underlie distinctive individual characteristics. These factors include the concepts people use for interpreting their experiences and their enduring expectancies about what they can and cannot do effectively. Research is also clarifying how such factors influence not only what people experience and feel, but also the effectiveness and adaptiveness (or maladaptiveness) of their behavior as they try to cope with life tasks and stressors.

For example, research has clarified the mental strategies that underlie "will power"—regulating one's own behavior to achieve difficult long-term goals. These strategies are the basis components of a well-functioning personality. Even at age four, children differ appreciably in the strategies they use; some can delay gratification to reach a long-term goal, but others cannot. Following the development of these children into young adulthood shows that these early self-regulatory skills foreshadow other indices of coping and personal efficacy, such as school success and college entrance, years later.

and ordinary families have demonstrated that genetic factors only moderately influence individual differences in most personality dimensions and that environmental factors are also important.

When the approaches of behavioral genetics and developmental psychology are combined, some novel findings emerge. For example, longitudinal studies of childhood temperament and early adult personality strongly suggest that personality stability over time stems more from genetic factors than from environmental constancy.

However, other studies suggest that genetic influences are dynamic—being activated at different times in life. For example, researchers have recently discovered that in newborns, individual differences in temperamental patterns such as activity level and irritability do not appear to be influenced by genes. Yet genes may influence these very same temperamental characteristics later in development. Scientists are now trying to understand how dynamic gene expression across the life span influences behavioral continuity and change.

Other issues currently under investigation concern genetic analyses of features of social life once considered to be "obviously" environmental in origin, such as divorce. Research suggests that many presumably social experiences can, in fact, be influenced by genes, which probably act indirectly through their influence on personality. Investigators have noted, for example, that pairs of identical twins are more likely to have the same divorce status than are pairs of fraternal twins, suggesting that genes may contribute to personality characteristics compatible with marriage.

To understand the mechanisms that link biology and behavior, more research is needed on the biological ties between genes and personality. Progress in this area will be helped by findings of the National Institutes of Health Human Genome Project, an ambitious attempt to map human chromosomes and to discover genes relevant to health and disease.

Experience and Environment

Ironically, studies in behavioral genetics provide strong evidence that the environment is influential in shaping behavior. Such research has shown, for example, that identical twins often have very different personalities, suggesting that environmental factors play a considerable role in personality differences.

Another important finding is that many key environmental influences on personality are experienced differently by various members of a given family. For example, for siblings growing up in the same family, the shared family environment seems less important for some aspects of intelligence and personality than is the unshared part (e.g., a child's unique relationships with parents and peers). Thus, a fruitful research direction would be to assess directly how the psychological environment varies across time and across individuals within a family unit.

Psychologists have found that many behaviors, such as aggression and altruism, that are often attributed to people's personality traits are also influenced by situational and environmental factors. For example, children who observe aggressive behavior on television are more likely to behave aggressively toward others, especially when frustrated, than those who have not seen such models. In one long-term study, researchers have found that—after controlling for baseline aggressiveness, intelligence, and socioeconomic status—the extent of viewing of TV violence at age 8 predicted the seriousness of criminal acts committed by age 30. This finding may have important implications for understanding and preventing the transmission of violence.

Attachment

Some of the most fruitful explorations of the close personal relationships moderating vulnerability and resilience involve studies of attachment, the special bond between infants and their caregivers. This relationship evolved both to meet the newborn infant's obvious physical needs and to provide security in the face of a complex and potentially dangerous environment.

When an attachment relationship is effective, the primary caregiver provides both a secure base for the infant's explorations and a safe haven the infant can return to when frightened, tired, or hungry. The more secure infants feel, the more willing they are to explore and interact with the physical and social world. As their physical and mental capabilities grow, infants increasingly direct their attention and activities away from their primary caregiver—as long as that person remains available in times of emotional need. When such emotional needs are not met, fear prevails and interferes with infants' exploration and interaction with others.

Consequences of Attachment Quality

Researchers have found that differences in infant attachment security, as measured on a brief behavioral test, can have long-term mental and emotional consequences. For example, children classified as securely attached to a caregiver during infancy will later approach problem-solving tasks more positively and with greater persistence than will children who are insecurely attached. Children with secure attachments are also likely to be more empathic, compliant, unconflicted, and generally competent in their relationships with adults and peers. Children with insecure attachments tend to have trouble relating to other people because their behavior is often either hostile and distant or overly dependent. These tendencies may extend into adolescence and adulthood, influencing significant social relationships as well as basic attitudes toward life.

Some researchers have hypothesized that the success or failure of an infant's early attachments establishes a cluster of expectations (internal working models) that set the stage for future social relationships. Some insecure and unhappy infants, for example, may have difficulty learning to deal with and trust others later in life.

An intriguing body of evidence from both human and animal studies suggests that early attachment relationships may be especially significant for later development of parenting skills. Some people who were neglected or abused as infants seem to have problems caring for their own children.

Other findings suggest a link between early attachment difficulties and risk for adolescent and adult mental health problems. Better understanding of the nature and extent of such links should aid in developing effective treatment and prevention programs for mental illness throughout the life span.

Researchers have been keenly interested in determining how differences in early attachment security arise. A key factor, according to the most widely accepted view, is the caregiver's sensitivity and responsiveness in interacting with the infant.

Building on such findings, one study found that, after a year of infant–parent psychotherapy, mothers of infants who had been anxiously attached showed greater empathy and were more interactive than untreated mothers of similar toddlers. The therapy focused on alleviating the mother's psychological conflicts about their children and on providing individually tailored information about child development. While the therapeutic effects need further validation, in this study the children of the treated mothers became more sociable and less angry than the children of the untreated mothers.

Insecure Attachment and Psychopathology

How much does the quality of attachment in infancy contribute to later personality and mental illness? Answers should become much clearer in the next decade, as researchers piece together a developmental story that is still unfolding. Data are just now being collected on the psychological health of a group of adolescents and young adults whose attachment relationships were studied 15 to 20 years earlier during infancy.

There is already evidence that severely disordered early attachment relationships (as seen in cases of physical or sexual abuse and neglect) are significant risk factors for certain mental disorders, such as borderline personality disorder. Research suggests that insecure attachment in infancy predicts childhood problems such as difficulties in peer relationships. Compared with children who were insecurely attached to their mothers at 12 months, those with

more secure attachments at that age were more resilient and cooperative, happier, and more likely to be leaders at three and six years.

The long-term mental health impact of various types of disturbed attachment has been examined through longitudinal studies of families affected by depression or maltreatment as well as families receiving therapy focused on low social support and certain behavior problems in children. Some major findings from these studies follow:

- Among children from low-income families, those who had been insecurely attached during infancy were, at ages 10 to 11 and 14 to 15, more dependent, less socially competent, and had lower self-esteem and resilience than those who had been securely attached. This study demonstrates striking consistency in individual adaptation between infancy and adolescence.

- Preschool children who had been maltreated by their parents were more likely than their peers to develop "fragmented relationships" in which, in a parent's presence, the child displays disorganized or disoriented behavior.

- Two-year-old children of mothers with major depression or manic-depressive illness had a higher proportion of insecure attachments than children of mothers with minor depression or no mood disorder. At five years of age, the children with disorganized attachment showed marked increases in hostility toward peers. Parental depression may contribute to children's insecure attachment through its influence on aspects of parent–child interaction and on broader aspects of the child-rearing environment, such as the psychological unavailability of the parent during periods of depression.

Self-Concept and Self-Esteem

Like the concept of attachment, the concept of self is central to our understanding of mental health and illness. In fact, attachment disturbances often

contribute to poor self-concepts. Progress in several research areas (e.g., self-regulation and perception of control, self-efficacy, and cultural influences on the self and identity) depends on understanding the factors and processes that regulate and occasionally distort people's self-concept. Research is clarifying how self-concept develops and functions normally, how the process can go awry, and what can be done to prevent or treat many forms of psychopathology (including borderline personality and sociopathy) that may be linked to disturbances of self-concept.

Researchers have concluded that, contrary to intuition, individuals have not one but several views of their selves, encompassing many domains of life, such as scholastic ability, physical appearance and romantic appeal, job competence, and adequacy as a provider. Further, self-esteem is often affected by social comparisons.

Studies in the academic domain have revealed, for example, that the self-esteem of African American students is higher in schools where they are numerically in the majority than where they are in the minority. The social comparison process that presumably contributes to these findings should be studied directly, however, since such research results have major implications for intervention. Other studies have revealed that, beginning in junior high school, many young girls reportedly feel inadequate in math, science, athletic ability, and physical appearance—a distressing set of findings that also deserves further exploration.

Researchers have discovered as well that, among a group of unpopular children, those deemed aggressive had relatively inflated self-esteem and overestimated their attributes and abilities in academics, appearance, athletics, and peer relations. By contrast, unpopular and withdrawn children had more negative —but accurate—conceptions of themselves, perhaps acknowledging their own deficiencies in social relationships. Children who are aggressive and unpopular are at increased risk for behavioral problems and juvenile delinquency, whereas withdrawn, unpopular children appear to sustain their low self-esteem through late childhood and are at increased risk for depression.

Pathways to Self-Esteem

Self-esteem begins to develop early in life; it has been studied in children as young as seven years of age. As children learn to describe aspects of themselves, such as their physical attributes, abilities, and preferences, they also begin to evaluate them. Becoming self-aware was once regarded as a uniformly positive step in development—a path to insight about one's own character. Recent research suggests that excessive self-awareness can interfere with concentration on important tasks in school, job, and social relationships and may undermine self-esteem. Indeed, overly harsh self-evaluation appears to be one cause of depression and suicidal behavior. Further study is needed of the boundaries between positive self-awareness, which can provide insights and promote healthy change, and negative self-consciousness, which can interfere with one's development.

Research findings have refuted the idea that a person's level of self-esteem is established in early childhood and remains stable throughout life. In many individuals, self-esteem changes dramatically over time. Long-term studies reveal that major transitions (e.g., marriage, parenthood, and job loss or promotion) are likely to provoke changes in self-esteem.

During the transition into junior high school, high school, or college, for example, the self-esteem of many students plummets. Some of them no longer feel competent scholastically (although they still value academic excellence), and others fail to gain the support of their new peer group. Still other students may respond to a school transition with enhanced self-esteem; they feel more competent in domains they value or they find themselves in a very supportive peer group.

The relationship of ethnicity and culture to self-esteem is complex. While one's ethnicity per se bears no natural relation to one's self-esteem, psychological factors associated with experience as a member of a particular ethnic or cultural group will influence self-esteem. However, across various ethnic populations, the same factors enhance children's self-esteem: their abilities in activities such as sports or academics that their culture values and the social support and approval of significant others.

Contributors to Low Self-Esteem

Low self-esteem plays an important role in mental illnesses. Research on self-esteem is beginning to explain interpersonal factors that lead people to devalue themselves, to become depressed, and even to consider suicide. Such factors include their assessments of their physical appearance, the behavior of parents and other caregivers, and the school environment.

Judgments of Physical Appearance

Beginning in preschool and continuing into middle age, people's evaluations of their physical appearance are inextricably linked to their self-esteem. Indeed, physical appearance is all-important, even in specific situations where one might expect other attributes—such as intelligence in a learning-disabled group—to be paramount. Cultural and media messages about the importance of good looks as a measure of self-worth appear to contribute strongly to our excessive valuation of physical appearance. People whose self-esteem depends on their appearance and who seek to reach standards of attractiveness (especially for women) that are virtually unattainable are vulnerable to low self-esteem, which in turn may contribute to the life-threatening eating disorders associated with slenderness, namely bulimia and anorexia nervosa.

Research has uncovered important individual differences in the links between self-esteem and assessments of attractiveness. Beginning at age four, some children's self-esteem depends on their view of how they look, while for others self-esteem is independent of appearance. The former orientation has been shown to be particularly pernicious for girls; as a group, they report more dissatisfaction with their appearance and more depressed mood than girls with the latter orientation. Greater knowledge about the factors underlying these different perspectives on the self should aid in encouraging young people to adopt standards for self-worth that are less superficial and less threatening to mental health.

Child-Rearing Practices

The behavior of parents and other caregivers also influences the early development of self-esteem. Recent studies reveal that children of depressed mothers in particular are at risk for low self-esteem; depressed mood; and lack of energy to engage in activities that foster physical, intellectual, and social development. However, more must be learned about which specific aspects of the parent–child relationship, in addition to genetic factors, contribute to these effects.

School Environment

A new line of research indicates how changes in the school environment influence self-esteem and motivation for learning. As children move from elementary to middle, junior, and high school, the school environment becomes increasingly more competitive and impersonal. In addition, growing emphasis is placed on social comparisons and scholastic ability.

The negative impact of this environment is most serious as students enter junior high school. Just as children are becoming more self-conscious, the emphasis on social comparison escalates, leading many students with lesser abilities to notice their deficiencies and possibly become "turned off" to school. Similarly, just as adolescents are trying to develop greater autonomy from their parents—and therefore need other adults to support their self-esteem—attention from teachers becomes less abundant, less personal, and more focused on the students' academic performance. These findings suggest that broader intervention efforts in schools, communities, and institutions outside the family may encourage a more positive self-concept in children and adolescents.

The finding that many women have a diminished sense of self-esteem compared with men invites further study of the social and other factors that contribute to this important difference. For example, in one long-term study, researchers found that during the adolescent years, self-esteem tends to increase in boys and decrease in girls. In another study, conducted at an all-women's college that became coeducational, women's self-esteem levels decreased after men were admitted. Following the men's arrival, the women also participated less in class discussions and showed less interest in the academic subject matter of their classes.

Such findings call for more research on how environments, including coeducational and same-sex school settings, influence and alter self-esteem. Since not all students are negatively affected by entering junior high, researchers may be able to reliably identify those whose self-esteem decreases, determine what factors and circumstances contribute to that outcome, and discover how to prevent that loss.

Research Directions

Important directions for future research on vulnerability and resilience include the following:

- Research has revealed that low self-esteem plays a powerful role in depression and eating disorders. Future research should explore the developmental pathways leading to low self-esteem and its maintenance. These pathways include comparisons to others in scholastic, athletic, social, and physical appearance domains. Self-esteem is also affected by specific socialization processes transmitted by parents, peers, schools, and the media. This is a vital research priority given the fact that low self-esteem is associated with self-destructive actions and antisocial behaviors.

- Considerable research suggests that complex relations exist among coping strategies, ethnicity, and culture. More research is needed to clarify different cultural orientations and define those cultural strengths that maintain a solid sense of self among members of ethnic minority groups, collectively and individually.

- Personality assessment can be useful in determining possible antecedents of mental illness as well as the outcomes of interventions intended to improve mental health. Future research in personality evaluation should move beyond the use of self-report questionnaires to the more frequent inclusion of judgments by other informants and observations of behavior in natural settings and in laboratory settings that can provide concurrent psychophysiological recordings. Such research will have practical applications in the prediction and diagnosis of psychopathological behavior.

- More precise theories of personality and more sophisticated and broadly based assessment tools must be developed to follow for extended periods individuals with specific personality patterns. Such studies can reveal how, when, and under what circumstances these patterns lead to harmful life outcomes and develop into mental disorders.

- Severe early problems in the emotional attachment between infant and caregiver create increased risk for certain mental disorders, such as borderline personality disorder, as well as impaired peer relations. Future studies of attachment need to examine in more detail both stability and change in parent–child attachment relationships. In addition, because, as their social network expands, children form attachments to siblings, friends, grandparents, day care personnel, and teachers, the developmental impact of these understudied aspects of attachment also requires examination.

- Confirmed connections between parental depression and disordered parent–child attachment raise the possibility that a mentally disturbed caregiver influences many aspects of the child-rearing environment. Future research should explore the possible contributions of other major life stressors, such as parental divorce and severe medical illness, to emerging attachment security.

References

Block, J. (1993). Studying personality the long way. In D. Funder, R. Parke, C. Tomlinson-Keasey, & K. Widaman (Eds.), *Studying lives through time: Personality and development.* Washington, DC: American Psychological Association.

Dunn, J. (1993). *Young children's close relationships: Beyond attachment.* Newbury Park, CA: Sage Publications.

Kagan, J. (1989). *Unstable ideas: Temperament, cognition, and self.* Cambridge, MA: Harvard University Press.

Loehlin, J. C. (1992). *Genes and environment in personality development.* Newbury Park, CA: Sage Publications.

Plomin, R. (1990). *Nature and nurture: An introduction to human behavioral genetics.* Pacific Grove, CA: Brooks/Cole.

Sampson, R. J., & Laub, J. H., II (1993). *Crime in the making: Pathways and turning points through life.* Cambridge, MA: Harvard University Press.

Werner, E. E., & Smith, R. S. (1992). *Overcoming the odds: High-risk children from birth to adulthood.* Ithaca, NY: Cornell University Press.

Article Review Form at end of book.

Why would a patient seeking treatment put up resistance to that treatment? What is repression as Freud describes it?

Resistance and Repression[1]

Sigmund Freud

Ladies and Gentlemen,—Before we can make any further progress in our understanding of the neuroses, we stand in need of some fresh observations. Here we have two such, both of which are very remarkable and at the time when they were made were very surprising. Our discussions of last year will, it is true, have prepared you for both of them.[2]

In the first place, then, when we undertake to restore a patient to health, to relieve him of the symptoms of his illness, he meets us with a violent and tenacious resistance, which persists throughout the whole length of the treatment. This is such a strange fact that we cannot expect it to find much credence. It is best to say nothing about it to the patient's relatives, for they invariably regard it as an excuse on our part for the length or failure of our treatment. The patient, too, produces all the phenomena of this resistance without recognizing it as such, and if we can induce him to take our view of it and to reckon with its existence, that already counts as a great success. Only think of it! The patient, who is suffering so much from his symptoms and is causing those about him to share his sufferings, who is ready to undertake so many sacrifices in time, money, effort and self-discipline in order to be freed from those symptoms—we are to believe that this same patient puts up a struggle in the

interest of his illness against the person who is helping him. How improbable such an assertion must sound! Yet it is true; and when its improbability is pointed out to us, we need only reply that it is not without analogies. A man who has gone to the dentist because of an unbearable toothache will nevertheless try to hold the dentist back when he approaches the sick tooth with a pair of forceps.

The patient's resistance is of very many sorts, extremely subtle and often hard to detect; and it exhibits protean changes in the forms in which it manifests itself. The doctor must be distrustful and remain on his guard against it.

In psycho-analytic therapy we make use of the same technique that is familiar to you from dream-interpretation. We instruct the patient to put himself into a state of quiet, unreflecting self-observation, and to report to us whatever internal perceptions he is able to make—feelings, thoughts, memories—in the order in which they occur to him. At the same time we warn him expressly against giving way to any motive which would lead him to make a selection among these associations or to exclude any of them, whether on the ground that it is too *disagreeable* or too *indiscreet* to say, or that it is too *unimportant* or *irrelevant,* or that it is *nonsensical* and need not be said. We urge him always to follow only the surface of his consciousness and to leave aside any criticism of what he finds, whatever shape that criticism may take; and we assure him that the success of the treatment,

and above all its duration, depends on the conscientiousness with which he obeys this fundamental technical rule of analysis.[3] We already know from the technique of dream-interpretation that the associations giving rise to the doubts and objections I have just enumerated are precisely the ones that invariably contain the material which leads them to the uncovering of the unconscious. [Cf. Lecture VII, p. 141.]*

The first thing we achieve by setting up this fundamental technical rule as that it becomes the target for the attacks of the resistance. The patient endeavors in every sort of way to extricate himself from its provisions. At one moment he declares that nothing occurs to him, at the next that so many things are crowding in on him that he cannot get hold of anything. Presently we observe with pained astonishment that he has given way first to one and then to another critical objection: he betrays this to us by the long pauses that he introduces into his remarks. He then admits that there is something he really cannot say—he would be ashamed to; and he allows this reason to prevail against his promise. Or he says that something has occurred to him, but it concerns another person and not himself and is therefore exempt from being reported. Or, what has now occurred to him is really too unimportant, too silly and senseless: I cannot possibly have meant him to enter into thoughts like that. So it goes on in innumerable

Note: footnotes are not included in this publication.

*Lectures and pages such as those referenced here are not included in this publication.

variations, and one can only reply that 'to say everything' really does mean 'to say everything.'

One hardly comes across a single patient who does not make an attempt at reserving some region or other for himself so as to prevent the treatment from having access to it. A man, whom I can only describe as of the highest intelligence, kept silence in this way for weeks on end about an intimate love-affair, and when he was called to account for having broken the sacred rule, defended himself with the argument that he thought this particular story was his private business. Analytic treatment does not, of course, recognize any such right of asylum. Suppose that in a town like Vienna the experiment was made of treating a square such as the Hohe Markt, or a church like St. Stephen's, as places where no arrests might be made, and suppose we then wanted to catch a particular criminal. We could be quite sure of finding him in the sanctuary. I once decided to allow a man, on whose efficiency much depended in the external world, the right to make an exception of this kind because he was bound under his oath of office not to make communications about certain things to another person. He, it is true, was satisfied with the outcome; but I was not. I determined not to repeat an attempt under such conditions.

Obsessional neurotics understand perfectly how to make the technical rule almost useless by applying their overconscientiousness and doubts to it.[4] Patients suffering from anxiety hysteria occasionally succeed in carrying the rule *ad absurdum* by producing only associations which are so remote from what we are in search of that they contribute nothing to the analysis. But it is not my intention to induct you into the handling of these technical difficulties. It is enough to say that in the end, through resolution and perseverance, we succeed in extorting a certain amount of obedience to the fundamental technical rule from the resistance—which thereupon jumps over to another sphere.

It now appears as an *intellectual* resistance, it fights by means of arguments and exploits all the difficulties and improbabilities which normal but uninstructed thinking finds in the theories of analysis. It is now our fate to hear from this single voice all the criticisms and objections which assail our ears in a chorus in the scientific literature of the subject. And for this reason none of the shouts that reach us from outside sound unfamiliar. It is a regular storm in a tea-cup. But the patient is willing to be argued with; he is anxious to get us to instruct him, teach him, contradict him, introduce him to the literature, so that he can find further instruction. He is quite ready to become an adherent of psycho-analysis—on condition that analysis spares him personally. But we recognize this curiosity as a resistance, as a diversion from our particular tasks, and we repel it. In the case of an obsessional neurotic we have to expect special tactics of resistance. He will often allow the analysis to proceed on its way uninhibited, so that it is able to shed an ever-increasing light upon the riddle of his illness. We begin to wonder in the end, however, why this enlightenment is accompanied by no practical advance, no diminution of the symptoms. We are then able to realize that resistance has withdrawn on to the doubt belonging to the obsessional neurosis and from that position is successfully defying us. It is as though the patient were saying: 'Yes, that's all very nice and interesting, and I'll be very glad to go on with it further. It would change my illness a lot if it were true. But I don't in the least believe that it *is* true; so long as I don't believe it, it makes no difference to my illness.' Things can proceed like this for a long time, till finally one comes up against this uncommitted attitude itself, and the decisive struggle then breaks out.[5]

Intellectual resistances are not the worst; one always remains superior to them. But the patient also knows how to put up resistances, without going outside the framework of the analysis, the overcoming of which is among the most difficult of technical problems. Instead of remembering, he *repeats* attitudes and emotional impulses from his early life which can be used as a resistance against the doctor and the treatment by means of what is known as 'transference'.[6] If the patient is a man, he usually extracts this material from his relation to his father, into whose place he fits the doctor, and in that way he makes resistances out of his efforts to become independent in himself and in his judgements, out of his ambition, the first aim of which was to do things as well as his father or to get the better of him, or out of his unwillingness to burden himself for the second time in his life with a load of gratitude. Thus at times one has an impression that the patient has entirely replaced his better intention of making an end to his illness by the alternative one of putting the doctor in the wrong, of making him realize his impotence and of triumphing over him. Women have a masterly gift for exploiting an affectionate, erotically tinged transference to the doctor for the purposes of resistance. If this attachment reaches a certain height, all their interest in the immediate situation in the treatment and all the obligations they undertook at its commencement vanish; their jealousy, which is never absent, and their exasperation at their inevitable rejection, however considerately expressed, are bound to have a damaging effect on their personal understanding with the doctor and so to put out of operation one of the most powerful motive forces of the analysis.

Resistances of this kind should not be one-sidedly condemned. They include so much of the most important material from the patient's past and bring it back in so convincing a fashion that they become some of the best supports of the analysis if a skillful technique knows how to give them the right turn. Nevertheless, it remains a remarkable fact that this material is always in the service of the resistance to begin with and brings to the fore a *façade* that is hostile to the treatment. It may also be said that what is being mobilized for fighting against the alterations we are striving for are character-traits, attitudes of the ego. In this connection we discover that these character-traits were formed in relation to the determinants of the neurosis and in reaction against its demands, and we come upon traits which cannot normally emerge, or not to the same extent, and which may be described as latent. Nor must you get an impression that we regard the appearance of these resistances as an unforeseen risk to analytic influence. No, we are aware that these resistances are bound to come to light; in fact we are dissatisfied if we cannot provoke them clearly enough and are unable to demonstrate them to the patient. Indeed we come finally to understand that the overcoming of these resistances is the essential function of analysis[7] and is the only part of our work which gives us an assurance that we have achieved something with the patient.

If you further consider that the patient makes all the chance events that occur during his analysis into interferences with it, that he uses as reasons for slackening his efforts every diversion outside the analysis, every comment by a person of authority in his environment who is hostile to analysis, any chance organic illness or any that complicates his neurosis and, even, indeed, every improvement in his condition—if you consider all this, you will have obtained an approximate, though still incomplete, picture of the forms and methods of the resistance, the struggle against which accompanies every analysis.[8]

I have treated this point in such great detail because I must now inform you that this experience of ours with the resistance of neurotics to the removal of their symptoms became the basis of our dynamic view of the neuroses. Originally Breuer and I myself carried out psychotherapy by means of hypnosis; Breuer's first patient[9] was treated throughout under hypnotic influence, and to begin with I followed him in this. I admit that at that period the work proceeded more easily and pleasantly, and also in a much shorter time. But results were capricious and not lasting; and for that reason I finally dropped hypnosis.[10] And I then understood that an insight into the dynamics of these illnesses had not been possible so long as hypnosis was employed.[11] That state was precisely able to withhold the existence of the resistance from the doctor's perception. It pushed the resistance back, making a certain area free for analytic work, and dammed it up at the frontiers of that area in such a way as to be impenetrable, just as doubt does in obsessional neurosis. For that reason I have been able to say that psycho-analysis proper began when I dispensed with the help of hypnosis.[12]

If, however, the recognition of resistance has become so important, we should do well to find room for a cautious doubt whether we have not been too light-heartedly assuming resistances. Perhaps there really are cases of neurosis in which associations fail for other reasons, perhaps the arguments against our hypotheses really deserve to have their content examined, and perhaps we are doing patients an injustice in so conveniently setting aside their intellectual criticisms as resistance. But, Gentlemen, we did not arrive at this judgement lightly. We have had occasion to observe all these critical patients at the moment of the emergence of a resistance and after its disappearance. For resistance is constantly altering its intensity during the course of a treatment; it always increases when we are approaching a new topic, it is at its most intense while we are at the climax of dealing with that topic, and it dies away when the topic has been disposed of. Nor do we ever, unless we have been guilty of special clumsiness in our technique, have to meet the full amount of resistance of which a patient is capable. We have therefore been able to convince ourselves that on countless occasions in the course of his analysis the same man will abandon his critical attitude and then take it up again. If we are on the point of bringing a specially distressing piece of unconscious material into his consciousness, he is extremely critical; he may previously have understood and accepted a great deal, but now it is just as though those acquisitions have been swept away; in his efforts for opposition at any price, he may offer a complete picture of someone who is an emotional imbecile. But if we succeed in helping him to overcome this new resistance, he recovers his insight and understanding. Thus his critical faculty is not an independent function, to be respected as such, it is the tool of his emotional attitudes and is directed by his resistance. If there is something he does not like, he can put up a shrewd fight against it and appear highly critical; but if something suits his book, he can, on the contrary, show himself most credulous. Perhaps none of us are very different; a man who is being analysed only reveals this dependence of the intellect upon emotional life so clearly because

in analysis we are putting such great pressure on him.

How, then, do we account for our observation that the patient fights with such energy against the removal of his symptoms and the setting of his mental processes on a normal course? We tell ourselves that we have succeeded in discovering powerful forces here which oppose any alteration of the patient's condition; they must be the same ones which in the past brought this condition about. During the construction of his symptoms something must have taken place which we can now reconstruct from our experiences during the *resolution* of his symptoms. We already know from Breuer's observation that there is a precondition for the existence of a symptom: some mental process must not have been brought to an end normally—so that it could become conscious. The symptom is a substitute for what did not happen at that point [p. 346 above]. We now know the point at which we must locate the operation of the force which we have surmised. A violent opposition must have started against the entry into consciousness of the questionable mental process, and for that reason it remained unconscious. As being something unconscious, it had the power to construct a symptom. This same opposition, during psycho-analytic treatment, sets itself up once more against our effort to transform what is unconscious into what is conscious. This is what we perceive as resistance. We have proposed to give the pathogenic process which is demonstrated by the resistance the name of *repression*.

We must now form more definite ideas about this process of repression. It is the precondition for the construction of symptoms; but it is also something to which we know nothing similar. Let us take as our model an impulse, a mental process that endeavours to turn itself into an action. We know that it can be repelled by what we term a rejection or condemnation. When this happens, the energy at its disposal is withdrawn from it; it becomes powerless, though it can persist as a memory. The whole process of coming to a decision about it runs its course within the knowledge of the ego. It is a very different matter if we suppose that the same impulse is subjected to repression. In that case it would retain its energy and no memory of it would remain behind; moreover the process of repression would be accomplished unnoticed by the ego. This comparison, therefore, bring us no nearer to the essential nature of repression.

I will put before you the only theoretical ideas which have proved of service for giving a more definite shape to the concept of repression. It is above all essential for this purpose that we should proceed from the purely descriptive meaning of the word 'unconscious' to the systematic meaning of the word.[13] That is, we will decide to say that the fact of a psychical process being conscious or unconscious is only one of its attributes and not necessarily an unambiguous one. If a process of this kind has remained unconscious, its being kept away from consciousness may perhaps only be an indication of some vicissitude it has gone through, and not that vicissitude itself. In order to form a picture of this vicissitude, let us assume that every mental process—we must admit one exception, which we shall mention at a later stage[14]—exists to begin with in an unconscious stage or phase and that it is only from there that the process passes over into the conscious phase, just as a photographic picture begins as a negative and only becomes a picture after being turned into a positive. Not every negative, however, necessarily becomes a positive; not is it necessary that every unconscious mental process should turn into a conscious one. This may be advantageously expressed by saying that an individual process belongs to begin with to the system of the unconscious and can then, in certain circumstances, pass over into the system of the conscious.

The crudest idea of these systems is the most convenient to us—a spatial one. Let us therefore compare the system of the unconscious to a large entrance hall, in which the mental impulses jostle one another like separate individuals. Adjoining this entrance hall there is a second, narrower, room—a kind of drawing-room—in which consciousness, too, resides. But on the threshold between the two rooms a watchman performs his function: he examines the differ-ent mental impulses, acts as a censor, and will not admit them into the drawing-room if they displease him. You will see at once that it does not make much difference if the watchman turns away a particular impulse at the threshold itself or if he pushes it back across the threshold after it has entered the drawing-room. This is merely a question of the degree of his watchfulness and of how early he carries out his act of recognition. If we keep to this picture, we shall be able to extend our nomenclature further. The impulses in the entrance hall of the unconscious are out of sight of the conscious, which is in the other room; to begin with they must remain unconscious. If they have already pushed their way forward to the threshold and have been turned back by the watchman, then they are inadmissible to consciousness;[15] we speak of them as *repressed.* But even the impulses which the watchman has allowed to cross the threshold are not on that account necessarily conscious as well; they can only become so if they succeed in catching the eye of consciousness. We are therefore justified in calling this second room the system of the *preconscious.* In that case becoming conscious retains its purely descriptive sense. For any particular impulse, however, the vicissitude of repression consists in its not being allowed by the watchman to pass from the system of the unconscious into that of the preconscious. It is the same watchman whom we get to know as resistance when we try to life the repression by means of the analytic treatment.

Now I know you will say that these ideas are both crude and fantastic and quite impermissible in a scientific account. I know that they are crude: and, more than that, I know that they are incorrect, and, if I am not very much mistaken, I already have something better to take their place.[16] Whether it will seem to you equally fantastic I cannot tell. They are preliminary working hypotheses, like Ampère's manikin swimming in the electric current,[17] and they are not to be despised in so far as they are of service in making our observations intelligible. I should like to assure you that these crude hypotheses of the two rooms, the watchman at the threshold between them and consciousness as a spectator at the end of the second room, must nevertheless be very far-reaching approximations to the real facts. And I should like to hear you admit that our terms, 'unconscious', 'preconscious' and 'conscious', prejudge things far less and are far easier to justify than others which have been proposed or are in use, such as 'subconscious', 'paraconscious', 'intraconscious' and the like.[18]

It will therefore be of greater importance to me if you warn me that an arrangement of the mental apparatus, such as I have here assumed in order to explain neurotic symptoms, must necessarily claim general validity and must give us information about normal functioning as well. You will, of course, be quite right in this. At the moment we cannot pursue this implication further; but our interest in the psychology of the forming of symptoms cannot but be increased to an extraordinary extent if there is a prospect, through the study of pathological conditions, of obtaining access to the normal mental events which are so well concealed.

Perhaps you recognize, moreover, what it is that supports our hypotheses of the two systems, and their relation to each other and to consciousness? After all, the watchman between the unconscious and the preconscious is nothing else than the *censorship,* to which, as we found, the form taken by the manifest dream is subject. [Cf. Lecture IX, p. 171 above.] The day's residues, which we recognized as the instigators of the dream, were preconscious material which, at night-time and in the state of sleep, had been under the influence of unconscious and repressed wishful impulses; they had been able, in combination with those impulses and thanks to their energy, to construct the latent dream. Under the dominance of the unconscious system this material had been worked over (by condensation and displacement) in a manner which is unknown or only exceptionally permissible in normal mental life—that is, in the preconscious system. We came to regard this difference in their manner of operating as what characterizes the two systems; the relation which the preconscious has to consciousness was regarded by us merely as an indication of its belonging to one of the two systems.[19] Dreams are not pathological phenomena; they can appear in any healthy person under the conditions of a state of sleep. Our hypothesis about the structure of the mental apparatus, which allows us to understand the formation alike of dreams and of neurotic symptoms, has an incontrovertible claim to being taken into account in regard to normal mental life as well.

That much is what we have to say for the moment about repression. But it is only the *precondition* for the construction of symptoms. Symptoms, as we know, are a substitute for something that is held back by repression. It is a long step further, however, from repression to an understanding of this substitutive structure. On this other side of the problem, these questions arise out of our observation of repression: what kind of mental impulses are subject to repression? by what forces is it accomplished? and for what motives? So far we have only one piece of information on these points. In investigating resistance we have learnt that it emanates from forces of the ego, from known and latent character traits [p. 360 above]. It is these too, therefore, that are responsible for repression, or at any rate they have a share in it. We know nothing more at present.

At this point the second of the two observations which I mentioned to you earlier [at the opening of this Lecture] comes to our help. It is quite generally the case that analysis allows us to arrive at the intention of neurotic symptoms. This again will be nothing new to you. I have already demonstrated it to you in two cases of neurosis.[20] But, after all, what do two cases amount to? You are right to insist on its being demonstrated to you in two hundred cases—in countless cases. The only trouble is that I cannot do that. Once again, your own experience must serve instead, or your belief, which on this point can appeal to the unanimous reports of all psycho-analysts.

You will recollect that, in the two cases whose symptoms we submitted to a detailed investigation, the analysis initiated us into these patients' most intimate sexual life. In the first case we further recognized with particular clarity the intention or purpose of the symptom we were examining; in the second case this was perhaps somewhat concealed by a factor which will be mentioned later [p. 371 below]. Well, every other case that we submit to analysis would show us the same thing that we have found in these two examples. In every instance we should be introduced by the analysis into the patient's sexual experiences and wishes; and in every instance we should be bound to see that the symptoms served the same intention. We find that this intention is the satisfaction of sexual wishes; the symptoms serve for the patients' sexual satisfaction; they are a substitute for satisfaction of this kind, which the patients are without in their lives.

Think of our first patient's obsessional action. The woman was without her husband, whom she loved intensely but with whom she could not share her life on account of his deficiencies and weaknesses. She had to remain faithful to him; she could not put anyone else in his place. Her obsessional symptom gave her what she longed for, set her husband on a pedestal, denied and corrected his weaknesses and above all his impotence. This symptom was fundamentally a wish-fulfilment, just like a dream—and moreover, what is not always true of a dream, an *erotic* wish-fulfilment. In the case of our second patient you could at least gather that her ceremonial sought to obstruct intercourse between her parents or prevent it from producing a new baby. You will also probably have guessed that it was at bottom endeavouring to put herself in her mother's place. Once again, therefore, a setting-aside of interferences with sexual satisfaction and a fulfilment of the patient's own sexual wishes. I shall soon come to the complication I have hinted at.

I should like to anticipate, Gentlemen, the qualifications which I shall have to make later in the universal validity of these statements. I will therefore point out to you that all I have said here about repression and the formation and meaning of symptoms was derived from three forms of neurosis—anxiety hysteria, conversion hysteria and obsessional neurosis—and that in the first instance it is also valid only for these forms. These three disorders, which we are accustomed to group together as 'transference neuroses',[21] also circumscribe the region in which psycho-analytic therapy can function. The other neuroses have been far less thoroughly studied by psychoanalysis; in one group of them the impossibility of therapeutic influence has been a reason for this neglect. Nor should you forget that psychoanalysis is still a very young science, that preparing for it costs much trouble and time, and that not at all long ago it was being practised single-handed. Nevertheless, we are everywhere on the point of penetrating to an understanding of these other disorders which are not transference neuroses. I hope later to be able to introduce you to the extensions of our hypotheses and findings which result from adaptation to this new material, and to show you that these further studies have not led to contradictions but to the establishment of higher unities.[22] If, then, everything I am saying here applies to the transference neuroses, let me first increase the value of symptoms by a new piece of information. For a comparative study of the determining causes of falling ill leads to a result which can be expressed in a formula: these people fall ill in one way or another of *frustration*, when reality prevents them from satisfying their sexual wishes.[23] You see how excellently these two findings tally with each other. It is only thus that symptoms can be properly viewed as substitutive satisfactions for what is missed in life.

No doubt all kinds of objections can still be raised to the assertion that neurotic symptoms are substitutes for sexual satisfactions. I will mention two of them to-day. When you yourselves have carried out analytic examinations of a considerable number of neurotics, you will perhaps tell me, shaking your head, that in a lot of cases my assertion is simply not true; the symptoms seem rather to have the contrary purpose of excluding or of stopping sexual satisfaction. I will not dispute the correctness of your interpretation. The facts in psycho-analysis have a habit of being rather more complicated than we like. If they were as simple as all that, perhaps it might not have needed psycho-analysis to bring them to light. Indeed, some of the features of our second patient's ceremonial show signs of this ascetic character with its hostility to sexual satisfaction: when, for instance, she got rid of the clocks and watches [p. 328], which had the magical meaning of avoiding erections during the night [p. 330], or when she tried to guard against flower-pots falling and breaking [p. 328], which was equivalent to protecting her virginity [p. 330]. In some other cases of bed-ceremonials, which I have been able to analyse, this negative character was far more outspoken; the ceremonial might consist exclusively of defensive measures against sexual memories and temptations. However, we have already found often enough that in psycho-analysis opposites imply no contradiction.[24] We might extend our thesis and say that symptoms aim either at a sexual satisfaction or at fending it off, and that on the whole the positive, wish-fulfilling character prevails in hysteria and the negative, ascetic one in obsessional neurosis. If symptoms can serve the purpose both of sexual satisfaction and of its opposite, there is an excellent basis for this double-sidedness or polarity

in part of their mechanism which I have so far not been able to mention. For, as we shall hear, they are the products of a compromise and arise from the mutual interference between two opposing currents; they represent not only the repressed but also the repressing force which had a share in their origin. One side or the other may be more strongly represented; but it is rarely that one influence is entirely absent. In hysteria a convergence of both intentions in the same symptom is usually achieved. In obsessional neurosis the two portions are often separated; the symptom then becomes diphasic [falls into two stages] and consists in two actions, one after the other, which cancel each other out.[25]

We shall not be able to dismiss the second objection so easily. If you survey a fairly long series of interpretations of symptoms, you will probably start by judging that the concept of a substitutive sexual satisfaction has been stretched to its extreme limits in them. You will not fail to emphasize the fact that these symptoms offer nothing real in the way of satis-

faction, that often enough they are restricted to the revival of a sensation or the representation of a phantasy derived from a sexual complex. And you will further point out that these supposed sexual satisfactions often take on a childish and discreditable form, approximate to an act of masturbation perhaps, or recall dirty kinds of naughtiness which are forbidden even to children—habits of which they have been broken. And, going on from this, you will also express surprise that we are representing as a sexual satisfaction what would rather have to be described as the satisfaction of lusts that are cruel or horrible or would even have to be called unnatural. We shall come to no agreement, Gentlemen, on this latter point till we have made a thorough investigation of the sexual life of human beings and till, in doing so, we have described what it is that we are justified in calling 'sexual'.

 Article Review Form at end of book.

What is the connection between keeping secrets and health? What is the effect of telling secrets?

Confession and Inhibition

The beginnings of an approach

J. W. Pennebaker

Long before the Spanish conquered the new world, Indians of North and South America had elaborate confession rituals wherein tribe members disclosed their transgressions to others. Indeed, rituals of confession are currently prominent among most Eastern and Western religions.

A growing number of Americans pay millions of dollars to therapists and self-help groups so that they can divulge their secret views of the world.

A large percentage of people write about their very deepest thoughts and feelings in diaries or letters but do not disclose the personal sides of themselves to the close friends they see every day.

On airplanes, buses, and trains, people are likely to disclose intimate sides of themselves to individuals they have never met before.

Why do people throughout the world seek to tell their untold stories? Is there some kind of urge to confess? Is it healthy for us to divulge our deepest thoughts and feelings? Or, conversely, is it unhealthy *not* to disclose the private side of our life? I have been fascinated by questions such as these for quite a while. Beginning in the late 1970s, I embarked on a large research project in an attempt to get some answers.

The main discoveries of this project indicate that actively holding back or inhibiting our thoughts and feelings can be hard work. Over time, the work of inhibition gradually undermines the body's defenses. Like other stressors, inhibition can affect immune function, the action of the heart and vascular systems, and even the biochemical workings of the brain and nervous systems. In short, excessive holding back of thoughts, feelings, and behaviors can place people at risk for both major and minor diseases.

Whereas inhibition is potentially harmful, confronting our deepest thoughts and feelings can have remarkable short- and long-term health benefits. Confession, whether by writing or talking, can neutralize many of the problems of inhibition. Further, writing our talking about upsetting things can influence our basic values, our daily thinking patterns, and our feelings about ourselves. In short, there appears to be something akin to an urge to confess. Not disclosing our thoughts and feelings can be unhealthy. Divulging them can be healthy.

Those are the most basic ideas of the book. But there is much more to the story. Before detailing the nature and implications of confession, let me explain how I got into this business. Several years ago, I became fascinated by three seemingly unrelated phenomena: the joy of talking, the nature of lie detection, and the role of self-understanding in affecting the mind-body link. Piecing together these observations laid the groundwork of an intriguing model of inhibition and confrontation.

I was originally trained as a social psychologist—someone who studies attitudes and social behaviors. After graduate school, I found myself teaching a class of three hundred freshmen about basic psychology at the University of Virginia. Because graduate training emphasizes research skills rather than teaching abilities, I quickly learned that class demonstrations were a wonderful way of hiding one's lack of knowledge about a topic. Further, if the demonstrations were set up right, I could actually conduct research and teach at the same time.

In one of the first class meetings, I split the students into small groups of people who didn't know one another. Once in their assigned groups, the students were told just to talk for fifteen minutes about anything they wanted. As you would expect, they talked about their hometowns, why they had come to college, what dormitory they lived in, friends they had in common, the weather, and related topics—the usual cocktail-party fare.

At the end of fifteen minutes, they all returned to their regular seats and estimated how much of the time every person in the group talked, how much they liked the group, and how much they learned from the group. Two rather surprising findings came from this and subsequent demonstrations. First, the more people talked, the more they liked the group. Second, the more they talked, the more they claimed to have learned from the group. In other words, as a group member, the more you dominate the conversation, the more you claim you have learned about the others.

In general, we would rather talk than listen. Most of us find that communicating our thoughts is a supremely enjoyable learning experience.

Not long after this, I was introduced to the world of lie detection. Up to that time, I had been interested in how students felt when they talked about superficial topics to their classmates. I was now in a position to learn what happened physiologically to people in the real world when they talked about crimes they may or may not have committed.

There is something frighteningly magical about the idea of lie detection. Machines that can accurately read others' private thoughts have been the basis of dreams by police officers, poker players, and parents. A crude approximation of this magical lie detector is the polygraph—an instrument that continuously measures several physiological indicators such as heart rate, blood pressure, breathing rate, and perspiration on the hand.

In law enforcement, polygraph exams and related lie-detector methods assume that when suspects try to deceive their interrogators, their biological stress levels will increase relative to when they tell the truth. Although numerous studies indicate that polygraph techniques do much better than chance at catching truly guilty suspects, they are far from perfect.

Ironically, the real value of the polygraph is in bringing about confessions. A particularly skilled polygrapher uses a suspect's biological responses to various questions as an indicator of what topics provoke the most anxiety. Once the "hot" questions are isolated, the polygrapher may note, "Gee, I really believe what you have told me, but my machine shows a huge reaction when you an-swered that question. Why do you think this is happening?" In more cases than not, deceptive suspects try to rationalize their physiological responses. In so doing, they often contradict their earlier stories. Finally, the more they are confronted with these contradictions, the more likely they are to ultimately break down and confess to the crime.

Because of my interest in physiological responses to stressors, I was invited to give a series of talks to some of the top-level polygraphers of the FBI, CIA, and other secret agencies with initials of which I had never heard. Fortunately, I spent several late evenings talking with the polygraphers about their job. As a group, these people were unusually bright and insightful. What most impressed me was a remarkably similar experience that many of the polygraphers reported in interrogating some of their suspects—something I call the polygraph confession effect.

A San Francisco-based polygrapher first alerted me to the polygraph confession effect in recounting an exam he had given to a forty-five-year-old bank vice-president who was a suspect in an embezzlement investigation. When initially run through the polygraph exam, the bank vice-president's heart rate, blood pressure, and other physiological levels were quite high. This is normal for both innocent and guilty people, because such an exam is almost always threatening. Nevertheless, the polygrapher suspected that the bank vice-president was lying or holding back information, because his physiological levels went even higher when the vice-president was asked about some of the details of the embezzlement. With repeated questions and prodding, the vice-president finally broke down and confessed to embezzling $74,000 over a six-month period.

In line with standard procedures, after the bank vice-president signed a written confession, he was then polygraphed again to be certain that his confession was itself not deceptive. When hooked up to the monitoring apparatus, his overall physiological levels were extremely low. His hands were no longer sweaty. His heart rate and blood pressure were extraordinarily low. His breathing was slow and relaxed.

You can appreciate the irony of this situation. This man had come into the polygrapher's office a free man, safe in the knowledge that polygraph evidence was not allowed in court. Nevertheless, he confessed. Now, his professional, financial, and personal lives were on the brink of ruin. He was virtually assured of a prison term. Despite these realities, he was relaxed and at ease with himself. Indeed, when a policeman came to handcuff and escort him to jail, he warmly shook the polygrapher's hand and thanked him for all he had done. This last December, the polygrapher received a chatty Christmas card written by the former bank vice-president with a federal penitentiary as the return address.

Even when the costs are high, the confession of actions that violate our personal values can reduce anxiety and physiological stress. Whereas dominating the conversation in a group may be fun, revealing pent-up thoughts and feelings can be liberating. Even if they send you to prison.

There was a third phenomenon that had a significant impact on my interest in confession and health. It dealt with the nature of psychological insight and the mind-body link. I was probably drawn to that area of psychosomatics by virtue of having asthma as a child. I grew up in West Texas, a very dry and flat part of the world. During my adolescence, asthma attacks became a routine feature of the windy part of winter (as opposed to the windy parts of spring, summer, and fall). Clearly, I reasoned, pollen and dust that had blown in from New Mexico and Nevada were to blame.

In college, I never had any wheezing bouts except when I went home for the Christmas holidays. The pollen and dust again. During my last year in college, however, my parents came to visit me in Florida in late November. The day they arrived, I developed asthma. All of a sudden, the profound realization hit me that there was more to asthma than pollen. Conflicts with my parents were undoubtedly linked to my upper respiratory system. Interestingly, once I saw the parent-asthma connection, I never again wheezed. It was too embarrassing.

Asthma, wheezing, congestion, and other respiratory changes have

Topic	Heart Rate	Warren's Comments
Girlfriend	77	Some disagreements about sexuality, but we are close.
College courses	71	Most have been interesting . . . tests have been another matter.
Failing exams	76	It's been hard on my ego. I can't explain it.
Parents	84	We were a close family until the divorce.
Parents' divorce	103	It was no big deal, really. They are a lot happier now.
The future	79	It scares me. I can't bear the thought of failing again.

long been known to be related to psychological conflict. In fact, two pioneers in psychosomatic medicine, Harold G. Wolff and Stewart Wolf, documented effects such as these in a book with the intriguing title *The Nose* (together and separately, they also published books entitled, *Headache, The Colon,* and, of course, *The Stomach*). In landmark studies spanning two decades, Wolff, Wolf, and their collaborators developed the stress interview, whereby volunteers would be asked a series of psychologically threatening questions while, at the same time, relevant bodily changes were monitored.

The stress interview serves as a medical version of a lie-detector exam. For most people, there are a limited number of psychological issues that account for most psychosomatic problems. Current stress interviews, for example, routinely touch on issues of loss, rejection, sexuality, parental problems, uncontrollable trauma, and failure. Depending on the person's health problem, the interviewer might measure muscle tension in the neck (for tension-headache sufferers), blood pressure and heart rate (for hypertensives), breathing rate or oxygen consumption (for those with respiratory problems or panic attacks), or one of a few dozen other biological indices.

As Wolff, Wolf, and a generation of psychosomatic researchers soon learned, different psychological conflicts are linked to specific changes in our bodies. One person's blood pressure may increase when he is forced to discuss the death of his parents, whereas another might respond to the same topic with the beginnings of a migraine headache. A third person may not show any biological changes to the death topic but may react selectively to issues surrounding sexuality.

That many, perhaps most, illnesses have a significant psychosomatic component is not surprising. More peculiar is that we rarely see the relationship between psychological events and illness in ourselves. When we do, however, the course of the illness often changes for the better.

Why are we blind to many of the psychological precursors to illness? One problem lies in our ability to perceive cause-effect relationships. When we see something happen, we naturally look for something that preceded the event by no more than a few seconds or, at most, hours. If our car doesn't start because of a dead battery, we might blame the battery's demise on the cold weather or our failure to turn off the headlights. It makes no sense to think back to the way we drove the car two weeks ago. Our body is a different story. If we come down with a cold, it probably has nothing to do with the last night's weather or what we had for breakfast. It could be that our immune system was compromised by the breakup of a significant relationship a week earlier.

Another reason for our myopia concerning the causal links between psychological issues and illnesses concerns denial. Virtually all of us have actively avoided thinking about unpleasant experiences. Some issues are so painful that we deceive ourselves into thinking that they don't exist. Sigmund Freud persuasively argued that we employ an arsenal of defense mechanisms, such as denial, compulsive behaviors, and even dwelling on physical symptoms, in order to screen out anxiety and psychological pain. Wheezing when around parents or headaches in sexually threatening situations can be safely attributed to purely physical causes (e.g., pollen or caffeine). Admitting to struggles concerning one's autonomy or sexuality will usually be avoided when less threatening alternative explanations exist.

Fortunately, once we become aware of the psychological causes of a recurring health problem such as headaches, back pain, or asthma, the problems often subside to some degree. There are several reasons for this. Once we see the psychological basis for a particular health problem, we can then use the health problem as a signal of distress. By focusing our energy on reducing the cause of the distress, we more quickly resolve the underlying psychological issues that we may not have known were issues in the first place. Another reason that seeing the cause-effect relationship is beneficial is that it makes the health problems more predictable and, hence, controllable. Perceptions of control and predictability over our world are essential to good psychological health.

One of my first experiences in discovering this sometimes invisible link between a psychological event and a biological activity was with Warren, an extremely bright student who had been the valedictorian of his high school class. After performing quite well his first year and a half of college, he suddenly developed test anxiety. Midway in his fourth semester of college, he began to fail every test he took. He was soon placed on academic probation and later forced to withdraw from school. Over the next year, Warren saw a therapist who specialized in behavioral treatments. Several weeks of relaxation training and behavior modification failed to produce significant improvement.

A year later, Warren visited me and explained his predicament. He agreed to be interviewed about his life while I measured his heart rate. Not until years later did I learn that heart rate was not the most reliable psychological indicator for most people. Warren, fortunately, was an exception. During the first hour-long interview, it became clear that Warren's body was telling a different story from Warren's words.

As is shown in the table (see p. 172), Warren's heart rate increased dramatically whenever the topic of his parents' divorce was discussed. No other issues influenced heart rate to a comparable degree. Despite the fact that Warren claimed to be unaffected by his parents' divorce, it was a significant event. Indeed, he first learned that they had separated about a week before his developing test anxiety. In the two intervening years, he never saw the relationship between the divorce and his poor performance during exams. When confronted with his heart-rate data, Warren was flabbergasted. Over the next few days, he discussed his feelings of anger and despair over the divorce with me and, later, with his parents. Although he still harbors some of those feelings, his text anxiety disappeared.

We are often blind to the psychological causes and correlates of our health problems. Many illnesses and recurring health problems have a psychosomatic component. Awareness or insight into the psychological bases of illness can help in the healing process. If we are aware of the conflicts influencing our bodies, we can act to overcome those conflicts.

These were the beginning pieces of the puzzle. When we talk a great deal in a group, we claim that we enjoy it and learn from it. After confessing a crime, our minds and bodies appear to be relaxed. Once we understand the link between a psychological event and a recurring health problem, our health improves.

Each of these phenomena deals with the psychological state of holding back versus opening up. As my students and I began systematically to examine the holding back-opening up continuum, an organizing framework began to emerge. Although it is still evolving, it can be summarized as follows:

Inhibition is physical work. To actively inhibit one's thoughts, feelings, or behaviors requires physiological work. Active inhibition means that people must consciously restrain, hold back, or in some way exert effort to *not* think, feel, or behave.

Inhibition affects short-term biological changes and long-term health. In the short run, inhibition is reflected by immediate biological changes, such as increased perspiration as that measured on lie-detector tests. Over time, the work of inhibition serves as a cumulative stressor on the body, increasing the probability of illness and other stress-related physical and psychological problems. Active inhibition can be viewed as one of many general stressors that affect the mind and body. Obviously, the harder one must work at inhibiting, the greater the stress on the body.

Inhibition influences thinking abilities. Active inhibition is also associated with potentially deleterious changes in the ways we think. In holding back significant thoughts and feelings associated with an event, we typically do not think about the event in a broad and integrative way. By not talking about an inhibited event, for example, we usually do not translate the event into language. This prevents us from understanding and assimilating the event. Consequently, significant experiences that are inhibited are likely to surface in the forms of ruminations, dreams, and associated thought disturbances.

The opposite pole of active inhibition is confrontation. For lack of a better term, confrontation refers to individuals' actively thinking and/or talking about significant experiences as well as acknowledging their emotions. Psychologically confronting traumas overcomes the effects of inhibition both physiologically and cognitively.

Confrontation reduces the effects of inhibition. The act of opening up and confronting a trauma immediately reduces the physiological work of inhibition. During confrontation, the biological stress of inhibition is immediately reduced. Over time, if individuals continue to confront and thereby resolve the trauma, there will be a lowering of the overall stress level on the body.

Confrontation forces a rethinking of events. Confronting a trauma helps people understand and, ultimately, assimilate the event. By talking or writing about previously inhibited experiences, individuals translate the event into language. Once it is language based, people can better understand the experience and ultimately put it behind them.

When first playing with these ideas, my students and I were exuberant. A number of potential experiments that could test and extend the framework popped into our minds. Despite similar theorizing by Aristotle, Freud, and several contemporary psychologists, many of my colleagues viewed the inhibition/confrontation approach as a bit extreme and even radical. Others viewed it with excitement. Given the polarized reception of the early work, I knew I was on to something.

After a boisterous meeting with colleagues where we debated the pros and cons of inhibition, I came home in a wonderful mood. I waltzed in the front door just as the phone began to ring. My brother, who is a graphic designer, called to ask what was new in my life. I excitedly told him about this new approach that I was playing with and its possible links to health, psychotherapy, religion, and, well, just about everything. Not swayed by my grandiosity, my brother asked about the specifics of the inhibition/confrontation framework. When I was finished, the phone was silent. "That's it?" my brother finally said. "What's the big deal? Everyone knows *that*."

He is right on a certain level. We do know that talking about our problems can be good for us. But we also know that we should put on a happy face and look at everything in a positive light. We also know that whining and complaining about our problems will get us nowhere. In other words, in these days of self-help popular psychology, there are often contradictory common sense views that explain everything. As our research journey into the inhibition/confrontation world began, my colleagues and I quickly learned that some common sense ideas were truer than others—indeed, some were completely false. In the remainder of this book, I would like to share with you some of the insights of this journey.

 Article Review Form at end of book.

What aspects of Mary's dream did Freud find important or interesting? What do you think of his interpretation of the dream?

Dream Analysis by Mail

An American woman seeks Freud's advice

Ludy T. Benjamin, Jr.
Texas A&M University

David N. Dixon
Ball State University

When a young American woman had a disturbing dream that continued to occupy her daily thoughts, she wrote to Sigmund Freud, sending him an account of her dream and asking for his help. This article reprints that 1927 letter to Freud and his reply, neither of which has been published before. This exchange of letters is discussed in the context of the popularity of psychology and psychoanalysis in America in the 1920s and in the context of Freud's letter writing habits and his life in 1927.

The 1920s were heady times for America. American military forces had turned the tide in Europe, helping to win the Great War and making the world safe for democracy—or so they believed. There was economic prosperity in the United States and a public euphoria that proclaimed the

Correspondence concerning this article should be addressed to Ludy T. Benjamin, Jr., Department of Psychology, Texas A&M University, College Station, TX 77843-4235. Electronic mail may be sent via Internet to ltb@psyc.tamu.edu.

validity of the American dream: that prosperity existed for all who would work hard enough to achieve it (Sokal, 1984).

Popularity of Psychology in the 1920s

Recall the nurturistic optimism of John B. Watson, who proclaimed in a 1925 book written for the American public:

Give me a dozen healthy infants, well-formed, and my own specified world to bring them up in and I'll guarantee to take any one at random and train him to become any type of specialist I might select—doctor, lawyer, artist, merchant-chief and, yes, even beggar-man and thief, regardless of his talents, penchants, tendencies, abilities, vocations, and race of his ancestors. (Watson, 1925, p. 82)

Watson was one of a number of psychologists who wrote for public consumption in the 1920s. And nonpsychologists also lent their voices to the growing chorus of those who touted the benefits of a life made better through psychology. The first American popular magazine on psychology appeared in 1923, and by the end of the decade it had been joined by two others. These magazines, a host of popular books, and several daily newspaper columns on psychology (one of them authored by

University of Wisconsin psychologist Joseph Jastrow) convinced much of the American public that the science of psychology held the keys to happiness and prosperity (Benjamin, 1986; Benjamin & Bryant, 1996). American businesses and schools were eager to adapt the military mental tests that had been developed during the war for use in their own settings, and the postwar publicity about the success of these tests encouraged their widespread use in American culture (Sokal, 1987).

Typical of the 1920s' claim for psychology's value were those made by Albert Wiggam, a popular science writer whose newspaper column argued that

Men and women never needed psychology so much as they need it today. . . . You can not achieve these things [effectiveness and happiness] in the fullest measure without the new knowledge of your own mind and personality that the psychologists have given us. (Wiggam, 1928, p. 13)

Not everyone shared Wiggam's (1928) enthusiasm. Writing in *Harpers*, Canadian humorist Stephen Leacock (1924) lamented that America was suffering from an unfortunate "outbreak of psychology" (p. 472). And more serious indictments came from Guernsey (1923), who warned the American public about psychology as pseudoscience, and from Stolberg (1930), who chastised legitimate psychologists for their failure to apprise the public of psychology's limitations. Yet prior to the stock market crash of 1929, these cautions were largely unheeded. People were interested in the applications of psychology, and when it was evident that too few academically trained psychologists existed, there were many without training who were willing to offer their services as psychologists. Newspaper classified sections were filled with advertisements for psychological services from individuals who identified themselves as clairvoyants, palmists, advisors, mediums, counselors, and psychologists (Benjamin, 1988). The Psychological Corporation (founded in 1921) and a certification procedure (begun in 1924 by the American Psychological Association) were two efforts by organized psychology to identify legitimate psychologists for the American public (Napoli, 1981). But both efforts failed: Demand was too great, and the public's ability to distinguish psychology from pseudopsychology was minimal.

The public interest in psychology included a fascination with psychoanalysis as well. Freud's ideas had been gaining recognition in America since his speeches at Clark University in the fall of 1909 (see Rosenzweig, 1992). By the 1920s there were a number of popular treatises on psychoanalysis available to the public, as well as English translations of most of Freud's principal works (Freud made the first of five appearances on the cover of *Time* magazine on October 27, 1924). Psychologist historian Gail Hornstein (1992) has written that by the 1920s in the United States, "psychoanalysis had so captured the public imagination that it threatened to eclipse experimental psychology entirely" (p. 254). The popular literature of the 1920s was filled with books and articles on applying psychoanalysis to the classroom, to businesses, and especially to everyday living.

Prominent in this popular psychoanalysis was encouragement for self-understanding and self-improvement through the interpretation of dreams. Many psychologists and psychoanalysts warned against amateur dream interpreters, including self-interpretation (see Valentine, 1922); however, public fascination with dreams and a belief in their validity as windows of the soul ensured the prosperity of those who invited individuals to enjoy the benefits of dream analysis (see Arnold-Foster, 1921; Tridon, 1921).

With belief in the validity of dreams, and especially with the public's growing acceptance of dreams as indications of unconscious wishes, anxiety dreams became even more disturbing. What did it mean to dream about your spouse dying or perhaps about murdering someone? Joseph Jastrow, in his daily Ann Landers-like newspaper column in the 1920s entitled "Keeping Mentally Fit," responded to a writer identified only as "Anxious" who wrote:

there's one thing that I can't get away from and that's paying attention to my dreams. I take them as warnings, and when I dream that something terrible is happening to me away from home, I have to struggle to go out the next day . . . How do you get over this? (Jastrow, 1928, p. 138)

In his published reply, Jastrow (1928) recounted several examples of dreams that had proved disturbing, and told how individuals had foolishly allowed these dreams to disrupt their lives. His not-so-helpful advice to "Anxious" and his other readers suggested that they just "dream of pleasant things and be thankful if they come true" (Jastrow, 1928, p. 140). And to amplify his message that concern with dream interpreta-tion was unnecessary, he informed his readers that "most of us in good health have no temptation to take dreams seriously" (p. 139). We do not know what impact Jastrow's advice had on "Anxious," but his discouragement did not curb the public's fascination with dreams, especially anxiety dreams, and so a dream-interpretation industry of books, magazine articles, local dream clubs, and "interpreters" flourished in the decades closely following Freud's only trip to America.

Mary Fields and Her Anxiety Dream

One of the many individuals who rejected Jastrow's advice to ignore dreams was Mary Fields,[1] a young woman working as a stenographer in a large midwestern city. Fields was an only child with a pharmacist father and a Victorian, homemaker mother. The family owned two homes, one in the city and the other a summer home in the country. The particular events Fields described in her dream apparently took place at the country home.

Fields, who was 20 years old at the time of her dream, was widely read. However, she never completed college because of a dispute about college choice with her parents. On the morning of October 18, 1927, Fields awakened early, disturbed by a dream that haunted her thoughts for weeks. She obsessed about it so much that it was interfering with her work. When it was evident that she could not stop worrying about this dream, she decided to get some relief through professional expertise. On November 11, she mailed a three-page typed letter to Sigmund Freud in Vienna, asking for his help.

[1]At the request of her surviving relatives, a pseudonym (Mary Fields) is used to identify the letter writer.

November 11, 1927.

Professor Sigmund Freud,
Bertggasse 19,
Vienna, Austria.

Dear Professor Freud:

I am writing you because I have read a great many of your books and admire you immensely and also because I hope you can help me. In the event that you find yourself too busy to do so I hope that you can tell me who I can go to that will be able to overcome the difficulty.

My desired information is concerning dreams, or rather a dream. First I should like to know the meaning of the dream and secondly whether it will have any direct meaning or reference on my future. I must sound as if I wanted you to be a fortune teller or the like but this is not so because I realize that a man of your fame certainly would be anything but. You see among your books I have read your views on dreams and because of my great respect for you and because of my interest in your work I thought you might be able to help me. Now to go on with the dream and the series of events connected with it. I mention the events previously connected with the dream because if I remember your text on Dream Psychology rightly, you spoke many times of previous occurrences often times having a great deal of influence on dreams. Now for the basis of this letter.

But a short two months ago I met a young man who since has held a great fascination for me. Not being of age as yet of course my parents tyranize over me in many respects and one of them happens to be the choosing of my friends. Possibly you may think me an ungrateful child but still it is only a few short months until I reach the age of independence. Perhaps also I ought to mention the fact that I am the only child in our family. In the case of this young gentleman there have been some very hard words spoken. The reason for this is that the young man in question is an Italian and of course is Catholic. My parents are thorough bred Americans and also are of a Protestant Religion and although they are not snobbish they feel that in going around with an Italian I am going around with some one who is not my equal. Of course the religious part of it comes in pretty strong as neither father or mother have a very strong love for the Catholic Religion. As for my self it does not bother me at all for I feel that because a person happened to be born into a family of the Catholic or Jewish Religion is nothing against them. In fact if I want to marry either a Jewish or Catholic fellow you may rest assured that I shall do so. But how well I shall accept that religion is another question.

The facination which this young man has for me has twice transported us into a forbidden paradise, it is also a fool's paradise, leaving us forgetful of every day morals and conventions. Before I met the young man in question he had been going steady with a girl of his own station in life and was going steadily enough with her so that she was wearing his ring, but since he has practically given her up entirely and devoted his time to me. Those are the circumstances leading up to the dream. Now for the dream.

I saw myself sitting in a place that was unfamiliar to me still I seemed to be very much at home. It seemed to be a place poorly furnished so it could not have been home for our place is very beautifully furnished. My uncle, rather my mother's brother, and my father were sitting on the front porch talking and as it was a very hot day I was seated inside by an open window fanning my self, and while I was dreaming as I sat there the door bell rang. Upon answering the ring I found the brother of my yourn Italian friend. He was dressed very peculiarly wearing the modern civilian clothes of the average American but with a large gaudy colored Mexican Sombrero on his head. We passed the time of day and for several minutes conversed politely on daily news topics of interest, the both of us standing up he on the porch and [me] in the house. He did not disclose the object of his visit until he was ready to depart when he handed me a letter saying that it was from his brother. As a parting remark he told me that he was coming into the city to see me next week and that probably there would be four or five other fellows along with him. To which I replied that I would be glad to see them. Upon that he left. In the meantime my father and uncle seemed to have disappeared when they went I have no recolection of but when I answered the door bell they were not upon the porch. The young man who called upon me lives in a small town not far from my summer home and that is why he told me he was coming in to see me.

Well I opened the letter and I can still see the expression of horror, dismay, and dispair which was shown on my face. The letter told me that this young Italian boy had been married on the afternoon of October 17 to a Miss Mildred Dowl. I cannot account for the girl's name because it is not the name of the girl to whom he was formerly engaged or even her initials. The name I cannot account for as I have never known anyone by the whole name given above or even the last name.

Well in my dispair I happened to look down on a small table standing near me and saw a large brass paper knife with a sharp edge. Grabbing the thing up I struck myself a hard blow around the region of the heart (I must sound quite dramatic, but I assure that I was and am far from feeling that way). I remember the sensation distinctly of the knife passing into my body. The first was the somewhat like the eternal thrill and it passed into something more powerful, lasting and serious, which cannot possibly be explained. I distinctly remember dropping to the floor without the slightest cry or shudder. I saw myself laying on the floor on my right side with my legs drawn up and my left hand outstretched and my right hand still clutching the paser knif. At this time I awoke and I was somewhat startled to find myself lying in the same position in bed as I was when I last saw myself lying on the floor presumably dead. Upon awakening I found the tears coursing down my face and it took me some little time before I could control myself. The next day I found myself thrown into the worst case of blues or dejection or whatever you want to call it and it was an impossibility to pull myself out of it. This comes back to me after I have been thinking about the dream and trying to find a solution of it myself.

This dream occurred during the early morning of the 18th of October. I hope that you will not think me bold for telling you the things I have and also for writing you and asking the favour that I have. If I have annoyed you with my troubles please dear Professor Freud forgive me I really did not intend to. Please believe me when I say that. And also please won't you help me for there seems to have been nothing on my mind but this confounded dream and as I am a stenographer it does not pay to have your mind occupied with anything other than business during business hours. I feel perhaps that just writing you and waiting a reply will relieve the sense of something formidable hanging over me which was caused by the dream.

Awaiting your reply, I am thanking you now for whatever help you can be to me, and begging you to pardon me for bothering you with my troubles.

Sincerely yours,

Mary Fields

PROF. D^R. FREUD   WIEN IX, BERGGASSE 19
Dec. 2nd 1927.

Dear Miss Fields,

I found your letter charming and I am willing to give you as much help as I can. Unhappily it does not reach very far. Dream interpretation is a difficult affair. As long as you cannot explain the name Mildred Dowl in your dream, find out what the source of these two names is, where you got it, a trustworthy explanation of the dream is not possible. You must have heard or read this name somewhere, a dream never creates, it only repeats or puts together. If you were here in Vienna and could talk to me in my study, we could detect where these names come from. But you are not here and the fact is, you have forgotten it and not yet remembered.

Now for the little I can grasp of the hidden meaning of your dream. I see your emotions towards the young Italian are not undivided, not free from conflict. Besides the love you feel for him there is a trend of perhaps distrust, perhaps remorse. This antagonistic feeling is covered up during your wake life by the love-attraction you undergo and by another motive, your resistance against your parents. Perhaps if your parents did not dislike the boy, it would be much easier for you to become aware of the splitting in your feelings. So you are in a conflict about him and the dream is a way out of the maze. To be sure, you will not leave him and fulfill your parent's request. But if he drops you this is a solution. I guess that is the meaning of the dream and your emotional reaction is produced by the intensity of your love while the content of the dream is the result of the repressed antagonism which yet is active in your soul.

Please write me another letter if after the receipt of mine you are able to explain the origin of the two names.

With best wishes

yours sincerely

freud

Fields's letter, which was found in the papers of Fields, was a carbon copy. On the basis of conversations with family members, it is likely that Fields corrected the spelling errors in the letter that she sent to Freud. Copyright of the letter to Sigmund Freud is held by the estate of the writer of the letter. Reprinted with permission. Freud's response is copyrighted 1995 A. W. Freud et al., by arrangement with Mark Paterson & Associates. Reprinted with permission.

Sigmund Freud in 1927

When the letter arrived in Vienna in 1927, the 71-year-old Freud was in poor health. In 1923 he had been diagnosed with cancer of the mouth, and between that date and his death in 1939 he underwent 31 separate surgeries, including those to create various jaw prostheses (Roazen, 1984). His health had worsened by 1927. In addition to the continued problems with his mouth and jaw, likely produced by the years of cigar smoking, he also suffered from angina, and these chest pains had returned in January 1927. His physicians urged him to rest and, after resisting for several months, he entered a sanitorium in April where he stayed a week for rest and treatment. But his health did not improve, and he wrote to Sandor Ferenczi in August that he was "eternally ill and plagued with discomfort" (Jones, 1957, p. 136).

Despite the illnesses, Freud maintained his practice, although he reduced it from five patients to three after his sanitorium visit. He also continued his professional writings. In 1927 he published an essay on fetishism and another on Michaelangelo's sculpture of Moses, extending an essay that he had written a decade earlier. He also published a small book, *The Future of an Illusion* (S. Freud, 1928), a book written in dialogue that pronounced religion an illusion with no future, emphasizing its failure, after centuries, to produce a world of happiness and contentment (see Malony & North, 1979).

In 1927 Freud also continued his battles on "the question of lay analysis." He had published a book by that title the previous year, prompted largely by a lawsuit against Theodor Reik for medical quackery. Newton Murphy, the American physician who brought the suit, had originally sought to be psychoanalyzed by Freud, but Freud referred him to Reik. Apparently dissatisfied with his psychoanalytic experience, Murphy's suit argued against the practice of psychoanalysis by those without a medical degree. Freud had battled the medical establishment on that issue throughout the 1920s. He saw no ne-cessity of medical training for practicing psychoanalysis and frequently argued that medicine could easily get in the way of psychoanalytic insights. In a letter to Paul Federn in 1926 Freud wrote, "As long as I live I shall balk at having psychoanalysis swallowed by medicine" (Gay, 1988, p. 491). Murphy lost his suit, but the medical establishment continued its battle, largely successfully, and most psychoanalysts, particularly the Americans, sided against Freud.

Freud's Correspondence

The letter from Fields that arrived in 1927 was one of many that Freud received in his daily mail. Most letters were sent to Freud in care of Verlag, the psychoanalytic publishing house that produced many of Freud's works. Freud's son Martin brought that mail to Freud twice daily. Mail also came directly to Freud's home, the 19 Berggasse address, and those letters tended to be the more important correspondence, including letters from friends and disciples (M. Freud, 1958). Fields's letter was sent to Freud's home.

In the early years of his career Freud handled his correspondence at the end of a long day of seeing patients, often after 10:00 at night. He used his study for his correspondence, often working there until quite late. Jones (1955) has written that Freud "was never in bed before one in the morning and often much later (p. 384). In those days mail was still a joy, as noted by Jones:

The daily arrival of the postman was an event he awaited with great eagerness. He not only greatly enjoyed getting letters but was apt to be impatient with his friends if they were not so swift in answering correspondence as he himself was. (p. 390)

But as Freud's fame grew so too did the volume of mail that he received. By the 1920s it had reached aversive proportions. In letters to colleagues at this time, Freud often lamented the burden of his fame. He wrote to Ernest Jones in 1922:

I am sorry I did not answer your last one. Sometimes my pen gets weary. I have so much business correspondence to do, warning patients not to come as I have not the time to treat them and declining flattering offers to write a paper on such a subject for a periodical. These are the drawbacks of popularity. I see not much of its blessings. (Jones, 1957, p. 83)

Freud commented similarly in a letter to Marie Bonaparte in 1927 that "the times of splendid isolation have been thoroughly overcome" (Jones, 1957, p. 133).

Despite these drawbacks, it is evident that Freud enjoyed writing, both the professional writing as well as the correspondence. Discussing Freud's writing habits, Jones (1955) has stated that "To judge from their extent and from his correspondence he must have been fond of the physical act itself of writing" (p. 395). Many of Freud's biographers, especially the more recent ones who have enjoyed better access to the Freud letters, have commented on the vitality in them. He was a ready correspondent who brought great energy to his letters. In an article discussing the art of Freud's letters, Grotjahn (1967) wrote, "Freud wrote his letters as he did his books, and his books often seemed like letters. He wrote with the ring of truth and with classical simplicity and with pictorial images" (p. 13).

As noted earlier, with fame came a multitude of unsolicited letters. And Freud attempted to answer every one of them. Even the letters from strangers often "moved him to long, thoughtful replies" (Gay, 1988, p. 610). He could no longer handle the volume of his correspondence by writing only late at night: he still used that time for letters, but he also wrote letters in between seeing patients. Throughout his career he had no secretary, nor did he ever learn to use a typewriter. The Freud home acquired a typewriter, although its arrival date is uncertain. Anna Freud used the typewriter and, with her father's increasing illness, she handled some of his correspondence (Roazen, 1984; Ruitenbeek, 1973).

Freud wrote most of his letters in German; however, his English was quite good, and he typically answered his English-language letters in turn. He kept a record of his correspondence in a large legal-sized ledger (Grotjahn, 1967). After 1923, Anna handled some of his correspondence, especially those items that did not require a personal reply. In later years he would dictate some letters to Anna, who would type them for his signature.

Freud's Interpretation of the Dream

It is likely that the reply to Fields was typed by Anna from her father's dictation. The page-and-a-half letter on Freud's personal stationery is double-spaced and dated December 2, 1927, three weeks after the date of the Fields letter.

The response is polite and gracious, which is consistent with the manner of Freud's replies, even to letters from strangers. Some readers would see the response as unusually reserved given the rich psychoanalytic symbolism of the dream (e.g., the guarded porch, the sombrero, the paper knife, the disparity in furnishings, and fanning in the hot room). But the limited interpretation seems typical of Freud's replies to strangers who sought his help via correspondence. Freud tells the woman that he can do little in the way of interpretation without a chance to see her and explore the dream content in a face-to-face encounter. So by letter he offers a minimal interpretation of the conflict indicated in the dream, an interpretation that seems likely to relieve some of her anxiety about the dream, and Freud invites her to write to him again should she have further insights to offer, including the possible meaning of the name, Mildred Dowl.[2]

Given the poor state of Freud's health in 1927, the considerable requirements of his professional practice and professional writing, his involvement in the ongoing political agenda for psychoanalysis, and many demands made on his time as a famous person, and the substantial volume of correspondence that he re-

[2]An attempt was made by the authors to discover the identity of Mildred Dowl by searching the back files of the principal newspaper of the midwestern city where Fields lived. A woman close in age and area of residence by the name of Mildred Dowling was located in the obituaries. A follow-up with family members and lifelong acquaintances of Fields uncovered no known connection between the two women.

ceived, it is perhaps amazing to think that he could find the time to help a young American woman unknown to him. But as many of Freud's biographers have noted, he was diligent in answering most of the letters he received. His son Ernst Freud (1975) wrote:

As a letter writer, my father was unusually prolific and conscientious . . . He answered every letter he received, no matter from whom, and as a rule this answer was in the post within twenty-four hours. (p. ix)

Sigmund Freud's reply and a copy of Fields's letter to Freud were found in her papers following her death in 1984. It is not known if Freud's words helped her forget the dream that was troubling her. But perhaps she felt gratified that so noteworthy an individual had taken the time to respond to her plea for help. Fields may have been emboldened by the response from Freud to her troublesome dream, so much so that some years later, when faced with a legal problem, she wrote to no less an authority than Clarence Darrow, whose reply was also found among her papers.

Conclusion

Fields worked as a professional secretary for her entire career. She never married and lived much of the latter part of her life in the setting of her dream—the country home of her parents—with a cat and a dog as companions. She greatly admired her parents, especially her father, and they continued to be a major focus for her life, even following their deaths. Her home changed little throughout her life, remaining frozen as a museum of the 1920s and 1930s. She continued to be a voracious reader of both fiction and nonfiction. During the last four years of her life, she lived in a nursing home, suffering from Alzheimer's disease.

Freud's response to Fields's letter reflects a remarkable personal and professional obligation. Despite failing health and a tremendous workload, he carefully read and thoughtfully responded to a letter from a 20-year-old American woman.

Also of interest is the initiative of Fields. When faced with a confus-

ing dream, she went to the world's leading expert for help. Perhaps this sequence primarily reflects psychological characteristics of these two people, that is, his compulsiveness and her inflated sense of place. Or perhaps it speaks to a sense of personal control and responsibility that were characteristic of the era. Despite the advances today in communication technology, whereas Freud could now be a frequent, featured visitor in our living rooms, there is something refreshing, yet melancholy, about this personal correspondence.[3]

References

Arnold-Foster, M. (1921). *Studies in dreams*. New York: Macmillan.

Benjamin, L. T., Jr. (1986). Why don't they understand us? A history of psychology's public image. *American Psychologist, 41*, 941–946.

Benjamin, L. T., Jr. (1988). Press coverage of psychology in the Rocky Mountains, 1885–1956. *Journal of the History of the Behavioral Sciences, 24*, 98–101.

Benjamin, L. T., Jr., & Bryant, W. H. M. (1996). The American public's need for health, happiness, and success: A history of popular psychology magazines. In W. Bringmann, H. E. Lück, R. Miller, & C. E. Early (Eds.), *A pictorial history of psychology* (pp. 585–593). Munich, Germany: Quintessenz.

Freud, E. (Ed.). (1975). *Letters of Sigmund Freud*. (T. Stern & J. Stern, Trans.). New York: Basic Books.

Freud, M. (1958). *Sigmund Freud: Man and father*. New York: Vanguard Press.

[3]For the past several years, we have used the two letters reprinted in this article as a device to generate class discussion about psychoanalytic theory and dream interpretation. We use the letters in our graduate courses (e.g., history of psychology and theory and methods of counseling psychology), in which students are reasonably familiar with Freudian theory. The Fields letter is given to each of the students, and they are asked to read it and then write out their interpretation of it. Parts of those interpretations are shared aloud (voluntarily) with the rest of the class, generating some very interesting class discussion. When that discussion has run its course, Freud's interpretation is distributed to each of the students. The discussion that follows focuses on a comparison of Freud's interpretation with their own, and the possible reasons for the differences. This classroom activity has proven quite popular with our students, and one of the reasons for publishing the letters now is to share this teaching resource with others.

Freud, S. (1927). *The problem of lay-analyses* (A. P. Maerker-Branden, Trans.). New York: Brentano's. (originally published in 1926).

Freud, S. (1928). *The future of an illusion* (W. D. Robson-Scott, Trans.). New York: Liveright Publishing Corporation. (Original work published 1927).

Gay, P. (1988). *Freud: A life for our time*. New York: W. W. Norton.

Grotjahn, M. (1967). Sigmund Freud and the art of letter writing. *Journal of the American Medical Association, 200,* 13–18.

Guernsey, M. (1923, July 11). Psychologists—so and pseudo. *Outlook, 134,* 364–365.

Hornstein, G. A. (1992). The return of the repressed: Psychology's problematic relations with psychoanalysis. *American Psychologist, 47,* 254–263.

Jastrow, J. (1928). *Keeping mentally fit: A guide to everyday psychology*. New York: Garden City Publishing Co.

Jones, E. (1955). *The life and work of Sigmund Freud: Years of maturity, 1901–1919* (Vol. 2). New York: Basic Books.

Jones, E. (1957). *The life and work of Sigmund Freud: The last phase, 1919–1939* (vol. 3). New York: Basic Books.

Leacock, S. (1924, March). A manual for the new mentality. *Harpers,* pp. 471–480.

Malony, H. N., & North, G. (1979). The future of an illusion—the illusion of the future: An historic dialogue on the value of religion between Oskar Pfister and Sigmund Freud. *Journal of the History of the Behavioral Sciences, 15,* 177–180.

Napoli, D. S. (1981). *Architects of adjustment: The history of the psychological profession in the United States*. Port Washington, NY: Kennikat Press.

Roazen, P. (1984). *Freud and his followers*. New York: New York University Press.

Rosenzweig, S. (1992). *Freud, Jung and Hall the king-maker: The expedition to America (1909)*. Toronto: Hogrefe and Huber.

Ruitenbeek, H. M. (1973). The professor. In H. M. Ruitenbeek (Ed.), *Freud as we knew him* (pp. 17–21). Detroit, MI: Wayne State University Press.

Sokal, M. M. (1984). James McKeen Cattell and American psychology in the 1920s. In J. Brozek (Ed.). *Explorations in the history of psychology in the United States* (pp. 273–323). Lewisburg, PA: Bucknell University Press.

Sokal, M. M. (Ed.). (1987). *Psychological testing and American society, 1890–1930*. New Brunswick, NJ: Rutgers University Press.

Stolberg, B. (1930, October 15). Degradation of American psychology. *The Nation, 113;* 395-398.

Tridon A. (1921). *Psychoanalysis, sleep and dreams*. New York: Alfred A. Knopf.

Valentine, C. W. (1922). *Dreams and the unconscious*. New York: Macmillan.

Watson, J. B. (1925). *Behaviorism*. New York: The People's Institute Publishing Co.

Wiggam, A. (1928). *Exploring your mind with the psychologists*. New York: Bobbs Merrill.

 Article Review Form at end of book.

WiseGuide Wrap-Up

- The study of personality has made large contributions to our understanding of such mental health outcomes as self-concept and self-esteem, drug abuse, depression, and relationship functioning.

- Freud argues that the normal psychotherapeutic process includes patients' putting up resistance to treatment. This resistance, he argues, protects repressed ideas and memories.

- "Telling" about negative events or secrets—either verbally or in writing—can have positive effects on one's mental *and* physical health.

- Freud regularly responded to letters requesting help or dream interpretations, even if those people were strangers. His interpretations, in such cases, were more conservative than those he might offer a patient with whom he had more contact.

R.E.A.L. Sites

This list provides a print preview of typical **coursewise** R.E.A.L. sites. There are over 100 such sites at the **courselinks**™ site. The danger in printing URLs is that web sites can change overnight. As we went to press, these sites were functional using the URLs provided. If you come across one that isn't, please let us know via email to: webmaster@coursewise.com. Use your Passport to access the most current list of R.E.A.L. sites at the **courselinks**™ site.

Site name: Successful Pathways Through Middle Childhood

URL: http://midchild.soe.umich.edu/index.html

Why is it R.E.A.L.? The site provides a wealth of information on recent research on development during middle childhood. Developmental researchers are interested in what makes for the successful negotiation of life transitions. One area of interest is the role that resilience plays in successful development. This site includes information on a host of current research projects in the area of middle childhood and includes links to researchers in the area. Studies covered include research on the immigrant experience, on hope for inner-city children, and on the successful transition to middle school and high school. Several of the many studies are bound to be of interest to you.

Key topics: personality development, resilience, adolescence

Site name: Association for the Study of Dreams

URL: http://www.asdreams.org/

Why is it R.E.A.L.? The association is dedicated to the investigation of dreams and dreaming. It is more reputable than many commercial "dream analysis" web sites you're likely to find on the web. Remember that the purpose of the commercial sites is to make money, and asses their value accordingly. The ASD site has information on its annual conference and journal, in which you can find information about dreams, dream analysis, and dreaming. In addition, it provides research reports for students, parents, and the general public, as well as links to sites on such diverse topics as dream sharing, dreams in film and art, and various analytic techniques.

Key topics: dreams and dream interpretation, Freud

section

8

Learning Objectives

- The ways in which our culture categorizes us—for instance, by race, gender, and ethnicity—can shape our experience in profound ways. Identify some of the ways described in these articles that discrimination can shape the lives of those discriminated against.

- Describe some of the unique struggles faced by parents of minority children in the United States.

- Characterize the "third gender" of India and how it differs from American conceptions of gender.

- Discuss how the concepts of self and community are different in Eastern and Western cultures.

Sociocultural Aspects of Personality

 WiseGuide Intro

The articles in this final section provide a bridge between personality psychology and sociology and social psychology. They ask us to think hard about the ways in which the culture in which we live shapes our personality. Culture includes both a society's beliefs and values and the ways a society is structured. Cultural beliefs and values include such ideas as how men and women are expected to behave and what kinds of demands we can appropriately place on our children. When we refer to the structure of a culture, we are speaking about whether one's opportunities or experiences are shaped by such characteristics as class, sex, race, ethnicity, and immigration status. In some cultures, it's very easy to see how the culture is structured. In cultures with slavery or castes, for example, the society is structured along those dimensions. When men and women have very different roles within a society, that is very easy to see. In other cultures, such as our own, it's more difficult to see the structure of the society. Sometimes the beliefs of a culture (e.g., "Anyone can get ahead in our culture, as long as he or she is willing to work hard" or "People should be free to speak their own minds, voice their opinions, and try to win support for their views") are easier to see than its structures (e.g., the different assumptions we hold about the appropriateness of different activities for men and women or about how the experiences of ethnic minority group members typically differ from those of ethnic majority members). The articles in this section explore some of the ways in which we can understand how a culture's beliefs and structures can influence the development of personality.

The first article in this section, "Commentary: Tending the Garden of Personality," is an excerpt of a longer work by Winter and Stewart in which they argue that personality psychology has not paid enough attention to how the structure of our society shapes individuals' personalities. They provide a brief case study of Maya Angelou, to show how her personality was shaped by her experiences and how many key experiences in her life were a direct result of her sex and ethnicity.

White and Williams provide first-person accounts of experiences that highlight the ongoing struggles faced by African Americans and many other ethnic minority members in the United States today. Although not psychologists, these authors offer moving accounts that demonstrate the way our lives are shaped by race and ethnicity. When the Williams reading has been used in class situations, it has provoked lively debate about how to interpret her experiences and how to understand what it says about our society. This work should help you to see different points of view on the subject.

Nanda's article, "The Hijras of India," provides insight into how our own understanding of the meaning of gender is shaped by the culture in which we live. In many cultures, gender is such a basic social category that it seems "natural" and even "biologically determined" to divide the world into two categories—men and women, girls and boys. This article demonstrates that gender is not such a simple, or "natural," category. Many cultures recognize a third or even a fourth gender. This article may challenge your beliefs about the relationship between biological sex and psychological gender.

Markus and Kitayama are among a growing group of psychologists whose goal is to understand how a culture's beliefs, values, and structure can shape our very conception of ourselves. If people in different cultures can have such radically different conceptions of self and psychological health, it suggests that environment and experience play a strong role in personality development. In their article, "A Collective Fear of the Collective," they discuss Americans' obsession with individualism and how American individualism differs from the beliefs of other cultures.

? Questions ? ? ?

Reading 27. What do the authors argue are two forces shaping personality that have remained largely unresearched? Describe two experiences that they suggest helped to shape the personality of Maya Angelou.

Reading 28. What are some of the struggles faced by parents of African American children? Why have the changes of the past 40 years not had much impact on the self-image of the African American children described in the article?

Reading 29. What do you think the store employee in this story was thinking about when he acted? What cumulative effect might many such experiences have on an individual's outlook or personality?

Reading 30. Describe two aspects of the Hijra role in India. Hijra life is described as being very different from male homosexuality—what are two of the ways it is different?

Reading 31. How do conceptions of self differ in Western and Eastern cultures? What are two ways the authors identify this difference?

What do the authors argue are two forces shaping personality that have remained largely unresearched? Describe two experiences that they suggest helped to shape the personality of Maya Angelou.

Commentary
Tending the garden of personality

David G. Winter
and Abigail J. Stewart

University of Michigan

Abstract

In this Commentary for the special issue of the Journal of Personality, *we discuss the uses and limitations of taxonomies in personality, drawing on the role of taxonomic efforts in other sciences. We endorse McAdams's concept of several "levels" (perhaps three: traits, motives and cognitive structures, and core unity themas or identity) for ordering and arranging the major variables of personality. We argue that these levels should be considered independent and distinct: Each level has its own range of convenience, and no level can be reduced to any other level. We suggest that the concept of conflict—within and across levels—is a useful way to understand certain problematic cases. Finally, we argue that the social macrocontext (gender, class, race, cultures, and history) has unfortunately been neglected in most personality theories and taxonomies of variables. We illustrate the importance of social macrocontext with a brief discussion of the case of Maya Angelou.*

Address all correspondence regarding this article to the first author at the University of Michigan, Department of Psychology, 525 E. University Avenue, Ann Arbor, MI 48109–1109.

On Description and Taxonomies

The articles in this special issue of the *Journal of Personality* address a set of questions posed by the editors (Emmons, this issue, p. (342):

> What kinds of constructs—and at what levels and in what domains—must be proposed to account for a human life and/or to predict what a person will do?
>
> What is needed to understand what a person is like?
>
> What is needed to account for human individuality?
>
> What is uniquely human about each human being?

Before taking stock of the insights and proposals contributed by these articles, we propose to raise two questions that will orient and situate this work in a larger context. While these questions are basic to the enterprise of personality psychology, they are seldom explicitly asked—probably because the answers are assumed to be obvious.

What Is It That Is Being Described?

"Persons" and *"personality."* This issue is focused on description, but of what? From Emmons's charge to the authors quoted above, the obvious answer is "individual persons." To be sure, most of the articles are concerned with identifying constructs and variables by which individual persons can be identified and described. A few even give illustrative case examples. Other articles, however, are more concerned with describing "personality"—that is, constructing an abstract model that explains how separate elements, mechanisms, and processes are integrated into a functioning whole within the person. (This concern is reflected in Emmons's fourth question quoted above.) We suggest that although these two concerns are related, they are not the same. As an analogy, the field and practice of medicine includes abstract, general descriptions of how the circulatory system, the nervous system, and the digestive system work, and work together; but it also requires descriptions (diagnoses, histories) of the health and illness of specific individual persons. Medical theorists debate about whether useful generalizations can be made beyond the individual case. Thus Hippocrates, the ancient Greek physician honored as the founder of medicine, is supposed to have said that "there are no diseases, only sick people" (Temkin, 1981, p. 261). The tension between describing the person and describing personality, which is an ancient one in the field, surfaces in several of the articles. We suggest that both concerns are valid and useful, that each can inform the other, but that they need to be understood as different.

Skin-Bounded Individual Bodies

And what is a "person"? In almost all of the present articles, a person is construed as a single body, bounded by skin. Connections to anything outside that body are construed either as internal representations (Ogilvie and Rose) or wholly external (Mayer). This is not surprising, for it is the seemingly natural, universal, and even inevitable practice of 20th-century American psychology. Yet from the diverse perspective of history and cultures, this is only one possible construction. In many cultures (China, for example) it would be unusual, if not impossible, to conceive of a skin-bounded individual body without at the same time considering the *family* (or kin-group, tribe, neighborhood, nation, and so forth). Even in the history of the West, the concept of individual skin-bounded "personality"—one to a body and one to every body—is a relatively recent legacy of the Renaissance, Reformation, and Industrial Revolution. As a result of these events, we have been taught, social complexity and differentiation resulted in a newly expanded range of individual variation and so made necessary a science of describing this variation. Here we suggest caution: It may be necessary to disentangle the post-Renaissance *ideology* of exuberant and expansive individualistic variation from the actual facts of social embeddedness, lest personality psychology be the servant of individualist ideology rather than the discipline of person description and analysis.

Two examples may illustrate the limits of the skin-bounded individual body conception of personality. First, there is blind and deaf social activist Helen Keller. She was surely an extraordinary and distinctive person; Mark Twain, for example, described her as one of "the two most interesting characters of the nineteenth century," along with Napoleon as the other (Keller, 1903, p. 286). Yet in her autobiography she clearly expressed an alternative perspective on her own personality:

My teacher [Anne Sullivan] is so near to me that I scarcely think of myself apart from her. . . . I feel that her being is inseparable from my own, and that the footsteps of my life are in hers.

It is certain that I cannot always distinguish my own thoughts from those I read, because what I read becomes the very substance and texture of my mind.

Thus it is that my friends have made the story of my life. (1903, pp. 39–40, 70, 140)

Perhaps Keller's handicaps made her more aware of the limits of an excessively individualistic conception of persons and personality than were most people of her time.

Second, we point to a concluding observation of Singer (this issue). After describing the measurement of people's self-defining memories—surely a concept toward the extreme end of expected individual variation—Singer concludes that "I have been overwhelmed by the narrative similarities they bring to the most important events of their lives. Their emphasis on the twin themes of achievement and relationship says as much about the design of our culture as it does about their individuality" (p. 452).

Personality in Its Social Context

Some of the articles in this special issue acknowledge the importance of situation and context as factors that shape and limit individual personality (see Veroff, 1983). Usually these references are to the immediate or short-term external situation. There is no sustained discussion of social structure and social class, race and ethnicity, or culture. These are social contexts of personality— "macrocontexts," in contrast to the "microcontexts" of the immediate situation. Cues suggesting social mobility are given in McAdams's discussion of Lynn, but social class does not play a major part in his program for the description and analysis of Lynn's personality. Although "gender," an important aspect of social context, is discussed extensively by Koestner and Aube, they treat it as a group of individual variables rather than as something that derives from a power-stratified gender *system* (as conceptualized by, for example, MacKinnon, 1987).

Please note that these comments are not criticisms of this particular set of articles; rather, they are comments directed to the field of personality more generally. Thus, for example, the words "class," "social class," "ethnicity," and "race" do not even appear in the index of Pervin's (1990) *Handbook of Personality Theory and Research*. Even that book's nine scattered references to "culture" contain only one extended discussion of a specific culture (two pages on Japanese vs. American conceptions of the self, by Markus & Cross, 1990). As long as personality is conceived— as it usually is—in terms of skin-bounded individual bodies (see above), this state of affairs is unlikely to change.

Social Context and Personality: The Case of Maya Angelou

We believe that attention to the social macrocontext is essential for the complete description and understanding of personality and prediction of behavior. In our view, this is the single greatest problem with an otherwise exceptionally broad and interesting set of concepts that illustrate the value of understanding personality and persons in complex, multilevel terms. Social contexts are the ultimate source of many personality variables and the patterned relationships among them; social contexts also shape and constrain the expression of almost all personality variables. We will illustrate this point with a brief discussion of Maya Angelou, the well-known African American writer and poet who wrote and read a poem, "On the Pulse of the Morning," at President Clinton's 1993 inaugural ceremony. The first volume of her autobiography, *I Know Why the Caged Bird Sings* (Angelou, 1970), has become a classic of African American memoirs. (See the fuller discussion of Angelou in Winter, 1995.)

Anyone who reads her autobiography will immediately recognize Angelou as a vivid, distinctive, and extraordinary person. She clearly "has a personality"—a personality that no doubt could be described in terms of many of the variables and concepts described in this special issue. However, we suggest that any real description of Angelou's personality must be grounded in several significant aspects of her social context. These are not simply "origins" or "sources" of internal personality variables; they *are a part of her personality.*

Angelou is a woman. Her story is saturated with references to gender and a gendered world—that is, a world in which relations of dominance and subordination are constructed upon gender. A few examples will illustrate the pervasiveness of gender. At age 8, she was psychologically and sexually abused and then raped by her mother's boyfriend. As a teenager, she fought to become the first woman ever employed as a street car conductor in San Francisco. Partly in response to anxieties about sexual identity, she maneuvered a friend into having sex with her and so became pregnant. Gender, then, is one aspect of the bird's "cage."

Race is clearly another aspect. As an African American growing up in a small southern town during the third and fourth decades of the 20th century, Angelou experienced the full impact of American racism. Like other structures of oppression, racism is not only a series of internal(ized) beliefs and values, but also a pervasive and powerful force, calling forth or demanding some features of Angelou's personality and imposing barriers on the expression of others. Race and gender often combine into a unique context that is greater than each alone; for example, in the case of rape (see Hine, 1989). Yet for Angelou, race also meant having the benefits of multiple nurturing mother-figures and a special "fluid" form of family (see Hunter & Ensminger, 1992) that were critical to her surmounting the oppression of sexism and racism in later life. Race combined with history as she came to young adulthood during the Civil Rights struggle, thereby incorporating positive images into her self-definition.

The Internalization of Social Context

In our view, the next big project for personality psychology is to work out the implications of social macrocontexts—gender, class, race, ethnicity, and history—for the field of personality psychology. Sometimes this may require suspending judgment or even revising previously settled issues. For example, if sustained relations of dominance and subordination are capable of producing some of the same personality characteristics that are imputed to differential parental investment (e.g., risk taking and urgency vs. conscientiousness and love; see MacDonald's contribution to this issue), then sex differences (and racial differences) in human traits may be underdetermined by past evolutionary pressures, and further determined by present structures of power and subordination.

The critical task is to work out the ways in which social macrocontexts are incorporated and reflected in personality. Gregg's (this issue) concept of cultural symbols that can "switch" from one script to another, from expression to control of an impulse, is a promising beginning. Mannheim's (1928/1952) concept of a critical stage, during which certain aspects of the social macrocontext are directly taken in to become the person's "entelechy" (loosely, mind-set or personality), may also suggest a model for this process (see Stewart & Healy, 1989).

The Garden of Personality

The articles in this issue encourage us to be excited by the state of personality psychology, and allow us to dream of an even richer field. Our own view of the past, present, and future of the field of personality can best be expressed metaphorically, building on Westen's (this issue) image of personality being buried in the "ice age" of situationist critique. Now it is spring, and the fields have awakened to a springtime of growth. Personality psychologists have cultivated a great diversity of plants, and we agree with Emmons and McAdams that some of the loveliest specimens—reflected in the articles in this issue—are drawn from the more motivational, developmental, and identity-based varieties. To some, the garden may seem in danger of becoming a "blooming, buzzing confusion." While we believe that some arranging, pruning, and cataloging may be appropriate in the garden of personality, we also (in agreement with the spirit of this spe-

cial issue) want to make sure that the garden is not dominated by a single variety of plant. Further, we suggest that the best gardeners maintain a sense of the whole garden—for example, by adopting mass plantings, and by defining the relations of all the plants to one another. Keeping these views in mind should enrich the beauty of the garden and the pleasure of all those who walk in it.

References

Allport, G. W. (1931). What is a trait of personality? *Journal of Abnormal and Social Psychology,* **25,** 368–372.

Allport, G. W. (1937). *Personality: A psychological interpretation.* New York: Holt.

Allport, G. W. (1961). *Pattern and growth in personality.* New York: Holt, Rinehart & Winston.

Allport, G. W. (1962). The general and the unique in psychological science. *Journal of Personality,* **30,** 405–422. (Reprinted in G. W. Allport, *The person in psychology* [pp. 81–102]. Boston: Beacon Press, 1968.)

Allport, G. W., & Allport, F. H. (1921). Personality traits: Their classification and measurement. *Journal of Abnormal and Social Psychology,* **16,** 6–40.

Angelou, M. (1970). *I know why the caged bird sings.* New York: Random House.

Block, J. (1971). *Lives through time.* Berkeley: Bancroft.

Block, J. (1985). A contrarian view of the five-factor approach to personality description. *Psychological Bulletin,* **117,** 187–215.

Briggs, S. R. (1989). The optimal level of measurement of personality constructs. In D. Buss & N. Cantor (Eds.), *Personality psychology: Recent trends and emerging directions* (pp. 246–260). New York: Springer-Verlag.

Briggs, S. R. (1992). Assessing the five-factor model of personality description. *Journal of Personality,* **60,** 253–293.

Cloninger, C. R. (1991). Brain networks underlying personality development. In B. J. Carroll & J. E. Barrett (Eds.), *Psychopathology and the brain* (pp. 183–208). New York: Raven.

Freud, S. (1957). Some character types met with in psycho-analytic work. In J. Strachey (Ed. and Trans.), *The standard edition of the complete psychological works of Sigmund Freud* (Vol. 14, pp. 309–333). London: Hogarth Press. (Original work published 1916)

Freud, S. (1959). Character and anal erotism. In J. Strachey (Ed. and Trans.), *The standard edition of the complete psychological works of Sigmund Freud* (Vol. 9, pp. 169–175). London: Hogarth Press. (Original work published 1908)

Freud, S. (1961). Libidinal types. In J. Strachey (Ed. and Trans.), *The standard edition of the complete psychological works of Sigmund Freud* (Vol. 21, pp. 215–220).

London: Hogarth Press. (Original work published 1931)

Gough, H. (1987). *The California Psychological Inventory: Administrator's guide.* Palo Alto, CA: Consulting Psychologists Press.

Hine, D. C. (1989). Rape and the inner lives of Black women in the Middle West. *Signs: Journal of Women in Culture and Society, 14,* 912–920.

Hogan, R. (1986). *Hogan Personality Inventory.* Minneapolis: National Computer System.

Hunter, A. G., & Ensminger, M. E. (1992). Diversity and fluidity in children's living arrangements: Family transitions in an urban Afro-American community. *Journal of Marriage and the Family, 54,* 418–426.

John, O. P., Winter, D. G., Stewart, A. J., Klohnen, E., Duncan, L., & Peterson, B. (1993). *Motives and traits in the explanation of behavior.* Unpublished manuscript, Universities of California and Michigan.

Jung, C. G. (1971). Psychological types. In H. Read, M. Fundham, G. Adler, & W. McGuire (Eds.), *The collected works of C. G. Jung* (Vol. 6, pp. 510–523). Princeton: Princeton University Press. (Original work published 1923)

Keller, E. F. (1985). *Reflections on gender and science.* New Haven: Yale University Press.

Keller, H. (1903). *The story of my life.* New York: Doubleday, Page.

Klein, H. G. (1980). *Making it perfectly clear.* Garden City, NY: Doubleday.

Lewin, K. (1935). *A dynamic theory of personality.* New York: McGraw-Hill.

MacKinnon, C. A. (1987). Difference and dominance: On sex discrimination. In *Feminism unmodified: Discourses on life and law* (pp. 32–45). Cambridge, MA: Harvard University Press.

Mannheim, K. (1952). The problem of generations. In *Essays on the sociology of knowledge.* New York: Oxford University Press. (Original work published 1928)

Markus, H., & Cross, S. (1990). The interpersonal self. In L. A. Pervin, *Handbook of personality theory and research* (pp. 576–608). New York: Guilford.

Mazlish, B. (1973). *In search of Nixon: A psychohistorical inquiry.* New York: Penguin. (Original work published 1972)

McAdams, D. P. (1985). *Power, intimacy, and the life story.* Homewood, IL: Dorsey.

McAdams, D. P. (1992). The five-factor model *in* personality: A critical appraisal. *Journal of Personality, 60,* 329–361.

Murray, H. A. (1938). *Explorations in personality.* New York: Oxford University Press.

Murray, H. A. (1981). An American Icarus. In E. S. Schneidman (Ed.), *Endeavors in psychology: Selections from the personology of Henry A. Murray* (pp. 535–556). New York: Harper & Row. (Original work published 1955)

Pervin, L. A. (1990). *Handbook of personality theory and research.* New York: Guilford.

Simonton, D. (1986). Presidential personality: Biographical use of the Gough Adjective Check List. *Journal of Personality and Social Psychology, 51,* 149–160.

Simonton, D. (1988). Presidential style: Personality, biography, and performance. *Journal of Personality and Social Psychology, 55,* 928–936.

Smith, C. P. (Ed.). (1992). *Motivation and personality: Handbook of thematic content analysis.* New York: Cambridge University Press.

Stewart, A. J., & Healy, J. M., Jr. (1989). Linking individual development and social change. *American Psychologist, 44,* 30–42.

Temkin, O. (1981). The scientific approach to disease: Specific entity and individual sickness. In A. L. Caplan, H. T. Engelhardt, & J. J. McCartney (Eds.), *Concepts of health and disease: Interdisciplinary perspectives* (pp. 247–263). Reading, MA: Addison-Wesley.

Thorne, A., & Gough, H. (1991). *Portraits of type: An MBTI research compendium.* Palo Alto, CA: Consulting Psychologists Press.

Veroff, J. (1983). Contextual determinants of personality. *Personality and Social Psychology Bulletin, 9,* 331–343.

Veroff, J., Kulka, R. A., & Douvan, E. (1981). *Mental health in America.* New York: Basic Books.

Wink, P. (1992). Three types of narcissism in women from college to mid-life. *Journal of Personality, 60,* 7–30.

Winter, D. G. (1987). Leader appeal, leader performance, and the motive profiles of leaders and followers: A study of American presidents and elections. *Journal of Personality and Social Psychology, 52,* 196–202.

Winter, D. G. (1990, July). *Presidential "scores" on the Eysenck Personality Inventory in relation to presidential behavior.* Paper presented at the annual meeting of the International Society of Political Psychology, Washington, DC.

Winter, D. G. (1995). *Personality: Analysis and interpretation of lives.* New York: McGraw-Hill.

Winter, D. G., & Carlson, L. (1988). Using motive scores in the psychobiographical study of an individual: The case of Richard Nixon. *Journal of Personality, 56,* 75–103.

Yang, K.-S., & Bond, M. H. (1990). Exploring implicit personality theories with indigenous or imported constructs: The Chinese case. *Journal of Personality and Social Psychology, 58,* 1087–1095.

York, K., & John, O. P. (1992). The four faces of Eve: A typological analysis of women's personality at mid-life. *Journal of Personality and Social Psychology, 63,* 494–508.

 Article Review Form at end of book.

What are some of the struggles faced by parents of African American children? Why have the changes of the past 40 years not had much impact on the self-image of the African American children described in the article?

Growing Up in Black and White

Jack E. White

"Mommy, I want to be white."

Imagine my wife's anguish and alarm when our beautiful brown-skinned three-year-old daughter made that declaration. We thought we were doing everything right to develop her self-esteem and positive racial identity. We overloaded her toy box with black dolls. We carefully monitored the racial content of TV shows and videos, ruling out *Song of the South* and *Dumbo*, two classic Disney movies marred by demeaning black stereotypes. But we saw no harm in *Pinocchio*, which seemed as racially benign as "Sesame Street" or "Barney," and a good deal more engaging. Yet now our daughter was saying she wanted to be white, to be like the puppet who becomes a real boy in the movie. How had she got that potentially soul-destroying idea and, even more important, what should we do about it?

That episode was an unsettling reminder of the unique burden that haunts black parents in America: helping their children come to terms with being black in a country where the message too often seems to be that being white is better. Developing a healthy self-image would be difficult enough for black children with all the real-life reminders that blacks and whites are still treated differently. But it is made even harder by the seductive racial bias in TV, movies and children's books, which seem to link everything beautiful and alluring with whiteness while often treating blacks as afterthoughts. Growing up in this all pervading world of whiteness can be psychologically exhausting for black children just as they begin to figure out who they are. As a four-year-old boy told his father after spending another day in the overwhelmingly white environment of his Connecticut day-care facility, "Dad, I'm tired of being black."

In theory it should now be easier for children to develop a healthy sense of black pride than it was during segregation. In 1937 psychologists Kenneth and Mamie Clark conducted a famous experiment that demonstrated just how much black children had internalized the hatred that society directed at their race. They asked 253 black children to choose between four dolls, two black and two white. The result: two-thirds of the children preferred white dolls.

The conventional wisdom had been that black self-hatred was a by-product of discrimination that would wither away as society became more tolerant. Despite the civil rights movement of the 1960s, the black-is-beautiful movement of the '70s, the proliferation of black characters on television shows during the '80s and the renascent black nationalist movement of the '90s, the prowhite message has not lost its power. In 1985 psychologist Darlene Powell-Hopson updated the Clarks' experiment using black and white Cabbage Patch dolls and got a virtually identical result: 65% of the black children preferred white dolls. "Black is dirty," one youngster explained.

Powell-Hopson thinks the result would be the same if the test were repeated today.

Black mental-health workers say the trouble is that virtually all the progress the U.S. has made toward racial fairness has been in one direction. To be accepted by whites, blacks have to become more like them, while many whites have not changed their attitudes at all. Study after study has shown that the majority of whites, for all the commitment to equality they espouse, still consider blacks to be inferior, undesirable and dangerous. "Even though race relations have changed for the better, people maintain those old stereotypes," says Powell-Hopson. "The same racial dynamics occur in an integrated environment as occurred in segregation; it's just more covert."

Psychiatrists say children as young as two can pick up these damaging messages, often from subtle signals of black inferiority unwittingly embedded in children's books, toys and TV programs designed for the white mainstream. "There are many more positive images about black people in the media than there used to be, but there's still a lot that says that white is more beautiful and powerful than black, that white is good and black is bad," says James P. Comer, a Yale University psychiatrist who collaborated with fellow black psychiatrist Alvin F. Poussaint on *Raising Black Children* (Plume).

The bigotry is not usually as blatant as it was in Roald Dahl's

Charlie and the Chocolate Factory. When the book was published in 1964, the *New York Times* called it "a richly inventive and humorous tale." Blacks didn't see anything funny about having the factory staffed by "Oompa-Loompas," pygmy workers imported in shipping cartons from the jungle where they had been living in the trees.

Today white-controlled companies are doing a better job of erasing racially loaded subtexts from children's books and movies. Yet those messages still get through, in part because they are at times so subtle even a specialist like Powell-Hopson misses them. She recently bought a book about a cat for her six-year-old daughter, who has a love of felines. Only when Powell-Hopson got home did she discover that the beautiful white cat in the story turns black when it starts behaving badly. Moreover, when the products are not objectionable, they are sometimes promoted in ways that unintentionally drive home the theme of black inferiority. Powell-Hopson cites a TV ad for dolls that displayed a black version in the background behind the white model "as though it were a second-class citizen."

Sadly, black self-hatred can also begin at home. Even today, says Powell-Hopson, "many of us perpetuate negative messages, showing preference for lighter complexions, saying nappy hair is bad and straight hair is good, calling other black people 'niggers,' that sort of thing." This danger can be greater than the one posed by TV and the other media because children learn so much by simple imitation of the adults they are closest to. Once implanted in a toddler's mind, teachers and psychologists say, such misconceptions can blossom into a full-blown racial identity crisis during adolescence, affecting everything from performance in the classroom to a youngster's susceptibility to crime and drug abuse. But they can be neutralized if parents react properly.

In their book, Comer and Poussaint emphasize a calm and straightforward approach. They point out that even black children from affluent homes in integrated neighborhoods need reassurance about racial issues because from their earliest days they sense that their lives are "viewed cheaply by white society." If, for example, a black little girl says she wishes she had straight blond hair, they advise parents to point out "in a relaxed and unemotional manner . . . that she is black and that most black people have nice curly black hair, and that most white people have straight hair, brown, blond, black. At this age what you convey in your voice and manner will either make it O.K. or make it a problem."

Powell-Hopson, who along with her psychologist husband Derek has written *Different and Wonderful: Raising Black Children in a Race-Conscious Society* (Fireside), takes a more aggressive approach, urging black parents in effect to inoculate their children against negative messages at an early age. For example, the authors suggest that African-American parents whose children display a preference for white dolls or action figures should encourage them to play with a black one by "dressing it in the best clothes, or having it sit next to you, or doing anything you can think of to make your child sense that you prefer that doll." After that, the Hopsons say, the child can be offered a chance to play with the toy, on the condition that "you promise to take the very best care of it. You know it is my favorite." By doing so, the Hopsons claim, "most children will jump at a chance to hold the toy even for a second."

White children are no less vulnerable to racial messages. Their reactions can range from a false sense of superiority over blacks to an identification with sports superstars like Michael Jordan so complete that they want to become black. But if white parents look for guidance from popular child-care manuals, they won't find any. "I haven't included it because I don't feel like an expert in that area," says T. Berry Brazelton, author of *Infants and Mothers* and other child-care books. "I think it's a very, very serious issue that this country hasn't faced up to." Unless it does, the U.S. runs the risk of rearing another generation of white children crippled by the belief that they are better than blacks and black children who agree.

As for my daughter, we're concerned but confident. As Comer says, "In the long run what children learn from their parents is more powerful than anything they get from any other source." When my little girl expressed the wish to be white, my wife put aside her anguish and smilingly replied that she is bright and black and beautiful, a very special child. We'll keep telling her that until we're sure she loves herself as much as we love her.

 Article Review Form at end of book.

What do you think the store employee in this story was thinking about when he acted? What cumulative effect might many such experiences have on an individual's outlook or personality?

The Death of the Profane

A commentary on the genre of legal writing

P. J. Williams

Buzzers are big in New York City. Favored particularly by smaller stores and boutiques, merchants throughout the city have installed them as screening devices to reduce the incidence of robbery: if the face at the door looks desirable, the buzzer is pressed and the door is unlocked. If the face is that of an undesirable, the door stays locked. Predictably, the issue of undesirability has revealed itself to be a racial determination. While controversial enough at first, even civil-rights organizations backed down eventually in the face of arguments that the buzzer system is a "necessary evil," that it is a "mere inconvenience" in comparison to the risks of being murdered, that suffering discrimination is not as bad as being assaulted, and that in any event it is not all blacks who are barred, just "17-year-old black males wearing running shoes and hooded sweatshirts."[1]

The installation of these buzzers happened swiftly in New York; stores that had always had their doors wide open suddenly be-

came exclusive or received people by appointment only. I discovered them and their meaning one Saturday in 1986. I was shopping in Soho and saw in a store window a sweater that I wanted to buy for my mother. I pressed my round brown face to the window and my finger to the buzzer, seeking admittance. A narrow-eyed, white teenager wearing running shoes and feasting on bubble gum glared out, evaluating me for signs that would pit me against the limits of his social understanding. After about five seconds, he mouthed "We're closed," and blew pink rubber at me. It was two Saturdays before Christmas, at one o'clock in the afternoon; there were several white people in the store who appeared to be shopping for things for *their* mothers.

I was enraged. At that moment I literally wanted to break all the windows of the store and *take* lots of sweaters for my mother. In the flicker of his judgmental gray eyes, that saleschild had transformed my brightly sentimental, joy-to-the-world, pre-Christmas spree to a shambles. He snuffed my sense of humanitarian catholicity, and there was nothing I could do to snuff his, without making a spectacle of myself.

I am still struck by the structure of power that drove me into such a blizzard of rage. There was almost nothing I could do, short of physically intruding upon him, that would

humiliate him the way he humiliated me. No words, no gestures, no prejudices of my own would make a bit of difference to him; his refusal to let me into the store—it was Benetton's, whose colorfully punish ad campaign is premised on wrapping every one of the world's peoples in its cottons and woolens—was an outward manifestation of his never having let someone like me into the realm of his reality. He had no compassion, no remorse, no reference to me; and no desire to acknowledge me even at the estranged level of arm's-length transactor. He saw me only as one who would take his money and therefore could not conceive that I was there to give him money.

In this weird ontological imbalance, I realized that buying something in that store was like bestowing a gift, the gift of my commerce, the lucre of my patronage. In the wake of my outrage, I wanted to take back the gift of appreciation that my peering in the window must have appeared to be. I wanted to take it back in the form of unappreciation, disrespect, defilement. I wanted to work so hard at wishing he could feel what I felt that he would never again mistake my hatred for some sort of plaintive wish to be included. I was quite willing to disenfranchise myself, in the heat of my need to revoke the flattery of my purchasing power. I was willing to boycott Benetton's,

1. "When 'By Appointment' Means Keep Out," *New York Times*, December 17, 1986, p. B1. Letter to the Editor from Michael Levin and Marguerita Levin, *New York Times*, January 11, 1987, p. E32.

random white-owned businesses, and anyone who ever blew bubble gum in my face again.

My rage was admittedly diffuse, even self-destructive, but it was symmetrical. The perhaps loose-ended but utter propriety of that rage is no doubt lost not just to the young man who actually barred me, but to those who would appreciate my being barred only as an abstract precaution, who approve of those who would bar even as they deny that they would bar *me.*

The violence of my desire to burst into Benetton's is probably quite apparent. I often wonder if the violence, the exclusionary hatred, is equally apparent in the repeated public urgings that blacks understand the buzzer system by putting themselves in the shoes of white storeowners—that, in effect, blacks look into the mirror of frightened white faces for the reality of their undesirability; and that then blacks would "just as surely conclude that [they] would not let [themselves] in under similar circumstances."[2] (That some blacks might agree merely shows that some of us have learned too well the lessons of privatized intimacies of self-hatred and rationalized away the fullness of our public, participatory selves.)

On the same day I was barred from Benetton's, I went home and wrote the above impassioned account in my journal. On the day after that, I found I was still brooding, so I turned to a form of catharsis I have always found healing. I typed up as much of the story as I have just told, made a big poster of it, put a nice colorful border around it, and, after Benetton's was truly closed, stuck it to their big sweater-filled window. I exercised my first-amendment right to place my business with them right out in the street.

So that was the first telling of this story. The second telling came a few months later, for a symposium on Excluded Voices sponsored by a law review. I wrote an essay summing up my feelings about being excluded from Benetton's and analyzing "how the rhetoric of increased privatization, in response to racial issues, functions as the rationalizing agent of public unaccountability and, ulti-

2. *New York Times,* January 11, 1987, p. E32.

mately, irresponsibility." Weeks later, I received the first edit. From the first page to the last, my fury had been carefully cut out. My rushing, run-on-rage had been reduced to simple declarative sentences. The active personal had been inverted in favor of the passive impersonal. My words were different; they spoke to me upsidedown. I was afraid to read too much of it at a time—meanings rose up at me oddly, stolen and strange.

A week and a half later, I received the second edit. All reference to Benetton's had been deleted because, according to the editors and the faculty adviser, it was defamatory; they feared harassment and liability; they said printing it would be irresponsible. I called them and offered to supply a footnote attesting to this as my personal experience at one particular location and of a buzzer system not limited to Benetton's; the editors told me that they were not in the habit of publishing things that were unverifiable. I could not but wonder, in this refusal even to let me file an affidavit, what it would take to make my experience verifiable. The testimony of an independent white bystander? (a requirement in fact imposed in U.S. Supreme Court holdings through the first part of the century[3]).

Two days *after* the piece was sent to press, I received copies of the final page proofs. All reference to my race had been eliminated because it was against "editorial policy" to permit descriptions of physiognomy. "I realize," wrote one editor, "that this was a very personal experience, but any reader will know what you must have looked like when standing at that window." In a telephone conversation to them, I ranted wildly about the significance of such an omission. "It's irrelevant," another editor explained in a voice gummy with soothing and patience; "It's nice and poetic," but it doesn't "advance the discussion of any principle . . . This is a law review, after all." Frustrated, I accused him of censorship; calmly he assured me it was not. "This is just a matter of style," he said with firmness and finality.

Ultimately I did convince the editors that mention of my race was

3. See generally *Blyew v. U.S.,* 80 U.S. 581 (1871), upholding a state's right to forbid blacks to testify against whites.

central to the whole sense of the subsequent text; that my story became one of extreme paranoia without the information that I am black; or that it became one in which the reader had to fill in the gap by assumption, presumption, prejudgment, or prejudice. What was most interesting to me in this experience was how the blind application of principles of neutrality, through the device of omission, acted either to make me look crazy or to make the reader participate in old habits of cultural bias.

That was the second telling of my story. The third telling came last April, when I was invited to participate in a law-school conference on Equality and Difference. I retold my sad tale of exclusion from Soho's most glitzy boutique, focusing in this version on the law-review editing process as a consequence of an ideology of style rooted in a social text of neutrality. I opined:

Law and legal writing aspire to formalized, color-blind, liberal ideals. Neutrality is the standard for assuring these ideals; yet the adherence to it is often determined by reference to an aesthetic of uniformity, in which difference is simply omitted. For example, when segregation was eradicated from the American lexicon, its omission led many to actually believe that racism therefore no longer existed. Race-neutrality in law has become the presumed antidote for race bias in real life. With the entrenchment of the notion of race-neutrality came attacks on the concept of affirmative action and the rise of reverse discrimination suits. Blacks, for so many generations deprived of jobs based on the color of our skin, are now told that we ought to find it demeaning to be hired, based on the color of our skin. Such is the silliness of simplistic either-or inversions as remedies to complex problems.

What is truly demeaning in this era of double-speak-no-evil is going on interviews and not getting hired because someone doesn't think we'll be comfortable. It is demeaning not to get promoted because we're judged "too weak," then putting in a lot of energy the next time and getting fired because we're "too strong." It is demeaning to be told what we find demeaning. It is very demeaning to stand on street corners unemployed and begging. It is downright demeaning to have to explain why we haven't been employed for months and then watch the job go to someone who is "more experienced." It is outrageously demeaning that none of this can be called racism, even if it happens only to, or to large numbers of, black people; as long as it's done with a smile, a handshake and a shrug; as long as the phantom-word "race" is never used.

The image of race as a phantom-word came to me after I moved into my late godmother's home. In an attempt to make it my own, I cleared the bedroom for painting. The following morning the room asserted itself, came rushing and raging at me through the emptiness, exactly as it had been for twenty-five years. One day filled with profuse and overwhelming complexity, the next day filled with persistently recurring memories. The shape of the past came to haunt me, the shape of the emptiness confronted me each time I was about to enter the room. The force of its spirit still drifts like an odor throughout the house.

The power of that room, I have thought since, is very like the power of racism as status quo: it is deep, angry, eradicated from view, but strong enough to make everyone who enters the room walk around the bed that isn't there, avoiding the phantom as they did the substance, for fear of bodily harm. They do not even know they are avoiding; they defer to the unseen shapes of things with subtle responsiveness, guided by an impulsive awareness of nothingness, and the deep knowledge and denial of witchcraft at work.

The phantom room is to me symbolic of the emptiness of formal equal opportunity, particularly as propounded by President Reagan, the Reagan Civil Rights Commission and the Reagan Supreme Court. Blindly formalized constructions of equal opportunity are the creation of a space that is filled in by a meandering stream of unguided hopes, dreams, fantasies, fears, recollections. They are the presence of the past in imaginary, imagistic form—the phantom-roomed exile of our longing.

It is thus that I strongly believe in the efficacy of programs and paradigms like affirmative action. Blacks are the objects of a constitutional omission which has been incorporated into a theory of neutrality. It is thus that omission is really a form of expression, as oxymoronic as that sounds: racial omission is a literal part of original intent; it is the fixed, reiterated prophecy of the Founding Fathers. It is thus that affirmative action is an affirmation; the affirmative act of hiring—or hearing—blacks is a recognition of individuality that re-places blacks as a social statistic, that is profoundly interconnective to the fate of blacks and whites either as sub-groups or as one group. In this sense, affirmative action is as mystical and beyond-the-self as an initiation ceremony. It is an act of verification and of vision. It

is an act of social as well as professional responsibility.

The following morning I opened the local newspaper, to find that the event of my speech had commanded two columns on the front page of the Metro section. I quote only the opening lines: "Affirmative action promotes prejudice by denying the status of women and blacks, instead of affirming them as its name suggests. So said New York City attorney Patricia Williams to an audience Wednesday."[4]

I clipped out the article and put it in my journal. In the margin there is a note to myself: eventually, it says, I should try to pull all these threads together into yet another law-review article. The problem, of course, will be that in the hierarchy of law-review citation, the article in the newspaper will have more authoritative weight about me, as a so-called "primary resource," than I will have; it will take precedence over my own citation of the unverifiable testimony of my speech.

I have used the Benetton's story a lot, in speaking engagements at various schools. I tell it whenever I am too tired to whip up an original speech from scratch. Here are some of the questions I have been asked in the wake of its telling:

Am I not privileging a racial perspective, by considering only the black point of view? Don't I have an obligation to include the "salesman's side" of the story?

Am I not putting the salesman on trial and finding him guilty of racism without giving him a chance to respond to or cross-examine me?

Am I not using the store window as a "metaphorical fence" against the potential of his explanation in order to represent my side as "authentic"?

How can I be sure I'm right?

What makes my experience the real black one anyway?

Isn't it possible that another black person would disagree with my experience? If so, doesn't that

4. "Attorney Says Affirmative Action Denies Racism, Sexism," *Dominion Post*, (Morgantown, West Virginia), April 8, 1988, p. B1.

render my story too unempirical and subjective to pay any attention to?

Always a major objection is to my having put the poster on Benetton's window. As one law professor put it: "It's one thing to publish this in a law review, where no one can take it personally, but it's another thing altogether to put your own interpretation right out there, just like that, uncontested, I mean, with nothing to counter it."[5]

Recently I got an urgent call from Thomas Grey of Stanford Law School. He had used this piece in his jurisprudence class, and a rumor got started that the Benetton's story wasn't true, that I had made it up, that it was a fantasy, a lie that was probably the product of a diseased mind trying to make all white people feel guilty. At this point I realized it almost didn't make any difference whether I was telling the truth or not—that the greater issue I had to face was the overwhelming weight of a disbelief that goes beyond mere disinclination to believe and becomes active suppression of anything I might have to say. The greater problem is a powerfully oppressive mechanism for denial of black self-knowledge and expression. And this denial cannot be separated from the simultaneously pathological willingness to believe certain things about blacks—not to believe them, but things about them.

When students in Grey's class believed and then claimed that I had made it all up, they put me in a position like that of Tawana Brawley. I mean that specifically: the social consequence of concluding that we are

5. These questions put me on trial—an imaginary trial where it is I who have the burden of proof—and proof being nothing less than the testimony of the salesman actually confessing yes I am a racist. These questions question my own ability to know, to assess, to be objective. And of course, since anything that happens to me is inherently subjective, they take away my power to know what happens to me in the world. Others, by this standard, will always know better than I. And my insistence on recounting stories from my own perspective will be treated as presumption, slander, paranoid hallucination, or just plain lies.

liars operates as a kind of public absolution of racism—the conclusion is not merely that we are troubled or that I am eccentric, but that we, as liars, are the norm. Therefore, the nonbelievers can believe, things of this sort really don't happen (even in the face of statistics to the contrary). Racism or rape is all a big fantasy concocted by troublesome minorities and women. It is interesting to recall the outcry in every national medium, from the *New York Post* to the *Times* to the major networks, in the wake of the Brawley case: who will ever again believe a black woman who cries rape by a white man? (See Chapter 9.*) Now shift the frame a bit, and imagine a white male facing a consensus that he lied. Would there be a difference? Consider Charles Stuart, for example, the white Bostonian who accused a black man of murdering his pregnant wife and whose brother later alleged that in fact the brothers had conspired to murder her. Most people and the media not only did not claim but actively resisted believing that Stuart represented any kind of "white male" norm. Instead he was written off as a troubled weirdo, a deviant—again even in the face of spousal-abuse statistics to the contrary. There was not a story I could find that carried on about "who will ever believe" the next white man who cries murder.

*Does not appear in this publication.

 Article Review Form at end of book.

Describe two aspects of the Hijra role in India. Hijra life is described as being very different from male homosexuality—what are two of the ways it is different?

The Hijras of India

Cultural and individual dimensions of an institutionalized third gender role

Serena Nanda

The hijra (eunuch/transvestite) is an institutionalized third gender role in India. Hijra are neither male nor female, but contain elements of both. As devotees of the Mother Goddess Bahuchara Mata, their sacred powers are contingent upon their asexuality. In reality, however, many hijras are prostitutes. This sexual activity undermines their culturally valued sacred role. This paper discusses religious meanings of the hijra role, as well as the ways in which individuals and the community deal with the conflicts engendered by their sexual activity.

The hijra, an institutionalized third gender role in India, is "neither male nor female," containing elements of both. The hijra are commonly believed by the larger society to be intersexed, impotent men, who undergo emasculation in which all or part of the genitals are removed. They adopt female dress and some other aspects of female behavior. Hijras traditionally earn their living by collecting alms and receiving payment for performances at weddings, births and festivals. The central fea-ture of their culture is their devotion to Bahuchara Mata, one of the many Mother Goddesses worshipped all over India, for whom emasculation is carried out. This identification with the Mother Goddess is the source both of the hijras' claim for their special place in Indian society and the traditional belief in their power to curse or confer blessings on male infants.

The census of India does not enumerate hijras separately so their exact numbers are unknown. Estimates quoted in the press range from 50,000 (*India Today*, 1982) to 500,000 (*Tribune*, 1983). Hijras live predominantly in the cities of North India, where they find the greatest opportunity to perform their traditional roles, but small groups of hijras are found all over India, in the south as well as the north. Seven "houses," or subgroups, comprise the hijra community; each of these has a guru or leader, all of whom live in Bombay. The houses have equal status, but one, Laskarwallah, has the special function of mediating disputes which arise among the others. Each house has its own history, as well as rules particular to it. For ex-ample, members of a particular house are not allowed to wear certain colors. Hijra houses appear to be patterned after the *gharanas* (literally, houses), or family lineages among classical musicians, each of which is identified with its own particular musical style. Though the culturally distinct features of the hijra houses have almost vanished, the structural features remains.[1]

The most significant relationship in the Hijra community is that of the *guru* (master, teacher) and *chela* (disciple). When an individual decides to (formally) join the hijra com-

[1] I would like to thank Veena Oldenburg for calling this to my attention. A similar pattern exists among the courtesans in North India (Oldenburg, 1984).

For their assistance in developing the ideas in this paper, grateful acknowledgement is made to Joseph Carrier, David Greenberg, A. M. Shah, Rajni Chopra, Evelyn Blackwood, John Money, the participants of the Columbia University Seminar on the Indian Self, and most especially, Owen Lynch and Alan Roland. I am also grateful to Mrs. Banu Vasudevan, Bharati Gowda, and Shiv Ram Apte, as well as my friends among the hijras, without whom this paper could not have been written.

munity, he is taken to Bombay to visit one of the seven major gurus, usually the guru of the person who has brought him there. At the initiation ritual, the guru gives the novice a new, female name. The novice vows to obey the guru and the rules of the community. The guru then presents the new chela with some gifts.

The chela, or more likely, someone on her behalf, pays an initiation fee and the guru writes the chela's name in her record book. This guru-chela relationship is a lifelong bond of reciprocity in which the guru is obligated to help the chela and the chela is obligated to be loyal and obedient to the guru.[2] Hijras live together in communes generally of about 5 to 15 members, and the heads of these local groups are also called guru. Hijras make no distinctions within their community based on caste origin or religion, although in some parts of India, Gujerat, for example, Muslim and Hindu hijras reportedly live apart (Salunkhe, 1976). In Bombay, Delhi, Chandigarh and Bangalore, hijras of Muslim, Christian, and Hindu origin live in the same houses.

In addition to the hierarchical guru-chela relationship, there is fictive kinship by which hijras relate to each other. Rituals exist for "taking a daughter" and the "daughters" of one "mother" consider themselves "sisters" and relate on a reciprocal, affectionate basis. Other fictive kinship relations, such as "grandmother" or "mother's sister" (aunt) are the basis of warm and reciprocal regard. Fictive kin exchange small amounts of money, clothing, jewelry and sweets to formalize their relationship. Such relationships connect hijras all over India, and there is a constant movement of individuals who visit their gurus and fictive kin in different cities. Various annual gatherings, both religious and secular, attract thousands of hijras from all over India.[3]

[2]Alan Roland (1982) has insightfully examined some of the emotional and psychological aspects of hierarchy within the Hindu joint family, and many of his conclusions could well be applied to the hijra hierarchy.

[3]Some of these religious occasions are participated in by non-hijras as well, while others celebrate events specific to the hijra community, such as the anniversary of the deaths of important gurus.

The extant literature on the hijras is scant, confusing, misleading, contradictory, and judgmental. With few exceptions (Salunkhe, 1976; Sinha, 1967) it lacks a basis in fieldwork or intensive interviewing. A major dispute in that literature has been whether or not the hijra role encompasses homosexuality.

In my view, the essential cultural aspect of the hijra role is its asexual nature. Yet, empirical evidence also indicates that many hijras do engage in homosexual activity. This difference between the cultural ideal and the real behavior causes a certain amount of conflict within the community. The present paper, based on a year's fieldwork among hijra communes in various parts of India, examines both the cultural ideal of asexuality and the behavioral dimension of homosexuality, and how the conflict is experienced and handled within the community.

Cultural Dimensions of the Hijra Role

Hijras As Neither Man nor Woman

A commonly told story among hijras, which conceptualizes them as a separate, third gender, connects them to the Hindu epic, the *Ramayana*:

In the time of the Ramayana, Ram . . . had to leave Ayodhya (his native city) and go into the forest for 14 years. As he was going, the whole city followed him because they loved him so. As Ram came to . . . the edge of the forest, he turned to the people and said, "Ladies and gents, please wipe your tears and go away." But these people who were not men and not women did not know what to do. So they stayed there because Ram did not ask them to go. They remained there 14 years and snake hills grew around them. When Ram returned from Lanka, he found many snake hills. Not knowing why they were there he removed them and found so many people with long beards and long nails, all meditating. And so they were blessed by Ram. And that is why we hijras are so respected in Ayodhya.

Individual hijras also speak of themselves as being "separate," being "neither man nor woman," being "born as men, but not men," or

being "not perfect men." Hijras are most clearly "not men" in relation to their claimed inability and lack of desire to engage in the sexual act as men with women, a consequence of their claimed biological intersexuality and their subsequent castration. Thus, hijras are unable to reproduce children, especially sons, an essential element in the Hindu concept of the normal, masculine role for males.

But if hijras are "not men," neither are they women, in spite of several aspects of feminine behavior associated with the role. These behaviors include dressing as women, wearing their hair long, plucking (rather than shaving) their facial hair, adopting feminine mannerisms, taking on women's names, and using female kinship terms and a special, feminized vocabulary. Hijras also identify with a female goddess or as wives of certain male deities in ritual contexts. They claim seating reserved for "ladies only" in public conveyances. On one occasion, they demanded to be counted as women in the census.[4]

Although their role requires hijras to dress like women, few make any real attempt to imitate or to "pass" as women. Their female dress and mannerisms are exaggerated to the point of caricature, expressing sexual overtones that would be considered inappropriate for ordinary women in their roles as daughters, wives, and mothers. Hijra performances are burlesques of female behavior. Much of the comedy of their behavior derives from the incongruities between their behavior and that of traditional women. They use coarse and abusive speech and gestures in opposition to the Hindu ideal of demure and restrained femininity. Further, it is not at all uncommon to see hijras in female clothing sporting several days growth of beard, or exposing hairy, muscular arms. The ultimate sanction of hijras to an abusive or unresponsive public is to lift their skirts and expose the mutilated genitals. The implicit threat of this shameless, and thoroughly unfeminine, behavior is enough to make most people give

[4]More recently, hijras have been issued ration cards for food in New Delhi, but must apply only under the male names.

them a few cents so they will go away. Most centrally, as hijras themselves acknowledge, they are not born as women, and cannot reproduce. Their impotence and barrenness, due to a deficient or absent male organ, ultimately precludes their being considered fully male; yet their lack of female reproductive organs or female sexual organs precludes their being considered fully female.

Indian belief and the hijra's own claims commonly attribute the impotence of the hijra as male to a hermaphroditic morphology and physiology. Many informants insisted "I was born this way," implying hermaphroditism; such a condition is the standard reason given for joining the community. Only one of 30 informants, however, was probably born intersexed. Her words clearly indicate how central this status is to the hijra role, and make explicit that hijras are not males because they have no male reproductive organ:

From my childhood I am like this. From birth my organ was very small. My mother tried taking me to doctors and all but the doctors said, "No, it won't grow, your child is not a man and not a woman, this is God's gift and all . . ." From that time my mother would dress me in girl's clothes. But then she saw it was no use. So she sent me to live with the hijras. I am a real hijra, not like those others who are converts; they are men and can have children, so they have the (emasculation) operation, but I was born this way. (Field notes, 1981–2)

Hijra Impotence and Creative Asceticism

If, in Indian reality, the impotent male is considered useless as a man because he is unable to procreate, in Indian mythology, impotence can be transformed into generativity through the ideal of *tapasya*, or the practice of asceticism. *Tapas*, the power that results from ascetic practices and sexual abstinence, becomes an essential feature in the process of creation. Ascetics appear throughout Hindu mythology in procreative roles. In one version of the Hindu creation myth, Siva carries out an extreme, but legitimate form of tapasya,

that of self-castration. Because the act of creation he was about to undertake had already been accomplished by Brahma, Siva breaks off his linga (phallus), saying, "there is no use for this linga . . ." and throws it into the earth. His act results in the fertility cult of linga-worship, which expresses the paradoxical theme of creative asceticism (O'Flaherty, 19973). This theme provides one explanation of the positive role given the hijras in Indian society. Born intersexed and impotent, unable themselves to reproduce, hijras can, through the emasculation operation, transform their liability into a source of creative power which enables them to confer blessings of fertility on others.

The link between the Hindu theme of creative asceticism and the role and power of the hijras is explicitly articulated in the myths connecting them to their major point of religious identification—their worship of Bahuchara Mata, and her requirement that they undergo emasculation. Bahuchara was a pretty, young maiden in a party of travelers passing through the forest in Gujerat. The party was attacked by thieves, and, fearing they would outrage her modesty, Bahuchara drew her dagger and cut off her breast, offering it to the outlaws in place of her body. This act, and her ensuing death, led to Bahuchara's deification and the practice of self-mutilation and sexual abstinence by her devotees to secure her favor.

Bahuchara has a special connection to the hijras because they are impotent men who undergo emasculation. This connection derives special significance from the story of King Baria of Gujerat. Baria was a devout follower of Bahucharaji, but was unhappy because he had no son. Through the goddess' favor a son, Jetho, was born to him. The son, however, was impotent. The King, out of respect to the goddess, set him apart for her service. Bahucharaji appeared to Jetho in a dream and told him to cut off his genitalia and dress himself as a woman, which he did. This practice has been followed by all who join the hijra cult (Mehta, 1945–1946).

Emasculation is the *dharm* (caste duty) of the hijras, and the chief source of their uniqueness. The

hijras carry it out in a ritual context, in which the client sits in front of a picture of the goddess Bahuchara and repeats her name while the operation is being performed. A person who survives the operation becomes one of Bahuchara Mata's favorites, serving as a vehicle of her power through their symbolic rebirth. While the most popular image of Bahuchara is that of the goddess riding on a cock, Shah (1961) suggests that her original form of worship was the *yantra*, a conventional symbol for the vulva. A relation between this representation of the goddess and emasculation may exist: emasculation certainly brings the hijra devotee into a closer identification with the female object of devotion.

Identification of the hijras with Bahuchara specifically and through her, with the creative powers of the Mother Goddess worshipped in many different forms in India, is clearly related to their major cultural function, that of performing at homes where a male child has been born. During these performances the hijras, using sexual innuendos, inspect the genitals of the infant whom they hold in their arms as they dance. The hijras confer fertility, prosperity, and health on the infant and family.

At both weddings and births, hijras hold the power to bless and to curse, and families regard them ambivalently. They have both auspicious functions and inauspicious potential. In regard to the latter, charms are used during pregnancy against eunuchs, both to protect against stillbirth, and a transformation of the embryo from male to female. Hiltebeitel (1980) suggests that the presence of eunuchs at birth and weddings:

marks the ambiguity of those moments when the nondifferentiation of male and female is most filled with uncertainty and promise—in the mystery that surrounds the sexual identity of the still unborn child and on that [occasion] which anticipates the re-union of male and female in marital sex. (p. 168)

Thus, it is fitting that the eunuch-transvestites, themselves characterized by sexual ambiguity, have ritual functions at moments that involve sexual ambiguity.

The eunuch-transvestite role of the hijras links them not only to the

Mother Goddess, but also to Siva, through their identification with Arjuna, the hero of the Mahabharata. One origin myth of the hijras is the story of Arjuna's exile. He lives incognito for one year as part of the price he must pay for losing a game of dice, and also for rejecting the advances of one of the celestial nymphs. Arjuna decides to hide himself in the guise of a eunuch-transvestite, wearing bangles made of white conch, braiding his hair like a woman, clothing himself in female attire, and serving the ladies of the king's court (Rajagopalachari, 1980). Some hijras say that whoever is born on Arjuna's day, no matter where in the world, will become a hijra. Hiltebeitel (1980) makes a persuasive case for the identification of Arjuna with Siva, especially in his singer/dancer/eunuch/transvestite role.

The theme of the eunuch state is elaborated in a number of ways in the Mahabharata, and it is Arjuna who is the theme's central character. Arjuna, in the disguise of eunuch-transvestite, participates in weddings and births, and thus provides a further legitimatization for the ritual contexts in which the hijras perform. At one point, for example, Arjuna in this disguise helps prepare the King's daughter for her marriage and her future role as mother-to-be. In doing this, he refuses to marry the princess himself, thus renouncing not only his sovereignty, but also the issue of an heir. His feigned impotence paves the way for the birth of the princess' child, just as the presence of the impotent hijras at the home of a male child paves the way for the child's fertility and the continuation of the family line.

This evidence suggests that intersexuality, impotence, emasculation and transvestism are all variously believed to be part of the hijra role, accounting for their inability to reproduce and the lack of desire (or the renunciation of the desire) to do so. In any event, sexual abstinence, which Hindu mythology associates with the powers of the ascetic, is in fact, the very source of the hijras' powers. The hijras themselves recognize this connection: They frequently refer to themselves as *sannyasin*, the person who renounces his role in so-

ciety for the life of a holy wanderer and beggar. This vocation requires renunciation of material possessions, the duties of caste, the life of the householder and family man, and, most particularly, the renunciation of sexual desire (*kama*). In claiming this vocation, hijras point out how they have abandoned their families, live in material poverty, live off the charity of others, and "do not have sexual desires as other men do."

Hijras understand that their "other-worldliness" brings them respect in society, and that if they do not live up to these ideals, they will damage that respect. But just as Hindu mythology contains many stories of ascetics who renounce desire but nevertheless are moved by desire to engage in sexual acts, so, too, the hijra community experiences the tension between their religious, ascetic ideal and the reality of the individual human's desire and sensuality.

Individual Dimensions of the Hijra Role

Hijras As Homosexuals

The remainder of this paper focuses on the sexual activities of hijras, and the ways in which the community experiences the conflict between the real and the ideal.

A widespread belief in India is that hijras are intersexed persons claimed or kidnapped by the hijra community as infants. No investigator has found evidence to support this belief. Given the large and complex society of India, the hijra community attracts different kinds of persons, most of whom join voluntarily as teenagers or adults. It appears to be a magnet for persons with a wide range of cross-gender characteristics arising from either a psychological or organic condition (Money & Wiedeking, 1980). The hijra role accommodates different personalities, sexual needs, and gender identities without completely losing its cultural meaning.

While the core of the positive meaning attached to the hijra role is linked to the negation of sexual desire, the reality is that many hijras do,

in fact, engage in sexual activities. Because sexual behavior is contrary to the definition of the role such activity causes conflict for both the individuals and the community. Individual hijras deal with the conflict in different ways, while the community as a whole resorts to various mechanisms of social control.

Though it is clear from the literature that some hijras engage in homosexual activity, there has been controversy over the centrality of this activity in the institutionalization of the role in India.[5] In his psychoanalytical study of high castes in a village in Rajasthan, Carstairs (1957) asserted that the hijra role is primarily a form of institutionalized homosexuality that developed in response to tendencies toward latent homosexuality in the Indian national character. Morris Opler (1960) contested both Carstairs' evaluation of Indian character and his assertion that hijras are primarily conceptualized as homosexuals or that they engaged in any sexual activity.

Opler argued that the cultural definition of their role in Indian society was only one of performers. Sinha (1967), who worked in Lucknow in North India, acknowledged their performing role, but treated hijras primarily as homosexuals who join the community specifically to satisfy their sexual desires. Lynton and Rajan (1974), who interviewed hijras in Hyderabad, indicate that a period of homosexual activity, involving solicitation in public, sometimes precedes a decision to join the hijras. Their informants led them to believe, however, that sexual activity is prohibited by hijra rules and that these are strictly enforced by the community elders. Freeman (1979), who did fieldwork in Orissa at the southern edge of North Indian culture, discusses hijras as transvestite prostitutes and hardly mentions their ritual roles.

My own data (Nanda, 1984), gathered through fieldwork in Bangalore and Bombay, and in several North Indian cities, confirm beyond doubt that, however deviant it may be regarded within the hijra

[5]A more detailed description of this literature is found in Nanda (1984) and Nanda (in press).

community, hijras in contemporary India extensively engage in sexual relations with men. This phenomenon is not entirely modern: 19th-century accounts (Bhimbhai, 1901; Faridi, 1899) claim that hijras were known to kidnap small boys for the purposes of sodomy or prostitution. Such allegations still find their way into the contemporary popular press (*India Today*, 1982).

Although hijras attribute their increased prostitution to declining opportunities to earn a living in their traditional manner, eunuch-transvestites in Hindu classical literature also had the reputation of engaging in homosexual activity. The classic Hindu manual of love, the *Kamasutra*, specifically outlines sexual practices that were considered appropriate for eunuch-transvestites to perform with male partners (Burton, 1962).[6] Classical Hinduism taught that there was a "third sex," divided into various categories, two of which were castrated men, eunuchs, and hermaphrodites, who wore false breasts, and imitated the voice, gestures, dress and temperaments of women. These types shared the major function of providing alternative techniques of sexual gratification (Bullough, 1976). In contemporary India, concepts of eunuch, transvestite and male homosexual are not distinct, and the hijras are considered all of these at once (O'Flaherty, 1980).

The term hijra, however, which is of Urdu origin and the masculine gender, has the primary meaning of hermaphrodite. It is usually translated as eunuch, never as homosexual. Even Carstairs' informants, among whom the homosexuality of the hijras was well known, defined them as either drum players at the birth of male children, or eunuchs, whose duty was to undergo castration. In parts of North India, the term

for effeminate males who play the passive role in homosexual relations is *zenanas* (women); by becoming a hijra, one removes oneself from this category (see also Lynton & Rajan, 1974). Furthermore, a covert homosexual subculture exists in some of the larger cities in North India (Anderson, 1977), but persons who participate in it are not called hijras. In fact, as in other cultures (Carrier, 1980; Wikan, 1977) men who play the insertor role in sexual activities between men have no linguistically or sociologically distinguished role. Unlike western cultures, in India sexual object choice alone does not define gender. In some South Indian regional languages, the names by which hijras are called, such as *kojja* in Telegu (Anderson, 1977), or *potee* in Tamil, are, unlike the term *hijra*, epithets used derogatorily to mean a cowardly or feminine male or homosexual. This linguistic difference, however, is consistent with the fact that in South India the hijras do not have the cultural role which they do in North India.

According to my research, homosexual activity is widespread among hijras, and teenage homosexual activity figures significantly in the lives of many individuals who join the community. As Sinha's interviews also indicate (1967), those hijras who engage in homosexual activity share particular life patterns before joining the community. Typically such individuals liked during childhood to dress in feminine clothes, play with girls, do traditionally female work, and avoid the company of boys in rough play. In lower class families, the boy's effeminancy is both ridiculed and encouraged by his peers, who may persuade him to play the insertee role for them, possibly with some slight monetary consideration. At this stage the boy lives with his family, though in an increasingly tense atmosphere. He thinks of himself as a male and wears male clothing, at least in public. As his interest in homosexual activity increases, and his relations with his family become more strained, he may leave home. In most cases their fami-

lies make serious attempts to inhibit their feminine activity with scoldings, surveillance, restrictions, and beatings, so that the boy finally has no choice but to leave.[7]

There are two modes of sexual relations among hijras. One is casual prostitution, the exchange of sexual favors with different men for a fixed sum of money, and the other is "having a husband." Hijras do not characterize their male sexual partners as homosexuals; they quite explicitly distinguish them as being different than homosexuals. One hijra, Shakuntala, characterizes the customers in the following way:

these men . . . are married or unmarried, they may be the father of many children. Those who come to us, they have no desire to go to a man . . . they come to us for the sake of going to a girl. They prefer us to their wives . . . each one's tastes differ among people. . . . It is God's way; because we have to make a living, he made people like this so we can earn. (Field notes, 1981–2)

Shakuntala clearly expressed a feminine gender identity and was, in fact, the person who came closest to what would be called in the west a transsexual; that is, experiencing himself as a "female trapped in a male body." She remembered having felt that she was a female since childhood, liking to dress in female clothing, doing woman's work inside the

---

[6] "Mouth Congress" is considered the appropriate sexual activity for eunuchs disguised as women, in the Kama Sutra. An Editor's note (Burton, 1962, p. 124) suggests that this practice is no longer common in India, and is perhaps being replaced by sodomy, which has been introduced since the Muslim period.

[7] Social class factors are relevant here. Boys who are born with indeterminate sex organs (I came across three such cases by hearsay) to upper middle class families would not be likely to join the hijras. In two of these cases the men in question were adults: one had been sent abroad to develop his career in science with the expectation that he would not marry, but at least would have the satisfaction of a successful and prestigious career. The other was married by his parents to a girl who, it was known, could not have children. The third is still a toddler and is being brought up as a boy. I also had the opportunity to interview a middle-aged, middle-class man who was desperately trying to find a doctor to perform the transsexual operation on him in a hospital. He chose not to join the hijras because of their "reputation" but envied them their group life and their ability to live openly as women.

house and playing with girls rather than boys. She was introduced to homosexual activity in her teens, which she claims "spoiled" her for the normal, heterosexual male role. She has a very maternal, nurturing temperament, and emphasizes the maternal aspect of the guru role to her young chelas.[8] She is currently involved in a long-term, monogamous relationship with a young man who lives in her neighborhood and whom she hopes will "marry" her. She underwent the emasculation operation because she wanted "to become more beautiful, like a woman." She was the only hijra interviewed who was taking hormones "to develop a more feminine figure." She always dressed as a woman and was very convincing in a feminine role, not exhibiting the more flamboyant mannerisms and gestures of the typical hijra. Because of her strong attachment to her present boyfriend, she is sometimes criticized by her hijra friends:

Those people, like Shakuntala, with husband fever, they are mad over their husbands, even to the point of suicide. If that fellow even talks to a[nother] girl, immediately they'll fight with him. If he is out at night, even if it is three o'clock in the morning, they'll go in search of him. They won't even sleep till he returns. (Field notes, 1981–2)

This devotion to one man is seen as typical of Shakuntala's extremely feminine identification.

Not all hijras who engage in sexual relations with other men express such complete feminine identification. One hijra, for example, explained the attraction of men to hijras on different grounds:

See, there is a proverb, "for a normal lady [prostitute] it is four annas and for a hijra it is twelve annas." These men, they come to us to have pleasure on their own terms.

[8]Gurus are sometimes considered like mothers, sometimes like fathers, and sometimes like husbands. Their female aspect is related to the nurturing and care and concern they have for their chelas; the male aspect refers more to the authority they have over their chelas and the obedience and loyalty that is due them.

They may want to kiss us or do so many things. For instance, the customer will ask us to lift the legs (from a position lying on her back) so that they can do it through the anus. We allow them to do it by the back [anal intercourse], but not very often. (Field notes, 1981–2)

This statement suggests that the attraction of the hijras is that they will engage in forms of sexual behavior in which Indian women will normally not engage. Several of my non-hijra male informants confirmed this view.

Having a husband is the preferred alternative for those hijras who engage in sexual relations. Many of my informants have, or recently had, a relatively permanent attachment to one man whom they referred to as their husband. They maintain warm and affectionate, as well as sexually satisfying and economically reciprocal, relationships with these men, with whom they live, sometimes alone, or sometimes with several other hijras. Lalitha, a very feminine looking hijra in her middle thirties, has had the same husband for nine years. He used to come for prostitution to the hijra commune in which Lalitha lived and then they lived together in a small house until he got married. Now Lalitha has moved back with the hijras, where she cooks their meals in return for free food and lodging, but she still maintains her relationship with her "husband":

My husband is a Christian. He works in a cigarette factory and earns 1000 rupees a month. He is married to [another] woman and has got four children. I encouraged him to get married and even his wife and children are nice to me. His children call me *chitti* [mother's sister] and even his wife's parents know about me and don't say anything. He gives me saris and flowers and whenever I ask for money he never says no. When he needs money, I would give him also. (Field notes, 1981–2)

Hijras who have husbands do not break their ties with the hijra community, although sometimes their husbands urge them to do so. Sushila, an attractive, assertive, and ambitious hijra in her early thirties has a husband who is a driver for a national corporation headquarters

and earns 600 rupees a month. She continues to be very active in the local hijra community, however, and even refuses to give up practicing prostitution in spite of her husband's objections:

My husband tells me, "I earn enough money. Why do you go for prostitution?" I tell him, "You are here with me today. What surety is there you will be with me forever? I came to you from prostitution, and if you leave me, I'll have to go back to it. Then all those other hijras will say, 'Oh, she lived as a wife and now look at her fate, she has come back to prostitution.' "So I tell him, "don't put any restrictions on me; now they all think of me as someone nice, but when I go back to prostitution, they will put me to shame." If he gives me too much back talk, I give him good whacks. (Field notes, 1981–2)

Sushila is saving the money she makes from prostitution and from that her husband gives her so that she can buy a business, probably a bathhouse for working class men. In Bangalore, bathhouses are commonly run by hijras.

Although many hijras complain that it is hard for them to save money, some have a good business sense and have invested in jewelry and property so that they can be relatively independent financially in their old age. For hijras who are not particularly talented singers and dancers, or who live in cities where their ritual performances are not in demand, prostitution provides an adequate way of earning a living. It is a demanding and even occasionally dangerous profession, however, because some customers turn out to be "rowdies." Although a hijra living in a commune has to pay 50% of her fees from prostitution to her household head, few of the younger hijra prostitutes can afford their own place; and living with others provides a certain amount of protection from rough customers and the police. In spite of the resentment and constant complaints by younger hijra prostitutes that they are exploited by their elders, they are extremely reluctant to live on their own.

Hijra Sexuality As a Source of Conflict

The attraction that the hijra role holds for some individuals is the opportunity to engage in sexual relations with men, while enjoying the sociability and relative security of an organized community; these advantages are apparent in contrast to the insecurity and harassment experienced by the effeminate homosexual living on his own. But, whether with husbands or customers, sexual relations run counter to the cultural definitions of the hijra role, and are a source of conflict within the community. Hijra elders attempt to maintain control over those who would "spoil" the hijras' reputation by engaging in sexual activity.

Hijras are well aware that they have only a tenuous hold on respectability in Indian society, and that this respectability is compromised by even covertly engaging in sexual relations. Ascetics have always been regarded with skepticism and ambivalence in Indian society. While paying lip service to the ascetic, conventional Hinduism maintained a very real hostility to it. It classed the non-Vedic ascetic with the dregs of society, "such as incendiaries, poisoners, pimps, spies, adulterers, abortionists, atheists and drunkards"; these fringe members of society found their most respectable status among the Siva sects (O'Flaherty, 1973, p. 67). This ambivalence toward ascetics accurately describes the response of Indian society to the hijra as well, who are also, not coincidentally, worshippers of Siva. In addition, the notion of the false ascetic (those who pretend to be ascetics in order to satisfy their lust) abounds in Hindu mythology. This contradictory attitude, a high regard for asceticism coupled with disdain for those who practice it, characterizes contemporary as well as classical India. Even those families who allow the hijras to perform at births and weddings ridicule the notion that they have any real power.

Indian audiences express their ambivalence toward the hijras by challenging the authenticity of hijra performers. The hijras' emasculation distinguishes them from *zenanas*, or practicing effeminate homosexuals,

who do not have the religious powers ascribed to the hijras, but who sometimes impersonate them in order to earn a living. Thus, hijras state that emasculation is necessary because, when they are performing or asking for alms, people may challenge them. If their genitals have not been removed, they will be reviled and driven away as imposters. Hijra elders themselves constantly deride those "men who are men and can have children" and join their community only to make a living from it, or to enjoy sexual relations with men. The parallel between such "fake" hijras and the false ascetics is clear.

Hijras consider sexual activity offensive to the hijra goddess, Bahuchara Mata. Upon initiation into the community, the novice vows to abstain from sexual relations or to marry. Hijra elders claim that all hijra houses lock their doors by nine o'clock at night, implying that no sexual activities occur there. In the cities where hijra culture is strongest, hijras who practice prostitution are not permitted to live with hijras who earn their living by traditional ritual performances. Those who live in these respectable or "family" houses are carefully watched to see that they do not have contact with men. In areas more peripheral to the core of hijra culture, including most of South India, prostitutes do live in houses with traditional hijra performers, and may, in fact, engage in such performances themselves whenever they have an opportunity to do so.

Sexually active hijras usually assert that all hijras join the community so that they can engage in sexual relations with men. As Sita, a particularly candid informant, said:

Why else would we wear saris? Those who you see who are aged now, when they were young they were just like me. Now they say they haven't got the sexual feeling and they talk only of God and all, but I tell you, that is all nonsense. In their younger days, they also did this prostitution and it is only for the sexual feeling that we join. (Field notes, 1981–2)

The hijras who most vehemently denied having sexual relations with men were almost always over 40. It appears that as they get older, hijras give up sexual activity. Such change over the life cycle parallels that in India generally; in the Hindu cultural

ideal, women whose sons are married are expected to give up sexual activity. In fact, not all women do so, but there is social pressure to do so. People ridicule and gossip about middle aged women who act in ways that suggest active sexual interest (Vatuk, 1985). The presentation of self as a non-sexual person that occurs with age also appears among the hijras. The elderly ones may wear male clothing in public, dress more conservatively, wearing white rather than boldly colored saris, act in a less sexually suggestive manner, and take on household domestic roles that keep them indoors.

Although hijra elders are most vocal in expressing disapproval of hijra sexual relations, even younger hirjas who have husbands or practice prostitution admit that such behavior runs counter to hijra norms and lowers their status in the larger society. Hijra prostitutes say that prostitution is a necessary evil for them, the only way for them to earn a living. They attribute the frequency of hijra prostitution to the declining economic status of the hijras in India since the time of Independence. At that time the rajas and nawobs in the princely states, who are important patrons of hijra ritual performances, lost their offices. Hijras also argue that in modern India, declining family size and the spread of Western values, which undermine belief in their powers, also contributes to their lowered economic position, making prostitution necessary.

India As an Accommodating Society

India is characteristically described as a sexually tolerant society (Bullough, 1976; Carrier, 1980). Indeed, the hijra role appears to be elastic enough to accommodate a wide variety of individual temperaments, identities, behaviors, and levels of commitment, and still function in a culturally accepted manner. This elasticity derives from the genius of Hinduism: although not every hijra lives up to the role at the highest level, the role nonetheless gives religious meaning to cross-gender behavior, that is despised, punished and pushed beyond the pale of the cultural system in other societies.

Several different aspects of Hindu thought explain both the ability of Indian society to absorb an institutionalized third gender role, as well as to provide several contexts within which to handle the tension between the ideal and real aspects of the role. Indian mythology contains numerous examples of androgynes (see O'Flaherty, 1980), impersonators of the opposite sex, and among both deities and humans individuals with sex changes. Myths are an important part of popular culture. Sivabhaktis (worshippers of Siva) give hijras special respect because one of the forms of Siva is Ardhanarisvara, ("the lord who is half woman"). Hijras also associate themselves with Vishnu, who transforms himself into Mohini, the most beautiful woman in the world, in order to take back the sacred nectar from the demons who have stolen it. Further, in the worship if Krishna, male devotees may imagine themselves to be female, and even dress in female clothing; direct identification with Krishna is forbidden, but the devotee may identify with him indirectly by identifying with Radha, that is, by taking a female form. Thousands of hijras identify themselves as Krishna's wives in a ritual performed in South India. These are only a few of the contexts within which the hijras link themselves to the Great Tradition of Hinduism and develop a positive definition for their feminine behavior.

In handling the conflict between the real and the ideal, hijras and other groups in the Indian population are confronted with the seemingly conflicting value which Hinduism places on both eroticism and procreation, on the one hand, and non-attachment and asceticism, on the other. Both Hinduism and Islam are what Bullough calls "sex-positive" religions (1976). Both allow for the tolerance of a wider range of sexual expression than exists in western culture with its restrictive Judeo-Christian, religious heritage. Hinduism explicitly recognizes that humans achieve their ultimate goals—salvation, bliss, knowledge and (sexual) pleasure—by following many different paths because humans differ in their special abilities and competencies. Thus, Hinduism allows a different ethic according to one's own nature and affords the individual temperament the widest latitude, from highly idealistic morality, through genial toleration, and, finally, to compulsive extremes (Lannoy, 1975).

Hindu thought attempts to reconcile the value conflict between sexuality and chastity through the concept of a life cycle with four stages. Each stage has its appropriate sexual behavior: In the first stage one should be a chaste student, in the second a married householder, in the third a forest dweller preparing for withdrawal from society, and in the final stage, a sannyasin, the ascetic who has renounced everything. Thus, the Hindu ideal is a fully integrated life in which each aspect of human nature, including sexuality, has its time. Hijras implicitly recognize these stages in their social organization through a hierarchy in which one begins as a chela and moves into the position of guru as one gets older, taking on chelas and becoming less sexually active.

Hindu mythology also provides some contexts within which the contradictions between the ascetic ideal and the sexual activity are legitimate: Siva himself is both the great erotic and the great ascetic. In myths he alternates between the two forms. In some mythic episodes Siva is unable to reconcile his two roles as ascetic and householder, and in others he is a hypocritical ascetic because of his sexual involvement with Parvati, his consort (O'Flaherty, 1973). Indian goddesses as sexual figures also exist in abundance and in some stories a god will take on a female form specifically to have sexual relations with a male deity.

Where Western culture feels uncomfortable with contradictions and makes strenuous attempts to resolve them, Hinduism allows opposites to confront each other without a resolution, "celebrating the idea that the universe is boundlessly various, and . . . that all possibilities may exist without excluding each other" (O'Flaherty, 1973, p. 318). It is this characteristically Indian ability to tolerate, and even embrace, contradictions at social, cultural and personality levels, that provides a context for hijras. Hijras express in their very bodies the confrontation of femaleness and maleness as polar opposites. In Indian society they are not only tolerated but also valued.

References

Anderson, C. (1977). *Gay men in India.* Unpublished manuscript, University of Wisconsin.

Bhimbhai, K. Pavayas. (1901). Gujarat population, Hindus. In J. M. Campbell (Compiler), *Gazetteer of the Bombay Presidency, 4,* part 1. Bombay: Government Central Press.

Bradford, N. J. (1983). Transgenderism and the cult of Yellamma: Heat, sex, and sickness in South Indian ritual. *Journal of Anthropological Research, 39,* 307–322.

Bullough, V. L. (1976). *Sexual variance in society and history.* Chicago: University of Chicago Press.

Carrier, J. (1980). Homosexual behavior in cross cultural perspective. In J. Marmor (Ed.), *Homosexual behavior: A modern reappraisal* (pp. 100–122). New York: Basic Books.

Carstairs, G. M. (1957). *The twice born.* London: Hogarth Press.

Faridi, F. L. (1899). Hijras. In J. M. Campbell (Compiler), *Gazetteer of the Bombay Presidency, 9,* part 2, Bombay: Government Central Press.

Freeman, J. M. (1979). *Untouchable: An Indian life history.* Stanford, CA: Stanford University Press.

Hiltebeitel, A. (1980). Siva, the goddess, and the disguises of the Pandavas and Draupadi. *History of Religions, 20*(1/2), 147–174.

India Today. Fear is the key. (1982, September 15), pp. 84–85.

The Kama Sutra of Vatsyayana. (1964). (R. F. Burton, Trans.). New York: E. P. Dutton.

Lannoy, R. (1975). *The speaking tree.* New York: Oxford University Press.

Lynton, H. S., & Rajan, M. (1974). *Days of the beloved.* Berkeley: University of California Press.

Mark, M. E. (1981). *Falkland Road: Prostitutes of Bombay.* New York: Knopf.

Mehta, S. (1945–1946). Eunuchs, pavaiyas and hijadas. *Gufarat ahitya Sabha,* Amdavad, Karyavahi, Part 2. Ahmedabad.

Money, J., & Wiedeking, C. (1980). *Handbook of human sexuality* (pp. 270–284). B. B. Wolman & J. Money (Eds.), Englewood Cliffs, N.J.: Prentice-Hall.

Nanda, S. (1984). The hijras of India: A preliminary report. *Medicine and Law, 3,* 59–75.

Nanda, S. (in press). Dancers only? In Murray (Ed.), *Cultural diversity and homosexualities.* New York: Longman.

O'Flaherty, W. (1973). *Asceticism and eroticism in the mythology of Siva.* London: Oxford University Press.

O'Flaherty, W. (1980). *Women, androgynes, and other mythical beasts.* Chicago: University of Chicago Press.

Oldenburg, V. (1984). *The making of colonial Lucknow.* Princeton, N.J.: Princeton University Press.

Opler, M. (1960). The hijara (hermaphrodites) of India and Indian national character: A rejoinder, *American Anthropologist, 62,* 505–511.

Rajagopalachary, C. (1980). *Mahabharata*. Bombay: Bharatiya Vidya Bhavan.

Roland, A. (1982). Toward a psychoanalytical psychology of hierarchical relationships in Hindu India. *Ethos, 10*(3), 232–253.

Salunkhe, G. (1976, August 8). The cult of the hijaras. *Illustrated Weekly*, pp. 16–21.

Shah, A. M. (1961). A note on the hijaras of Gujerat. *American Anthropologist, 61*, 1325–1330.

Sinha, A. P. (1967). Procreation among the eunuchs. *Eastern Anthropologist, 20*, 168–176.

The Tribune. (1983, August 26). Five eunuchs in India, Pak. p. 2.

Vatuk, S. (1985). South Asian cultural conceptions of sexuality. In J. K. Brown & V. Kerns (Eds.). *In her prime: A new view of middle-aged women* (pp. 137–152).

Wikan, U. (1977). Man becomes woman: Transsexualism in Oman as a key to gender roles. *Man, 12*, 304–319.

 Article Review Form at end of book.

How do conceptions of self differ in Western and Eastern cultures? What are two ways the authors identify this difference?

A Collective Fear of the Collective

Implications for selves and theories of selves

Hazel Rose Markus
Stanford University

Shinobu Kitayama
Kyoto University

Drawing on recent analyses of the self in many cultures, the authors suggest that the cultural ideal of independence of the self from the collective has dominated European-American social psychological theorizing. As a consequence, the existence of considerable interdependence between the self and the collective has been relatively neglected in current conceptual analysis. The authors (a) argue that a group's cultural ideal of the relation between the self and the collective is pervasive because it is rooted in institutions, practices, and scripts, not just in ideas and values; (b) show how a given cultural ideal, whether it is independence or interdependence, can shape the individual's experience and expression of the self; and (c) discuss how a comparative approach may enrich and expand current theory and research on the interdependence between the self and the collective.

Authors' Note: The authors would like to acknowledge the support of the National Science Foundation Grant #BNS9010754 during the time this article was written.

Our cultural nightmare is that the individual throb of growth will be sucked dry in slavish social conformity. All life long, our central struggle is to defend the individual from the collective.

—Plath, 1980, p. 216

Selves, as well as theories of selves, that have been constructed within a European-American cultural frame show the influence of one powerful notion—the idea that people are independent, bounded, autonomous entities who must strive to remain unshackled by their ties to various groups and collectives (Bellah, Madsen, Sullivan, Swidler, & Tipton, 1985; Farr, 1991; Sampson, 1985; Shweder & Bourne, 1984). This culturally shared idea of the self is a pervasive, taken-for-granted assumption that is held in place by language, by the mundane rituals and social practices of daily life, by the law, the media, the foundational texts like the Declaration of Independence and the Bill of Rights, and by virtually all social institutions. The individualist ideal as sketched in its extreme form in the opening quotation might not be explicitly endorsed by many Americans and Europeans. Some version of this view is, however, the basis of social science's persistent belief in the person as a rational, self-interested actor, and it occasions a desire not to be defined by others and a deep-seated wariness, in some instances even a fear, of the influence of the generalized other, of the social, and of the collective.

Asocial Social Psychology

Although a diverse group of European and American theorists (e.g., Geertz, 1973; Gergen & Gergen, 1988; Gilligan, 1982; Icheiser, 1943; Moscovici, 1984; Shweder & Bourne, 1984; Tajfel & Turner, 1985) have found fault with the individualist model of self and its ability to reflect and account for social behavior, for the most part this critique has gone unheeded in the empirical analysis of behavior. A scrutiny of any current American textbook in social psychology reveals that social psychologists, the very group committed to understanding the social nature of the mind, approach the analysis of social behavior with a distinctly asocial model of the self.

In current social psychology, the healthy self is characterized as one that can maintain its integrity across diverse social environments and can successfully fend off challenge and attacks from others (Greenwald, 1980; Markus, 1977; Rosenberg, 1979; Tesser & Campbell, 1983). Although "social" identities are regarded as significant in some situations, they are typically viewed as separate from the more important and more defining "personal" identities (Crocker & Luhtanen, 1990;

Markus, Hazel Rose, and Kitayama, Shinobu (1994). "A Collective Fear of the Collective: Implications for Selves and Theories of Selves." *Personality and Social Psychology Bulletin*, 20, 568–579. Copyright © 1994 by the Society for Personality and Social Psychology, Inc. Reprinted by permission of Sage Publications, Inc.

Oyserman & Markus, 1993; Tajfel, 1981). Moreover, in many textbooks, there is an abiding concern that the social group will somehow overwhelm or disempower the autonomous, agentic self. It is the troublesome aspects of social behavior—conformity, obedience, groupthink, deindividuation, risky shift, diffusion of responsibility, and stereotyping—that are the main focus of conceptual analysis (see, e.g., Myers, 1993). Social behavior is very often presented as in opposition to individual behavior and construed as compromising individual behavior. This perspective, we contend, follows directly from a culturally held view of the self as distinctly separate from the exogenous collective.

Further, we suggest here that one major stumbling block to realizing the goal of this special issue—understanding how social aggregates influence individuals' thoughts and actions—and, in fact, to developing a comprehensive and fully "social" social psychology, is the unchallenged, heavily scripted, cultural view that the individual is, a priori, separate and self-contained and must resist the collective This individualist view, what might be called America's civil religion (Gates, 1993), works to keep many of the social and interdependent aspects of the self relatively invisible.

Recent analyses of the self in cultures other than the European-American (e.g., Daniels, 1984; Derné, 1992; Markus & Kitayama, 1991; Triandis, 1990; White & Kirkpatrick, 1985) reveal some very different perspectives on the relation between the self and the collective. Japanese culture, for example, emphasizes the *inter*dependence of the individual with the collective rather than independence from it. The analysis of non-European-American views of self has two notable benefits. First, such an analysis can illuminate some central characteristics of these non-Western cultures themselves. Second, and more important for our purposes, it can help uncover some aspects of European-American social behavior that are not well captured in the current social psychological theories.

Culture and Self

Independence of Self from the Collective—A Cultural Frame

The model that underlies virtually all current social science views the self as an entity that (a) comprises a unique, bounded configuration of internal attributes (e.g., preferences, traits, abilities, motives, values, and rights) and (b) behaves primarily as a consequence of these internal attributes. It is the individual level of reality—the thoughts and feelings of the single individual—that is highlighted and privileged in the explanation and analysis of behavior; the collective level of reality recedes and remains secondary. The major normative task is to maintain the independence of the individual as a self-contained entity or, more specifically, to be true to one's own internal structures of preferences, rights, convictions, and goals and, further, to be confident and to be efficacious. According to this *independent* view of the self, there is an enduring concern with expressing one's internal attributes both in public and in private. Other people are crucial in maintaining this construal of the self, but they are primarily crucial for their role in evaluating and appraising the self or as standards of comparison (see Markus & Kitayama, 1991; Triandis, 1990, for a discussion of the independent or individualist self). Others do not, however, *participate* in the individual's own subjectivity.

The independent view of self does not, of course, argue for a permanent separation of self from the collective, but it strictly prescribes the terms of the relationship between the two. According to this model of the self and the collective, there are indeed positive outcomes of the social matrix of behavior—people cooperate, they love one another, they show concern and sympathy, they value friendship, they help each other, they care about those in need, they volunteer, they give to charity, they are compassionate, and at times they perform heroic acts in behalf of

others. In fact, according to many recent analyses, North Americans are among the most concerned and committed people in the world (Bellah et al., 1985; Withnow, 1992). For the most part, however, from the perspective of the individualist ideal, such prosocial behavior is *intentional* and *voluntary*, treated more as an exception to be admired and rewarded. It is not to be taken for granted, as it is in more collectively oriented cultures. Acts that are motivated primarily by the desire to improve another person's situation are seen as opposing self-interest and as costly to the individual. In many respects, interdependence is cast as a matter of personal discretion, not a moral imperative (Miller, Bersoff, & Harwood, 1990). Similarly, European-Americans also value groups and group activity (de Tocqueville, 1835/1969), especially when such activity involves pulling together to solve a difficult problem or overcome a barrier. Again, however, collectively oriented behavior is typically understood as voluntary and as purposely and temporarily engaging the separate self to participate in the collective for the purpose of realizing a shared goal.[1]

Interdependence of the Self and the Collective—An Alternative Frame

The pervasive influence of the individualist ideal in many aspects of European-American social behavior has appeared in high relief as we have carried out a set of studies on the self and its functioning in a variety of Asian countries, including Japan, Thailand, and Korea (Kitayama & Markus, 1993; Kitayama, Markus, & Kurokawa, 1991; Markus & Kitayama, 1991, 1992). What has become apparent is that the European-American view of the self and its relation to the collective is only *one* view. There are other, equally powerful but strikingly different, collective notions about the self and its relation to the collective.

From one such alternative view, the self is viewed not as an independent entity separate from the collective but instead as a priori fundamentally interdependent with others. Individuals do not stand in opposition to the confines and constraints of the external collective, nor do they voluntarily choose to become parts of this external collective. Instead, the self *is* inherently social—an integral part of the collective. This interdependent view grants primacy to the *relationship* between self and others. The self derives only from the individual's relationships with specific others in the collective. There is no self without the collective; the self is a part that becomes whole only in interaction with others (e.g., Kondo, 1990; Kumagai & Kumagai, 1985; Lebra, 1992). It is defined and experienced as inherently connected with others. In contrast to the European-American orientation, there is an abiding fear of being on one's own, of being separated or disconnected from the collective. A desire for independence is cast as unnatural and immature.

The major normative task of such a self is not to maintain the independence of the individual as a self-contained entity but instead to maintain *inter*dependence with others. Rather than as an independent decision maker, the self is cast as "a single thread in a richly textured fabric of relationships" (Kondo, 1990, p. 33). This view of the self and of the collective requires adjusting and fitting to important relationships, occupying one's proper place in the group, engaging in collectively appropriate actions, and promoting the goals of others. One's thoughts, feelings, and actions are made meaningful only in reference to the thoughts, feelings, and actions of others in the relationship, and consequently others are crucially important in the very definition of the self. (For more detailed descriptions of the interdependent self, see Hsu, 1953; Kondo, 1990; Markus & Kitayama, 1991.)

Interdependence in this sense is theoretically distinct from social identity (e.g., Tajfel & Turner, 1985; Turner & Oakes, 1989), which refers to social categorizations that define a person as a member of particular social categories (e.g., American, male,

Protestant, engineer). Social identity, in the framework of Turner and colleagues, is always defined in counterpoint to personal identity, which is all the ways a person is *different* from his or her in-groups. The key feature of interdependence is not distinctiveness or uniqueness but a heightened awareness of the other, and of the nature of one's relation to the other, and an expectation of some mutuality in this regard across all behavioral domains, even those that can be designated as private or personal.

Rooted in a Cartesian tradition, most European-Americans never question the natural and obvious separation of self and the collective. The notion of a self that in some respects transcends the limits of the individual's physical body and is inherently connected with others can be partly demystified by envisioning different ways of experiencing or knowing the self. Neisser (1988), for example, makes a useful distinction among five types of self-knowledge—ecological (i.e., the self as perceived with respect to the physical environment), interpersonal (i.e., a sense of self in human interchange), extended (i.e., a sense of self based on personal memories and anticipations), private (i.e., an awareness of self based on experiences not shared with others), and conceptual (i.e., one's theory of self). Building on the idea that self-representation is a plural phenomenon and can assume a diversity of forms, it is possible to hypothesize that although everyone has some store of private and ecological self-knowledge, from the interdependent perspective it is the self-in-human-interchange, or self-in-relation, that is granted primacy in individual experience. In this view, a type of *intersubjectivity*, rather than a private subjectivity, would be the strongest, most elaborated aspect of self.

Differences in the Enculturation of the "Basic" Tasks

Although both European-American and Asian cultural groups recognize that independence from others and

interdependence with others are essential human tendencies or tasks, these two tasks are weighted and organized quite differently in the two groups. The notion of the autonomous individual in continuous tension with the external collective is "natural" only from a particular cultural perspective. From an alternative perspective, such an arrangement appears somewhat unnatural and contrived. In Japan, for example, the culture in its dominant ideology, patterns of social customs, practices, and institutions emphasizes and foregrounds not independence from others but interdependence with others. Interdependence is the first goal to be taken care of; it is crafted and nurtured in the social episodes and scripted actions of everyday social life, so that it becomes spontaneous, automatic, and taken for granted. Although independence is also essential for social functioning, it remains a tacit and less culturally elaborated pursuit. It is left to the intentions and initiatives of each individual member, and so its pursuit is relatively optional and is the focus of personal and unofficial discourse because it is not strongly constrained or widely supported by socially sanctioned cultural practices.[2]

The Cultural Shaping of Psychological Processes

In Figure 1, we have illustrated how the "reality" of independence is created and maintained in selves, as well as in theories of selves. According to this view, a cultural group's way of self-understanding is simultaneously related to a set of macrolevel phenomena, such as cultural views of personhood and their supporting collective practices, and to a set of microlevel phenomena, like individual lives and their constituent cognitive, emotional, and motivational processes.

Collective Reality

Under the heading "collective reality" we have included cultural values and their related ecological, historical, economic, and sociopolitical factors. For example, the United States is a nation with a rich tradition

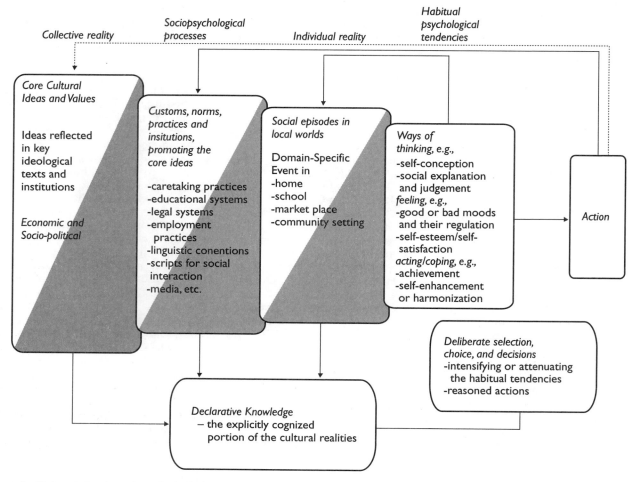

Figure 1. Cultural shaping of psychological reality.

of moral imperatives, but the most well elaborated is the need to protect the "natural rights" of each individual. This core cultural ideal is rooted most directly in the Declaration of Independence and the Bill of Rights, which protect certain inalienable rights, including life, liberty, and the pursuit of happiness. This highlighting of individuals and their rights is objectified and reified in a variety of democratic political institutions and free-market capitalism. In Japan, as throughout Asia, the prevalent ideological and moral discourses are not tied to individual rights but to the inevitability of a strict hierarchical order and to the achievement of virtue through cultivation of the individual into a "social man" (Yu, 1992). This core cultural ideal is anchored in the works of Confucius and Mencius and finds expression in an array of

economic, political, and social institutions.

Sociopsychological Products and Processes—Transmitting the Core Ideas

The cultural ideals and moral imperatives of a given cultural group are given life by a diverse set of customs, norms, scripts, practices, and institutions that carry out the transformation of the collective reality into the largely personal or psychological reality. These sociopsychological products and processes objectify and make "real" the core ideas of the society (Bourdieu, 1972; D'Andrade, 1984; Durkheim, 1989/1953; Farr & Moscovici, 1984; Geertz, 1973; Oyserman & Markus, in press). For example, in the United States, the idea of human rights (including lib-

erty from the thrall of the collective) as inherent and God-given gains its force from a large array of legal statutes protecting individual rights. In this way the individual gains superiority to the collective.

Child-rearing practices in the United States, rooted in Freudian theory and filtered through Dr. Spock and most recently the self-esteem movement, also work to develop the constituent elements of the self and to reinforce the importance of having a distinct self that the individual can feel good about. A recent study (Chao, 1993), for example, found that 64% of European-American mothers, in comparison with 8% of Chinese mothers, stressed building children's "sense of themselves" as an important goal of child rearing. Many American mothers take every opportunity to praise children and to help them realize the ways in which they are positively unique or different from their peers. Training in autonomy and the development of the appreciation of being alone also comes early. Day-old children sleep alone in their cribs, often in separate rooms from their parents (Shweder, Jensen, Goldstein, in press). On the playground, children are taught to stand up for themselves and fight back if necessary (Kashiwagi, 1989).

Another important quality of personhood, from the independent perspective, is the capacity to make one's own choice. In much of Western culture, but especially in North America, there are numerous examples of everyday scripts that presuppose the actor's right to make a choice. It is common for American hosts to instruct their guests, "Help yourself." With this suggestion, the host invites the guest to affirm the self by expressing some of those preferences that are thought to constitute the "real self." American children, then, are socialized to have distinct preferences. Long before the child is old enough to answer, caretakers pose questions like "Do you want the red cup or the blue cup?" With such questions, mothers signal to children that the capacity for independent choice is an important and desirable attribute. And the availability of choice gives rise to the need for preferences by which to make choices.

The practices of the media further create and foster the objectivity of the autonomous, independent self. Advertising in the United States makes appeals to nonconformity, originality, and uniqueness. A hard-sell approach is common in which the product is presented as the best or the leader of its kind, and purchasing it is claimed to reveal that the consumer has the "right" preferences or attitudes (Mueller, 1987; Zandpour, Chang, & Catalano, 1992). For example, Chanel recently marketed, in both the United States and Europe, a men's cologne with the strikingly unsubtle name of *Egoïste* and the slogan "For the man who walks on the right side of the fine line between arrogance and awareness of self-worth."

Perhaps the most powerful practice of all for the purpose of creating a shared concern with independence is that of advancing, promoting, and compensating people according to their "merit." This practice places a lifelong emphasis on inner attributes, capacities, and abilities as the "real" measure of the self and encourages people to define and develop these attributes.

In many Asian cultures, there is an equally diverse and powerful set of sociopsychological processes in each of these corresponding domains, but these practices are rooted in a view of the self as an interdependent entity. For example, in place of (or, to a certain extent, in addition to) the emphasis on human rights, there exist dense systems of rules and norms that highlight the duties of each individual to the pertinent collective, whether it is the company, school, or nation. Moreover, there are many fewer statutes protecting individual rights, and the Japanese resort to court suits to secure their rights far less readily than European-Americans (Hideo, 1988).

In the course of interpersonal interaction, the Japanese are encouraged to try to read the partner's mind and to satisfy what is taken as the partner's expectations or desires. A Japanese mother does not ask for a child's preference but instead tries to determine what is best for the child and to arrange it. Rather than asking a guest to make a choice, Japanese hosts do their best to prepare and offer what they infer to be the best possible meal for the guest, saying, for example, "Here's a turkey sandwich for you. I thought you said you like turkey better than beef last time we met."

Child rearing in many Asian cultures places a continual emphasis on understanding and relating to others, first to the mother and then to a wide range of others. The rules of interdependence are explicitly modeled, and the goal is to maintain harmonious relationships (Hsu, 1953). Interdependence can be found in all domains. In stark opposition to American practices and Freudian wisdom, cosleeping and cobathing are common in Japanese families. The emphasis is not on developing a good, private sense of self but on tuning in to and being sensitive to

others. Punishing or reprimanding Japanese children often involves not the withholding of rights and privileges but a threat to the relationship. Mothers will say, "I don't like children like you" or "People will laugh at you" (Okimoto & Rohlen, 1988).

With respect to media practices, Japanese advertising often uses soft-sell appeals that focus on harmony or connection with nature or with others (Mueller, 1987). In classified ads, employers explicitly seek individuals with good interpersonal relations, as opposed to self-starters or innovators (Caproni, Rafaeli, & Carlile, 1993). A focus on relationships is also evident in all types of business practices. Japan stands out from all countries in the West because of its emphasis on durable and pervasive ties between government and industry, between banks and businesses, and among corporations. Okimoto and Rohlen (1988) contend that the emphasis on organizational networks and human relationships is so strong that Japanese capitalism can be labeled *relational capitalism*. In the pursuit of long-term relationships and mutual trust, Japanese corporations operate quite differently, often, for example, forgoing the maximization of short-term profits with the hope of gaining a long-term market share. And in contrast to the European-American emphasis on merit for promotion and compensation, wages and advancement in the majority of Japanese companies and institutions are tied to seniority in the system. In addition, employment in large corporations is typically permanent, and there is little lateral entry from the outside—all publicly scripted collective practices that foster and promote a view of the self as inherently relational and interdependent.

Beyond the caretaking, legal, business, and media practices we have alluded to are a host of others, including educational and linguistic practices, and all the scripts and institutions that structure everyday social interactions. An important element in understanding which practices will become socially established is how the practices reflect and carry the group's underlying cultural values. Americans, for example, will be particularly susceptible to ideas and practices that directly follow from individualism (Sperber, 1985). Other practices—welfare and universal health care programs are good examples—will have a more difficult time taking hold in the United States.

Local Worlds—Living the Core Ideas

The third segment of Figure 1 represents the specific settings, circumstances, and situations of everyday life that make up an individual's immediate social environment and in which particular customs, norms, and practices become lived experience. The local worlds—home, school, the workplace, the community center, the church, the restaurant, bar, or café, the marketplace—and the specific activities or episodes they support—helping a child with homework, shopping for a gift, drinking with friends, discussing politics, playing baseball, working with others to meet a deadline—demand specific, culturally appropriate responses if a person is to become a valued member of the family, school, workplace, or community.

It is within the demands and expectations of these domain-specific, recurrent social episodes that people, often quite unknowingly, live out the core cultural values. So Americans are likely to create and live within settings that elicit and promote the sense that one is a positively unique individual who is separate and independent from others. For example, in many American schools, each child in the class has the opportunity to be a "star" or a "Very Special Person" for a week during the school year. Likewise, Japanese will create and live with situations that promote the sense of self as interdependent with others. In Japanese schools, children routinely produce group pictures or story boards, and no child leaves to go to the playground or lunch until all members of the group are ready to leave.

Habitual Psychological Tendencies Reflecting the Core Ideas

As a result of efforts to respond or adjust to the set of specific episodes that constitute the individual's life space, episodes that have themselves been shaped by norms, practices, and institutions supporting the cultural group's core ideas, a set of habitual psychological tendencies is likely to develop. The final segment of Figure 1 represents the individual's "authentic" subjective experience—particular, proceduralized ways of thinking, feeling, striving, knowing, understanding, deciding, managing, adjusting, adapting, which are, in some large part, structured, reinforced, and maintained by the constraints and affordances of the particular social episodes of the individual's local worlds. In this way, people who live within a society whose daily practices and formal institutions all promote independence will come not just to believe that they are, but to experience themselves as, autonomous, bounded selves who are distinct from other members of the collective. This will be evident in many ways of thinking, feeling, and acting, but it is particularly evident when people are asked to characterize themselves.

For example, by the time they are young adults, many Americans will seek an optimal distinctiveness from others (Brewer, 1990) and will "naturally" experience an ambivalence about their collective nature and a deep concern with being categorically perceived or socially determined. The journalist Barbara Ehrenreich (1992) describes an interchange with an acquaintance who has just rediscovered her own ethnic and religious heritage and now feels in contact with her 2000-year ancestral traditions. The acquaintance asks about Ehrenreich's ethnic background. The first word to come out of Ehrenreich's mouth in answer to the question is "None." She is surprised at how natural and right her answer seems, yet slightly embarrassed. She reflects and decides that her response when asked the nature of her ethnicity was quite correct. Her identity, she claims, comes from the realization that "we are the kind of people that whatever our distant ancestors' religions—we do not believe, we do not carry on traditions, we do not do things just because someone has done them before." Her ethnicity, she contends, is rooted not in a given group but in the ideas "Think for yourself" and "Try new things." In conclusion, Ehrenreich tells of asking her own children whether they ever had any stirring of "ethnic or religious identity." "None," they all conclude, and she reports, "My chest swelled with pride as would my mother's to know that the race of 'None' marches on."

A tendency to define one's "real" self as distinct from one's social groups and obligations is characteristic of both younger and older cohorts of Americans as well. In a series of studies with young children, Hart and his colleagues (Hart, 1988; Hart & Edelstein, 1992) asked American children to imagine a "person machine" that makes the original person disappear but at the same time manufactures other people, copies of the original, which receive some but not all of the original person's characteristics. The respondent's task is to judge which new manufactured person—the one with the same physical attributes (looks like you), the one with the same social attributes (has the same friends and family), or the one with the same psychological attributes (same thoughts and feelings)—will be most like the original person. By ninth grade, Hart et al. (Hart, Fegley, Hung Chan, Mulvey, & Fischer, 1993) finds that most respondents believe it is the copy with the original's psychological characteristics that is the most similar to the original.

These findings are consistent with those of several other studies of cultural variation in self-categorization (Cousins, 1989; Triandis, 1990) and suggest that, for American students, it is the internal features of the self—the traits, attributes, and attitudes—that are privileged and regarded as critical to self-definition. From this perspective, the significant aspects of the self are those that are the inside, the private property—one's characteristic ways of behaving, one's habitual thoughts, feelings, and beliefs (e.g., think for yourself, try new things)—the elements that do not explicitly reference others or the social world. Such internal attributes are also mentioned by the Japanese, but they appear to be understood as relatively situation specific and therefore elusive and unreliable (Cousins, 1989) as defining features of self. For the Japanese, the critical features are those attributes—social roles, duties, obligations—that connect one to the larger world of social relationships. (For other detailed examples of the cultural shaping of judgment, self, and emotion, see Kitayama & Markus, 1993, in press; Markus & Kitayama, 1994.) In a study examining response time for self-description, Kitayama et al. (1991) find that Japanese respondents are decidedly slower to characterize themselves than American respondents and that this is particularly true for positive attributes.

The top level of Figure 1 indicates feedback loops from each individual's action. The most immediate and frequent feedback occurs at the micro level. Most obviously, what an individual does influences the very nature of the situation in which he or she has acted. There are, however, people who at times contribute, through their actions, not just to the micro level but also to the more macro level. The bottom level of Figure 1 represents a more cognitive influence. Some portion of the social realities—both macro and micro—can be represented cognitively. This cognized portion of culture is shaded in each segment of the figure. The articulated, declarative knowledge of cultural values, practices, and conventions may be recruited in modulating social action, either facilitating or inhibiting the automatized psychological tendencies. Importantly, however, psychological tendencies can develop independently of this second, articulated route of cultural influence. In this way, cultural values and beliefs can cause differences in psychological processes even when these beliefs (e.g., a fear of influence by the collective) are not cognitively encoded and overtly articulated. Of course, the values and beliefs often are encoded cognitively, but this current analysis implies that cognitive representations need not be central in the cultural shaping of psychological processes. Instead, we suggest that psychological processes and behavior can be best understood as an important, but only partial, element of the dynamic cultural and historical process that involves the systematic (though by no means error-free or "faxlike") transmission of cultural imperatives to shape and define the nature of the specific, immediate life space—the microlevel reality—for each individual.

Implications of a Collective Fear of the Collective for Psychological Theorizing

Using Asian cultures, particularly Japan, as a point of reference and standard, we have sketched how the European-American fear of the collective may arise and how it is naturalized, enacted, and embodied so that people rarely see or feel the collective nature or source of their behavior and instead experience themselves as separate and self-contained entities. A large set of mutually reinforcing everyday rituals, social practices, and institutions work together to elaborate and objectify the culture's view of what the self is and what it should be. Independence and autonomy are thus the "natural" mode of being—in Geertz's (1975) terms, they become "experience near" phenomena. The subjective authenticity or "naturalness" of this mode, however, is a function of the degree of fit between habitual psychological tendencies and the cultural and social systems that are grounded in these cultural imperatives.

Theorists of European-American behavior have also been extremely influenced by the prevailing ideology of individualism. They have often viewed the self as in tension, or even as in opposition, to the "ruck of society" (Plath, 1980) or the "thrall of society" (Hewitt, 1989). The source of all important behavior is typically "found" in the unique configuration of internal attributes—thoughts, feelings, motives, abilities—that form the bounded, autonomous whole. As a consequence, the ways in which the self is, in fact, quite interdependent with the collective have been underanalyzed and undertheorized. It is our view that there are a number of important reasons for theorists to go beyond theories that are directly shaped by the cultural ideal of individualism and to consider a broader view of the self.

First, and most obviously, although current descriptions of the largely independent and autonomous self could be argued to be reasonably adequate for European-American

selves, a growing body of evidence suggests that they are simply not valid for many other cultural groups (see extended discussions of this point in Markus & Kitayama, 1991; Triandis, 1990; Triandis, Bontempo, & Villareal, 1988). Second, although the cultural ideal of independence is very influential in the nature and functioning of the European-American self, it does not determine it completely. For example, with respect to the bounded or fixed nature of the self, there are a variety of studies that reveal the self as decidedly malleable and its content and functioning as dependent on the social context. Typically these studies are not integrated with the literature that suggests stability of the self (e.g., Fazio, Effrein, & Falender, 1981; James, 1993; Jones & Pittman, 1982; Markus & Kunda, 1986; McGuire & McGuire, 1982; Schlenker, 1980).

Third, at least in the United States, the analysis of the selves of those groups in society that are somewhat marginalized—women, members of nondominant ethnic groups, the poor, the unschooled, and the elderly—reveals a more obvious interdependence between the self and the collective. For example, women describe themselves in relational terms (Gilligan, 1982; Jordan, Kaplan, Miller, Stivey, & Surrey, 1991), and they do not reveal the "typical" preference for being positively unique or different from others (Josephs, Markus, & Tafarodi, 1992). Other studies reveal that those groups that are in the minority with respect to language, skin color, or religion are decidedly more likely to define themselves in collective terms (Allen, Dawson, & Brown, 1989; Bowman, 1987; Husain, 1992). Further, Americans with less schooling are more likely to describe themselves in terms of habitual actions and roles, and less likely to characterize themselves in terms of psychological attributes, than those with more schooling (Markus, Herzog, Holmberg, & Dielman, 1992). And those with low self-esteem show a marked tendency to describe themselves as similar to others (Josephs et al., 1992). These findings suggest that those with power and privilege are those most likely to internalize the prevailing European-American cultural frame to achieve Ehrenreich's "ethnicity of none" and to "naturally" experience themselves as autonomous individuals.

Fourth, a number of recent studies show many Americans to be extremely concerned about others and the public good (Bellah et al., 1985; Bellah, Madsen, Sullivan, Swidler, & Tipton, 1991; Hewitt, 1989; Withnow, 1992) and to characterize themselves in interdependent terms. For example, a recent representative sample of 1,500 adults, aged 30 or over, found that although Americans indeed characterized themselves in terms of trait attributes and not social roles or obligations, the most frequently used attributes were *caring, responsible, loved*—all terms that imply some concern with a connection to the collective (Markus et al., 1992). Even if, as we have suggested, this connection is clearly voluntary and done on one's own terms, the prevailing model of the self could be modified.

And finally, increasingly throughout social psychology, there are indications that the individualist model of the self is too narrow and fails to take account of some important aspects of psychological reality. For example, within social psychology specifically, there is a great deal of evidence that people are exquisitely sensitive to others and to social pressure. People conform, obey, diffuse responsibility in a group, allow themselves to be easily persuaded about all manner of things, and become powerfully committed to others on the basis of minimal action (Myers, 1993). Despite the powerful cultural sanctions against allowing the collective to influence one's thoughts and actions, most people are still much less self-reliant, self-contained, or self-sufficient than the ideology of individualism suggests they should be. It appears in these cases that the European-American model of self is somewhat at odds with observed individual behavior and that it might be reformulated to reflect the substantial interdependence that characterizes even Western individualists.

Alternative Views of the Self and the Collective

In trying to formulate the collective sources of the self among Europeans or Americans, models of the self and the collective "Asian style" may be particularly informative.[3] If we assume, as does Shweder (1991), that every group can be considered an expert on some features of human experience and that different cultural groups "light up" different aspects of this experience, then Asian cultures may be an important source of conceptual resources in the form of concepts, frameworks, theories, or methods that can be employed to "see" interdependence. Even though interdependence American style will doubtlessly look quite different from interdependence Japanese style, an analysis of divergent cultural groups may further any theorist's understanding of the possibilities, potential, and consequences, both positive and negative, for socialness, for engagement, for interdependence, and for the ties that bind.[4]

The first step in expanding theories of the self and the collective seems to require being deliberately self-conscious about what is being taken for granted in the initial formulation of the problem and about the labels that are used. If a theorist accepts the notion that the self is constantly striving to defend itself from the collective, then influence by others is viewed as a weakness or as failure. Looking for possible consequences of such behavior will be seen as just so much rationalization. Yet, from the perspective of a model that acknowledges interdependence between the self and the collective, social influence, acknowledgment of others, attunement with others, imitation of others, the inhibition of private thoughts or feelings, even yielding to others can be framed quite differently. Such actions can be construed as essential, positive, and empowering (Azuma, 1986; Weisz, Rothbaum, & Blackburn, 1984).

Consider the phenomenon of conformity. It typically occurs when there is an ambiguous stimulus situation. Although conformity is obvi-

ously a necessary integrative mechanism, it is often cast as yielding to the collective, and investigators work to explain why it is that individuals feel the need to give in. This same behavior could be viewed as the mutual negotiation of social reality or as attunement with the other. Indeed, in Japan giving in to another is typically not a sign of weakness; rather, it can reflect tolerance, self-control, maturity. A recent study by Horike (1992) revealed that "conforming naturally to others" was the most important factor underlying humanness among Japanese respondents.

Or consider the phenomenon of groupthink. This occurs when members are deeply involved in a very cohesive group. It is said to occur when "members striving for unanimity override their motivation to realistically appraise alternative courses of action" (Janis, 1982, p. 9). Here, as with conformity, groupthink is viewed as a weakness, a failure of the autonomous self. Even given negative consequences like the Bay of Pigs invasion (said to be a result of groupthink), this same behavior could be analyzed as consensual decision making. By reconstituting "conformity" and "groupthink" as socially legitimate processes of mutual negotiation for consensual understanding and definition of the focal situation or issue, it may be possible to advance a somewhat different perspective on the link between the collective and individual thought and to more fully consider the nature and consequences of socially induced thought. Similarly, deindividuation could be seen from an alternative perspective on the self and the collective, not as a loss of self—the ultimate failure from the perspective of individualist ideology—but as the purposeful inhibition of one's thoughts and feelings, a clearing of the screen, to allow one to be receptive to others.

Another model of the self and the collective could also provide an alternative view of two of psychology's oldest problems—the inconsistency between attitudes and behavior and the inconsistency between personality and behavior. From an interdependent perspective, such behavior does not have to be framed negatively and does not have to give rise to great theoretical consternation. Interdependent selves do not prescribe or require consistency between one's internal attributes and one's actions. In fact, such consistency may reflect, not authenticity, but a lack of flexibility, rigidity, or even immaturity.

We have argued here that the cultural frame of individualism has put a very strong stamp on how social psychologists view the individual and his or her relation to the collective. Although this individualist view has provided a powerful framework for the analysis of social behavior, it has also, necessarily, constrained theories, methods, and dominant interpretations of social behavior. Because individualism is not just a matter of belief or value but also one of everyday practice, including scientific practice, it is not easy for theorists to view social behavior from another cultural frame, and it is probably harder still to reflect a different frame in empirical work. But the comparative approach that is characteristic of the developing cultural psychology (e.g., Cole, 1990; Stigler, Shweder, & Herdt, 1990) may eventually open new and productive possibilities for the understanding and analysis of behavior.

For example, just as social influence, from the perspective of an interdependent cultural frame, can be seen as the mutual negotiation of social reality, helping can be seen as a result of obligation, duty, or morality, rather than as voluntary or intentional (e.g., Miller et al., 1990). Similarly, emotion can be viewed as an enacted interpersonal process (Rosaldo, 1984) or as an interpersonal atmosphere, as it is characterized in some non-Western theories (White, 1990). Further, cognition can be seen as an internalized aspect of communication (Zajonc, 1992), and the early idea of the social and interactive nature of the mind (e.g., Asch, 1952; Bruner, 1990; Vygotsky, 1978) can be taken much more seriously than it has been. In general, viewing the self and social behavior from alternative perspectives may enable theorists to see and elaborate at least one important and powerful universal that might otherwise be quite invisible—

the ways in which psychological functioning (in this case, the nature of the self), as well as theories about psychological functioning (here, theories of the nature of the self), are in many ways culture specific and conditioned by particular, but tacit and taken-for-granted, meaning systems, values, and ideals.

Notes

1. For an analysis of the failure of teamwork in American corporations, see Hackman (1993), who argues that many American corporate teams are teams in name only. Typically, they are not stable or meaningfully interdependent. Moreover, they do not have control over their own affairs and rewards and incentives are not at the team level but are given to individuals.

2. The reason that some cultural groups "do independence," highlighting in their practices and institutions the separation between the self and the collective, while others, "do interdependence," highlighting in their practices and institutions the interconnection between the self and the collective, is a mystery that is only now being analyzed (see, e.g., Fiske, 1990; Taylor, 1989). These analyses begin with the notion that groups everywhere have a need to solve some questions about social existence. One of the most significant questions is, What is the self and what is not the self? In approaching this question, different groups make very different ideological commitments, drawing on diverse ontologies and philosophies.

    According to one account, European-American culture naturally elaborates the individual level of reality—the person's seemingly separate and private store of thoughts, feelings, and proclivities—because it is rooted in an ontological tradition that favors, according to Lebra (1992), the "theistic/Cartesian split self." (Here *split* refers to the mind/body split and the self/other split as well as the cognitive/affective split.) Lebra argues that the goal of this ontological system is self-objectification. In this view, there is a highlighting of division between the experiencer and what is experienced, and becoming separate and independent from the surrounding context (both the natural and the interpersonal) is emphasized.

    Lebra (1976) contends that Asian cultural groups, in contrast to those in the West, will more readily elaborate a social or interpersonal level of reality—the way in which the self is a connected and relational phenomenon—because they

are tied to an ontological tradition that favors a notion of the submerged self, in which the goal is not self-objectification but instead freedom from self. Lebra argues that the perspective of the "Shinto-Buddhist submerged self" downplays division between the experiencer and what is being experienced. It is connection with others and the surrounding context, rather than separation, that is emphasized.

3. Some of the most important work suggesting the need for alternative models of the self comes from feminist theorists who have argued in the last 15 years that relations have a power and significance in women's lives that has gone unrecognized (Belenky, Clinchy, Goldberger, & Tarule, 1986; Gilligan, 1982; Jordan et al., 1991). The development of a psychology of women has shown that the "Lone Ranger" model of the self simply does not fit many women's experience because women's sense of self seems to involve connection and engagement with relationships and collective. In this work, being dependent does not invariably mean being helpless, powerless, or without control. It often means being interdependent—having a sense that one is able to have an effect on others and is willing to be responsive to others and become engaged with them (Jordan, 1991).

4. Interdependence in Japan is a collective, multiply represented and reinforced goal. As interdependence is the prescribed way of being a self, there is relatively little ambivalence about it in public discourse. It is hard to be otherwise, and interdependence seldom seems a matter of conscious, active choice. Yet, in many European and American groups, interdependence is for the most part not culturally sanctioned and maintained, and it is left for people to deliberately negotiate on their own terms.

References

Allen, R. L., Dawson, M. C., & Brown, R. E. (1989). A schema based approach to modeling in African American racial belief system. *American Political Science Review, 83,* 421–442.

Asch, S. E. (1952). *Social psychology.* Englewood Cliffs, NJ: Prentice-Hall.

Azuma, H. (1986). Why study child development in Japan? In H. Stevenson, H. Azuma, & K. Hakuta (Eds.), *Child development and education in Japan* (pp. 3–12). New York: Freeman.

Belenky, M. F., Clinchy, B. M., Goldberger, N. R., & Tarule, J. M. (1986). *Women's ways of knowing: The development of self, voice, and mind.* New York: Basic Books.

Bellah, R. N., Madsen, R., Sullivan, W. M., Swidler, A., & Tipton, S. M. (1985). *Habits of the heart: Individualism and commitment in American life.* Berkeley: University of California Press.

Bellah, R. N., Madsen, R., Sullivan, W. M. Swidler, A., & Tipton, S. M. (1991). *The good society.* New York: Knopf.

Bourdieu, P. (1972). *Outline of a theory of practice.* Cambridge: Cambridge University Press.

Bowman, P. J. (1987). Post-industrial displacement and family role strains: Challenges to the Black family. In P. Voydanoff & L. C. Majka (Eds.), *Families and economic distress.* Newbury Park, CA: Sage.

Brewer, M. B. (1990, August). *The social self: On being the same and different at the same time.* Presidential address to the Society for Personality and Social Psychology presented at the annual meeting of the American Psychological Association, Boston.

Bruner, J. (1990). *Acts of meaning.* Cambridge, MA: Harvard University Press.

Caproni, P., Rafaeli, A., & Carlile, P. (1993, July). *The social construction of organized work: The role of newspaper employment advertising.* Paper presented at the European Group on Organization Studies conference, Paris, France.

Chao, R. K. (1993). *East and West: Concepts of the self reflected in mothers' reports of their child-rearing.* Unpublished manuscript, University of California, Los Angeles.

Cole, M. (1990). Cultural psychology: A once and future discipline? In J. J. Berman (Ed.), *Nebraska Symposium on Motivation, 1989* (Vol. 37, pp. 279–336). Lincoln: University of Nebraska Press.

Cousins, S. (1989). Culture and selfhood in Japan and the U.S. *Journal of Personality and Social Psychology, 56,* 124–131.

Crocker, J., & Luhtanen, R. (1990). Collective self-esteem and ingroup bias. *Journal of Personality and Social Psychology, 58,* 60–67.

D'Andrade, R. (1984). Cultural meaning systems. In R. A. Shweder & R. A. LeVine (Eds.), *Cultural theories: Essays on mind, self, and emotion* (pp. 88–119). New York: Cambridge University Press.

Daniels, E. V. (1984). *Fluid signs: Being a person the Tamil way.* Berkeley: University of California Press.

Derné, S. (1992). Beyond institutional and impulsive conceptions of self: Family structure and the socially anchored real self. *Ethos, 20,* 259–288.

de Tocqueville, A. (1969). *Democracy in America* (J. P. Mayer, Ed.; G. Lawrence, Trans.). Garden City, NY: Anchor. (Original work published 1835)

Durkheim, E. (1953). Individual representations and collective representations. In E. Durkheim (Ed.), *Sociology and philosophy* (D. F. Pocok, Trans.) (pp. 1–38). New York: Free Press. (Original work published 1898)

Ehrenreich, B. (1992, March). The race of none. *Sunday New York Times Magazine,* pp. 5–6.

Farr, R. M. (1991). Individualism as a collective representation. In V. Aebischer, J. P. Deconchy, & M. Lipiansky (Eds.), *Idéologies et représentations sociales* (pp. 129–143). Cousset (Fribourg), Switzerland: Delval.

Farr, R. M., & Moscovici, S. (Eds.), (1984). *Social representations.* Cambridge: Cambridge University Press.

Fazio, R. H., Effrein, E. A., & Falender, Y. J. (1981). Self-perceptions following social interactions. *Journal of Personality and Social Psychology, 41,* 232–242.

Fiske, A. P. (1990). *Making up society: The four elementary relational structures.* New York: Free Press.

Gates, H. L., Jr. (1993, September 20). Let them talk. *New Republic,* pp. 37–49.

Geertz, C. (1973). *The interpretation of cultures.* New York: Basic Books.

Geertz, C. (1975). On the nature of anthropological understanding. *American Scientist, 63,* 47–53.

Gergen, K. J., & Gergen, M. M. (1988). Narrative and the self as relationship. In L. Berkowitz (Ed.), *Advances in experimental social psychology* (Vol. 21, pp. 17–56). New York: Academic Press.

Gilligan, C. (1982). *In a different voice: Psychological theory and women's development.* Cambridge, MA: Harvard University Press.

Greenwald, A. G. (1980). The totalitarian ego: Fabrication and revision of personal history. *American Psychologist, 35,* 603–618.

Hackman (1993, October). Why groups don't work. Paper presented at the ICOS, University of Michigan, Ann Arbor.

Hart, D. (1988). The adolescent self-concept in social context. In D. Lapsley & F. Power (Eds.), *Self, ego, and identity: Integrative approaches* (pp. 71–90). New York: Springer-Verlag.

Hart, D., & Edelstein, W. (1992). Self understanding development in cultural context. In T. M. Brinthaupt & R. P. Lipka (Eds.), *The self: Definitional and methodological issues.* Albany: State University of New York Press.

Hart, D., Fegley, S., Hung Chan, Y., Mulvey, D., & Fischer, L. (1993). *Judgment about personal identity in childhood and adolescence.* Unpublished manuscript.

Hewitt, J. P. (1989). *Dilemmas of the American self.* Philadelphia: Temple University Press.

Hideo, T. (1988). The role of law and lawyers in Japanese society. In D. I. Okimoto & T. P. Rohlen (Eds.), *Inside the Japanese system: Readings on contemporary society and political economy* (pp. 194–196). Stanford, CA: Stanford University Press.

Horike, K. (1992, July). *An investigation of the Japanese social skills: What is called "hito-atari-no-yosa" (affability).* Paper presented at the 25th International Congress of Psychology, Brussels, Belgium.

Hsu, F. L. K. (1953). *Americans and Chinese: Two ways of life.* New York: H. Schuman.

Husain, M. G. (1992, July). *Ethnic uprising and identity.* Paper presented at the 11th Congress of the International Association for Cross-Cultural Psychology, Liege, Belgium.

Icheiser, G. (1943). Misunderstandings in human relations: A study in false social perception. *American Journal of Sociology, 55* (suppl.).

James, K. (1993). Conceptualizing self with in-group stereotypes: Context and esteem precursors. *Personality and Social Psychology Bulletin, 19,* 117–121.

Janis, I. L. (1982). *Groupthink: Psychological studies of policy decisions and fiascoes.* Boston: Houghton Mifflin.

Jones, E. E., & Pittman, T. S. (1982). Towards a general theory of strategic self-preservation. In J. Suls (Ed.), *Psychological perspectives on the self* (Vol. 1, pp. 231–262). Hillsdale, NJ: Lawrence Erlbaum.

Jordan, J. V. (1991). Empathy and self boundaries. In J. V. Jordan, A. G. Kaplan, J. B. Miller, I. P. Stivey, & J. L. Surrey (Eds.), *Women's growth in connection* (pp. 67–80). New York: Guilford.

Jordan, J. V. Kaplan, A. G. Miller, J. B. Stivey, I. P. & Surrey J. L. (Eds.). (1991). *Women's growth in connection.* New York: Guilford.

Josephs, R. A., Markus, H., & Tafarodi, R. W. (1992). Gender differences in the source of self-esteem. *Journal of Personality and Social Psychology, 63,* 391–402.

Kashiwagi, K. (1989, July). *Development of self-regulation in Japanese children.* Paper presented at the tenth annual meeting of the International Society for the Study of Behavioral Development, Jväskylä, Finland.

Kitayama, S., & Markus, H. (1993). Construal of the self as a cultural frame: Implications for internationalizing psychology. In J. D'Arms, R. G. Hastie, S. E. Hoelscher, & H. K. Jacobson (Eds.), *Becoming more international and global: Challenges for American higher education.* Manuscript submitted for publication.

Kitayama, S., & Markus, H. (in press). A cultural perspective on self-conscious emotions. In J. P. Tangney & K. W. Fisher (Eds.), *Shame, guilt, embarrassment and pride: Empirical studies of self-conscious emotions.* New York: Guilford.

Kitayama, S., Markus, H., & Kurokawa, M. (1991, October). *Culture, self, and emotion: The structure and frequency of emotional experience.* Paper presented at the biannual meeting of the Society for Psychological Anthropology, Chicago.

Kondo, D. (1990). *Crafting selves: Power, gender, and discourses of identity in a Japanese work place.* Chicago: University of Chicago Press.

Kumagai, H. A., & Kumagai, A. K. (1985). The hidden "I" in *amax.* "Passive love" and Japanese social perception. *Ethos, 14,* 305–321.

Lebra, T. S. (1976). *Japanese patterns of behavior.* Honolulu: University of Hawaii Press.

Lebra, T. S. (1992, June). *Culture, self, and communication.* Paper presented at the University of Michigan, Ann Arbor.

Markus, H. (1977). Self-schemas and processing information about the self.

Journal of Personality and Social Psychology, 35, 63–78.

Markus, H., Herzog, A. R., Holmberg, D. E., & Dielman, L. (1992). *Constructing the self across the life span.* Unpublished manuscript, University of Michigan, Ann Arbor.

Markus, H., & Kitayama, S. (1991). Culture and the self: Implications for cognition, emotion, and motivation. *Psychological Review, 98,* 224–253.

Markus, H., & Kitayama, S. (1992). The what, why and how of cultural psychology: A review of R. Shweder's *Thinking through cultures. Psychological Inquiry, 3,* 357–364.

Markus, H., & Kitayama, S. (1994). The cultural construction of self and emotion: Implications for social behavior. In S. Kitayama & H. R. Markus (Eds.), *Emotion and culture: Empirical studies of mutual influence* (pp. 89–130). Washington, DC: American Psychological Association.

Markus, H., & Kunda, Z. (1986). Stability and malleability in the self-concept in the perception of others. *Journal of Personality and Social Psychology, 51,* 1–9.

McGuire, W. J., & McGuire, C. V. (1982). Significant others in self space: Sex differences and developmental trends in social self. In J. Suls (Ed.), *Psychological perspectives on the self* (Vol. 1, pp. 71–96). Hillsdale, NJ: Lawrence Erlbaum.

Miller, J. G., Bersoff, D. M., & Harwood, R. L. (1990). Perceptions of social responsibilities in India and in the United States: Moral imperatives or personal decisions? *Journal of Personality and Social Psychology, 58,* 33–46.

Moscovici, S. (1985). The phenomena of social representations. In R. M. Farr & S. Moscovici (Eds.), *Social representations* (pp. 3–69). Cambridge: Cambridge University Press.

Mueller, B. (1987, June/July). Reflections of culture: An analysis of Japanese and American advertising appeals. *Journal of Advertising Research,* pp. 51–59.

Myers, D. (1993). *Social psychology* (4th ed.). New York: McGraw-Hill.

Neisser, U. (1988). Five kinds of self-knowledge. *Philosophical Psychology, 1,* 35–59.

Okimoto, D. I., & Rohlen, T. P. (Eds.). (1988). *Inside the Japanese system: Readings on contemporary society and political economy.* Stanford, CA: Stanford University Press.

Oyserman, D., & Markus, H. R. (in press). Self as social representation. In S. Moscovici and U. Flick (Eds.), *Psychology of the social.* Berlin: Rowohlt Taschenbuch Verlag Gmbh.

Oyserman, D., & Markus, H. R. (1993). The sociocultural self. In J. Suls (Ed.), *Psychological perspectives on the self, volume 4: The self in social perspective.* Hillsdale, NJ: Erlbaum.

Plath, D. W. (1980). *Long engagements: Maturity in modern Japan.* Stanford, CA: Stanford University Press.

Rosaldo, M. (1984). Toward an anthropology of self and feeling. In R. A. Shweder & R. A. LeVine (Eds.), *Culture theory: Essays on mind, self, and emotion* (pp. 137–157). Cambridge: Cambridge University Press.

Rosenberg, M. (1979). *Conceiving the self.* New York: Basic Books.

Sampson, E. E. (1985). The decentralization of identity: Toward a revised concept of personal and social order. *American Psychologist, 40,* 1203–1211.

Schlenker, B. R. (1980). *Impression management.* Pacific Grove, CA: Brooks/Cole.

Shweder, R. A. (1991). *Thinking through cultures: Expeditions in cultural psychology.* Cambridge, MA: Harvard University Press.

Shweder, R. A., & Bourne, E. (1984). Does the concept of the person vary cross-culturally? In R. A. Shweder & R. A. LeVine (Eds.), *Culture theory: Essays on mind, self, and emotion* (pp. 158–199). Cambridge: Cambridge University Press.

Shweder, R. A., Jensen, L. A., & Goldstein, W. M. (in press). Who sleeps by whom revisited: A method for extracting the moral goods implicit in practice. In J. Goodnow, P. Miller, & F. Kessel (Eds.), *Cultural practices as contexts for development.* San Francisco: Jossey-Bass.

Sperber, D. (1985). Anthropology and psychology: Towards an epidemiology of representations. *MAN, 20,* 73–89.

Stigler, J. W., Shweder, R. A., & Herdt, G. (Eds.). (1990). *Cultural psychology: Essays on comparative human development.* London: Cambridge University Press.

Tajfel, H. (1981). *Human groups and social categories: Studies in social psychology.* Cambridge: Cambridge University Press.

Tajfel, H., & Turner, J. C. (1985). The social identity theory of intergroup behavior. In S. Worchel & W. G. Austin (Eds.), *Psychology of intergroup relations* (pp. 7–24). Chicago: Nelson-Hall.

Taylor, C. (1989). *Sources of the self: The making of modern identities.* Cambridge, MA: Harvard University Press.

Tesser, A., & Campbell, J. (1983). Self-definition and self-evaluation maintenance. In J. Suls & A. Greenwald (Eds.), *Psychological perspectives on the self*

(Vol. 2, pp. 1–31). Hillsdale, NJ: Lawrence Erlbaum.

Triandis, H. C. (1990). Cross-cultural studies of individualism and collectivism. In J. J. Berman (Ed.), *Nebraska Symposium on Motivation, 1989* (Vol. 37, pp. 41–143).

Triandis, H. C., Bontempo, R., & Villareal, M. (1988). Individualism and collectivism: Cross-cultural perspectives on self-ingroup relationships. *Journal of Personality and Social Psychology, 54,* 323–338.

Turner, J. C., & Oakes, P. J. (1989). Self-categorization theory and social influence. In P. B. Paulus (Ed.), *The psychology of group influence* (2nd ed.). Hillsdale, NJ: Lawrence Erlbaum.

Vygotsky, L. S. (1978). *Mind in society: The development of higher psychological processes* (M. Cole, V. John-Steiner, S. Scribner, & E. Souberman, Eds.). Cambridge, MA: Harvard University Press.

Weisz, J. R., Rothbaum, F. M., & Blackburn, T. C. (1984). Standing out and standing in: The psychology of control in America and Japan. *American Psychologist, 39,* 955–969.

White, G. M. (1990). Moral discourse and the rhetoric of emotion. In C. Lutz & L. Abu-Lughod (Eds.), *Language and the politics of emotion.* Cambridge: Cambridge University Press.

White, G. M., & Kirkpatrick, J. (Eds.). (1985). *Person, self, and experience: Exploring Pacific ethnopsychologies.* Berkeley and Los Angeles: University of California Press.

Withnow, R. (1992). *Acts of compassion.* Princeton, NJ: Princeton University Press.

Yu, A. B. (1992, July). *The self and life goals of traditional Chinese: A philosophical and cultural analysis.* Paper presented at the 11th Congress of the International Association for Cross-Cultural Psychology, Liege, Belgium.

Zajonc, R. B. (1992, April). *Cognition, communication, consciousness: A social psychological perspective.* Invited address at the 20th Katz-Newcomb Lecture at the University of Michigan, Ann Arbor.

Zandpour, F., Chang, C., & Catalano, J. (1992, January/February). Stories, symbols, and straight talk: A comparative analysis of French, Taiwanese, and U.S. TV commercials. *Journal of Advertising Research,* pp. 25–38.

 Article Review Form at end of book.

WiseGuide Wrap-Up

- Personality theorists have not paid much attention to how such social categorizations as race, ethnicity, and gender shape our experiences and how these experiences, in turn, shape personality. Winter and Stewart argue that this is an area that needs further attention.

- Although much has changed over the past 40 years, members of ethnic minority groups still face many experiences of discrimination over the course of their lives, and these experiences can have an

impact on how they perceive themselves and the world around them. The frequency of such experiences is frustrating and emotionally exhausting at best—and enraging and embittering at worst.

- The Hijras of India represent a distinct "gender" within that culture—biological males with very feminine styles of dress and ways of behaving. Such "mixed" genders exist in many cultures around the world, and they challenge the American notion that men and

women belong in two, and only two, distinct gender categories.

- Western—and especially American—conceptions of psychological health include such ideas as "being your own person" and not bending to the will of others. These are radically different from conceptions of psychological health in other—particularly Eastern—cultures, which focus more on being a responsible member of important social groups, such as one's family.

R.E.A.L. Sites

This list provides a print preview of typical **coursewise** R.E.A.L. sites. There are over 100 such sites at the **courselinks™** site. The danger in printing URLs is that web sites can change overnight. As we went to press, these sites were functional using the URLs provided. If you come across one that isn't, please let us know via email to: webmaster@coursewise.com. Use your Passport to access the most current list of R.E.A.L. sites at the **courselinks™** site.

Site name: International Association for Cross-Cultural Psychology
URL: http://www.fit.edu/CampusLife/clubs-org/iaccp/
Why is it R.E.A.L.? The group's purpose is to future communication between people interested in cross-cultural psychology. The web site contains information about recent conferences, books published in the area, and graduate programs and provides links to related web sites.
Key topics: culture and personality

Site name: Society for the Psychological Study of Social Issues
URL: http://www.umich.edu/~sociss/
Why is it R.E.A.L.? This society is focused on encouraging and disseminating quality psychological research into pressing social issues, including issues of gender, ethnicity, and poverty. It has published much of the important work in this area in its *Journal of Social Issues*. The web site offers information on the organization, recent conferences and publications, and "hot topics" and links to other psychological organizations and the United Nations.
Key topics: gender, race and ethnicity, social justice

Index

Note: Names and page numbers in **bold** type indicate authors and their articles; page numbers in *italics* indicate illustrations; page numbers followed by *t* indicate tables; page numbers followed by *n* indicate notes.

Putting it in *Perspectives*
-Review Form-

Your name:_____   Date: _____

Reading title: _____

Summarize: Provide a one-sentence summary of this reading. _____

_____

_____

_____

Follow the Thinking: How does the author back the main premise of the reading? Are the facts/opinions appropriately supported by research or available data? Is the author's thinking logical?

_____

_____

_____

_____

_____

Develop a Context (answer one or both questions): How does this reading contrast or compliment your professor's lecture treatment of the subject matter? How does this reading compare to your textbook's coverage?

_____

_____

_____

_____

_____

Question Authority: Explain why you agree/disagree with the author's main premise.

_____

_____

_____

_____

_____

_____

COPY ME! Copy this form as needed. This form is also available at http://www.coursewise.com
Click on: *Perspectives.*